Innovative Methods in Media and Communication Research

D1826490

Sebastian Kubitschko • Anne Kaun
Editors

Innovative Methods in Media and Communication Research

palgrave
macmillan

Editors
Sebastian Kubitschko
University of Bremen (ZeMKI)
Bremen, Germany

Anne Kaun
Södertörn University
Huddinge, Sweden

ISBN 978-3-319-40699-2   ISBN 978-3-319-40700-5   (eBook)
DOI 10.1007/978-3-319-40700-5

Library of Congress Control Number: 2016956372

This Palgrave Macmillan imprint is published by Springer Nature
The registered company is Springer International Publishing AG
The registered company address is: Gewerbestrasse 11, 6330 Cham, Switzerland

Foreword to 'Innovative Methods in Media and Communication Research'

How we research the social world can seem to be the concern only of professional academics. Even among academics, books about methods tend to be the books you consult only when you have to, while debates *about* methods (methodological debates), although they sometimes come to the fore in particular academic fields, generally do so under disguise, as disputes about 'ontology', new paradigms, and the like. A major collection of essays by young scholars on what is at stake in innovative methods is therefore a notable event.

The context indeed could not be more urgent. The transformations of what we still try to call the 'media' environment over the past quarter-century have been profound. Twenty-five years ago the challenge for media and communications scholars was to reflect on the implications of expanding television channels and everyday video recording. In the early years of the internet's commercialization, modes of internet access seemed to play out in a parallel world of their own—the world of 'cyberspace'—which attracted its explorers and methodological pioneers. Yet their work could safely be ignored by the mainstream of media research, although by 2000 it was clear that the internet was going at some point to bring major transformations.

Those times of 'normal science' and quarantined exploration seem unrecognizable today. The past fifteen years have disturbed the comfortable division of labor in media research between mainstream and innovative margins, and in their course dismantled the boundaries around media research itself. No actual or would-be researcher of 'media' today can avoid the questions of *where exactly* to 'cut in' to our lives with media, *why* make *that* cut exactly, and relying on *what* combination of research techniques and skills. Not only have the *surface features* of media, the range of their contents, the modes of their production or delivery to audiences, and the complexity of their intertextual connections changed hugely in the past fifteen years, but so too has the way in which media contents, media choices, and media-related practices are embedded in daily life. Entirely new portals of media consumption now exist (such as YouTube and social media platforms); meanwhile, the options for, in some sense, 'producing' media content, or distributing it on a significant scale, have also expanded massively. The result is a complexity, a flux, that is genuinely puzzling at times, posing major difficulties in how to capture it.

Yet this is only the *first* transformation whose impacts on how we research the social world must be considered. Two further transformations stem from the nature of the internet itself, distinctive features that have only become clear, to most of us at least, in the past five to eight years. During its first few years, the internet was predominantly discussed as a space of freedom, a space into which human agency could expand by acquiring more information, making personal connections, joining up information and things in new ways: a 'technology of freedom', in Ithiel de Sola Pool's resonant phrase. As the size, depth, and multi-layeredness of internet space expanded, it increasingly became clear that much work is needed simply to keep track of the proliferating variety of the things we do online, or with/through media reached online: this was the so-called practice turn in media research that has broken apart the traditional boundaries of media studies since the early 2000s.

Looking back, however, this transformation was to be succeeded by a further transformation potentially much more disruptive to the study not just of media, but of the social world in all its forms. This third transformation has reconfigured the specialist space of media research as part of a wider continuum in which information and computer science, sociology of the economy and information, legal studies, and many other disciplinary traditions converge. This third transformation derived from changes deep *within* the production of online content and online interaction spaces, which have profoundly altered the nature of the internet as an infrastructure. The impetus came primarily from a crisis in the advertising industries, which could no longer reliably reach their audiences in a world of proliferating informational content: the result was the construction, over time, of ever more sophisticated ways of tracking automatically what people do online, as they do it, and the distribution of that data for value within and beyond the media industries, a story that Joseph Turow in particular has told brilliantly. The corporate gathering of consumer data goes back to the late 1980s, as Turow's former Annenberg School colleague Oscar Gandy uncovered, and states have, of course, for two centuries tried to gather data about citizens. However, the latter state-based gathering was for a very long time confined to discrete chunks of information related to isolated moments, aggregated only with difficulty, and affording only broad snapshots of populations. Automated tracking of computer-based action, driven by corporate innovations (cookies and the like) and combined with huge increases in networked computing power, has, however, in the past decade normalized continuous data gathering in every domain of online life. The embedded software that gathers and processes such data has become a banal, if often hidden, element of doing anything online.

The resulting rise of data collection has been so profound that it is now driving new types of object in the world. The 'internet of things' is just a catchy phrase for something rather more interesting: the routine embedding not simply of online connection, but automated data gathering and data processing in an infinitely expandable set of everyday objects and tools. Parallel transformations in information gathering and processing have been under way in specialized domains, such as the physical and medical sciences, trading markets, and so on. From the combination of these many 'local' transformations has come the phenomenon of 'Big Data' and the banal installation of automated data surveillance in every stream of social life.

The methodological challenges that flow from this profound transformation in how the world is 'mediated' through online infrastructures are twofold: first, we have at work in daily life devices and systems for tracking people, bodies, and objects, which may, or may not, generate social knowledge; second, and *not* tracked by the new devices and systems themselves, there are the social, political, and cultural *adjustments* to the presence of such tracking in daily life, which generate new types of reflexive problem for human subjects that, in turn, require new ways of studying those problems and how they are, or are not, resolved.

In response to these more recent transformations and challenges, some commentators seem to have lost their head completely. When Chris Anderson, the editor of *Wired* magazine, proclaimed Big Data as the harbinger of the 'End of Theory' (a claim noted, and rejected, in this book's introduction), he mistook the role of commentator for legislator; fortunately, until now, the world has ignored his imperious proposal. Much more interesting have been the adjustments to the universalization of data tracking by multiple scholars across many parts of the social sciences, which are reflected in this book. Far from leading to the 'end of theory' or—Anderson's rhetoric had gone even wider—the redundancy of all hermeneutic approaches to the world, the emergence of 'big' data (which is never quite as comprehensive as its proselytes claim) becomes itself an important issue to be thought about in terms of the changes it brings to the texture of the social world.

In addressing these challenges, themselves driven by deep changes in the technologies through which the world is mediated, there is no way of avoiding thinking about the consequences of *Technology* for innovations in method, the topic of this book's Part II. Yet the consideration of technology, as I have implied, is inadequate unless grounded in an understanding of the stuff out of which the world is put together (in part a matter of prior naturalizations of technology), addressed in the book's Part I on *Materiality*. None of this would be so interesting if we insisted on ignoring its consequences for our experience of the social world, which is addressed in the book's Part III on *Experience*. The result, undeniably, is to increase massively the scale of information about the social world that requires interpretation, necessitating in turn better ways of presenting the data of social research (and indeed corporate and state research too), discussed in Part IV on *Visualization*.

The richness of this book's explorations is hugely to be welcomed. At a time emphatically *not* of 'normal science', whether in media research or the social sciences generally, we need a book like this that brings together young scholars in a collective endeavor to discover how much method— and sophisticated, theoretically informed innovation in method—matters for the quality of social life.

April 2016   Nick Couldry
                    London School of Economics and Political Science

Contents

Notes on Contributors

Jess Baines is Lecturer in Cultural and Historical Studies at London College of Communication, University of the Arts, UK. Her doctoral project at the London School of Economics and Political Science centers on the history of the UK's late twentieth-century radical and community printshops. MA in Contemporary Art History and Theory from Goldsmiths College, London. Prior to contact with higher education, she was a participant in various radical printing collectives.

Nicolas Baya-Laffite holds degrees in Political Science and Urban Environmental Management and a PhD in History of Science and Technology. His main research focus is on the political history of the environment as an object of conflict and government. After three years at the Médialab Sciences Po, he is now postdoctoral research fellow at the Institut Francilien Recherche Innovation Société (IFRIS), Université Paris-Est, France. Based at the Laboratoire Interdisciplinaire Sciences Innovations Sociétés (LISIS), he works on mapping international controversies on sustainability and adaptation using digital methods and tools.

Liliana Bounegru is a PhD candidate at the University of Groningen, the Netherlands, and the University of Ghent, Belgium, and researcher at the Digital Methods Initiative, University of Amsterdam. Her current research focuses on data journalism, digital methods and new media studies. She is also visiting researcher at the Médialab Sciences Po and a research fellow at the Tow Center for Digital Journalism at Columbia University.

Taina Bucher is Assistant Professor of Communication and IT at the University of Copenhagen, Denmark. She holds a PhD in Media Studies from the University of Oslo and an MSc in Culture and Society from the London School of Economics and Political Science. Her work focuses on the cultural and social implications of digital infrastructure, in particular, on the power and politics of algorithms in the contemporary media environment.

Paolo Ciuccarelli is Associate Professor at Politecnico di Milano, Italy, where he is Head of the Communication Design Research group. His research and publishing activities focus on the development of data, information and knowledge visualization tools and methods to support decision-making processes in complex systems. He is the founder and scientific coordinator of POLIteca, the Design Knowledge Centre of Politecnico di Milano, and has been visiting lecturer at Universidad de Malaga, Spain, and the Royal Institute of Art, Stockholm.

Jean Philippe Cointet holds degrees in Engineering and a PhD in Complex Systems. Since 2010, he is a researcher at Institut National de la Recherche Agronomique (INRA), France. Based at the Laboratoire Interdisciplinaire Sciences Innovations Sociétés (LISIS) he works on knowledge production dynamics in various kinds of communities forming socio-semantic systems. He participates to the development in the CorText platform that provides social science scholars online capacities for multi-source textual corpora analysis, including natural language processing tools, corpus collection and exploration, temporal analysis, and network mapping.

Nick Couldry is Professor of Media, Communications and Social Theory at the London School of Economics and Political Science, UK, where is also Head of the Department of Media and Communications. He was previously Professor of Media and Communications and joint Head of the Department of Media and Communications at Goldsmiths, University of London. He is the author or editor of eleven books including *Ethics of Media* (Palgrave Macmillan 2013), *Media, Society, World: Social Theory and Digital Media Practice* (2012) and *Why Voice Matters: Culture and Politics after Neoliberalism* (2010) and more than 100 peer-reviewed journal articles and book chapters. He is currently completing a book *The Mediated Construction of Reality* (2016) with Andreas Hepp, which revisits the work of social phenomenology for an age of digital media.

Erin Despard holds a PhD from Concordia University, Canada, and has been a visiting researcher and postdoctoral fellow at UC Berkeley, UCLA, and McGill University. Despard's research on the communicative functioning of parks, gardens and other urban environments has appeared in *Environment and Planning D: Space and Society*, *The Journal of Aesthetics and Culture*, *Landscape Research* and *Space and Culture*, among others. She is currently an adjunct professor in the Departement d'histoire at the Université de Sherbrooke, Quebec, Canada, where she is working on a book manuscript entitled *Montréal, la ville fleurie: An Archaeology of Urban Landscape and Horticultural Media*.

Alberto Frigo is a doctoral candidate in Media and Communication Studies at Södertörn University, Sweden. He has been project leader at MIT, USA, and has taught at Tongji University in Shanghai. Frigo's early interest in lifelogging has resulted in http://2004-2040.com, a 36 years depiction of himself and his surroundings. The project includes, for instance, a record of his activities based on the photos of all the objects his right hand uses. Exhibited worldwide, the project was awarded the prestigious Prix Ars Electronica in 2006. As part of his PhD thesis, Frigo investigates meaning-making of manually compiled lifelogs such as the one he is creating.

Jonathan Gray is a postdoctoral researcher at the University of Amsterdam, the Netherlands. He is also Research Associate at the Digital Methods Initiative, University of Amsterdam, and Director of Policy and Research at Open Knowledge. His current research focuses on the politics of data.

Richard Huskey is a doctoral candidate at the University of California Santa Barbara's Media Neuroscience Lab, and incoming Assistant Professor at the School of Communication, the Ohio State University, USA. Richard is the principle investigator at the Cognitive Communication Science Lab and the digital media coordinator for the International Communication Association's Communication Science and Biology Interest Group. His research lies at the intersection of media psychology and cognitive neuroscience with a particular focus on how media content influence human cognition and behavior. Philosophically grounded in an understanding of the mind (and the communication phenomena it enables) as a physical property of the brain, his research investigates three core topics: attitude and behavior change, media enjoyment and influence of moral narratives.

Neha Kumar is Assistant Professor at Georgia Tech, USA, jointly appointed at the schools of International Affairs and Interactive Computing. Her research focuses on human-centered computing for global development. She holds a PhD from UC Berkeley's School of Information. Before she came to Georgia Tech, she was a postdoctoral researcher both at the University of Washington's Computer Science & Engineering Department and the Annenberg School of Communication, University of Southern California.

Emily LaDue is a doctoral candidate at the Annenberg School for Communication, University of Pennsylvania, USA. She is currently researching the cultures, conditions, and discourses of contemporary urban development in deindustrialized US cities, with emphasis on the role of nonprofits in the political and economic processes of gentrification. She is also a documentary producer and uses video as one research method and medium in her work.

Katharina Lobinger is a postdoctoral research fellow at the Centre for Media, Communication and Information Research (ZeMKI), University of Bremen, Germany, and Associated Junior Fellow at the Institute for Advanced Study Delmenhorst (HWK). She works in the research area of communication and media studies with a special focus on visual research, social communication and mediatization research. In 2011 she was awarded the Doctoral Dissertation Award 'Media–Culture– Communication' for her doctoral thesis 'Visual Communication Research' (2012). Currently, she is the chair of the Visual Communication division of the German Communication Association (DGPuK). Her research interests include networked visual communication, mediatized everyday communication and visual methodologies.

Lev Manovich is Professor of Computer Science at the Graduate Center, City University of New York, USA. Manovich is the founder and director of Software Studies Initiative that uses methods from computer science, media design and humanities to analyze big cultural data such as millions of Instagram images. The lab's most recent projects were commissioned by the Museum of Modern Art (MoMA), New Public Library, and Google. He is the author and editor of eight books including *Data Drift* (2015), *Software Takes Command* (2013), *Soft Cinema: Navigating the Database* (2005) and *The Language of New Media* (2001).

Noortje Marres is Associate Professor at the University of Warwick, UK, where she is based at the Centre for Interdisciplinary Methodology. Her work investigates intersections between technology, knowledge, engagement and environments. She was trained in Science and Technology Studies at the University of Amsterdam and the Ecole des Mines, Paris, and has worked at the Department of Sociology at Goldsmiths, University of London, where she directed the interdisciplinary research at Centre for the Study of Invention and Social Process. Her first book was *Material Participation: Technology, the Environment and Everyday Publics* (Palgrave 2012).Currently she is writing a book on *Digital Sociology: The Reinvention of Social Research* (forthcoming).

Stefania Milan is Assistant Professor of New Media and Digital Culture at the University of Amsterdam, and Principal Investigator of the DATACTIVE project, funded with a Starting Grant of the European Research Council (data-activism.net). Her research explores technology and participation, cyberspace governance and emerging data epistemologies.

Paolo Patelli is an architect and researcher. His current interests include the role of design and legibility in promoting assemblages and networked publics across the geography and the media of the contemporary city. He investigates the ways urban publics reconnect to the physical dimension of the city through the affordances of a networked public sphere. He earned a PhD in Architectural and Urban Design from the Politecnico di Milano, Italy. He is half of La Jetée, a collaborative design practice based in Milan and Eindhoven. He has exhibited projects, contributed articles, lectured and offered workshops internationally.

Sarah Pink is RMIT Distinguished Professor and Director of the Digital Ethnography Research Centre in the School of Media and Communication, RMIT University, Melbourne, Australia. Her research is usually interdisciplinary and often brings together academic scholarship and applied practice. She has (co)authored and (co)edited *Digital Ethnography: Principles and Practice* (2016), *Screen Ecologies* (2016), *Digital Materialities* (2016), *Media Anthropology and Public Engagement* (2015), *Un/Certainty* (2015) and *Doing Sensory Ethnography* (2015, 2nd edition).

Segah Sak is an instructor at Faculty of Art, Design and Architecture, Department of Architecture, Bilkent University, Turkey. She holds a PhD in Art, Design and Architecture from Bilkent University. Following her dissertation she was a postdoctoral researcher at the University of Warwick's Centre for Interdisciplinary Methodologies. Her research lies in the intersection of memory, media and urban studies.

Paola Sartoretto holds a PhD from Karlstad University, Sweden, with a thesis analyzing communicative processes in the Brazilian Landless Workers Movement (MST). She is an associated researcher at the Institute of Latin American Studies, Stockholm University, and her research focuses on media practices among insurgent youth collectives.

Saskia Sassen is the Robert S. Lynd Professor of Sociology and Chair, the Committee on Global Thought, Columbia University, USA. Her new book is *Expulsions: Brutality and Complexity in the Global Economy* (2014). Recent books are *Territory, Authority, Rights: From Medieval to Global Assemblages* (2008), *A Sociology of Globalization* (2007), and the fully updated fourth edition of *Cities in a World Economy* (2012). Among older books are *The Global City* (1991/2001), and *Guests and Aliens* (1999). Her books are translated into over 20 languages. She is the recipient of diverse awards and mentions, including multiple doctor honoris causa, named lectures and being selected as one of the top global thinkers on diverse lists. Most recently she was awarded the Principe de Asturias 2013 Prize in the Social Sciences and made a member of the Royal Academy of the Sciences of Netherland.

Luca Simeone is a doctoral candidate in Interaction Design at Malmö University, Sweden. Luca's trajectory crosses design research and design practice. He has conducted research and teaching activities in leading international centers (Harvard, MIT, Polytechnic University of Milan and University of the Arts London), and has (co)authored and (co)edited some 70 publications. His latest book on *Visualizing the Data City* (2014) explores the potential of data visualizations for more inclusive urban design, planning, management processes. He has founded and managed six companies, including Vianet, an interaction design agency focused on delivering advanced technology and design solutions based on ethnographic research methods.

Pablo R. Velasco is a doctoral candidate at the Centre for Interdisciplinary Methodologies, University of Warwick, UK. His current research explores the materiality of digital currencies observed as political devices. He is interested in the rationale behind cryptocurrencies' design and in the interwoven relations between the state, borders, politics and cryptocurrencies' distribution of power. He recently participated in *Transmediale 2016: Conversation Piece* (Haus der Kulturen der Welt, Berlin) and collaborated in *APRJA: Excessive Research Journal* (Digital Aesthetics Research Centre, Aarhus University), and the *Moneylab Reader* (Institute of Network Cultures, Amsterdam).

LIST OF FIGURES

LIST OF TABLES

EDITOR Biography

Sebastian Kubitschko is a post-doctoral researcher at the University of Bremen's Centre for Media, Communication and Information Research, Germany. The main focus of his research is on hacker cultures, politics and democratic constellations. Kubitschko holds degrees from Goldsmiths, University of London, UK (PhD), the University of Melbourne, Australia (MA) and the Free University of Berlin, Germany (BA).

Anne Kaun is an associate professor in Media and Communication Studies at Södertörn University, Sweden. Her research is concerned with media and political activism and the role of technology for political participation from a historical perspective. Kaun holds degrees from Örebro University and Södertörn University, Sweden (PhD) and the University of Leipzig, Germany (MA).

CHAPTER 1

An Introduction to Innovative Methods in Media and Communication Research

Sebastian Kubitschko and Anne Kaun

As we are writing, media—or rather, their manifestations in the form of digital devices, online platforms, software, and algorithms—continue their triumphal march by increasingly penetrating social life in all its facets. It is understood that the near future will see more of an intensification than an alleviation of what is commonly referred to as mediatization, digitalization, or datafication. It is also understood by now that contemporary developments are far from being a linear, flat, or evenly distributed progression. Contemporary constellations contest the separation between discursive/digital/virtual/technical and material/embodied/physical/social spheres. As a consequence thereof, the emphasis of empirical research is shifting from interpreting 'life online' to researching a far broader range of 'mediated life' (Hand 2014). The insight that offline and online activities do not belong to separate worlds but in fact blend into one and the same 'reality' that constitutes people's everyday life has certainly intensified this dynamic. Along with these developments there have been diversification

S. Kubitschko (✉)
University of Bremen (ZeMKI), Bremen, Germany
e-mail: sebastian.kubitschko@uni-bremen.de

A. Kaun
Södertörn University, Stockholm, Sweden
e-mail: anne.kaun@sh.se

S. Kubitschko, A. Kaun (eds.), *Innovative Methods in Media and Communication Research*, DOI 10.1007/978-3-319-40700-5_1

and multiplication of research methods in media and communication studies, along with other disciplines that have an increasing interest in media and communication phenomena. As media technologies and infrastructures become inseparably interwoven with societal constellations, scholars from varying disciplines increasingly investigate their characteristics, functioning, relevance, and impact.

Contemporary developments are opening up the potential for change in both the methods and the objects of analysis in social science research. It is certainly the case that there is more opportunity to develop and make use of innovative methods now than at any other point in the history of media and communication research. At the same time, over the past years it has become a kind of truism to state that the quasi-omnipresence of media technologies and infrastructures poses challenges to empirical investigations (for valuable contributions see Rieder and Röhle 2012; Ruppert et al. 2013; Marres and Gerlitz 2015). The aim of this volume is to approach these challenges and opportunities actively and prolifically by bringing together empirical research *about* media transformations as well as studies that do research *through* media. The guiding aim of this volume is to provide methodological toolkits for investigating contemporary media and communication phenomena.

Research methods lay the foundation of almost every empirical endeavor and constitute an essential building block of science per se. The acquisition of knowledge about contemporary social, cultural, political, and economic constellations goes hand in hand with the implementation of appropriate methods. They might be considered a more or less welcome necessity, but they can also be stimulating, inspiring, and provoking. Research about media stretches back at least over a century and has involved most of the human and social sciences, as do the methods employed to study media. More recently, however, the process of innovating empirical research has gained considerable pace. This dynamic has led some commentators to attest a fundamental shift in the very way we should access our social world.

As a recent heatedly debated polemic declared: 'Who knows why people do what they do? The point is they do it, and we can track and measure it with unprecedented fidelity. With enough data, the numbers speak for themselves' (Anderson 2008, n.p.). Such empiricist epistemology might hold a lot of promise, but, as critical observers have rightfully argued, it is based on fallacious thinking in at least four ways: data are not simply essential elements that are abstracted from the world in objective ways; identifying patterns within data is discursively framed by previous findings, theories, and training; data cannot speak for themselves free of human bias or framing; and data cannot be interpreted without domain-specific knowledge (Kitchin 2014, pp. 4–5). At the same time, it is critical to acknowledge that empirical methods are, and in fact need to be, always in motion. This is far from saying that methodological innovations are the answer to all scientific quests. All the same, faced with 'a newly coordinated reality, one that is open, processual, non-linear and constantly on the move' (Adkins and Lury 2009, p. 18), researchers are asked to develop and implement methods that suit the contemporary media environment. Accordingly, instead of entering deeply into highly optimistic or deeply pessimistic visions of empirical research, we see a substantial need and demand for doing innovative research as well as for critical reflection on the epistemological implications of the acute change in the media environment.

The best way forward is not necessarily, to paraphrase Friedrich Nietzsche's famous aphorism in *The Gay Science*, to set sail after we have destroyed the bridge and demolished the land behind us (2001[1882], p. 119). We do not have to travel toward an uncertain no-man's-land and leave all we know behind. It appears to be much more fruitful to determinedly rethink and make valuable changes to established methods, to develop methodological approaches that break out from their conventional surroundings while remaining sensible to history and context. In fact, reconsidering, adjusting, and advancing research methods is a critical element of making significant findings possible in the first place. As it is understood that neither methods nor the people who develop and apply them emerge out of nowhere, the volume at hand emphatically implements the integration of emerging and established methods. Hence, the book gathers chapters about emerging methods in media and communication studies, while embedding these new ways of investigating current phenomena in the rich history of interdisciplinary empirical research in various fields.

With that in mind, this volume provides an encounter of current trajectories that we conceive as innovating media and communication research. Here, we do not simply insert innovation as an empty signifier celebrating everything new simply for the sake of newness, we explicitly employ the term to denote the lively and productive qualities of emerging methods. As Emma Hutchinson puts it: 'The drive for innovation appears misplaced, especially when the "new" aspects of online interaction are constantly overemphasized to the point where existing social research methods are ignored' (Hutchinson 2016, p. 143). Accordingly, we advocate an inclusive understanding of innovation, positioned between the notion that innovation is reserved for new research methods (see Wiles et al. 2013) and the idea that innovation is simply an extension of existing methodologies (see Taylor and Coffey 2008). Innovation here is a call for widening and rethinking research methods to further understanding of the role that media technologies and infrastructures play in society. Above all, methodological innovation takes place in doing. To innovate one has to develop, apply, and critically reflect on research methods.

The vast majority of empirical studies gathered in this volume are accomplished through early career scholars—doctoral and postdoctoral researchers, as well as assistant professors—who strive to advance fresh, cutting-edge, and at least partially also provocative approaches to the study of media and communication. Giving early career scholars a voice on research methods explicitly acknowledges their expertise in the field of methodology. To advocate innovative inquiries that are beneficial for social inquiry also means to be methodologically inclusive and receptive. Reflecting the need for suitable methods to answer emerging questions that result from the ever-changing media landscape, this book brings together researchers from varying scholarly traditions, theoretical backgrounds, and empirical training. The book thus provides unique insights into innovative methodological approaches at the intersection of media and communication studies, information science, urban studies, cultural studies, and neuroscience, as well as science and technology studies (STS) that all deal with media technologies and infrastructures.

Where We Are and Where We Want to Go

The study of media technologies and infrastructures is without doubt a rapidly growing field of inquiry in scientific and increasingly also in corporate settings. Research methods are the site where theory and practice merge into one often hardly distinguishable unit. Ideally they do so in a forward-thinking, critical, and engaged way. There is a plethora of handbooks dedicated to methodological questions in the social sciences and humanities as well as more specifically in media and communication studies. Yet, when revisiting existing methods books that dominate the field, we have been surprised that there are only a few dedicated publications on the issue of innovating methods that bring together interdisciplinary methodological perspectives (see Lury and Wakeford 2012; Snee et al. 2016).

The characteristics that the majority of available handbooks share are that they tend to engage in depth with one particular, traditional method like content analysis, interviewing, or participant observation and tend to lack comparative or overview aspects (Krippendorf 2013). Another corpus of publications shares a very generic perspective on media and communications and does not necessarily take into account contemporary methodological developments (Hansen and Machin 2013; Berger 2014). Still other methodology handbooks focus exclusively on particular approaches like visual methods (Banks and Zeitlyn 2015) or online qualitative methods (Salmons 2015), zero in on a singular technology like mobile media (Büscher et al. 2011), or introduce specific digital tools and methods to study 'new' media and communication phenomena such as issue networks (Rogers 2013; Bellotti 2015). Then again, scholars have modified methodological guidelines like ethnographic research to investigate the internet's role in present-day social worlds (Horst and Miller 2012; Hine 2015; Kozinets 2015; Pink et al. 2016). In their respective field of inquiry these methods books have proven to be highly valuable sources of inspiration and guidance.

Publications that share features with our approach of bringing inventive methods into dialogue with established ones from a critical cultural perspective tend to leave aside an explicit contextualizing of media and communications (Strydom 2011; Amelina et al. 2014; Kara 2015). While Bonnie Brennen's (2012) work on *Qualitative Research Methods for Media Studies* comes closer to our own approach within the realm of media and communications, her volume focuses on integrating practice and theory. What distinguishes this volume from many existing books is that it seeks to explore both the conceptual and the practical aspects of innovative methods for media and communication research. On the one hand, we aim to give researchers input for critical reflection and are taking stock of currently evolving methods in the field. On the other hand, we wish to give readers the hands-on research literacies essential for planning and conducting research. The purpose of this book is to feature a body of research that shines a light on the diversity and liveliness of contemporary methods in media and communication studies. What we aim to emphasize is that there is not one singular answer to the questions raised by the constantly changing media environment. In other words, this book is not about one-dimensionality but about multi-facetedness.

The overall subject that holds the project together is therefore less issue oriented than thematically structured. Rather than structuring the book along strict disciplinary boundaries, its component parts encompass a range of methodological approaches to the contemporary contexts and future directions of media technologies and infrastructures. It would be naïve to expect that the contributing authors provide definite answers to all of the current research questions and challenges around media environments. Neither does this volume incorporate all possible and meaningful methods that are currently employed or emerging in media and communications. What the contributions in this volume do establish, however, are some of the critical junctures and key resources for rethinking existing and traditional methods to research media and communications. Accordingly, with this book we aim to stimulate a more sophisticated debate on and exploration of contemporary research methods for scholars at various levels of academic life—from undergraduates and postgraduates to junior and senior researchers.

It is often challenging to find, let alone to develop, adequate research methods to analyze social practices and structures under apparently fast-moving and 'complex' conditions. In particular, postgraduate and doctoral students might be intimidated or even frightened to leave common ground and establish research projects off the beaten track. It can be difficult to convince peers and supervisors of the benefit, usability, and reliability of inventive research practices. We hope that the writings of the authors in this book, most of whom are early career scholars themselves, give young researchers the confidence to break new ground. At the same time, the book aims to inspire scholars who continue to apply classic research methods to take into consideration upcoming tendencies that might enrich their scholarship. The objective of the volume is to give students, young scholars as well as experienced academics, insights into up-to-date research methods and an overview of what might work best for their own research projects.

Research methods are 'tools of investigation and vehicles for thought' (Back and Puwar 2012, p. 6). Echoing this viewpoint, we are keen to argue that the volume at hand should be seen as an inspiration and a guide to emerging methodological possibilities and thinking. This book is intended specifically to intrigue, provoke, and encourage readers to a degree that lets them reflect about their own approach, and perhaps even try out something new. Ideally, the chapters that lay ahead of us will inspire scholars to revisit their research repertoire and to expand their methodological craft. We also aim to assist teaching by providing a methods book that draws together a diverse and eclectic range of material that is presented in an accessible and stimulating form. In each chapter the authors position their research within existing, comparable, and competing approaches and by doing so give the reader the possibility of digging deeper into a specific field of inquiry.

To familiarize the reader in more depth with the road ahead, we now proceed to give a brief overview of the chapters that actually bring the book's objectives into being.

The Structure of the Book

As we set great value on preventing the establishment of theoretical and methodological silos, this book is a heterogeneous collection of exciting empirical research projects brought together from a variety of academic traditions. Overall the volume comprises twenty-four early career and prominent scholars from twenty institutions spread across eleven countries. The contributing authors are united in their endeavor to engage with the complexities of methodological possibilities and challenges with which researchers from across diverse areas in the field of media and communication are dealing. To integrate the different approaches and to make the content readily accessible, the chapters are allocated into four sections that resemble dominant tropes in media and communication research: Materiality (Part I), Technology (Part II), Experience (Part III), and Visualization (Part IV).

The distinctions between the four parts are, at least to a certain degree, arbitrary, as the different methods across the sections and chapters often interrelate. While the volume does not claim completeness—an impossible task to achieve, considering the diversity and complexity of research in media and communication studies—one of the book's distinguishing features is that it includes a wide range of perspectives to mirror the increasing interconnection of media technologies and infrastructures (instead of artificially narrowing the field of inquiry). At the same time, the volume brings together methods that relate to each other, affect one another, and are vital when considering innovative research in media and communications.

Dividing the book into distinct domains does not only provide readers with a better overview, it also underlines the references the researchers make to particular approaches, theoretical traditions, and fields of inquiry, since each section has its own focal point. The respective focal points are explicitly addressed in concise introductions that precede each section. To provide further validation of the notion that innovative research methods are often modifications and transmutations of established paths of investigation, introductory chapters written by experienced scholars in the field yield a fruitful contextualization of the innovative approaches presented by early career researchers. Besides serving a framing function, the idea here is also to create a dialogue between young and more senior scholars.

Part I on *Materiality* is introduced by Saskia Sassen, one of the world's leading scholars for rethinking conceptualizations of metropolitan areas and urbanizing technologies over the past two decades. In Chap. 2, Jess Baines employs the wiki as a method *for* research to mobilize its 'participatory' potential through the instigation of the open access wiki radicalprintshops.org. Without losing sight of the potential and actual value for the principled and instrumental aims of the wiki, Baines also discusses the methodological and ethical challenges and contradictions that the experiment raised. In Chap. 3, Erin Despard develops an approach for the empirical study of site-specific media relations. The methodological strategy she advances based on theories of an inclusive materialist media ecology is designed to grapple with the political implications inherent in the mediation of public places. Chap. 4 handles digital media research through an architectural/urban viewpoint. More concretely, Segah Sak shows how media and communication studies can benefit from socio-spatial approaches to urban, environmental, and behavioral research. The chapters gathered in Part I tackle questions of how media shape their material, spatial surroundings. How do media technologies contribute to the constitution and experience of space and place? How are space and place produced as political sites in and through media technologies?

Part II on *Technology* is introduced by Noortje Marres, who is renowned for investigating the intersections between technology, knowledge, engagement, and environments in innovative ways that often relate to digital social research. In Chap. 5, Taina Bucher uses the concept of the black box as a heuristic device to discuss the nature of algorithms in contemporary media platforms, and how researchers might investigate algorithms despite, or even because of, their seemingly secret nature. Moving beyond the notion that algorithms *are* black boxes, Bucher asks instead what is at stake in framing algorithms in this way, and what such a framing might possibly distract us from asking. Pablo R. Velasco devotes his research in Chap. 6 to identifying native social structures in cryptocurrencies. Based on digital research that is directed toward socio-political inquiries, he develops indicators and a method to map entities of the Bitcoin network on a geographic canvas. In Chap. 7, Richard Huskey examines the neural basis of human communication behavior by explaining how psychophysiological interaction analyses (PPI) can be used to assess communication questions with functional magnetic resonance imaging (fMRI) data. Huskey discusses how investigations of neural connectivity add crucial information about how neural structures enable higher-order communication processes. Alberto Frigo makes use of Chap. 8 to provide an alternative way to look at lifelogging and goes as far as proposing it as an indispensable method for scholars to better sense and understand the complex media-generated landscape around them. Through a historical contextualization of lifelogging and an invitation to embrace technical complexity in an autoethnographic fashion, Frigo introduces a set of instructions on how to get started on lifelogging as a research method. Unifying questions that concern the authors in this section are: How is technology enabling us to capture everyday life and mundane communicative practices? How is everyday life constitutive of and constituted by technologies?

Part III on *Experiences* is introduced by Sarah Pink, one of the most eminent social anthropologists in the field of visual methods and renowned for advocating ethnographic research to investigate the contemporary media environment. In Chap. 9, Emily LaDue critically examines the reflexive turn in ethnographic methods and the gentrification critique of urban development. Based on research on a community organization, LaDue explicates how this examination may offer visual ethnographers and urban ethnographers insight into the (political) shortcomings of work that relies on reflexivity and a critique of gentrification alone. In Chap. 10, Paola Sartoretto focuses on the experiences of marginalized groups that are geographically isolated and do not have access to the most advanced technologies, in order to broaden the horizons of analysis of the interplay between social action and media. Sartoretto positions non-media-centric multi-media ethnography as a helpful way to include experiences outside the Western context in the process of theory and knowledge building. By presenting field experiences from non-Western and relatively under-studied contexts in Chap. 11, Neha Kumar demonstrates the relevance of ethnographically oriented approaches and in-person interviews in light of the increasing preponderance of quantitative, data-driven methodologies. Kumar also accentuates that conducting interviews is not always straightforward and can bring unforeseeable challenges when the researcher and field sites are separated by geographic, cultural, gender, or class-based differences. The three chapters applying ethnographic methods that are gathered in this section concern experiences that emerge while engaging with different media technologies, in terms of both content and infrastructures. How are meaningful experiences produced? How can we capture the broad range of political experiences through the lens of media? How are communal experiences produced through media practices?

Part IV on *Visualization* is introduced by Lev Manovich, a pioneer in computational analysis of large data sets and visualization techniques. In Chap. 12, Jonathan Gray, Liliana Bounegru, Stefania Milan, and Paolo Ciuccarelli underline the importance of developing a critical literacy to read, understand, and work with data visualizations in contemporary information environments. By proposing a three-part heuristic framework, the chapter contributes toward a critical literacy for data visualizations as research objects and devices in order to support their critical and reflexive use. In Chap. 13, Luca Simeone and Paolo Patelli build on their experience as designers and researchers within Urban Sensing, a research project aimed at creating software that gathers and analyzes geo-located information posted on social networks. Simeone and Patelli provide helpful empirical material for researchers to reflect on the potential and limitations of social network analysis and data visualization as research methods in urban studies. In Chap. 14, Nicolas Baya-Laffite and Jean-Philippe Cointet map the United Nations Climate Convention's negotiations topic structure and evolution over twenty years using a digital corpus. The methodological strategy that Baya-Laffite and Cointet explore is based on computer-assisted tools and techniques of text mining, semantic network analysis, and data visualization that allow both quantitative and qualitative insights to be obtained. In Chap. 15, Katharina Lobinger discusses the advantage of creative *visual* methods beyond the image-centered scopes of visual communication research. More concretely, Lobinger puts emphasis on different forms of participatory approaches, on visual Q-sort studies and card-sorting procedures, and on creative drawing-based exercises to signal the relevance of *visual* methods for audience studies in media and communication research. The chapters share an interest in investigating visualizations as means of making sense of the world. Visualizations and visual methods in that sense become a way of knowing the world as well as creating new ecologies to be known.

The concluding chapter acts in the first instance as an amalgamating entity. Even more importantly, it articulates a methodological 'advisory register' and formulates a (more or less) provoking outlook on the road ahead of media and communication research.

Now, before we give the stage to the empirical chapters, we want to thank all the contributing authors for their commitment to and belief in this project. Without your drive for deepening understanding of the contemporary media environment and its role in the social world, this book would not exist—it's as simple as that. We want to thank the three reviewers for their productive and supportive feedback, which has without doubt enhanced this volume considerably. Thanks to Felicity Plester and Sophie Auld at Palgrave Macmillan, who have supported and guided us not only in a very professional but also a kindly and dedicated way. We also want to give thanks to Aram Bartholl (and Janet Leyton-Grant) for giving us the possibility to use his humorous, critical, and fitting artwork and Lisa Jung for her wonderful support on the cover design. Finally, we want to thank all the brilliant colleagues who have supported the publication of this volume early on by stating their interest in the project.

Acknowledgment Sebastian Kubitschko's contribution to editing this book took place in the context of the Creative Unit IV 'Communicative Figurations' at ZeMKI (Centre for Media, Communication and Information Research), University of Bremen, which is supported by the institutional strategy 'Ambitious and Agile' of the University of Bremen, funded within the frame of the Excellence Initiative by the German Federal and State Governments.

REFERENCES

Adkins, L. and Lury, C. (2009) Introduction: What is the Empirical? *European Journal of Social Theory* 12(1): 5–20.

Amelina, A., Nergiz, D., Faist, T., et al. (Eds.) (2014) *Beyond Methodological Nationalism: Social Science Research Methods in Transition* (London: Routledge).

Anderson, C. (2008) The End of Theory: The Data Deluge Makes the Scientific Method Obsolete. *Wired* 23 June: http://www.wired.com/2008/2006/pb-theory/ (accessed 10 March 2016).

Back, L. and Puwar, N. (2012) A Manifesto for Live Methods: Provocations and Capacities. *The Sociological Review* 60(S1): 6–17 .

Banks, M. and Zeitlyn, D. (2015) *Visual Methods in Social Research.* 2nd ed. (London: Sage).

Bellotti, E. (2015) *Qualitative Networks: Mixing Methods in Social Research* (New York: Routledge).

Berger, A. (2014) *Media and Communication Research: An Introduction to Qualitative and Quantitative Approaches.* 3rd ed. (London: Sage).

Brennen, B. (2012) *Qualitative Research Methods for Media Studies* (London: Routledge).

Büscher, M., Urry, J. and Witchger, K. (Eds.) (2011) *Mobile Methods* (London: Routledge).

Hand, M. (2014) From Cyberspace to the Dataverse: Trajectories in Digital Social Research. In: M. Hand and S. Hillyard (Eds.), *Big Data? Qualitative Approaches to Digital Research* (Bingley: Emerald), pp. 1–27.

Hansen, A. and Machin, D. (2013) *Media and Communication Research Methods* (London: Palgrave Macmillan).

Hine, C. (2015) *Ethnography for the Internet: Embedded, Embodied and Everyday* (London: Bloomsbury).

Horst, H. and Miller, D. (Eds.) (2012) *Digital Anthropology* (London: Berg).

Hutchinson, E. (2016) Digital Methods and Perpetual Reinvention? Asynchronous Interviewing and Photo Elicitation. In: H. Snee, C. Hine, Y. Morey, et al. (Eds.), *Digital Methods for Social Science: An Interdisciplinary Guide to Research Innovation* (London: Palgrave Macmillan), pp. 143–56.

Kara, H. (2015) *Creative Research Methods in the Social Sciences: A Practical Guide* (Bristol: Policy Press).

Kitchin, R. (2014) Big Data, New Epistemologies and Paradigm Shifts. *Big Data & Society* (April–June): 1–12.

Kozinets, R. (2015) *Netnography: Refined.* 2nd ed. (London: Sage).

Krippendorf, K. (2013) *Content Analysis: An Introduction to its Methodology.* 3rd ed. (London: Sage).

Lury, C. and Wakeford, N. (Eds.) (2012) *Inventive Methods. The Happening of the Social* (London: Routledge).

Marres, N. and Gerlitz, C. (2015) Interface Methods: Renegotiating Relations Between Digital Social Research, STS and Sociology. *The Sociological Review* 64(1): 21–46.

Nietzsche, F. (2001[1882]) *The Gay Science* (Cambridge: Cambridge University Press).

Pink, S., Horst, H., Postill, J., et al. (2016) *Digital Ethnography: Principles and Practice* (London: Sage).

Rieder, B. and Röhle, T. (2012) Digital Methods: Five Challenges. In D. M. Berry (Ed.), *Understanding Digital Humanities* (London: Palgrave Macmillan), pp. 67–84.

Rogers, R. (2013) *Digital Methods* (Cambridge, MA: MIT Press).

Ruppert, E., Law, J. and Savage, M. (2013) Reassembling Social Science Methods: The Challenge of Digital Devices. *Theory, Culture & Society* 30(4): 22–46.

Salmons, J. (2015) *Doing Qualitative Research Online* (London: Sage).

Snee, H., Hine, C., Morey, Y., et al. (Eds.) (2016) *Digital Methods for Social Science: An Interdisciplinary Guide to Research Innovation* (London: Palgrave Macmillan).

Strydom, P. (2011) *Contemporary Critical Theory and Methodology* (London: Routledge).

Taylor, C. and Coffey, A. (2008) *Innovation in Qualitative Research Methods: Possibilities and Challenges. Working Paper 121* (Cardiff: Cardiff University).

Wiles, R., Bengry-Howell, A., Crowe, G., et al. (2013) But is it Innovation? The Development of Novel Methodological Approaches in Qualitative Research. *Methodological Innovations Online* 8(1): 18–33.

PART I

Materiality

Saskia Sassen

THE ASSEMBLAGES WITHIN WHICH THE DIGITAL FUNCTIONS

The technical properties of digital domains deliver their utilities through complex ecologies that include non-technological variables, such as the social and the subjective, as well as the particular cultures of use of different actors. This is particularly strong in interactive domains. When we consider digital spaces as part of such ecologies, rather than as a purely technical condition, we make conceptual and empirical room for a range of conditions and vectors that are not part of the technology. Such conditions include the broad range of cultures of use through which these technologies are engaged by different actors and entities across variable settings. In this analytic move lies the possibility of theorization (Sassen 2016).

These larger ecologies remain under-recognized, under-studied, and under-theorized in the social science literature. The more typical approach is to use technical categories to analyze digital space. There is a need to develop more social categories to study and theorize digital space. The three chapters in this part do this and make an important contribution to a more theorized approach to the subject.

S. Sassen (✉)
Columbia University, New York City, NY, USA
e-mail: sjs2@columbia.edu

One way in which this partial reshaping of the technical by social logics of users and/or settings becomes evident is that similar, and even the same, technical properties can produce strikingly different outcomes across diverse settings. Depending on the logics guiding use, digital capabilities can contribute to very diverse outcomes. They can contribute to distributive outcomes, for instance by enabling greater participation of local organizations in global networks; thereby they can help constitute transboundary public spheres or forms of globality centered in multiple localized types of struggles and agency.

However, these same properties can also lead to higher levels of control and concentration in the global capital market (Sassen 2012). And they can do so even though the power of these financial electronic networks rests on a kind of distributed power; that is, millions of investors distributed around the world and their millions of individual decisions. Thus, while digitization of instruments and markets was critical to the sharp growth in the value and power of the global capital market, this outcome was shaped by interests and logics that typically had little to do with digitization per se. This brings to the fore the extent to which digitized markets are embedded in complex institutional settings, cultural frames, and even intersubjective dynamics. In turn, much place boundedness is today increasingly—although not completely—inflected or inscribed by the hypermobility of some of its components, products, and outcomes. More than in the past, both fixity and mobility are located in a temporal frame where speed is ascendant and consequential, but immobilities and slow-downs are also very much part of it all.

When it comes to very practical issues, there is often a poverty of social imagination in the analysis—it is all flattened into description even when the case includes very complex systems. For instance, we have enormously detailed descriptions of how and why local governments deploy all kinds of digital sensors—for fire, floods, deterioration of key components of mechanical systems, all part of the smart city. Yet these are descriptions, and we need to go beyond descriptions and explore whether these practical applications lend themselves to interpretations that might include social variables and theorized examinations of the larger settings within which they are inserted. The city puts technologies to a test: it is one window into understanding successful technological innovations for urban systems and urban life. Here the chapter 'Engaging (Past) Participants: The Case of radicalprintshops.org' by Jess Baines makes a very good contribution: it focuses on a wiki and its practical applications, but then takes these on a theoretical walk that brings in the social.

Socio-political processes can emerge from the use of even a simple technology, especially if they involve people. We must capture these effects in our analyses of the technologies, even if they are peripheral. Further, they can also mobilize across neighborhoods, because the tech enables that. I find that one key issue is the need to urbanize these technologies; that is to say, to bring them out of the techie zone and into the messy urban zone. The active and mutually shaping interaction of the digital and place or, more generically, material spaces is at work in the chapter 'A Materialist Media Ecological Approach to Studying Urban Media in/of Place' by Erin Despard. One effect is changes in conceptions of place and their role in mediated communication. The chapter 'Socio-Spatial Approaches for Media and Communication Research' by Segah Sak brings to the fore that research on digital media benefits from socio-spatial analyses, and offers the elements of such an approach.

Cities will almost inevitably leave an imprint on most technologies—it is rarely feasible simply to plop down a new technology, for example, in an urban space. I would argue that these kinds of analyses also signal the need to push the urbanizing of technology further, and in different directions—including settings we have neglected, for instance low-income neighborhoods and workplaces, and settings in other parts of the world that are radically different from those described in all three chapters. Diverse ecologies of meaning may be generated from similar technical capabilities. We can think of these cultural and spatial differences as pushing the open sourcing of at least some technologies by mobilizing the intelligences, the needs, and the imaginations of residents.

The DNA of the city is more akin to open source technology. An approach that takes this factor into account would enable interactions between the technology and the user beyond those already pre-programmed within these systems. Historically, I find that it is the combination of the incompleteness and the complexity of major cities that has enabled them to outlive enterprises, kingdoms, and nation-states. These are all rather closed formal systems, and this has made them rigid and more susceptible to disintegration. One implication of this development (there are more) is that the new trend toward installing a growing range of closed, controlled intelligent systems in cities puts those cities at risk of becoming obsolete themselves when the technologies become obsolete.

Across time, cities have complicated the straightforward implementation of technologies. Elsewhere I have examined this through the question 'Does the City have Speech?' (Sassen 2013). The mix of urban materialities and people's cultures in a city is not quite predictable, and hence can unsettle or disrupt the best designs. This holds at many levels—from a vast structural transportation system and so-called intelligent systems installed in buildings, to a minimalist pothole-detection wiki. The city puts technologies to the test: it is one window into understanding successful technological innovations for urban systems and urban life. Therewith the city also is a lens that allows us to understand the diverse interactions between users (whether systems, organizations, or people) and the design and implementation of the technologies used in cities.

Recognizing that digital technologies often engage socio-material conditions opens up a research agenda about their access and use. It is not simply about the fact that such digital capabilities exist. These capabilities are made and so are their infrastructures and software, and since societies contain vastly different opportunities as well as marginalization structures, we must allow for the fact that not all potential users and potential types of uses are necessarily in play. Further, some types of potential uses may not be sustained by existing software, and some users may lack access.

Getting to the heart of these diverse engagements with digital capabilities requires not only understanding the particular features of cities, but also 'seeing' the issue as if one were a city. In other words, it requires a juggling of the diversity of elements that constitute urban space, which inevitably means a multi-perspective approach. The city is a generous partner in this work: it offers a lens into larger realities, many non-urban but that in today's economic structuring have an urban moment in their trajectories. This type of analysis keeps us from simply being technologists. It helps us factor in the friction and obstacles that even the most advanced technologies or engineering confront in urban environments.

References

Sassen, S. (2016) Digital Cultures of Use and Their Infrastructures. In J. Wajcman and N. Dodd (Eds.), *The Sociology of Speed* (Oxford: Oxford University Press).

Sassen, S. (2013) Does the City have Speech? *Public Culture* 25(2): 209–21.

Sassen, S. (2012) Interactions of the Technical and the Social: Digital Formations of the Powerful and the Powerless. *Information, Communication and Society* 5(4): 455–78.

CHAPTER 2

Engaging (Past) Participants: The Case of radicalprintshops.org

Jess Baines

In the assembly of contemporary digital technologies, wikis are among those heralded for their democratic and 'participatory' potential. From the ambitious scale of Wikipedia to the more modest scope of the school classroom, wikis have been adopted to co-produce and share knowledge. In relation to the latter, Robert Fitzgerald argues that 'the wiki approach' (2007, p. 680) to learning is consistent with the constructionist educational theory perspective that knowledge is 'neither received or found', but produced in interaction with other humans and tools. There has been significant research into the use of wikis in a variety of contexts, as the nine thousand pages of WikiPapers testify.[1] Regarding the use of wikis *in* academic research, they are mostly utilized as a means for closed groups to manage research data rather than as a method *for* research. This chapter describes an experiment to mobilize this potential through the instigation of an open access wiki, radicalprintshops.org. This wiki was conceived as an adjunct to and part of a research project I had recently undertaken. It was partly an attempt to balance the nature of the academic research process and final form with something that was more aligned to the collectivist politics and practices of my subjects. The aspiration was also that

J. Baines (✉)
London School of Economics and Political Science, London, UK
e-mail: j.baines@lse.ac.uk

© The Author(s) 2016   17
S. Kubitschko, A. Kaun (eds.), *Innovative Methods in Media and Communication Research*, DOI 10.1007/978-3-319-40700-5_2

it would engender their interest and generate new empirical material on which to draw. Without losing sight of the potential and actual value for the principled *and* instrumental aims of radicalprintshops.org, the developing challenges and contradictions that the experiment raised will also be discussed throughout this chapter.

SOMEONE SHOULD DO A HISTORY BEFORE WE ALL DIE

The subject of my research was the history of the radical printshops collectives that had proliferated during the 1970s in the UK. Along with scores of other people, I had spent several years working in them. The impetus to make them a subject of research grew out of conversations at a 2007 anniversary celebration of one of the last remaining shops (Calverts Press in East London, 1977 to today). While marveling at how this printshop had survived, we gossiped about all the others that had long since disappeared. One person said, half-jokingly, 'somebody should do a history before we all die'; there was a murmur of concurrence. 'Yeah, but who would do it?' I asked. 'You could!'[2] The event itself and this exchange planted the seeds for my research proposal. Ideas for an oral history project, an exhibition, and a book of images and anecdotes were all considered before I eventually decided that the research should take a conventional academic form. I felt that this would allow me to better explore the questions that were starting to present themselves. It was treating the history of the printshops, our history, as worthy of rigorous and sustained attention. I had also begun to think that given my own involvement, some kind of distance would better serve the endeavor. The decision to take this direction was not without ambivalence.

PROBLEM CONTEXT NO. 1

My own experience in the printshops was mostly one of little respect for academic inquiry. During the 1980s there was spate of academic study into 'industrial democracy' and researchers frequently contacted the printshop where I worked. We constantly refused them, seeing it as a waste of our productive time and of no benefit. Underlying our dismissal was the view that the researcher's interest was probably a career-serving fad. Commitment meant 'doing', not 'observing' on a university grant or salary to produce information we knew already. Concern about academic research and its subsequent 'value' for its subjects has become an ongoing theme in social movement studies, with much discussion about ethics, reciprocity, positionality, identity, and so on (Croteau 2005; Khasnabish and Haiven 2012; Milan 2014). While scholars of radical movements and organizations might hope that their assiduously researched and analytic studies will in some way assist the future of progressive movements and organizations, their efforts tend to remain in inaccessible journals and textbooks. It is not simply the final form and dissemination of the research that may be at issue, but the manner in which the research is conducted, and thus the kind of knowledge produced (Chesters 2012). As Gillan and Pickerill (2012) state, a key question becomes: Who is the research for? Many of those engaged in such research are politically sympathetic to the movements and groups they study and, as in my own case, have often been or are involved in them, which can make these issues especially resonant. The ways in which the issues can be addressed partly depends on the type of research and the researcher's relationship to the subjects of study. While there is not space to expand on this here, various propositions and approaches have been advocated, such as participatory action research (PAR) and militant research, which in various ways are about politically engaged research that is 'with' rather than 'about' its subjects (see Kindon et al. 2010; Shukaitis and Graeber 2007; Garelli and Tazzioli 2013). Once I had eventually embarked on the research, recurring questions from people with printshop associations were: 'Where can we see what you are doing?', 'How will you make it available?', and 'Will we understand it?'.

Problem Context No. 2

The printshops themselves had developed alongside the growth of 'history from below', oral history, community history, and 'community archives', and the importance of these challenges to conventional history were assumed. Nevertheless, like most organizations of the alternative left, the printshops did not consider their own historical record, and as such—as I soon discovered—scant documentary evidence of them existed in archives and repositories. This presented one part of the ensuing research challenge. The problem of elusive remains is one common to historians both of grassroots activity and of marginalized lives (Black and MacRaild 2000). 'Fringe' social movement groups and 'alternative' organizations often fall into this category and, as Bosi and Reiter point out, due to their often 'informal and fragmented nature produce and leave behind only in a limited way the same kind of evidence as classical organisations' (2014, p. 129). Few do what they do with 'heritage' in mind, and they may even deliberately leave minimal evidence for reasons of safety (Flinn 2008). The alternative left culture that grew up in the printshops was also one in which an 'anti-bureaucratic' ethos often prevailed (Landry et al. 1985), with little importance attached to keeping records (Chong 2011; Swash 2011). While independent community and radical archives can sometimes provide vital sources of marginal or otherwise overlooked activity, such resources frequently exist in precarity due to lack of economic resources, scarcity of space, and the fluctuations of interested volunteers (Bosi and Reiter 2014). Furthermore, ideological or idiosyncratic rejections of storage, handling, access, and cataloguing conventions can also frustrate the academic researcher's expectations.

What evidential traces that still existed of the printshops were likely to be mainly in the hands (or dusty boxes) of ex-participants. This connected to another problem: I had only a small handful of ex-printshop contacts. The aims of my research were congruent with a qualitative rather than quantitative approach, in that I sought to elicit detail, texture, experience, and diversity to build a nuanced historical analysis (Flick 2007). The qualitative approach means that the numbers of respondents or cases are 'necessarily small' (Bauer and Gaskell 2009, p. 42). However, not only were my contacts limited, they were inevitably prejudiced toward particular organizations. As Jolly et al. (2012) have discussed in relation to their Women's Liberation Movement research, the recent history of radical organizations and movements raises particular problems of representation—who speaks or gets asks to speak, and within that whose version of the past prevails. If my research was going to be based on empirical data, be 'properly historical' rather than a more abstract theoretical consideration that drew on loose generalizations, there was an arduous task ahead of tracing as many ex-members as I could, and of persuading them to share information and be interviewed. Interviews would be a crucial tool for research given the apparently thin documentation of the printshops.

The issue of both finding interviewees and convincing them of the value of giving me their time was serious. This is a common problem for researchers (Seale et al. 2007), and with regard to locating subjects of marginal and no longer existing activities, it can be especially so (Rubin and Rubin 2011). However, my own background as an ex-printshop participant gave me a relatively privileged starting position in that (a) I had some names and a few contacts already; and (b) our common history *might* provide some basis for trust. The printshops were also part of a wider alternative left milieu of politics, shared living, friendships, and relationships, and as such I anticipated that there would be some vestiges of this that would assist with a 'snowball' of contacts. The 'snowball sample' is typically useful when, as Lorenzo Mosca puts it, 'focusing on hard to reach populations [… and] where the members know each other' (2014, p. 409). Concerning the issue of what value potential interviewees might cede to the research, the casual conversation that had prompted it provided some encouragement. Ex-members would also be of an age where their involvement might now be viewed as a distinct and possibly significant part of their own life history. Whether they would value an academic research project, or want to discuss this period in their life or share their shoebox archives with me, was of course another matter. It was a long time ago and it was not part of a history that had been culturally validated since. For well over twenty years the collective experiments of the 1970s and 1980s in working and living differently had essentially been consigned to the history dustbin marked 'uncool' (Sholette 2011; see also Hesmondhalgh 2000). Edward Thompson's memorable words that presaged the simultaneously flourishing movement for 'history from below' might well be applied to these attempts: 'Only the successful (in the sense of those whose aspirations anticipated subsequent evolution) are remembered. The blind alleys, the lost causes and the losers themselves are forgotten' (1968, p. 12). As recently as 2007, Colin MacCabe and Stuart Hall agreed that the reason that these experiments had gone unwritten by those involved was that 'it was too painful' (MacCabe 2007, p. 27). It is only recently, and really after I began the research, that this situation has been noticeably reversed.

The combination of these factors led to the decision to experiment with building a preliminary online resource, the open wiki radicalprintshops.org, as an adjunct and possible aid to the academic research. In the first instance the site would serve to publicly share the material I was finding. The anticipated 'audience' was printshop members and a wider activist and radical lay audience. The site seemed like a way to begin to bridge the gap between the formal process and outcome of the academic project and its subjects. It would hold documents, images, and maybe participant accounts, operating as an organically developing open archive, a sort of niche knowledge commons. It would also start to give the history of the printshops a visible and affirmative online presence that printshop members unknown to me might encounter. I hoped that it would stimulate interest from ex-participants, individually and collectively, in the *general* value of producing such a history. By setting the site up as a *wiki*, it also held the possibility for them to contribute in their own time and terms, a sort of micro 'crowdsourcing' (Howe 2006) to begin to generate a loosely collaborative history.[3] That in turn might provide new sources of information for my academic research. A wiki was not just practical for the task, its affordances for content collaboration seemed ideologically resonant with the historical background of the printshop collectives. The congruence of wikis with horizontal organizational structures and collective knowledge building does of course have historical precedence in their use by the Indymedia Documentation Project, as well as ESF (European Social Forum) groups in the early 2000s (Ebersbach and Glaser 2004; Milberry 2012). More recently wikis are being used for a growing number of participatory digital history projects, from FoundSF (http://foundsf.org), which gathers the history of alternative San Francisco, to the LGBT History Project (http://lgbthistoryuk.org). As Andrew Flinn (2007) has articulated, the upsurge more generally of online 'community archives' and digital history projects is driven by the same impetus as the radical, community, and oral history initiatives that were developed in the 1970s and 1980s. The recent growth is not least because of the affordances of online technologies in creating virtual space for deposits and dispersed collaboration and access, overcoming some of the problems inherent to their location-bound counterparts. Flinn has argued that the 'community archive', digital or not, presents a crucial challenge and opportunity for the mainstream archive by exposing its historical exclusion of 'the voices of non-elites, the grassroots and the marginalised' (Flinn 2007, p. 152; see also Vincent 2014). Within recent years the archiving profession has grappled with notions of 'Archives 2.0', which Joy Palmer described as 'less about the integration of Web 2.0 technologies […] and more related to a fundamental shift in perspective, to a philosophy that privileges the user and promotes an ethos of sharing, collaboration and openness' (2009, n.p). The use of digital technology has played a core role in facilitating institutional attempts at this democratization, from the digitization of and online access to archives to the trialing of tools including 'wiki layers'[4] on such archives that enable users (lay or academic) to add supplementary content or tags, and the creation of personal workspaces within archive sites (Howard et al. 2011; Ridge 2014; Craven 2012).

Setting Up the Wiki

To some extent, 'everyone' knows roughly what a wiki is, mainly because of Wikipedia (launched in 2001). In brief then, the first wiki software (WikiWikiWeb) was developed by Ward Cunningham in the mid-1990s to enable a community of software developers to work together. Wikis are web-based content management systems that allow users to collaborate on content asynchronously. They contain a series of extendable hyperlinked pages on which users can add, edit, and delete information, alter the structure, and so on. Every change is automatically recorded, viewable and reversible by users. Wikis use a very simplified markup language and as such users require no knowledge of code, nor any specialist software or plugins. Cunningham described wikis as the 'simplest online database that could possibly work' (2002, n.p.). Up to the present, two basic applications for wikis have emerged. One is for a closed group to collaborate or share information, and these have been taken up and promoted in various educational, workplace, and community settings to this effect. The other application, exemplified by Wikipedia but also by some of the examples already mentioned, is the open model that allows anyone to contribute. A wiki also might be viewable across the web, but only open to a closed group of contributors. Since Cunningham's WikiWikiWeb, numerous types of wiki clone software have been developed, including Mediawiki (which powers Wikipedia), TikiWiki, and Foswiki. TikiWiki (or Tiki) is complex, all-in-one content management system (CMS), wiki, and groupware software that can be used for a wide variety of applications (websites, portals, intranets, extranets), including online collaboration. Foswiki is designed for intraorganizational collaboration and sharing.

The decision about what particular wiki software to use for radicalprintshops.org was important. It had to be free for economic reasons, open source for ideological reasons, and simple for practical reasons. Although I had a technically superior friend who volunteered to help me set up the wiki, I had to be able to administrate it myself without a steep learning curve. Equally, it had to be as accessible as possible for potential contributors. A key rule of any software implementation is undoubtedly to 'know your users'. Knowledge of my potential users was limited. What I did know was that they were aged between 45 and 65. I suspected that those most likely to contribute would be those for whom the printshops were a significant part of their life. Given that the 'heyday' of the printshops was between the early 1970s and 1980s, these users would probably be nearer the middle and older end of that age range. The 'internet revolution' had occurred during their adult lives, but the degree of their active engagement with its tools and platforms for either work or play was unknown to me. However, given their technical background of printing and related processes (and developments within that such as desktop publishing), it was conceivable that at least some of them would have been early adopters.

As for the 'gender technology' issue, despite it being a conventionally male trade, many women were involved in the printshops, actively challenging the stereotype (Cadman et al. 1981; Baines 2012, 2015). It was *possible* that this had built confidence that carried over into using digital technologies. On the other hand, involvement in printing could have been at least twenty years previously and, as I later found out, few women continued to do any sort of technical job. Based on these factors, along with observations of colleagues and friends in this demography, striving for lowest common denominator accessibility was clearly paramount. After research into the various forms of wiki software, their requirements, affordances, and ease of use, we decided on the free, open-source DokuWiki, because it has low system requirements, does not require a database, and is particularly simple to use.

It also seemed important to try to make the site *look* accessible and 'attractive', subjective though the latter is. The typical appearance of an unadorned wiki interface can be dull and 'techy' and thus potentially alienating for users. This concern also related to the shared print media background of members: working with type, images, and color mostly develops some sort of design awareness. We adapted a 'skin' in DokuWiki to give the site a distinctive appearance. The theme colors were red and black, perhaps a little obvious for radical printshops with political origins that bore symbols of those colors, but it was also probably the most common color combination of 'radical print'. This aestheticization was not just 'marketing' but also a sort of basic 'branding', indicating that this was a particular history, not simply 'so much data'.

The radicalprintshops wiki went live in February 2009 (Fig. 2.1). Next to an image of the cheap, dilapidated press that was typical and the phrase 'the freedom of the press belongs to those who run it', taken from a 1970s poster made in one of the printshops called See Red Women's Workshop, the text on the homepage declared:

> This site is devoted to building a history of London's late 20th century radical and community printing collectives […]. This is a history that doesn't exist except in the memories of ex-workers, friends and clients. The idea is that people who were involved in the printshops can create and edit the pages.

Following instructions on how to register as a user, the home page showed the index of the different pages so far created ('namespaces' in wiki language). These were for the printshops I already knew: names, locations,

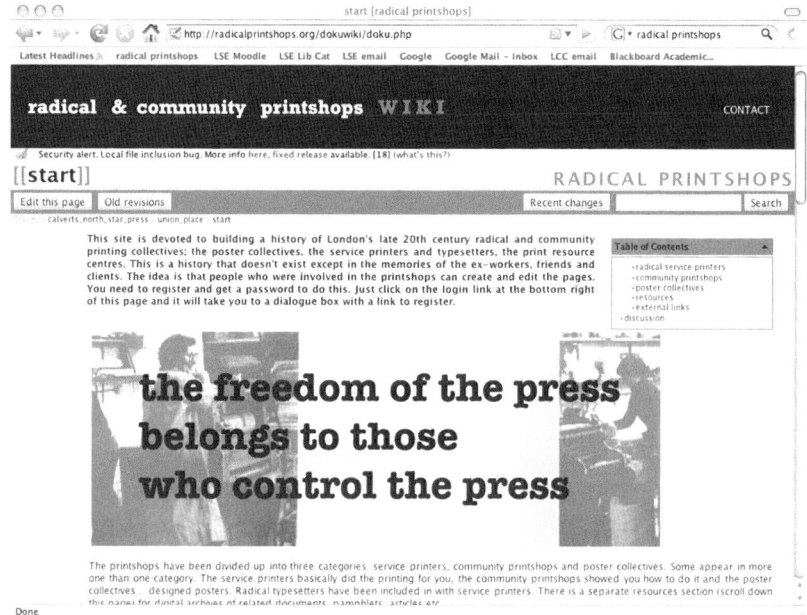

Fig. 2.1   Screenshot of radicalprintshops.org wiki

and approximate duration. I uploaded pictures and documents from my personal archive along with images of materials that bore the imprint of specific printshops. I created lists of links to radical archives and libraries, along with articles relating to the history of alternative print media. I added more of everything as I found it. I worked on the assumption that the more content the site had, the more it would encourage others to contribute. Sometimes the only information I had was the name of a printshop and very approximate dates, but setting up pages in advance also made it simpler for people to add content.

Once the site had sufficient information to look like a viable concern, I began publicizing it. I left messages and links on politically resonant sites, where printshop members might lurk or have friends that did, such as marxists.org and libcom.org, and continued to do so as new radical history sites sprang up. I emailed the slowly growing number of print-shop workers for whom I was obtaining contacts. The link to the wiki served to introduce the idea of a history of the printshops, and showed the beginnings of a visible and accessible outcome, which I hoped might be a hook to encourage participation. If people were interested in the wiki they might also be interested further down the line in being interviewed by me, and I used this email to introduce the research project. The response to both the wiki and the academic research was generally encouraging. At this stage I had not put any information on the site about who had instigated it, or that its instigator was doing academic research into the subject, although this information appeared elsewhere online (for example, my university profiles).

Over a four-year period about thirty-five people registered as radicalprintshop.org users, most of them within the first two years after its inception. Although not a large number, it was more than I had expected. Throughout this time I periodically emailed my contact list of printshop members with updates about the wiki and to encourage contributions. Twenty-three of the thirty-five registered actually *contributed* content, ten of them by directly uploading and the remaining thirteen by sending contributions through the wiki's contact form or by email, for me to upload. The explanation given by some for the latter was that they either were not confident enough to upload themselves or that they had tried and failed. By the end of 2013, eight of the forty pages/namespaces on the wiki had been set up by registered users and twenty-five different pages/namespaces had been contributed to. There were perhaps four 'super contributors', although I remained the key contributor by far. Content added ranged from cursory to extensive printshop biographies, personal photographs and memories, lists of printing equipment, and images of work printed. Some pages bulged; some were still scant. There was a marked profile of those who contributed: they had either worked in several printshops or had been a founder member of a press. This was unsurprising, as greater length of involvement and/or intense 'start-up' commitment would have made their time in the printshops a significant period in their lives and as such probably led to a greater motivation or interest in the printshops' 'historicization'. Those who registered were overwhelmingly male, but two (half) of the 'super contributors' were female. Of the people who uploaded, I was in contact with only two of them when the wiki launched. Overall I had previously known less than a quarter of those who contributed and over half of those who contributed had found the site independently.

The wiki was almost universally appreciated by the ex-members with whom I made contact ('great stuff'; 'brilliant'; 'it's nice to be acknowledged!'; 'so much of this history is invisible'). As such it was productive in gathering support and interest for the research and helped both to introduce and legitimize it. My knowledge of the scope of different printshops significantly expanded and the wiki quickly began to function as a useful *organizational* tool for the research, revealing gaps and relationships. Interest from printshop members in different parts of the UK enlarged the scope of the wiki and the research beyond its original London focus. It developed many fruitful new contacts who were more than willing to be interviewed and to share old documents with me, offline. It also generated wider interest and connections, especially from peers in the USA with similar printshop interests and backgrounds, and led to ongoing reciprocal information sharing and support.

Challenge No. 1

One of the risks of initiating a 'collaborative history', however informally, is that conflicting versions of events lead to unresolved and confusing content, can cause friction between individuals, and can deter involvement. The 'edit war' is of course a well-known phenomenon of Wikipedia (Tkacz 2014). In the case of radicalprintshops.org this could take on a very different tenor, because the subject was people's *own* history and personal understanding of what 'had happened' and/or why and with people they had once known or still knew. While the site was intended to be a positive recognition of that history, like most collective projects (or indeed any kind of organization) the printshops had their share of internal conflicts, people who did not get on. In my academic research this was of interest—and the responsibility for a broader interpretation was mine. The wiki was another matter. Concern about this had been flagged up early on after a reunion of some print co-op members, with one person emailing me to say: 'I must admit I was slightly concerned how time had changed some events and facts, but hopefully you will solve all that.' The wiki certainly could not 'solve all that'.

This aspect of co-writing history remained a particularly hindering factor for a couple of contributors and came up in several email exchanges: 'Such a wiki raises all sorts of questions about who and what exactly can be mentioned/quoted/talked about without their permission. Also about who writes which history'; 'how is collective writing managed in "ethical" and practical terms […] perhaps there is a universally known manual of such things somewhere on the web?'; 'still somewhat perplexed as to how a wiki works in terms of contributions, reconciling everyone's tendency to rewrite history'. Although one of these people made a significant entry about the printshop in which he was involved, uncertainty about these questions meant that he felt unable to encourage the contribution of others from the press, as he did not consider he could offer them any guidance.

Given the amount of time that had passed, I had hoped that old conflicts would be 'water under the bridge' by now. With regard to different versions of events, I had attempted to set the namespaces/pages to allow for multiple perspectives. Cap (2012) has since suggested something similar with his proposal for 'every point of view' (EPOV) knowledge bases rather than the 'neutral point of view' (NPOV) target of Wikipedia. This seemed more appropriate for a collaborative history of this kind, given that the history was that of the people contributing. I doubted that people would want to contribute particularly 'contentious' content, although that was always a risk. The individual printshop pages had been set up with sections for 'background', 'narratives', 'images', 'discussion', and 'sources/links'. I had imagined that the general history would go into 'background' and personal stories into 'narratives', which is mainly what happened. Conceivably the latter would also be the space where specific versions of events could live. In actuality, the issue barely arose. Also, despite or because of the anxieties discussed, there was minimal editing of what others had written; people added without deletion. Where there were differences or (mild) criticism of content, these came through to me to manage and I ended up editing the text to fit both accounts. Nobody used the available discussion space.

Although the wiki enabled collaborative content, there was not in any sense a *group* of 'committed users', either in relation to a particular press or of the site overall. Even though there were certainly users from some of the same presses, they never got into working together. In that sense the mode of participation was contributory rather than genuinely collaborative or co-creative (see Bonney et al. 2009). Furthermore, the wiki was not conceived of or set up collectively; there was no group discussion about how it might operate, the shape it should take, or whether there should be some sort of code of conduct. It was set up as a sort of 'probe' or experiment driven by my agenda, parts of which I hoped others might share. I was the unelected, unaccountable, and effectively sole admin. I could block users, limit access rights, delete namespaces, and of course take down the site. This obviously is not an egalitarian situation. I had hoped that in time others might emerge as co-admins, but had devised no strategy to especially encourage this—and no one was putting themselves forward. In a sense, I was pleased that anyone else contributed at all.

Preparatory research into setting up the wiki had been primarily technical. I provided no FAQs (frequently asked questions), guidelines, or support manuals about how or what to write or edit. This was for various reasons: (a) I wanted to see what happened; (b) I did not know what such guidance would look like; (c) I did not want to hinder participation through creating 'rules' that might be felt to be patronizing; (d) I hoped that how to do this would reveal itself (to me as well) through experiment rather than direction; and (e) there was already enough to do! Retrospectively, more support around the process in the provision of this sort of material is likely to have encouraged people to contribute rather than dissuading them. It would not have been a case of reinventing the wheel, given that various existing wikis provide such guidelines that I could have drawn on and adapted.

Challenge No. 2

The other and more overwhelming issue that emerged was spam; the site was increasingly subject to attacks. Pages were frequently hijacked and filled with all manner of commercial junk. The emails that told me a new user had registered poured in from marauding bots. Block deleting them was risky, in case they contained a message from a human user. There might be two hundred to go through at any one time. Open registration on wikis makes them especially vulnerable to spambots, unless like Wikipedia you have the resources and technical infrastructure to counteract them. The time I spent on wiki admin, essentially clearing junk, increased exponentially, leaving little time for developing the site, leave alone encouraging people to contribute. I became cautious about publicizing the site in case I had not had time to remove offending spam. While I had the support of my technically superior comrade, who tried to help resolve these issues—we experimented with different CAPTCHA plugins, for example—they inevitably returned. This is something that would have been eased with more sustained user commitment; removing spam from pages at least is a basic editing task. While 'wiki-gnome' and 'wiki-fairy' tasks were relatively satisfying, the lone role of 'housework zombie' was not.

The obvious way to address this would have been to cease open registration, as this was what allowed spam into the site. Those already registered would still have their password and new users would make contact with the site admin to acquire one, which would be a sort of filtering process. It creates another admin task, but is far less onerous than dealing with spam. It also creates a direct relationship between the admin/myself and prospective contributors that on the one hand *may* have encouraged greater involvement. On the other hand, it removes a level of autonomy and possible anonymity from the process, which might deter some people.

CHALLENGE No. 3

The third challenge took a rather different shape. As the main contributor to the wiki, I had been sharing materials gathered in pursuit of my 'original' and far from completed academic research. I had assumed that interest in the wiki would be from ex-participants, the lay field of radical historians, artists and activists, and curious others (a few of whom were my students), but mainly beyond the bounds of serious professional and institutional interests. Within the field of media and communication studies too, my 'old media' subject was a marginal curio at best. However, a revival of craft-based radicalism and an upsurge of art world interest in collectives of the 1970s and 1980s began to generate a small but steady stream of attention and requests from this direction. Even the phrase 'radical and community printshops' that I had used—and that had long ceased to exist as a meaningful coupling—began to circulate. A trickle of students from different art institutions now emailed me to help with their dissertations on 'radical and community printshops', having discovered the wiki. In 2012, a new book on radical posters came out and, while skimming for possible research leads, I had the dawning realization that significant information must have been derived from the wiki, and more precisely from what I had written. I scanned the bibliography for acknowledgment of this, but there was none. With some trepidation, I contacted the author, who admitted that the wiki had indeed been a great help, and apologized for not having got in touch. A few months later another situation arose with a professional in the cultural field whose funded and well-regarded project was based on their 'research into radical and community printshops'. Again, the sources of this research were derived from the wiki, similarly unacknowledged. More occurrences of this ilk arose.

On the one hand it was cheering that in a small way, the subject of the printshops had started to become 'hot' and I seemed to have helped this along by making publicly accessible hitherto unknown information and source material. It indicated that the research subject was timely and that there was probably a wider audience than I had imagined. While I positively liked the fact that bits from the wiki were being pasted across the web on various radical websites or individuals' blogs, unacknowledged use of its content by paid 'professionals', particularly when presented as their own research, was disconcerting. I had spent a lot of unpaid time on the wiki, not just uploading and writing but managing the tech issues as well as supporting and encouraging other users. My own academic work was a long way from completion, and its main strength was its original subject matter. As Dunleavy (2003) cautions, research that is empirically rather than theoretically original is always vulnerable to losing this claim. A tension had emerged between the aspirations for the wiki and the possible need to 'protect' my academic research interests. In their user analysis of the Old Bailey Proceedings Online, Howard and her colleagues also found that academics were put off from using the wiki function in part because 'they are unwilling to share rough drafts of work with all comers (and in any case would probably not post something they may want to publish in a more formal context later on)' (Howard et al. 2011, p. 8).

During this time I decided that it was prudent to put my own name somewhere on the wiki, and to state that I had initiated it and that it was an adjunct to academic research on the subject. However, I could have put a request on the site for professionals in the academic and cultural field to reference it. We had set a Creative Commons 'non-commercial reuse' and 'attribution required' terms of reuse for the site content, but this lingered as a tiny logo at the bottom of scrollable pages and was not drawn attention to. We could have made more of this.

Under Maintenance

After four years, user contributions to the wiki had dwindled to near zero and the time I spent on it was mostly dealing with spam. Maintaining it with limited time, knowledge, resources, and support was becoming untenable. Added to this was the lingering concern about the extent to which I might have unwittingly been undermining my academic research and future publishing opportunities by making such a range of source material so publicly available, before the completion of my academic research project. Until I could work out a way to resolve these very different issues, I decided to archive the site and temporarily take it offline. This raised a new ethical consideration. Did taking it down invalidate the ethics of reciprocity that I had hoped the wiki might partially serve? What in this context was the site instigator and admin's responsibility to the others who contributed to the wiki? The situation exposed the asymmetric relationship between myself, as sole admin, and the registered users, in terms of agenda, authority, and labor. Unless users were willing or able to get more involved, they had little say in decisions about the overall site management.

Conclusion

There is much that might be said in terms of how the radicalprintshops. org wiki could be better set up to facilitate a collaborative knowledge base, and I have covered some aspects of this already. In the context of this book, however, it is on the brief evaluation of it as an aid to academic research that I want to end. First, the wiki helped to *socialize* the idea of a history of printshops among ex-participants. It enabled the renewal of communications with ex-colleagues and associates and the introduction to many more whom I had never known. While the wiki's value for *direct* information gathering was limited, my knowledge of the scope of different printshops significantly expanded, which was invaluable for my research. The wiki also quickly began to function as a useful *organizational* tool for the research, revealing gaps and relationships. Finally, and perhaps most instrumental to the research, it developed many fruitful new contacts who were more than willing to be interviewed and dig through their personal documents to assist me. For many of them in fact this was preferable to contributing to the wiki. During the course of the research I interviewed about seventy people, double the number of registered wiki users.

Initially the wiki had helped address my ambivalence regarding the distance between academic process and form and my subject/s. The timing of it for generating interest and contacts was at the right stage of the research: early on, while I was working out what shape the project should take, what my questions were, and what methods I was going to use. On the other hand, it was possibly too early to experiment with building a collaborative history. I did not have sufficient resources (time and knowledge) to maintain the site effectively or to support contributors properly. I was also ignorant at the outset of what that might actually mean. It was probably too early as well to be sharing so much original research data on a public site. None of these issues is insurmountable, but all require pre-emptive consideration.

Notes

1. The WikiPapers site was set up in 2010 by Emilio Rodríguez-Posada 'to create the most comprehensive literature compilation for this research area' (see http://wikipapers.referata.com).
2. The suggestion was based on a haphazard career trajectory that led to employment as a lecturer in the printing trades college, now London College of Communication (LCC), as well as involvement in small publications and exhibitions.
3. Howe, who coined the term crowdsourcing in a 2006 *Wired* article, defines it as 'the act of taking a job traditionally performed by a designated agent (usually an employee) and outsourcing it to an undefined generally large group of people in the form of an open call' (Howe 2006, n.p.). The term has been taken up by Mia Ridge (2014) in particular to describe initiatives toward digital participation in institutional cultural heritage projects.
4. In the UK, for example, the 'Your Archives' part of the National Archives site and the Old Bailey Proceedings Online instigated wiki layers for users between 2007 and 2012 and 2009 and 2011, respectively (see http://webarchive.nationalarchives.gov.uk/+/http://yourarchives.nationalarchives.gov.uk, accessed 10 August 2016; see also Howard et al. 2011).

References

Baines, J. (2015) Nurturing Dissident? Community Printshops in 1970s London. In J. Uldam and A. Vestergaard (Eds.), *Engagement and Social Media: Political Participation Beyond Protest* (London: Palgrave Macmillan), pp. 174–93.

Baines, J. (2012) Experiments in Democratic Participation: Feminist Printshop Collectives. *Cultural Policy, Criticism & Management Research* 6(Autumn): 29–51.

Bauer, M. and Gaskell, G. (2009) *Qualitative Researching with Text, Image and Sound* (London: Sage).

Black, J. and MacRaild, D. (2000) *Studying History* (Basingstoke/New York: Palgrave).

Bonney, R. Ballard, H., Jordan, R. et al. (2009) Public Participation in Scientific Research: Defining the Field and Assessing Its Potential for Informal Science Education. A CAISE Inquiry Group Report (Washington, DC: Center for Advancement of Informal Science Education).

Bosi, L. and Reiter, H. (2014) Historical Methodologies: Archival Research and Oral History in Social Movement Research. In D. della Porta (Ed.), *Methodological Practices in Social Movement Research* (Oxford: Oxford University Press), pp. 117–43.

Cadman, E., Chester, G. and Pivot, A. (1981) *Rolling Our Own: Women as Printers, Publishers and Distributers* (London: Minority Press Group).

Cap, C. H. (2012) Towards Content Neutrality in Wiki Systems. *Future Internet* 4: 1086–104.

Chong, D. (2011) Interview with author, 27 September.

Craven, L. (2012) *What are Archives?: Cultural and Theoretical Perspectives: A Reader.* (Aldershot: Ashgate).

Croteau, D. (2005) Which Side Are You On? The Tension Between Movement Scholarship and Activism. In C. David, W. Hoynes and C. Ryan (Eds.), *Rhyming Hope and History: Activists, Academics, and Social Movement Scholarship* (Minneapolis: University of Minnesota Press), pp. 20–40.

Chesters, G. (2012) Social Movements and the Ethics of Knowledge Production. *Social Movement Studies* 11(2): 145–60.

Cunningham, W. (2002) What is Wiki. Available at: http://www.wiki.org/wiki.cgi?WhatIsWiki (accessed 3 March 2015).

Ebersbach, A. and Glaser, M. (2004) Towards Emancipatory Use of a Medium: The Wiki. *International Journal of Information Ethics* 2(11).

Dunleavy, P. (2003) *Authoring a PhD* (London: Palgrave Macmillan).

Fitzgerald, R. (2007) Wikis as an Exemplary Model of Open Source Learning. In K. St Amant and B. Still (Eds.), *Handbook of Open Source Software: Technological, Economic and Social Perspectives* (London: Information Science Reference), pp. 681–9.

Flick, U. (2007) *Designing Qualitative Research* (London: Sage).

Flinn, A. (2007) Community Histories, Community Archives: Some Opportunities and Challenges. *Journal of the Society of Archivists* 28(2): 151–76.

Flinn, A. (2008) Other Ways of Thinking, Other Ways of Being. Documenting the Margins and the Transitory: What to Preserve, How to Collect. In L. Craven (Ed.), *What are Archives? Cultural and Theoretical Perspectives: A Reader* (Aldershot: Ashgate), pp. 109–28.

Garelli, G. and Tazzioli, M. (2013) Challenging the Discipline of Migration: Militant Research in Migration Studies. *Postcolonial Studies* 16(3): 245–9.

Gillan, K. and Pickerill, J. (2012) The Difficult and Hopeful Ethics of Research on, and with, Social Movements. *Social Movement Studies* 11(2): 133–43.

Hesmondhalgh, D. (2000) Alternative Media, Alternative Texts? Rethinking Democratisation in the Cultural Industries. In J. Curran (Ed.), *Media Organisations in Society* (London: Arnold), pp. 107–26.

Howard, S., Hitchcock T. and Shoemaker, R. (2011) *Crime in the Community: Enhancing User Engagement for Teaching and Research with the Old Bailey Online.* Available at: http://www.hrionline.ac.uk/san/hridigital/uploads/crimeinthecommunitycasestudy.pdf (accessed 18 September 2015).

Howe, J. (2006) *The Rise of Crowdsourcing.* In *Wired* 1 June: http://www.wired.com/2006/06/crowds (accessed 10 June 2015).

Jolly, M., Russell, P. and Cohen, R. (2012) Sisterhood and After: Individualism, Ethics and an Oral History of the Women's Liberation Movement. *Social Movement Studies* 11(2): 211–26.

Landry, C., Morley, D., Southwood, R., et al. (1985) *What a Way to Run a Railroad: An Analysis of Radical Failure* (London: Comedia).

Khasnabish, A. and Haiven, M. (2012) Convoking the Radical Imagination: Social Movement Research, Dialogic Methodologies, and Scholarly Vocations. *Cultural Studies – Critical Methodologies* 12(5): 408–21.

Kindon, S., Pain, R. and Kesby, M. (Eds.) (2010) *Participatory Action Research Approaches and Methods: Connecting People, Participation and Place* (London: Routledge).

MacCabe, C. (2007) Interview with Stuart Hall. *Critical Quarterly* 50(1–2): 12–42.

Milan, S. (2014) Ethics of Social Movement Research. In D. della Porta (Ed.), *Methodological Practices in Social Movement Research* (Oxford: Oxford University Press), pp. 446–64.

Milberry, K. (2012) Hacking for Social Justice. In A. Feenberg and N. Friesen (Eds.), *(Re)Inventing the Internet: Critical Case Studies* (Rotterdam: Sense Publishers), pp. 109–26.

Mosca, L. (2014) Methodological Practices in Social Movement Online Research. In D. della Porta (Ed.), *Methodological Practices in Social Movement Research* (Oxford: Oxford University Press), pp. 397–417.

Palmer, J. (2009) *Archives 2.0: If We Build It, Will They Come? Ariadne* 60: http://www.ariadne.ac.uk/issue60/palmer (accessed 17 September 2015).

Ridge, M. (Ed.) (2014) *Crowdsourcing Our Cultural Heritage* (Farnham: Ashgate).

Rubin, H. and Rubin, I. (2011) *Qualitative Interviewing: The Art of Hearing Data* (London: Sage).

Seale, C., Silverman, D., Gubrium, J., et al. (2007) *Qualitative Research Practice* (London: Sage).

Sholette, G. (2011) *Dark Matter: Art and Politics in an Age of Enterprise Culture* (London: Pluto Press).

Shukaitis, S. and Graeber, D. (Eds.) (2007) *Constituent Imagination: Militant Investigations/Collective Theorization* (Edinburgh: AK Press).

Swash, T. (2011) Interview with author, 22 September.

Thompson, E.P. (1968) *The Making of the English Working Class* (London: Penguin).

Tkacz, N. (2014) *Wikipedia and the Politics of Openness* (Chicago: University of Chicago Press).

Vincent, J. (2014) *LGBT People and the UK Cultural Sector: The Response of Libraries, Museums, Archives and Heritage since 1950* (Farnham: Ashgate).

CHAPTER 3

A Materialist Media Ecological Approach to Studying Urban Media in/of Place

Erin Despard

The rise of pervasive, embedded, mobile, and locative media in cities has greatly increased interest in questions of space and place in relation to communication. As Scott McQuire (2008) asserts, the juxtaposition of spaces and temporalities enabled by these new, or newly situated, media forms shifts and disrupts the spatial orientations and boundaries that have traditionally structured social relations. At the same time, attention to the spatial dimensions of media is a way of revealing the politics of their geographically (and therefore, socially and economically) differential effects (Couldry and McCarthy 2004). Of particular interest to many communication researchers are changing conceptions of place and the role of particular places within processes of mediated communication. The massive uptake of mobile media, and particularly smartphones, has enabled the production of seemingly infinite volumes of 'geocoded' metadata that are not only economically but, increasingly, socially and culturally valuable. In what is more and more an era of 'conspicuous mobility', images of and references to places are framing and providing the content for a variety of communicative processes (Wilson 2012). At the same time, the installation and use of media in new places change how places and media alike

E. Despard (✉)
University of Glasgow, Glasgow, Scotland, UK
e-mail: Erin.Despard@glasgow.ac.uk

© The Author(s) 2016
S. Kubitschko, A. Kaun (eds.), *Innovative Methods in Media and Communication Research*, DOI 10.1007/978-3-319-40700-5_3

function (McCarthy 2001; McQuire 2006). There are as such proliferating grounds for recognizing the co-constitution of media and place.

On the one hand, this recognition promises to democratize the shaping of urban public culture and social life by giving rise to media-based projects that encourage a more active interaction with, and collective interpretation of, shared urban spaces (for example, de Lange and de Waal 2013; McQuire 2006; Murthy 2006). Especially in the case of mobile and locative media, it is possible to view such projects as reflective of a growing creative potential in everyday media use (Berry and Schleser 2014). On the other hand, media and places alike are increasingly *coded* to channel and constrain communication and interaction. For example, while social media platforms are designed to maximize the production of social and location data useful to commercial applications (Wilson 2014), public places are designed not only to prioritize particular viewpoints and enable certain activities, but (at least in North America, the UK, and Australia) also to prevent crime, terrorism, and 'undesirable' uses such as sleeping, drug use, skateboarding, and graffiti (Schneider 2005). In this context, and given that such coding is invisible to most users (Boulton and Zook 2013), the co-constitution of media and place may produce a doubling of obscurity in relation to the conditions that shape the possibilities of public life in mediated cities.

From both these perspectives, developing a means of perceiving and analyzing the interactivity of media and place would be beneficial. Not only does such interaction constitute a potential site of political action (whether creative or resistant in character), it may also enable an improved critical perception that is similar to what Marshall McLuhan observed with respect to the overlapping of old and new media forms: '[t]he moment of the meeting of media is a moment of freedom and release from the ordinary trance and numbness imposed by them on our senses' (1964, p. 63). That is, developing a means of studying the functioning of media and place *together* promises to improve our understanding of both. However, as I discuss here, in the empirical research concerned with media and place to date there is very little in the way of precedent for an interactive or holistic approach, despite renewed interest in media ecological perspectives such as McLuhan's.

In this chapter, I develop an approach to studying the interactivity of media and place together based on theories of an inclusive, *materialist* media ecology. I understand 'material' in an expansive sense that, in addition to the 'new materialisms' (Coole and Frost 2010) that inflect the work of media theorists such as Jussi Parikka, also encompasses the socio-political significance given to it by Tony Bennett and Patrick Joyce (2010), and the 'elemental' or infrastructural meaning elaborated by John Durham Peters (2015). It implies an attention to what different sites and communication technologies can *do* as opposed to (or at least *before*) what they mean, as well as to the relations of production and circulation that enable and sustain those capacities. When I look at photographs of a public park, for example, I wonder how their content has been constrained or enabled by things like the spatial organization and appearance of the park itself, as well as by the technical specifications of the camera and the circumstances of display and circulation. Revealing such conditions provides a means of pursuing a relational and politically differentiated perspective on place-based processes of communication. This is particularly important in the study of media in relation to public places, where different publics (Staeheli and Mitchell 2008) and their public cultures (Amin 2008) are made, contested, and celebrated.

An analysis of material conditions must always be to a certain degree tailored to the site and specific media under consideration: here, I present a strategy for developing site- and media-specific methods capable of both describing and critically exploiting the interactivity of place, practice, and technology. I begin by reviewing some of the existing literature on media and place, with a focus on studies that take an integrative approach. This is followed by a discussion of the relevance of materialist media ecologies to the difficulties of studying media and place together, and key insights issuing from the work of Matthew Fuller and Jussi Parikka in particular. I synthesize these in an open-ended strategy for the development of site- and media-specific methods. Finally, I present the outlines of an ongoing project focusing on the affordances and constraints of Instagram in relation to the visibility of a contested public place in Glasgow, Scotland, as a means of demonstrating the forms of insight and avenues for artistic or activist intervention that such methods may yield.

Methodological Orientations of Existing Research on Urban Places

In the context of increasing attention to the socio-spatial dimensions and implications of communication media (noted earlier), the work of theorists such as Doreen Massey (1994) and Tim Ingold (2009) has enabled a reinvigoration of the concept of 'place' within communication and media studies. Once understood as that which is stable and bounded, place is increasingly seen as relational, multiplicitous, and temporally as well as spatially constituted (Forlano 2013; Pink 2011; Wilken 2009). It is, in other words, *practiced*—not only through various forms of social and practical use, but also through the representational activities of users. This more nuanced and complex understanding of place has informed numerous books and edited collections in which 'place' serves as a central concept for understanding the social and cultural impact of new media technologies and practices in relation to themes such as everyday life, the city, mobility, and so on (Couldry and McCarthy 2004; Darroch and Marchessault 2014; Evans 2015; Wilken and Googin 2012).

While a comprehensive survey of communication research concerned with place is beyond the scope of this chapter, I note that the majority of empirical research to date has focused on the influence of either media *or* place (for example, the impact of media on the shaping, use, and interpretation of place, or the changing/continuing importance of place in mediated processes of communication). Here I present a more focused discussion of a selection of studies that attempt to analyze media and place together. Each of these investigates what media *do* as opposed to what they mean. In making this selection, I have passed over some frameworks for the production of integrated analyses—for example, practice theory (Rodgers 2014) and socio-semiotic or functionalist approaches (Bolin 2004)—in order to focus on those that are more directly relevant to the materially oriented analysis that I am advocating. Given that the studies I discuss all draw from several different methodologies in order to produce a more holistic or integrated reading of media and place, I organize the discussion in terms of overarching frameworks rather than specific methods and position my approach in relation to them.

A Comparative Approach to the Study of Site-Specific Media

Anna McCarthy's seminal *Ambient Television* (2001) provides a comprehensive analysis of how what televisions can do in public is shaped in part by the environments in which they appear. Working within a cultural studies framework, she draws on a range of historical and contemporary texts to identify the meanings associated with the use of television in different kinds of public space, and on socio-spatial and visual analyses to identify differences in their functioning at different sites. This enables an integrated analysis of media discourse, ideology, practices of production, and the material specificities of place. She argues that it is the simultaneously physical and subjective positioning of television viewers that enables her analysis, and gives considerable attention to the placement of televisions and the visual, aural, and atmospheric effects that they produce in relation to the space in which they appear. I think that all media that are embedded in, or enable engagement with, the specificities of place can be considered similarly site specific or environmental in their functioning—it is just a question of identifying where or when the relevant differences become visible as such. The approach I describe here is intended precisely as a strategy for producing such visibility.

Actor–Network Theory and the Inclusion of Non-Human Actors in the Making of Place

As Nick Couldry (2008) argues, actor–network theory (ANT) constitutes a powerful tool for countering the effects of naturalization within media studies, and critically interrogating the social effects of media. This is particularly relevant to studies of media and place for three reasons. First, the methods employed to identify the relationships and material circumstances underpinning the production of meaningful practices necessarily situate ANT analyses in both time and space. Second, the specificity of media effects is potentially doubly obscure in relation to particular places. As Morris (2010) points out, places go through a process of naturalization in which particular meanings and site-specific practices become durably associated with them. Third, the inclusive definition of 'actors' constituting a given network means that the contributions of place and its material constituents can be taken into consideration. This is of special relevance to vegetated places such as the one I consider in this chapter, but it also serves to complicate consideration of other urban places where non-human nature has a muted role (Tosoni and Tarantino 2013), and makes visible a broader range of effects than those intended in the design of specific technologies (Morris 2010).

All this said, there are important limitations associated with ANT-based analyses of media and place. For example, as Couldry (2008) notes, ANT analyses are not very good at accounting for changes in networks over time, or—I would add—for effects and practices that are excessive of or resistant to established networks.[1] In contrast, and as I discuss later, within a materialist media-ecological approach, attention to non- and more-than-human agencies and effects is precisely a means of foregrounding what is excessive and generative of change within a given media ecology.

Locative and Place-Based Media Experiments

These are artistic experiments with media that *take place*—which is to say, they consist in events that rely on the participation of people and place alike. The necessarily open-ended character of such works enables them to reveal—and often to disrupt or amplify—the site-specific affordances and constraints of a particular media form. Thus, for example, as Scott McQuire (2006) argues, based in part on a historically contextualized reading of 'Body Movies' by Rafael Lozano-Hemmer (2001), interactive screens in public places may stage unexpected encounters that are both revealing of existing conventions for interaction in public, and provide an opportunity to experiment collectively with new forms. Such experiments may take a more explicitly political dimension. For example, as Andrea Zeffiro (2014) argues in relation to GPS-enabled projects such as the Transborder Immigrant Tool (by Electronic Disturbance Theatre and b.a.n.g. lab in 2007), place-based interventions guided simultaneously by aesthetic and activist concerns make visible the spatio-political implications of media and place alike. In contrast, as Beiguelman (2006) shows via a series of works using public participation to hack digital billboards, *taking place* in a context that is self-consciously placeless can disrupt the otherwise durable association between activities of creation, contemplation, and occupation, suggesting avenues for the invention of new activities appropriate to those places we are encouraged to disregard as such.

Such experiments provide a bodily or affective as opposed to analytic insight, often pointing to or affording critical and synthetic analyses rather than fully accomplishing them. A similar observation could be made of the example I present in this chapter, which attempts to find a means for researchers to experiment with media and place in a creatively analytic manner. Two important differences are that I undertake this as an individual, non-expert practitioner relatively unconcerned with the participation of others, and that mundane failure, as opposed to artistic success, is what enables the generation of insight for me. I theorize this deliberately naïve media experiment via the work of Fuller and Parikka, who have done a great deal of thinking about media via critical interpretation of media experiments.

Having positioned and contextualized some of the motivations for my approach, I turn now to a very brief discussion of the concept of 'media ecology' in media and communication studies, and its recent revision by theorists such as Fuller and Parikka. I then discuss their interpretative work as inspiration for a media-ecological approach to studying communication media in and of place, and propose an over-arching strategy for generating site- and media-specific methods.

MATERIALIST MEDIA ECOLOGIES

Although there is no single agreed definition of 'media ecology' as a field of, or conceptual framework for, communication research, most work under this umbrella takes off from the observation (attributed largely to McLuhan 1964) that media function in terms that are environmental as well as instrumental—that is, not only recording, storing, and transmitting information, but also shaping perception, practice, and social relations in lasting ways. Much of this work is sympathetic, if not explicitly indebted, to ecological thought more generally, seeing in the rapid evolution of new communication technologies a variety of social, cultural, and environmental dangers. As Neil Postman put it, 'Media ecology looks into the matter of how media of communication affect human perception, understanding, feeling, and value; and how our interaction with media facilitates or impedes our chances of survival' (1970, p. 161).

That said, some researchers object to the humanist underpinnings and normative aims of this version of media ecology. Influenced by the technologically focused histories provided by media archaeologists such as Friedrich Kittler and Wolfgang Ernst as well as new materialist and vitalist philosophies, authors such as Fuller and Parikka have elaborated more inclusively materialist versions of media ecology, seeking to identify new potentials of media technology and practice and, thereby, to encourage experimentation and enable critique. Rather than, for example, a more media-savvy or less technologically determined society, they seek to identify and facilitate the new forms of collective organization opened by media-based experiments.

They do so in part on the basis of defining media ecologies more broadly—taking interest not only in the interaction of different technologies and practices, but also active materials (Fuller 2005) and non-human modes of communication and perception (Parikka 2011, 2013). Each elaborates a point of view that is relational in an open-ended sense: to mediate is not only to produce effects, but also to be affected and thereby to produce specific relational possibilities. The media relations they describe are thus ecological in a concrete and local as opposed to metaphorical sense (for the latter, see Heise 2002).

Both Fuller and Parikka base their theorizing for the most part on media experiments undertaken by artists and activists. Through the incorporation of communication media in an artistic practice, or in collective activities not envisioned in their design, the material, practical, and social affordances of specific technologies can be tested and made to reveal relations of production and circulation otherwise obscured in everyday media use. While this perspective opens a rich terrain for interdisciplinary, activist investigations, it is not immediately clear how it may be used to ground empirical investigation of less expert or more mundane forms of media use. I am particularly interested in the way an inclusively materialist conception of media ecology suggests an avenue for investigating the interactive effects of media and place. If 'media' is defined more broadly (as in Peters 2015), then aspects of the place itself may be understood to mediate in a manner comparable with communication technologies. Next I present an orientation to empirical research inspired by the work of Fuller and Parikka, which provides the means of developing methods for the study of site-specific media relations.

NAÏVE EXPERIMENTATION AS METHOD

In the most general sense, Fuller and Parikka shift the analytic focus from intentional actors and discrete media forms to media relations, and from effects to events. Similar to other integrative approaches (already discussed), this implies an interest in what media can do, rather than what they mean. The media experiments these authors write about are precisely a means of producing events—or, rather, effects of novelty and disjunction that reveal an ongoing eventfulness of media production and circulation otherwise obscured by habits of use and received categories of analysis. In my own research on the interaction between designed landscapes and different forms of photography, I have explored different ways of producing a similar eventfulness in non-artistic, empirical contexts. The observations that this enables—for example, with respect to how photographic social media both afford and constrain the aestheticization of urban land—are somewhat more subtle and inconclusive than those enabled by artistic media experiments, but are nonetheless useful to an excavation of political possibilities in everyday media use.

Producing an eventfulness within non-artistic modes of communication poses a methodological problem that requires strategies tailored not only to the location and media forms in question, but to the specific challenge to critical perception posed by their interaction. For example, at the site of an overgrown Scottish woodland, where attempts by myself and a colleague to photographically analyze a 19th century landscape were frustrated simultaneously by rhododendron thickets and discourses of invasiveness, a historical 'eventalization' of the landscape—to borrow Foucault's (1991) term—is what enabled an analysis of interactions between rhododendrons, landscape, and camera (Despard and Gallagher 2014). In general, it is a question of determining what will enable perception of a given media ecology in terms of events, rather than users and content, or forms and effects.

Sometimes this can be accomplished by doing something counter to the conventions of normal media use and interpretation (see Despard 2015). At other times a strategy based on pushing the terms of 'normal' use to their fullest expression may work best. In the example presented here, I took an approach that combined these two strategies—on the one hand, trying to make Instagram do something it was not intended to do (advance a political cause); and on the other, using its inbuilt features and prescribed conventions of use to do so. In other words, I used Instagram in a deliberately naïve fashion, suspending my skepticism about its utility and my expectations of failure, as a means of creating openings for an eventful learning process. I contend that a degree of naïvety enables an otherwise mundane use of media to register the force of specific processes, affordances, and constraints that shape the possibilities for its use and broader effects. This is particularly useful in relation to social media, since the functioning of these platforms is characterized by multiple layers of obscurity, and their newness means that the broader social and cultural effects of their massive uptake are unknown.

Before turning to this example, I present a very brief discussion of Instagram use in relation to urban public places as a means of contextualizing my motivations for the project described in the example.

Instagram as a Way of Seeing the City

Instagram is an application that enables mobile photo capture, editing, and sharing. It was launched in 2010, bought by Facebook in 2012 (for $1 billion), and as of this writing claims 400 million active users who upload, on average, 80 million photographs a day.[2] On its own website (www.instagram.com) it is promoted as a *photographic* social media platform in which the social and the aesthetic are effortlessly blended, providing 'a new way to see the world'. Its restriction to mobile use, and its highly streamlined functionality (relative to Facebook or Flickr, for example), makes it particularly conducive not only to instantaneous sharing of personal news (of the 'where I am and what I am doing right now' variety), but also to a photographic engagement with places. In this context, and given its aesthetic capabilities (for example, via filters and other editing tools), it provides a means of aestheticizing and elevating the social and cultural value of particular places, and the qualities and events associated with them.

In the course of these communicative and interpretative activities, many users choose to share the location of their photographs.[3] Even if they do not, however, that location information is *always* included in the metadata that, for those users whose profile is public, is provided to anyone accessing Instagram's API (application programming interface).[4] This is because location data is increasingly crucial not only to location-based advertising, but also to market research, much of which is based on geographically organized demographic data—since where you are says a great deal about your age, income, lifestyle, and so on (Phillips and Curry 2002). With some exceptions (Gibbs et al. 2015; Hochman 2014; Hochman and Manovich 2013; Schwartz and Halegoua 2015; Willim 2013), much of the research on Instagram to date has focused on how to make best use of this data (for example, Latorre-Martínez and Iñiguez-Berrozpe 2014; Silva et al. 2013; Schwartz and Hochman 2014; Zhang et al. 2013). While such research must presume certain conventions of use, I wondered in contrast about the potential for a heterogeneous use of Instagram: Might the simplicity of the platform enable its diversion toward more explicitly political ends than it was designed to serve? In particular, I wanted to explore whether the aesthetic capacities of Instagram might be deployed in the service of producing alternative visibilities of contested public spaces. Suspending my doubts with respect to the prospects of success, I undertook the pursuit of this naïve hope as a means to make clear some of the application's affordances and constraints for political intervention at a specific site.

The North Kelvin Meadow Campaign

The North Kelvin Meadow is the name given to a meadow and urban wood that have grown up at the site of an abandoned playing field in the west end of Glasgow, Scotland. Since 2008, the meadow has been the focus of a conflict between Glasgow City Council, which wants to sell the land to a developer, and community members, who value it as an open, semi-natural community space and have been working to establish its social and environmental value through a variety of initiatives. This has included the planting of wild flowers and a community orchard, allotment and collective food gardening, the installation and maintenance of composting facilities, cultural events (such as film screenings and seasonal celebrations), and ongoing educational activities for children. I see these activities, combined with others (for example, vandalism, littering, drinking), as reflective of a community that is struggling to become visible in a form of its own choosing. On the one hand, many interventions defensively seek to make the meadow look more like other urban landscapes—by tidying it up in various ways, planting flowers, and so on. On the other, there has been a determined avoidance of any form of regulation and a broad commitment to preserving a looser, less defined aesthetic as a means to honor a diversity of tastes and uses.

The meadow has, however, seen surprisingly little in the way of media-based representational activities. While news pertaining to the conflict over the meadow or its events is sometimes covered in the local press, communications have otherwise been limited to the maintenance of a website[5] and Facebook pages. Thus, for example, Instagram searches yield little in the way of photographs tagged for the meadow. It is in this context, as a volunteer helping to care for the meadow, that I started a dedicated Instagram account (see Fig. 3.1) and began uploading photographs on a regular basis.[6] In doing so I hoped not simply to bring *greater* visibility to the meadow's cause, but to contribute to an alternative visibility—one that registers an aesthetic value in its open-ended, constantly shifting character. While these efforts have failed to produce concrete results to date (for example, in the form of increased support for the campaign or a substantial group of followers), they provide an opportunity to sketch the outlines of what I think is to be gained by a naïve cultivation of eventfulness between media and place. I begin by considering some of the factors contributing to the shaping of what kind of photographs are taken—between the place itself and Instagram's expansion of the camera phone's capabilities—and then consider what particular mechanisms of circulation reveal about the constraints on political engagement generated through Instagram use.

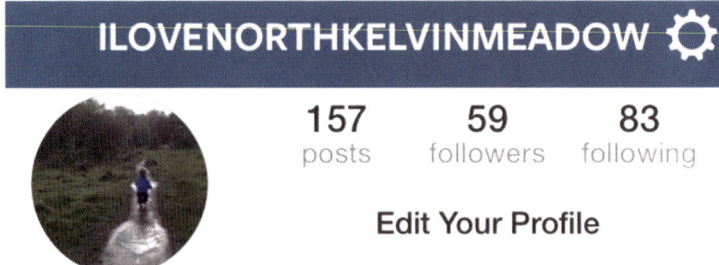

Fig. 3.1   Screenshot of @ilovenorthkelvinmeadow's profile

@ILOVENORTHKELVINMEADOW: AN AMBIVALENT REVALUATION AND FAILED POLITICIZATION OF PLACE VIA INSTAGRAM

As a start, I note my surprise at the variation in color that these photographs present on the whole (see Fig. 3.2). An abundance of wild vegetation makes the meadow quite a *green* landscape. The fact that this greenness is not fully reflected in my photographs is a testament to my efforts to include other colors. This was not because I dislike green, but because its predominance produced a field of vision quite low in contrast. In many areas of the meadow, subtle variations in green blend together in front of the camera (phone) lens, making it hard to produce photographs with adequate contrast and color to be at least visually legible and interesting, if not spectacularly beautiful.

I also observe that one of my strategies for producing interesting photographs is particularly instructive with regard to the affordances and constraints at work between the meadow and Instagram (not to mention the camera phone, my personal tastes, and relative lack of photographic expertise, none of which I consider here). That is, I have included many flowers, as well as objects and structures introduced into the meadow. While this helps to capture the meadow's dynamic character, and incorporates colors other than green or brown, this strategy also responds to two additional constraints. First, the square cropping of the image that Instagram requires (which responds in turn to the constraints of a smartphone's display) is well suited to close-up photographs of single objects or structures (rather than those separated in space, or extending in height or length). Second, the event-based structure of social media generally, and the fact that Instagram photos are distributed and archived chronologically, as a 'feed', encourages attention to what is new. As a result, in my collection I have ended up with relatively few photographs of the larger landscape.[7]

All in all, the subjects of these photographs are quite mundane. There is a certain charm in them, I think, but only rarely does this constellation of affordances and constraints produce what I would characterize as a beautiful or truly interesting photograph. That said, Instagram provides some pretty convincing tools for aestheticization. For one, the filters that can be applied before posting a photograph make it possible to enhance the existing contrast in a given image, and to boost particular colors; this makes many of the photographs in my collection more dramatic and bright than they would otherwise be, thus modifying the constraints imposed by the

Fig. 3.2   Screenshot of @ilovenorthkelvinmeadow's gallery

meadow's greenness. For another, Instagram's display format, which puts the uploaded images in a 'gallery' viewable as a whole, further aestheticizes them by showing their variety and making the perception of overarching themes possible.

However, putting these photographs side by side also generates a certain ambivalence of effect, showing that beauty is here measured in small degrees of difference as opposed to memorable events. Thus, while Instagram enables the production of the meadow as an aesthetic space, the fact that it does so within a self-consciously competitive 'market' of images[8] reveals the distance between my efforts and what is available elsewhere (for example, in the feeds of other users). While I intend my photographs to demonstrate an aesthetic value (if not conventional beauty), once uploaded to Instagram they show something else: that is, a *work* of beautification whose potential is relatively limited in relation to the visual effects otherwise widely valued (for example, in photographs of colorful and well-demarcated landscapes). As such, and at least as presented on Instagram, these photos are *ambivalent* with respect to the qualities of place they present. These qualities are both made beautiful and diminished by having the marginality of that beauty made apparent. When I look at them, I feel at turns pleasantly surprised and disappointed—as if I have been tricked into finding them beautiful.

In wanting this aesthetic work to contribute more broadly to the articulation of alternative visibilities—relevant not only to the meadow but to other landscapes like it—I experimented with hashtags as a means of contextualizing my photographs in particular ways.[9] For example, in addition to tagging every one of my photos with #northkelvinmeadow (thus creating an archive for photos of the meadow), I frequently used tags that have an explicitly socio-political significance, such as #urbancommons. Yet, while this tag references academic discourses about environmental justice and the 'right to the city' as well as the history of open-space politics in the UK, it is not very frequently used by other users, and draws very little in the way of 'likes' by users who are not already following me. In contrast, apolitical tags, such as those with specific plant names, frequently get 'likes' from non-followers. There is as such no indication that political hashtags increased the viewing of my photographs by users who appreciate their political significance.

I turn now to a consideration of the kinds of observation that this failed politicization, and the ambivalence of my attempts to aestheticize the meadow, may enable.

Learning from the Surprises and Failures of a Naïve Experimentation with Instagram

Naïvely taking Instagram for what it promises to be—that is, a tool of image creation and sharing adaptable to a range of expressive and communicative uses—while also putting it into (inter)action with a particular place, produces surprises and failures that help to reveal the specific affordances and constraints of media and place alike. This brings extra-intentional aspects of representation to the forefront of analysis (such as the proliferation of flowers and found objects in my photographs), and demonstrates some of the limits of what has been effectively decided ahead of time through the coding of possible uses and outputs—for example, through the square format of the photographs, and the use of searchable hashtags to archive them. At the same time, it helps to identify the specific qualities and circumstances that are communicative, or that mediate processes of communication, at a given location. For example, attempting to represent the beauty and vitality of the meadow in photographs turns its 'greenness' into a problem. Given that most people in the neighborhood value the meadow in large part precisely for its wild vegetation, this suggests that there are serious limitations on what can be accomplished on its behalf through photographs alone.

More generally, the aesthetically ambivalent outcome of my attempt to enhance the perceived value of the meadow through photographic means points to the longstanding role of specific technologies in reproducing aesthetic tastes and cultural values (with respect to landscape, see Cosgrove 1998). This suggests that one way to develop alternative aesthetics and/or cultural values in relation to a contested public place such as the North Kelvin Meadow is to design interventions that make a critical and reflexive, or inventive, use of visual technologies (for example, using technologies associated with other visual regimes, or modifying existing ones; see Parikka 2011).

Similarly, the relative failure of my attempts to politicize certain qualities of the meadow via hashtags enables a reflection on the cultural and political implications of Instagram's primary function: the production of large quantities of user-generated data. The commercial value of this data is such that *all* use is forced to be productive—or, at least, the platform works best when use conforms to those conventions that enable the production of data amenable to aggregation. So, for example, you can take pictures of whatever you want and tag them however you want, but if you care about being followed, and having your photos viewed and/or liked, you need either (a) friends who are also on Instagram (and with whom you likely share many interests, not to mention demographic characteristics); or (b) images and tags that are both interesting and recognizable to other Instagram users. In both cases, using Instagram effectively requires that you associate your data—that you interpret your experience of the world—in ways that are compatible with those of existing groups.

In this sense, while Instagram provides anyone with a smartphone and data plan access to a virtual gallery space, free advertising, and/or a soap-box (depending on your purposes), such uses are ultimately constrained by the same market-based imperatives as other forms of publishing: as Instagram advises, effective hashtags are specific but 'relevant'; they 'stand out and connect with the people most like you' (Instagram Help website). This effectively constrains the forms of visibility that can be produced or reproduced through the application, which suggests that just as alternative aesthetics require alternative technologies, so the production of an alternative visibility—at least through Instagram—needs to be thought about in terms other than the multiplication of views.

While we may simply conclude that Instagram is not the most productive avenue through which to bring an alternative visibility of contested urban places to light, being able to identify the specific constraints at work within it is instructive with regard to knowing what we want when we look for or devise new tools. How can a more nuanced visibility of a place such as the North Kelvin Meadow be brought to a broader audience, if not through advertising on social media? The point here is less to criticize the performance of a given platform or the appropriateness of a given media practice, and more to identify openings for further research and intervention on behalf of creative and critical mediations of public places.

Conclusion

At the outset of this chapter, I observed both an increasing recognition of the co-constitutive nature of media and place, and a lack of conceptual and methodological tools for the empirical study of site-specific media relations. The methodological strategy I have advanced in response is designed in particular to grapple with the political implications inherent in the mediation of public places. While mobile social media would seem ideal for the purpose of democratizing the use and interpretation of public places, the obscurity of their material relations to specific places makes it difficult to critically evaluate or facilitate such processes.

Experimenting with media such as Instagram in a reflexively naïve manner is a way of creating events of surprise, learning, and failure. However modest, these events in turn create openings for a critical perception of relations between place and media. The specific affordances and constraints that are made visible in this manner in turn point to the ways in which media and place alike (though to varying degrees) can be coded or otherwise structured to serve imperatives that are often quite different from those discursively associated with them. For example, just as Instagram's functionality is shaped by commercial imperatives as well as the specific communicative and expressive activities it enables, public places are frequently designed to constrain as well as enable collective processes of communication (which is why the open-ended use of the North Kelvin Meadow is at once so valuable and so contentious). Finding a means of analyzing the relations between media and place is one way of making the influence of such imperatives more apparent, and of finding openings for interventions that disrupt them or experiment with alternatives.

Notes

1. Timeto (2013) provides a good example of how such shortcomings can be addressed through strategic couplings of ANT with non-representational theory – in this case, via software studies and a reading of activist urban art practices as performative.
2. See 'Stats' on www.instagram.com/press (accessed 10 November 2015). These numbers would seem to reflect a disproportionate number of people under the age of 30 (Raine et al. 2012).
3. Or at least, the location at the time the photograph was uploaded, which is not always the same as where it was taken.
4. In November 2015, Instagram announced new limitations on the purposes for which it will provide access to its API. As of this writing, it is not clear whether requests to conduct scientific (as opposed to journalistic) research will be granted.
5. http://www.northkelvinmeadow.com (accessed 10 March 2016).
6. The gallery can be viewed at https://www.instagram.com/ilovenorthkelvinmeadow (accessed 10 March 2016).
7. The frequently flat, gray, or white Glasgow sky is also a contributing factor in the lack of these photographs.
8. This is reflected, for example, not only in the prominent display of the number of followers for a given account and the number of 'likes' a given photograph receives, but also in the capacity to track who else your followers have recently 'liked'.

9. Similar to Twitter, hashtags assemble a continuously updated 'conversation' or archive of images created by different users, which are searchable within Instagram and third-party applications. They provide a means of locating content relevant to specific interests and, as such, are one of the main ways in which Instagram can be used for purposes that exceed interpersonal communication.

REFERENCES

Amin, A (2008) Collective Culture and Urban Public Space. *City* 12(1): 5–24.

Beiguelman, G. (2006) For an Aesthetics of Transmission. *First Monday* Special Issue #4: http://journals.uic.edu/ojs/index.php/fm/article/view/1553 (accessed 10 January 2016).

Bennett, T. and Joyce, P. (2010) Material Powers. In T. Bennett and P. Joyce (Eds.), *Material Powers: Cultural Studies, History and the Material Turn* (London: Routledge), pp. 1–22.

Berry, M. and Schleser, M. (2014) *Mobile Media Making in an Age of Smartphones* (New York: Palgrave Macmillan).

Bolin, G. (2004) Spaces of Television: The Structuring of Consumers in a Swedish Shopping Mall. In N. Couldry and A. McCarthy (Eds.), *MediaSpace: Place, Scale and Culture in the Digital Age* (London: Routledge), pp. 126–44.

Boulton, A. and Zook, M. (2013) Landscape, Locative Media, and the Duplicity of Code. In N. C. Johnson, R. H. Schein and J. Winders (Eds.), *The Wiley-Blackwell Companion to Cultural Geography* (Oxford: Wiley-Blackwell), pp. 437–51.

Coole, D. and Frost, S. (2010) *New Materialisms: Ontology, Agency and Politics* (Durham: Duke University Press).

Cosgrove, D. (1998) *Social Formation and Symbolic Landscape* (Madison and London: The University of Wisconsin Press).

Couldry, N. (2008) Actor Network Theory and Media: Do They Connect and on What Terms?. In A. Hepp, F. Krotz, S. Moores and C. Winter (Eds.), *Connectivity, Networks and Flows: Conceptualizing Contemporary Communications* (Cresskill, NJ: Hampton Press), pp. 93–110.

Couldry, N. and McCarthy, A. (2004) Introduction. In N. Couldry and A. McCarthy (Eds.), *MediaSpace: Place, Scale and Culture in a Digital Age* (London: Routledge), pp. 1–18.

Darroch, M. and Marchessault, J. (2014) *Cartographies of Place: Navigating the Urban* (Montreal and Kingston: McGill-Queens University Press).

de Lang, M. and de Waal, M. (2013) Owning the City: New Media and Citizen Engagement in Urban Design. *First Monday* 18(11): http://journals.uic.edu/ojs/index.php/fm/article/view/4954/3786 (accessed 10 January 2016).

Despard, E. (2015) Photographic Social Media, Designed Urban Landscapes and Place-based Visibilities: In Search of Friction. *Journal of Aesthetics and Culture*

7: http://www.aestheticsandculture.net/index.php/jac/article/view/28242 (accessed 10 January 2016).

Despard, E. and Gallagher, M. (2014) Media Ecologies of Landscape and the Co-production of Photographic Knowledge of Invasive Species. Presentation at the annual meeting of the RGS-IBG, August 26–29, London, UK.

Evans, L. (2015) *Locative Social Media: Place in the Digital Age* (London: Palgrave Macmillan).

Foucault, M. (1991) Questions of Method. In G. Burchell, C. Gordon and P. Miller (Eds.), *The Foucault Effect: Studies in Governmentality* (Chicago: University of Chicago Press), pp. 73–86.

Forlano, L. (2013) Making Waves: Urban Technology and the Co-production of Place. *First Monday* 18(11): http://journals.uic.edu/ojs/index.php/fm/article/view/4968/3797 (accessed 10 January 2016).

Fuller, M. (2005) *Media Ecologies: Materialist Energies in Art and Technoculture* (Cambridge, MA: MIT Press).

Gibbs, M., Meese, J., Arnold, M., Nansen, B. and Carter, M. (2015) #Funeral and Instagram: Death, Social Media and Platform Vernacular. *Information, Communication and Society* 18(3): 255–68.

Heise, U. (2002) Unnatural Ecologies: The Metaphor of the Environment in Media Theory. *Configurations* 10(1): 149–68.

Hochman, N. (2014). The Social Media Image. *Big Data and Society* 1.

Hochman, N. and Manovich, L. (2013) Zooming into an Instagram City. *First Monday* 18(7): http://journals.uic.edu/ojs/index.php/fm/article/view/4711 (accessed 10 January 2016).

Instagram Help Website (no date) Best Practices for Using Hashtags, retrieved from https://help.instagram.com/365080703569355/ (accessed 10 November 2015).

Ingold, T. (2009) Against Space: Place, Movement, Knowledge. In P. Kirby (Ed.), *Boundless Worlds* (New York: Berghahn), pp. 29–44.

Latorre-Martínez, M.P. and Iñiguez-Berrozpe, T. (2014) Image-focused Social Media for a Market Analysis of Tourism Consumption. *International Journal of Technology Management* 64(1): 17–30.

Massey, D. (1994) *Space, Place and Gender* (Minneapolis: University of Minnesota Press).

McCarthy, A. (2001) *Ambient Television* (Durham and London: Duke University Press).

McLuhan, M. (1964) *Understanding Media: The Extensions of Man* (New York: McGraw-Hill).

McQuire, S. (2006) The Politics of Public Space in the Media City. *First Monday* Special Issue #4: http://journals.uic.edu/ojs/index.php/fm/article/view/1544 (accessed 10 January 2016).

McQuire, S. (2008) *The Media City: Media, Architecture and Urban Space* (London: Sage).

Morris, B. (2010) Un/wrapping Shibuya: Place, Media and Punctualization. *Space and Culture* 13(3): 285–303.

Murthy, R. (2006) Story Space: A Theoretical Grounding for the New Urban Annotation. *First Monday* Special Issue #4: http://journals.uic.edu/ojs/index.php/fm/article/view/1547/1462 (accessed 10 January 2016).

Parikka, J. (2011) Media Ecologies and Imaginary Media: Transversal Expansions, Contractions, and Foldings. *Fibrecultures* 17: 34–50.

Parikka, J. (2013) Insects and Canaries: Medianatures and the Aesthetics of the Invisible. *Angelaki: Journal of the Theoretical Humanities* 18(1): 107–19.

Peter, J. (2015) *The Marvelous Clouds: Towards a Philosophy of Elementary Media* (Chicago: University of Chicago Press).

Phillips, D. and Curry, M. (2002) Privacy and the Phenetic Urge: Geodemographics and the Changing Spatiality of Local Practice. In D. Lyon (Ed.), *Surveillance as Social Sorting: Privacy, Risk, and Automated Discrimination* (London: Routledge), pp. 137–52.

Pink, S. (2011) Sensory Digital Photography: Re-thinking 'Moving' and the Image. *Visual Studies* 26(1): 4–13.

Postman, N. (1970) The Reformed English Curriculum. In A.C. Eurich (Ed.), *High School 1980: The Shape of the Future in American Secondary Education* (New York: Pitman), pp. 160–8.

Rainie, L., Brenner, J. and Purcell, K. (2012) Photos and Videos as Social Currency Online. Report published as part of Pew Research Center's *Internet & American Life Project*, http://www.pewinternet.org/files/old-media//Files/Reports/2012/PIP_OnlineLifeinPictures_PDF.pdf (accessed 10 March 2016).

Rodgers, S. (2014) The Architectures of Media Power: Editing, the News Room and Urban Public Space. *Space and Culture* 17(1): 69–84.

Schneider, R. (2005) Crime Prevention Through Environmental Design: Themes, Theories, Practices, and Conflict. *Journal of Architectural and Planning Research* 22(4): 271–83.

Schwartz, R. and Halegoua, G. (2015) The Spatial Self: Location-based Identity Performance on Social Media. *New Media and Society* 17(10): 1643–60.

Schwartz, R. and Hochman, N. (2014) The Social Media Life of Public Spaces: Reading Places Through the Lens of Geo-Tagged Data. In R. Wilken and G. Goggin (Eds.), *Locative Media* (New York: Routledge), pp. 52–65

Silva, T., Vaz de Melo, P., Almeida, J., et al. (2013) A Picture of Instagram is Worth a Thousand Words: Workload Characterization and Application. In *Proceedings of the 2013 IEEE International Conference on Distributed Computing in Sensor Systems*, pp. 123–32.

Staeheli, L. and Mitchell, D. (2008) *The People's Property? Power, Politics, and the Public* (London: Routledge).

Timeto, F. (2013) Redefining the City Through Social Software: Two Examples of Open Source Locative Art in Italian Urban Space. *First Monday* 18(11):

http://journals.uic.edu/ojs/index.php/fm/article/view/4952 (accessed 10 March 2016).

Tosoni, S. and Tarantino, M. (2013) Space, Translations and Media. *First Monday* 18(11): http://journals.uic.edu/ojs/index.php/fm/article/view/4956 (accessed 10 March 2016).

Wilken, R. (2009) Mobilizing Place: Mobile Media, Peripatetics, and the Renegotiation of Urban Places. *Journal of Urban Technology,* 15(3): 39–55.

Wilken, R. and Goggin, G. (Eds.) (2012) *Mobile Technology and Place* (New York: Routledge).

Willim, R. (2013) Enhancement or Distortion? From the Claude Glass to Instagram. In Raqs Media Collective and S. Sarda (Eds.), *Sarai Reader 09,* (The Sarai Programme, CSDS), pp. 353–9.

Wilson, M. (2012) Location-based Services, Conspicuous Mobility, and the Location-aware Future. *Geoforum* 43(6): 1266–75.

Wilson, M. (2014) Morgan Freeman is Dead and Other Big Data Stories. *Cultural Geographies* 22(2): 345–9.

Zeffiro, A. (2014) Locative Praxis: Transborder Poetics and Activist Potential of Experimental Locative Media. In R. Wilken and G. Goggin (Eds.), *Locative Media* (New York: Routledge), pp. 66–80.

Zhang, J., Zhao, H. and Xie, Y. (2013) Follow You From Your Photos. In *Proceedings of the 2013 IEEE International Conference on Green Computing and Communications and IEEE Internet of Things and IEEE Cyber, Physical and Social Computing,* pp. 985–92.

CHAPTER 4

Socio-spatial Approaches for Media and Communication Research

Segah Sak

Digital media can be considered as the focus of contemporary research on media and communication. This is related not only to the significance of digital media on its own, but also to its invasion of other mass media. On the one hand, media and communication research handle a wide array of subjects such as interface design, architecture of information and communication technologies (ICT), or audience reception. On the other hand, as digital media are now part of a fundamental dynamic of contemporary culture, it is a subject of research in a wide array of disciplines.

Digital media is an issue of discussion for architectural and urban research, since spaces not only are computable through digital media, but also accommodate various forms of digital media. Although there is a significant body of works that keep their distance from digital media in the theoretical discussions of the concepts of space and place, most of the research on socio-spatial issues, particularly human geography, handles digital media and communication technologies as a fundamental part of contemporary urban space and life. In the meantime, media and communication research has almost always been inclusive of spatial issues. Especially after William Gibson developed the concept of cyberspace in his

S. Sak (✉)
Bilkent University, Ankara, Turkey
e-mail: segah@bilkent.edu.tr

© The Author(s) 2016
S. Kubitschko, A. Kaun (eds.), *Innovative Methods in Media and Communication Research*, DOI 10.1007/978-3-319-40700-5_4

literary work—first in his short story 'Burning Chrome' (1982) and then in the well-known science-fiction novel *Neuromancer* (1984)—academic research embraced the association of physical space and the digital realm.

In this chapter, I engage with digital media research through an architectural/urban viewpoint. My argument is that research on digital media does and can further benefit from socio-spatial approaches to research. The chapter will start by explaining the socio-spatial attributes of the digital realm. In the following section, I will discuss the ways in which methods and approaches of urban, environmental, and behavioral studies are being and can be further adopted for digital media and communication research. Finally, I will suggest an alternative approach—namely, considering digital spaces as *places of memory*—to be employed by further research on the digital realm.

Socio-spatial Attributes of the Digital Realm

Transcending simple information flows in their functioning, information, and communication technologies provides societies with the digital realm where various social interactions are realized. Even before the sprawl of social media, the social dimensions of the digital realm have been subject to many discussions. Not only are various phenomena related to digital media explained in relation to social dynamics, but social phenomena are also elaborated in relation to digital media. For example, Featherstone and Burrows explain *cyberspace* as an information space 'in which data is configured in such a way as to give the operator the illusion of control, movement and access to information, in which he/she can be linked together with a large number of users' (1995, p. 3). Although maintained through individual use, the digital realm implies collectivity and connectivity—a network of individual agents (see McBeath and Webb 2005).

Castells (2010) argues that in network societies, the logic of the space of flows prevails against the logic of the space of places. The digital realm establishes a new kind of movement through time and space that implies the flow of data and is dependent on flows rather than pauses. This flow reflects on human experience through which the human consciousness moves to witness close and distant spaces and times. Stephen Graham states that 'both urban places and electronic spaces are subject to similar processes of interlinked social struggle, as between the demands of social equity, public space and local accountability and the commodifying tendencies of global commercialization' (Graham 2005, p. 47). Accordingly, understandings of space and the social production of space are altered in the contemporary world.

The potential of integrating a socio-spatial approach into media and communication research can be traced back to theories that account for space as being mainly socially produced. Henri Lefebvre, in *The Production of Space*, explains that 'a social space is constituted neither by a collection of things or an aggregate of (sensory) data, nor by a void packed like a parcel with various contents, and that it is irreducible to a "form" imposed upon phenomena, upon things, upon physical materiality', arguing that 'social space implies a great diversity of knowledge' (Lefebvre 2007, p. 27 and p. 73). The existence of a space does not solely depend on its architectural production; rather, a space needs to be experienced, adopted, and eventually produced by users for a meaningful presence. Ultimately, the digital realm owes its strength and sustainability to social involvement. It consequently resembles physical spaces in the realization of collective productions and experiences, therefore in its social production and publicness. Furthermore, diversity of information constitutes a fundamental feature of the digital realm, supporting its functioning as a social space.

It is possible to elaborate on social production in the digital realm with two approaches. First, *social production* is provided through new forms of communication. Social networks comprise communication and interaction tools that enable the creation of affinity among members. Peter Nieckarz states that 'it is the web of social interactions that determines the boundaries of a community and not vice versa' (2005, p. 405) and explains that internet communities are 'in many ways are not very different from non-Internet community networks in their characteristics' (Nieckarz 2005, p. 405). The variety and quality of the personal communications in which individuals take part are thought to be sufficient for the creation of 'a *sense* of a community' (Rotman et al. 2009, p. 48), if not for the creation of a community. Correlatively, because the digital realm is undoubtedly public, it provides a sense of place, if not *places*. Or maybe, after all, 'social relations are not fixed or located in place', because 'all social relationships always involve diverse "connections", which are more or less at a distance, more or less intense, and more or less mobile' (Urry 2010, p. 144).

The digital realm also has the potential to extend to the physical space, and to mediate and increase face-to-face communication. In a study carried out by Driskell and Lyon, the respondents reported that 'the Internet has had a modestly positive impact on both increasing contact with others and communicating more with family' (2002, p. 385). Self-help groups are one significant example of such communication: they provide people with the support that they lack because of the unavailability of similar cases in the same locality or because of their drawbacks for some reason (King and Moreggi 2007). Virtual teams are another example of networks that benefit highly from communication through the internet escaping the limitations of physical space, time, and organizational boundaries, lowering travel and facility costs, reducing project schedules, and improving decision-making time (Shayo et al. 2007).

Secondly, the digital realm allows the creation and representation of cultural texts. Featherstone and Burrows (1995) point out the possibility of post-bodied form of existence, which can strengthen bodily existence in the physical public space by encouraging creativity and freedom in communication, interaction, and production. Just as Nieckarz argues, the internet 'provides a means for people to resist a centralized culture and actively create and define things on their own' (2005, p. 421). It provides opportunities for individuals to be able to express themselves freely and to reach out for anything and anyone across the globe, contributing to the collaborative creation of social capital.

Depending on the arguments used, it is possible to assert that there is social production within the digital realm with respect to relationships among people, and between people and their physical and digital environment. The digital realm, involving collective experiences and being precisely socially produced, inherits the attributes of space.

Merging the Approaches of Socio-spatial and Media Research

Whereas it certainly is not possible to treat physical space and the digital realm as identical phenomena, depending on the socio-spatial characteristics that the digital realm possesses it is viable to merge research in both areas. Digital media in everyday life mostly operate through the visual. Jussi Parikka argues that 'the visual as part of the wider financial, urban and security regimes cannot be neglected as one fold in the topological continuum between spatial architectures and informational ones' (Parikka 2015, p. 213). Such an approach, revealing the cultural landscape of the contemporary world, superposes the virtual on the spatial. In this respect, theories and methods of socio-spatial research provide grounds for studies on the digital realm in various ways. Whereas it is not the subject of this chapter, it should be mentioned that contemporary socio-spatial research, in exchange, gets notable enhancement from media and communication research.

The digital realm, being public, encompasses social processes, which, as explained previously, designate its spatial character. Correspondingly, there is a growing body of research concentrating on various aspects of *social production* of the digital realm. Although this research often does not mention the concept of social production, it does study the formation of socio-cultural products or of communities and social groups, which almost always touch on the *spaces/places* of these formations. The former being related to *representational spaces* and the latter to *social practices*, these studies, which are mostly either urban or sociological, lead us to an understanding of social production—in the sense in which Lefebvre (2007) discusses the concept—within the digital realm.

As communication can be considered to be the fundamental social practice within the digital world, studies regarding people relating to each other and to information eventually provide us with insight about the social production of digital spaces. One fundamental question that is widely discussed concerning the relationship between the digital realm and people's relation to each other is the possibility of forming communities. Driskell and Lyon (2002) juxtapose three components of traditional communities: *a specific place*, *common ties*, and *social interaction*. For the formation of online communities the most problematic component is locality, whereas globality, rather than locality, is the essence of the digital realm. However, it is a well-established thought that online communities are possible. This viewpoint depends on the argument that social cohesion and common values take the place of geographic proximity and physical presence, consequently making relationships and communications the crucial component of society (for example, Rotman et al. 2009; Papadopoulos et al. 2012). Therefore, relationships within social networks are suitable to be analyzed as social phenomena.

One of the most prevalent areas of research in this context considers the digital realm as a public sphere in relation to democracy. The first accounts of research on the politics of the digital realm explore the potential of democracy, freedom, and access to information more on a theoretical basis (for example, Papacharissi 2002). Research on varied arenas including news media (for example, Braun and Gillespie 2011), corporate policies (Ihlen 2008), and e-government applications (for example, Bertot et al. 2010) emphasizes the significance of digital politics for the contemporary public. As could be expected, recent research discusses political issues related to specific digital agoras such as Twitter (for example, Ausserhofer and Maireder 2013) or specific cases that take place in the physical space (for example, Nanabhay and Farmanfarmaian 2011). In the work of Nanabhay and Farmanfarmaian (2011), the uprising in Tahrir

Square in Egypt is discussed as having revealed the topological continuum between the physical space and the digital realm. Deuze, with a similar understanding of such a continuum, states that 'media are becoming invisible, as media are so pervasive and ubiquitous that people in general do not even register the presence of media in their lives' (2011, p. 143).[1] As a consequence thereof, theories on social and political practices have been widely adopted in the public digital realm.

Where such theoretical frameworks of socio-spatial research are adopted, a ground for the analysis of certain formations in digital media is enabled. Lev Manovich, through referencing Michel de Certeau's influential text *The Practice of Everyday Life*, discusses how 'the logic of tactics has now become the logic of strategies' (2009, p. 324) in the media of everyday life. De Certeau (1984) refers to strategies as being of agents of power and to tactics as being of individual or group subjects. Manovich adopts this approach and integrates it into his work, explaining how, for example, companies offer customization tools in their digital products as a tactic to cover the demands of users, who would in any way develop tactics to appropriate the given products. In the light of the validity of this paradigm, it is possible to track the reflections of socio-spatial studies on research related to the development of marketing strategies or ideological and political discourses.

A number of studies on the digital realm adopt not only the theoretical framework but also the methods of environmental and behavioral research. Empirical studies of people's preferences for or behaviors in the digital realm frequently focus on the cognitive processes that guide certain practices within spaces. Intrinsically related to cognitive processes, *wayfinding/navigation* and *cognitive/mental maps* are among concepts that are inherited by digital media research from the terminology of spatial research toward the end of the 1990s. Downs and Stea explain that 'human spatial behavior is dependent on the individual's cognitive map of the spatial environment' (1973, p. 9). Cognitive/mental maps are constituted by the routes and reference points that are reflected into the mind, and are referred to for navigating within spaces. Navigation is defined as 'the act, activity, or process of finding the way to get to a place when you are travelling in a ship, airplane, car, etc.'.[2] Wayfinding, on the other hand, is defined as 'the process of determining and following a path or route between an origin and a destination' (Golledge 1999, p. 6). Dahlbäck puts forward two assumptions that lie behind the use of the same methods for physical and digital spaces: geographic and electronic worlds are similar, and 'the *activities* of wayfinding and navigation are similar to the information seeking activities of users of information spaces' (Dahlbäck 1998, p. 15). Although these concepts are primarily used in studies on virtual worlds (for example, Kohler et al. 2011), research on wayfinding and navigation, in general, present models for better evaluating or designing the digital realm depending on human behavior (for example, Dieberger 1997; Spence 1999). In such research, the cases are handled as means of information architecture, and the patterns in the ways in which visual data guide movement are studied in various contexts and scales. The technical computational aspects of information architecture can be put aside within this chapter, and the primary subject matter can be defined as the cues present in the space of the movement and the navigational reactions of users to these cues. Here, the challenge in adopting methods of navigation research lies in the dichotomy of virtual and physical. The relevant behaviors and the entities that govern movement within physical spaces and digital spaces have different dimensionalities. Interface, which is the medium of interaction with the digital realm, and the cues involved are still two dimensional. Movement, on the other hand, is realized in a different dimension. In other words, interaction with data and movement within data are not realized in the same dimensions. Consequently, approaching with a socio-spatial point of view, the methods of spatial research on navigation and wayfinding are rendered inadequate for the digital realm. This is not because these methods do not work for the navigational aspects of behavior in the digital realm, but because they do not deal with the social aspects, which provide the required dimension for the spatiality of digital spaces.

A socio-spatial approach to media and communication research can be verified only by considering the multi-layered constitution of complex human behavior. At this point, Dourish and Chalmers's (1994) differentiation between *spatial*, *semantic*, and *social* forms of navigation provides an endorsement. The authors explain that although spatial models can be used for virtual environments and for digital maps of physical spaces, the systems that arrange information objects spatially and hypertext systems require semantic navigation. At the same time, they propose social navigation for the information systems that extend to collaborative activity. Such a deconstruction abides by the complexity of human behavior within both physical and digital spaces, and, in a way, reconstructs the extensive concept of *spatial cognition* for contemporary media, which is immensely social.

Where we handle the digital realm as a social space, the destinations at which we arrive in our daily movement within it can be considered to be random and unexpected. Unless we search for specific information, and therefore act toward a certain destination, we are like wanderers rather than residents in the physical space. In the governance of search engines, arriving at a certain destination, finding the required information within the digital realm, is no longer a fundamental problem. For a wanderer, for a digital destination (for example, a web page, a video, a blog entry, and so on) to be reachable, links to it strongly require to be shared or promoted, and so to be connected and communicated in social media (see van Dijck 2013). The promotion of digital destinations is a subject of research on digital marketing strategies. Sharing, on the other hand, is instead realized through social tactics by users for the utilization of the digital realm. *Tags* and *hashtags,* which are for identifying and grouping data and so for making them socially accessible, constitute significant tools of navigation in both semantic and social forms. There is a growing body of research on hashtags, which elaborate on the relation between specific events, concepts, or social groups and on the hashtags used for them (for example, Romero et al. 2011). Although it has been the subject of a few social navigation–related research projects (for example, Nizam et al. 2014), the use of hashtags is yet to be explored in much more depth to understand how people behave in the digital realm.

Socio-spatial research on people's behaviors within spaces concentrates on the interrelations of individuals and social groups, and on their relations to their environment. How public spaces mediate various social acts and activities, and how people utilize and use the environmental elements, are the subject matter of socio-spatial research that handles space as a network of people and physical spatial elements. For the digital realm, hashtags provide fruitful data to be analyzed to understand these networks. They guide the researcher through the network of users and data, which corresponds to the network of people and spaces in the physical world. Although they can be subjected to debates on the ethics of research, hashtags provide relevant information about practices well accessible to the researcher. However, since data are extensively available and can be considered to be speculative, there is a need for careful analysis and elimination to ensure the validity of research.

Approaching the network of people and spaces, the subject of socio-spatial research, from a broad perspective, hyper-dimensional relation building to the environment should be considered as a fundamental feature of spatial cognition. When viewed from this aspect, the conception of a *mental image* provides a rather integrative understanding of these networks in question. Based on *The Image of the City* by Kevin Lynch (1960), the mental image of the city can be defined as a combination of the understanding of the structure of the city, the perception of the identity of urban elements, and the meanings that people attach to spaces. Cognitive processes related to the digital realm can be explained in the light of this trilogy, which Lynch proposed to provide a holistic understanding of people's relation to their environment. Accordingly, research on the relations of people to digital spaces can be developed by studying related perceptions and meanings among navigational issues. A thorough discussion of the influence of Lynch's work on the development and research of digital visual data is provided by Orit Halpern (2015). She explains that the studies of Lynch, along with the studies of Kepes and Eames, 'contributed in complicated ways to producing perception as a channel to scale between individuated bodies and vast networks, and a pedagogy and epistemology that reworked space through a new way territory of algorithmic logics and cognitive processes' (Halpern 2015, p. 136).

Perception within the digital realm has been a popular subject for many researchers, most of whom, utilizing methodologies from environmental psychologists, explore how users perceive websites—especially corporate ones—and what makes websites usable, attractive, and engaging (for example, Wang and Li 2012). The studies in question mostly explain usability and navigation as the key features that influence people's perceptions of websites. In addition, the findings propose personalization/customization and enjoyment as features that have a positive effect on people's perceptions. These findings reveal that the formation of people's mental images of the digital realm resembles that for physical space. Consequently, it becomes expedient to suggest that adapting methods of environmental psychology research can be significantly constructive for media and communication research.

The relevant methods used in previous research involve surveys that are realized through observations of behaviors of informed subjects as well as of the object, which is the urban space, and through conducting interviews and questionnaires with a sample of respondents. In Lynch's research, for example, individuals are expected to navigate within the urban space while explaining their decisions about taking certain routes, their perceptions of and/or their emotional or evaluative approaches toward urban elements. They are also asked to respond to questions that are posed to reveal how they perceive, remember, and reflect on their experiences of the relevant urban spaces. Depending on the findings, he sets forth the fundamental constituents of the image of the city, and elaborates on the elements that have a strong influence on the formation of mental images to propose features of a better urban design. Kaplan et al. (1998), in parallel, utilize the data that they gather from their respondents to create a preference matrix for the design of the urban space. Although similar methods and the underlying theoretical frameworks have been adopted by a few researchers for digital media research (for example, Rosen and Purinton 2004), considering the extensive insight that is provided through such research, the adaptation and development of corresponding methods for media and communication research could be of great help both for the understanding of the network of people and the digital realm and for the design and improvement of data spaces.

Approaching the Digital Realm as a Place of Memory

These discussions designate established and developing mergers in the approaches of socio-spatial and media research. At this point, to potentially extend the scope of superposition of the virtual on the spatial, I will set forth an alternative approach to understanding the digital realm. The argument here is that media and communication research can also handle the digital realm as a *place of memory*.

The idea about memory's relation to place is an ancient one, since Aristotle, Cicero, and Quintilian suggested the ordering and placement of mental images within mental spaces for better remembrance. The association of individual memory with mental places is mainly established through studies of the *art of memory*. Frances Yates (1969) studied the art of memory, elaborating on the mnemonic practices for remembering developed by Cicero, Quintilian, and later by Matteo Ricci and Giordano Bruno. In a brief explanation, she states that 'this art seeks to memorize through a technique of impressing *places* and *images* on memory' (Yates 1969, p. 11). Those places are not always three-dimensional ones. Yates argues that the art of memory mostly adopts architectural mnemonics and uses architectural structures to order the *images* of the things to be remembered. The art of memory refers to places as *loci* that are 'easily grasped by the memory' (Yates 1969, p. 22), such as 'a house, an intercolumnar space, a recess, an arch, or the like', and the images are 'a figure, mark, or portrait of the object we wish to remember' (Cicero 2007, p. 44).

Cicero (2007) highlights that there should be various loci for disposition of different groups of images and those loci should somehow be connected, as if they were the different rooms of a structure. In her study of the art of memory in different time periods, Yates makes a significant statement, and asserts that the art of memory always uses 'contemporary architecture for its memory places and contemporary imagery for its images' (1969, p. 11) and therefore has its artistic periods.

In its classic and Renaissance periods, the art of memory was the method 'of memorizing the encyclopaedia of knowledge, of reflecting the world in memory' (Yates 1969, p. 355). Later in the 17th century, the method became 'an aid for investigating the encyclopaedia and the world with the object of discovering new knowledge' (Yates 1969, p. 355) and led to the scientific method. The method indicated by the art of memory is the method of loci, which became the subject of many psychological studies to understand how the act of remembering is realized and to propose ways to practice and improve memory against an increasing number of mental disorders.

For collective memory, the art of memory is reflected in collective practices that facilitate remembering through the experience of urban spaces. In *The City of Collective Memory*, Christine Boyer handles cities as places of the art of collective memory: 'the city [...] carries in the weaving and unravelling of its fabric the memory traces of earlier architectural forms, city plans, and public monuments' (1994, p. 31). In parallel, Aldo Rossi, in his pioneering work *The Architecture of the City*, states that 'the city is the *locus* of collective memory' (Rossi 1982, p. 130).

Hebbert (2005) focuses on streets and explains that a public space can be a locus of collective memory in two ways. First, it can operate as a memory space through its structures, monuments, symbols, and their syntax. In this way, the urban space becomes a place in which memorial and cultural *texts* that help societies remember are exhibited. Those cultural texts depend on contemporary technologies and ideologies. Secondly, it accommodates collective *social practices* and acts as a public sphere, providing a stage for public debates or gatherings (Boyer 1994, p. 7). In a similar approach, Casey (2004) sees public places as a component of public memory where a public is embodied and public interaction takes place. Boyer (1994) emphasizes this second aspect for deepening understanding of the art of collective memory. Boyer's argument is that the contemporary approach to the art of collective memory reveals a paradox in its assumption that museums are the places where the images—or the artifacts—of the past are to be ordered. Museums, nevertheless, are curated in such a way that those artifacts are no longer a part of spatial, temporal, or social continuity; therefore, they are not themselves socially produced, as a place would be, to become loci of collective memory. Loci of collective memory need to be accommodating collective social practices and so necessarily have to be social spaces that are collectively produced. Only in this way can they make the functioning of collective memory possible.

Where the art of memory uses contemporary architecture for its places, it is reasonable to consider the digital realm as a locus for contemporary collective memory. If the art of memory aims at remembering better, the contemporary art of collective memory, to which digital media is integral, aims at articulation. The digital realm offers places for the *ordering* and *imprinting* of *digital images*—places that are socially produced, and are not at all more virtual than the *mental places* of the art of memory. In other words, the digital realm has the potential to operate as a locus where images, 'forms, marks or simulacra of what we wish to remember' (Yates 1969, p. 22), are placed. The strength of the digital realm as a locus of memory is based on its features that make it a social space: its publicness and accessibility, its social production, and so its integration into daily life. Cicero (2007), for individual rhetorical memory, explains that conscious organization of images in significant places is required. The digital realm, then, can be evaluated and developed through architectural mnemonics considering its organization as a socially produced space where articulation is to be made possible. Although architectural mnemonics is not an extrinsic concept for virtual worlds, the research on the digital realm in its broadest context and also on specific digital spaces can further benefit from this method.

As better remembering depends on the encoding and organization of information through order, orientation, grouping, association, affect, and repetition, a combination of the theoretical grounds and methods discussed in the previous part of the chapter eventually reflects the principles of the art of memory. In fact, these principles are all very well handled and explored by the agents involved in the construction and development of digital infrastructures. The techniques of better remembering can further be utilized to develop guidelines for the design of digital spaces. Research on digital spaces, on the other hand, can embrace inclusive methods considering the aspects mentioned together for the understanding of the audience's use and experience of certain digital spaces. In this way, criteria regarding analysis in relevant academic research as well as efforts to ensure articulation of websites, services, or portals can be based on solid grounds and be systematized. This approach does not necessarily suggest the use of alternative methods for media and communication; however, it proposes an alternative disposition that would help cope with the dichotomy of the physical and the virtual in the potential adoption of methods of socio-spatial research.

Conclusion

The objective of this chapter was to provide an overview of studies integrating socio-spatial approaches into digital media research, and to elaborate on how the methods of media and communication research can be enriched with socio-spatial approaches. The basis of this disposition is built on the line of reasoning that the digital realm inherits a number of socio-spatial attributes of physical spaces. Architectural and urban studies have long been nourished by the acknowledgment of space as being socially produced. As a fundamental feature of contemporary digital media, social production of the digital realm is realized through social practices and representational spaces, which are both proposed by Lefebvre (2007) as components of social spaces. Consequently, various issues related to physical spaces can be observed in the digital realm, leading us to consider the digital realm as a social space in research.

There is a body of research that focuses either on the cognitive processes or on the social processes within the digital realm. Studies on cognitive processes are related to the ways in which people experience and perceive the digital realm, and adopt various methods of environmental and behavioral studies. On the other hand, works on questions of social processes question or explore how people form communities or cultural texts that are traditionally accepted to be closely related to the spaces in which they are formed. I believe that an overview of these studies can explain and inspire merging of the approaches of socio-spatial and media research.

In the last part of the chapter, to extend the scope of superposition of the virtual on the spatial for further research, I discuss the potential of approaching the digital realm as a place of memory. This potential is originated again on the spatiality of the digital realm. As the digital realm embraces acts, tools, and objects of remembering just like physical spaces do, such an integrative approach paves the way for evaluating and developing the digital realm for better articulation of digital spaces and therefore for better functioning of digital life, which is integral to contemporary daily life. The discussion of socio-spatial approaches in this chapter aims at encouraging the use and development of innovative methods for media and communication research, and also at paving the way for comprehending the significant influence of media on spatial practices for socio-spatial research.

Notes

1. For a critique of Mark Deuze's argument, see Kubitschko and Knapp (2012).
2. See *Navigation*, in Merriam-Webster dictionary; http://www.merriam-webster.com/dictionary/navigation (accessed 10 January 2016).

References

Ausserhofer, J. and Mairede, A. (2013) National Politics on Twitter. *Information, Communication & Society* 16(3): 291–314.

Bertot, J., Jaeger, P. and Grimes, J. (2010) Using ICTs to Create a Culture of Transparency: E-government and Social Media as Openness and Anti-corruption Tools for Societies. *Government Information Quarterly* 27(3): 264–71.

Boyer, M. (1994) *The City of Collective Memory: Its Historical Imagery and Architectural Entertainments* (Cambridge, MA: MIT Press).

Braun, J. and Gillespie, T. (2011) Hosting the Public Discourse, Hosting the Public. *Journalism Practice* 5(4): 383–98.

Casey, E. (2004) Public Memory in Place and Time. In: K. Phillips (Ed.), *Framing Public Memory* (Tuscaloosa: University of Alabama Press), pp. 17–44.

Castells, M. (2010) *The Rise of the Network Society. The Information Age: Economy, Society and Culture*. Vol. 1 (Oxford: Blackwell).

Cicero (2007) From Ad Herennium. In M. Rossington and A. Whitehead (Eds.), *Theories of Memory: A Reader* (Edinburgh: Edinburgh University Press), pp. 43–9.

Dahlbäck, N. (1998) On Spaces and Navigation in and Out of the Computer. In N. Dahlbäck (Ed.), Exploring Navigation: Towards a Framework for Design and Evaluation of Navigation in Electronic Spaces (Kista, Sweden: SICS), pp. 15–29.

De Certeau, M. (1984) The Practice of Everyday Life (Berkeley: University of California Press).

Deuze, M. (2011) Media Life. *Media, Culture & Society* 33(1): 137–48.

Dieberger, A. (1997) Supporting Social Navigation on the World Wide Web. *International Journal of Human Computer Studies* 46(6): 805–25.

Dourish, P. and Chalmers, M. (1994) Running out of Space: Models of Information Navigation. *Human Computer Interaction Conference*, HCI 94 (Glasgow).

Downs, R. and Stea, D. (1973) Cognitive Maps and Spatial Behaviour: Process and Products. In: R. Downs and D. Stea (Eds.), *Image and Environment: Cognitive Mapping and Spatial Behavior* (Chicago: Aldine Press), pp. 8–26.

Driskell, R. and Lyon, L. (2002) Are Virtual Communities True Communities? Examining the Environments and Elements of Community. *City& Community* 1(4): 373–90.

Featherstone, M. and Burrows, R. (1995) Cultures of Technological Embodiment: An Introduction. In: M. Featherstone and R. Burrows (Eds.), *Cyber Space/ Cyber Bodies/ Cyber Punk: Cultures of Technological Embodiment* (London: Sage), pp. 1–20.

Golledge, R. (1999) Human Wayfinding and Cognitive Maps. In R. G. Golledge (Ed.), *Wayfind Behavior: Cognitive Mapping and Other Spatial Processes* (Baltimore: Johns Hopkins University Press), pp. 5–45.

Graham, S. (2005): Imagining the Real-Time City: Telecommunications, Urban Paradigms and the Future of Cities. In: S. Westwood and J. Williams (Eds.), *Imagining Cities: Scripts, Signs, Memory* (London: Routledge), pp. 31–47.

Halpern, O. (2015) Beautiful Data: A History of Vision and Reason Since 1945 (Durham: Duke University Press).

Hebbert, M. (2005) The Street as a Locus of Collective Memory. *Environment and Planning D* 23(4): 581–96.

Ihlen, Ø. (2008) Mapping the Environment for Corporate Social Responsibility. *Corporate Communications: An International Journal* 13(2): 135– 46.

Kaplan, R., Kaplan, S. and Ryan, R. (1998) *With People in Mind: Design and Management of Everyday Nature* (Washington, DC: Island Press).

King, S. and Moreggi, D. (2007) Internet Self-Help and Support Groups: The Pros and Cons of Text-Based Mutual Aid. In: J. Gackenbach (Ed.), *Psychology and the Internet: Intrapersonal, Interpersonal, and Transpersonal Implications* (Boston: Elsevier), pp. 221–44.

Kohler, T., Fueller, J., Matzler, K., et al. (2011) Co-Creation in Virtual Worlds: The Design of the User Experience. *MIS Quarterly* 35(3): 773–88.

Kubitschko, S. and Knapp, D. (2012) An Invisible Life? A Response to Mark Deuze's 'Media Life'. *Media, Culture & Society* 34(3): 359–64.

Lefebvre, H. (2007) *Production of Space* (Oxford: Wiley-Blackwell).

Lynch, K. (1960) *The Image of the City* (Cambridge, MA: MIT Press).

Manovich, L. (2009) The Practice of Everyday (Media) Life: From Mass Consumption to Mass Cultural Production? *Critical Inquiry* 35(2): 319–31.

McBeath, G. and Webb, S. (2005) Cities, Subjectivity and Cyberspace. In: S. Westwood and J. Williams (Eds.), *Imagining Cities: Scripts, Signs, Memory* (London: Routledge), pp. 249–60.

Nanabhay, M. and Farmanfarmaian, R. (2011) From Spectacle to Spectacular: How Physical Space, Social Media and Mainstream Broadcast Amplified the Public Sphere in Egypt's 'Revolution'. *The Journal of North African Studies* 16(4): 573–603.

Nieckarz, P. (2005) Community in Cyber Space? The Role of the Internet in Facilitating and Maintaining a Community of Live Music Collecting and Trading. *City & Community* 4(4): 403–23.

Nizam, N., Watters, C. and Gruzd, A. (2014) Link Sharing on Twitter During Popular Events: Implications for Social Navigation on Websites. In: *System Sciences, 47th Hawaii International Conference on System Science* (HICSS), pp. 1745–54.

Papacharissi, Z. (2002) The Virtual Sphere: The Internet as a Public Sphere. *New Media & Society* 4(1): 9–27.

Papadopoulos, S., Kompatsiaris, Y., Vakali, A., et al. (2012) Community Detection in Social Media. *Data Mining and Knowledge Discovery* 24(3): 515–54.

Parikka, J. (2015) The City and the City: London 2012 Visual (Un)Commons. In: D. M. Berry and M. Dieter (Eds.), *Postdigital Aesthetics: Art, Computation and Design* (Basingstoke: Palgrave Macmillan), pp. 203–18.

Romero, D., Meeder, B. and Kleinberg, J. (2011) Differences in the Mechanics of Information Diffusion Across Topics: Idioms, Political Hashtags, and Complex Contagion on Twitter. In: Proceedings of the 20th International Conference on World Wide Web (Hyderabad, India), pp. 695–704.

Rosen, D. and Purinton, E. (2004) Website Design: Viewing the Web as a Cognitive Landscape. *Journal of Business Research* 57(7): 787–94.

Rossi, A. (1982) *The Architecture of the City* (Cambridge, MA: MIT Press).

Rotman, D., Golbeck, J. and Preece, J. (2009) The Community is Where the Rapport Is – On Sense and Structure in the YouTube Community. In: *Proceedings of the Fourth International Conference on Communities and Technologies*, pp. 41–50.

Shayo, C., Olfman, L., Iriberri, A. and Igbaria, M. (2007) The Virtual Society: Its Driving Forces, Arrangements, Practices, and Implications. In: J. Gackenbach (Ed.), *Psychology and the Internet: Intrapersonal, Interpersonal, and Transpersonal Implications* (Boston: Elsevier), pp. 187–219.

Spence, R. (1999) A Framework for Navigation. *International Journal of Human Computer Studies* 51(5): 919–45.

Urry, J. (2010) Connections. In: G. Bridge and S. Watson (Eds.), *The Blackwell City Reader*. 2nd ed. (Malden: Wiley-Blackwell), pp. 144–51.

van Dijck, J. (2013) *The Culture of Connectivity: A Critical History of Social Media* (Oxford: Oxford University Press).

Wang, W.-T. and Li, H.-M. (2012) Factors Influencing Mobile Services Adoption: A Brand-equity Perspective. *Internet Research* 22(2): 142–79.

Yates, F. (1969) *The Art of Memory* (Harmondsworth: Penguin).

PART II

Technology

Noortje Marres

Experiments in Interpretation: Researching Media, Society, and Culture with Technology

Are methods continuously emerging in the age that comes after the internet, digital media, and 'pervasive computing'? There is something curious about the question of method as it arises at the interface of social research, media technologies, and computing today: on the one hand, the use of digital techniques in the conduct of social and cultural inquiry is becoming ever more common and routine. Few people would expect social, media, and cultural researchers *not* to use search engines, analyze online materials, or interact electronically as part of the research process. Indeed, the attempt to avoid such technological mediations altogether would likely result in a highly artificial methodology and affect the very credibility of the research. On the other hand, however, the uptake of computational techniques in social and cultural research continues to unsettle established methodologies and, as I would like to argue here, forces the development of more experimental ways of knowing.

This puzzle of method arises from the following circumstances. Most importantly, so-called technology-driven forms of inquiry that some years ago were heralded as 'radically innovative' have been shown to be less of a novelty than previously proclaimed. Approaches like the

N. Marres (✉)
University of Warwick, Coventry, UK
e-mail: N.Marres@warwick.ac.uk

'new network science' and 'natively digital' methods such as Google Trends have been shown to contain many elements deriving from long-standing methodological traditions in social research, including social network analysis and sample survey analysis. Notwithstanding its declared ambition to revolutionize social and cultural science, this work replicates key analytic and methodological presumptions from a pre-digital age, such as the notions that all actors are human and that data can be presumed to be passive. This insight into the methodological inertia of at least some parts of computational social and cultural science is liberating in some respects, insofar as it turns the tables on 'innovation' in social and cultural inquiry. Many of the technology-driven approaches have been developed in collaboration with tech industries and, while these industries certainly have access to more powerful machines, larger volumes of data, and more sophisticated analytics than most social and cultural researchers, this does *not* necessarily mean that they have the methodological edge.

It is becoming increasingly clear, then, that the uptake of digital techniques, data, and methods in social and cultural research compels a more fundamental interrogation of the analytic assumptions guiding social and cultural inquiry than previously recognized. Digital data prove to be heavily formatted by technology, and digital objects of inquiry are marked by 'interactivity effects': the internet, social media, and sensor networks do not just make the social world available for empirical analysis, they disclose phenomena that are themselves shot through with media-technological dynamics, like linking, tagging, and ranking. In brief, this means that the uptake of computational techniques, data, and methods in social research disrupts the assumptions and ideals of *representational* social science. Digital machines do not just qualify as windows on the social world, but present us with ambiguous instruments of social media research. As such, they invite us to explore alternative methodologies, for example by turning to interpretative approaches in social and cultural inquiry that explicitly recognize the possibility of the type of interactivity effects already noted: interpretative methodology has long emphasized that the categories used to describe social life may affect its very enactment, at least since the beginning of the 20th century. This form of reflexivity is proving all the more pernicious in relation to interactive technology.

How can we deal with this? Insight into the historicity of computational social and cultural research—the realization that it is animated by deeply familiar methodological concerns and problems—does not cancel out the provocation that technology presents to social and cultural inquiry. Insofar as it compels us to recognize openly the role of technology in social life (as well as in social research), it invites and indeed forces us to experiment with alternative research designs, ones that explicitly recognize the participation of technologies, environments, and formats in social and cultural life. Each of the contributions collected in this volume in its different way takes up this challenge by adopting and developing experimental strategies of researching media, technology, and society. While many of us trained in qualitative methodology have grown accustomed to viewing experimental methods with trepidation, the contributors to this section courageously take up computational methods, data, and techniques that require them to cross into alien methodological territory, as they experiment with tools from the domains of information science, human–computer interaction, and network analysis: they compare social media feeds, take up self-tracking applications, model connectivity, and automatically extract (scrape) data from peer-to-peer networks. As such, these contributions follow the intuition that the development of social and cultural research methods 'with technology' must be a creative as well as an interdisciplinary project.

Why call these research projects at the interface of digital media, computing, and social research experimental? Their willingness to take up unfamiliar research techniques—the application of which therefore inevitably involves trying and tinkering—is certainly part of the answer. But another is their reliance on basic research protocols to generate empirical objects. As social and cultural researchers capture and analyze data by computational means, their research acquires a formal character, following a series of steps and implementing technical instructions. Taina Bucher compares social media feeds (one unfiltered, one curated) for six months; Pablo Velasco relies on 'the public transaction information displayed in the blockchain' to map socio-technical networks. As social and cultural researchers curate and analyze digital data in this way, they are likely to generate empirical objects that did not exist prior to the research: they actively produce phenomena that are *not* already given in the data or in the machine. In doing so, these projects move beyond the descriptive or observational modes of qualitative inquiry, and unsettle—if not reject—the anti-methodical impulse in much qualitative research, even as they conduct their experiments in order *to produce interpretations of an exploratory kind*.

What is critical, then, is that efforts to develop more experimental ways of doing social and cultural research 'with technology' should not be equated, as a matter of course, with the uptake of methodological frameworks taken from the sciences. These efforts are better understood as attempts to configure 'experiments in interpretation', as heeding the call to cultivate distinctively experimental forms of social and cultural inquiry that has been voiced by philosophers and sociologists since the early 20th century. Pragmatist thinkers like John Dewey, the ethnomethodology of Harold Garfinkel, and the social studies of science and technology (STS) undertaken by Susan Star, Bruno Latour, and others have long argued that we need to move beyond description and observation to intervention—or provocation—in order to truly know social, political, and public life. They also made the case for a broader analytic sensibility for the 'experimentality' of social, political, and public life itself: in their views, ongoing disruptions, breakdowns, surprises, and controversies—in short, the disturbance of taken-for-granted ways of doing—mean that experimental moments proliferate in our worlds, and these present positive, enabling occasions for interpreting the world, for social research but also in social life, more widely defined.

How does social research at the interface of computing, digital media, and social life take this broad approach forward? On the one hand, this work focuses our attention on the experimentality of phenomena in digital societies. Velasco shows how the emerging socio-technical infrastructure of Bitcoin unsettles the very notion of 'currency'. Alberto Frigo conceptualizes lifelogging as a social and cultural practice that seeks the transformation of habit through measurement. Richard Husky invites us to include neural networks among the heterogeneous formations that inform and inflect life and media in digital societies. The experimental quality of these methodological propositions, to be sure, gives them a rather slippery status—but social and cultural research conducted with computational technologies is able to translate this constraint into an empirical brief. They invite us to ask: What are the relevant constraints—algorithms, social structures, standards, resources, interests, and so on—that come together in a socio-computational phenomenon like a distributed transactional network, a social media recommender system?

Approaching such a question experimentally, it should then be clear, does *not* mean that it becomes our aim to implement maximally 'controlled' research procedures (the digital networked environment as social science laboratory). Experiments in social and cultural research have various merits, but one of them surely is that they take experimental inquiry into an opposite direction from the presumption that conducting an experiment requires that the researcher control the setting and gain full and complete access to the data. Rather, it is to pursue exploratory knowledge through the active configuration and combination of networks, data, feeds, and measures and by deploying the ongoing provocations of life in technological societies in order to generate partial empirical objects.

CHAPTER 5

Neither Black Nor Box: Ways of Knowing Algorithms

Taina Bucher

Consider the following tweets: 'The suggested algorithm on Facebook confuses me. It thinks I need to lose weight, am pregnant, broke, and single.' 'I hate Facebook's algorithm so much. My followers aren't seeing my posts on my FB page.' 'I feel like the Facebook algorithm doesn't know me at all.'[1] Every single day, social media users feel compelled to express their feelings and observations about the ways in which systems like Facebook work. Searching Twitter for mentions of the Facebook algorithm solicits an impressive list of beliefs, questions, opinions, and observations concerning the algorithms animating the platform. The stream provides a rare glimpse into the everyday experiences that people have with algorithmic media. I say rare, because as it stands we do not know much about the ways in which people experience algorithms in their everyday life. There are many reasons for this lack of knowledge about the contours of algorithmic life, some of which I will address as part of this chapter. The most straightforward reason, perhaps, is the only very recent uptake of algorithms as a field of research within the social science and humanities.

During the past few years, however, there has been a significant upsurge in academic and public interest. Algorithms have been described as playing

T. Bucher (✉)
University of Copenhagen, Copenhagen, Denmark
e-mail: wfg568@hum.ku.dk

© The Author(s) 2016
S. Kubitschko, A. Kaun (eds.), *Innovative Methods in Media and Communication Research*, DOI 10.1007/978-3-319-40700-5_5

81

an increasingly important role in shaping the world of finance (Karppi and Crawford 2015; Lenglet 2011), journalism (Anderson 2013; Diakopoulos 2015), the media sector, and social media in particular (Gillespie 2014). When computer scientists speak of software, they generally refer to machine-readable instructions that direct the computer to perform a specific task. The algorithm, simply put, is just another term for those carefully planned instructions that follow a sequential order (Knuth 1998). When a social scientist talks about software, however, it often has less to do with the mechanical term or the nature of those machine-readable instructions, and more with the ways in which 'software conditions our very existence' (Kitchin and Dodge 2011, p. ix). Thus, the nature of research into algorithms differs across these disciplinary boundaries. While computer scientists are generally concerned with the design and development of algorithms, aimed at making them more efficient, social scientists and humanities scholars tend to be interested in the 'social phenomenon that is driven by and committed to algorithmic systems' (Gillespie 2016). For the latter, what is at stake are not so much the mathematical-logical coded instructions per se, but how these instructions have the power to shape the world in specific ways.

From the important work that has already emerged in the social study of algorithms (for example, Anderson 2013; Beer 2009; Diakopoulos 2015; Gillespie 2014; Kitchin 2016; McKelvey 2014; Napoli 2014; Pasquale 2015; Seaver 2013), what has become clear is that algorithms seem to pose some serious conceptual, epistemological, and methodological challenges when it comes to actually studying and knowing them. What is remarkable about the tweets quoted is not so much *that* people have an opinion about the media they are using, but the ways in which they are starting to decode and make sense of the operational logic that experts routinely describe as *unknowable*. Following the lead of social media users, this chapter makes a case for not letting the seemingly unknowable and hidden aspects of software and algorithms constrain scientific inquiry and creative explorations. The question is thus: When confronted with the seemingly obscure and hidden, what are our methodological options?

In this chapter I use the concept of the black box as a heuristic device to discuss the nature of algorithms in contemporary media platforms, and how we, as scholars and students interested in this nature, might attend to and study algorithms, despite, or even because of, their seemingly secret nature. The argument is made that despite the usefulness in pointing out some of the epistemological challenges relating to algorithms, the figure of the black box constitutes somewhat of a 'red herring'. Understood as a figure of speech, a red herring is a piece of information that distracts from other, perhaps more pressing, questions and issues. Moving beyond the notion that algorithms *are* black boxes, this chapter asks instead what is at stake in framing algorithms in this way, and what such a framing might possibly distract us from asking. The chapter unfolds as follows. First I address the alleged problematic of the black box, arguing that algorithms are neither as black or as boxed as they are sometimes laid out to be. Next, I discuss three ways of knowing algorithms, each of which addresses the challenges associated with the black box in more detail. Synthesizing and extending existing approaches, the chapter makes a case for using well-known methods in new domains, not only generating knowledge about emerging issues and practices, but contributing to (re)inventing methods.

Revisiting the Black-Boxed 'Nature' of Algorithms

The concept of the black box has become a commonplace for all the things we (seemingly) cannot know. Black box refers to an opaque technical device of which only the inputs and outputs are known. It is an entity whose inner functioning cannot be known, at least not by observation, as the blackness of the box obscures vision. Historically, the black box refers quite literally to a physical black box containing war machinery and radar equipment during World War II. In tracing the genealogy of the black box, von Hilgers (2011) describes how the term initially referred to a 'black' box that had been sent from Britain to the USA as part of the so-called Tizard Mission, which sought technical assistance for the development of new technologies for the war effort. This black box that was sent to the radiation lab at Massachusetts Institute of Technology (MIT) contained another black box, the Magnetron. During wartime, crucial technologies had to be made opaque in case they fell into enemy hands. Conversely, if confronted with an enemy's black box one would have to assume that the box could contain a self-destructing device, thus making it dangerous to actually open it. As a consequence, what emerged was a culture of secrecy, or what Galison (1994) has termed 'radar philosophy', a model of thought that paved the way for the emergence of cybernetics and the analysis and design of complex man–machine systems. In his 1956 book *An Introduction to Cybernetics*, Ashby dedicates a whole chapter to the problem of the black box, presented as a challenge to the engineer who had 'to deduce what he can of its contents' (1956, p. 86).

What is interesting about Ashby's early writings is how the black box is not necessarily presented as an obstacle, but simply as part of everyday life. What early cyberneticians like him recognized is that the black box is not an exception, but rather the norm.

We may see how the black box has become a metaphor for the secret, hidden, and unknown. In everyday parlance, everything from the brain, markets, and totalitarian nation-states is now conceptualized as a black box. Algorithms are no different. The media routinely call algorithms the 'secret sauces' that make companies tick (Colett 2007; Kincaid 2010; Oremus 2014; Vanhemert 2013). If the workings of algorithms are kept 'behind veils of trade secrecy' (Pasquale 2015, p. 2), scholars worry that algorithms cannot be held accountable or critically scrutinized. What happens when algorithms suddenly start to make discriminatory inferences based on certain data sets and design decisions? The lack of transparency and accountability of 'black box algorithms' (Pasquale 2015) is fundamentally seen as a democratic problem. For Tufekci (2014), the 'opaque algorithms' of Facebook and Twitter have 'enormous consequences for political speech' as they 'determine the visibility of content and can be changed at will'. Because of the ways in which commercial platforms now tailor and personalize content to individual users, the fear is that 'the opacity of algorithms and private control of platforms alters the ability of the *public* to understand what is ostensibly a part of the public sphere' (Tufekci 2014, p. 9). What seems to be at stake is not only the regulatory or political challenge related to algorithmic discrimination or the undermining of the public sphere. More fundamentally, our most trivial everyday experiences are mediated, augmented, and conditioned by algorithms. For Striphas (2010), what need critical scrutiny are the ways in which algorithms increasingly measure and shape cultural taste. As he writes: 'I don't fear the machine. What I do fear, though, is the black box of algorithmic culture' (Striphas 2010, n.p.).

While it is true that proprietary algorithms are hard to know, that does not make them unknowable. There are many ways of knowing algorithms (if broadly understood) besides opening the black box and reading the exact coded instructions telling the machine what to do. Algorithms are not as secretive as the metaphor of the black box makes them out to be. Indeed, while some things are 'fundamentally not discoverable' (von Hilgers 2011, p. 42), the widespread notion of algorithms as black boxes may prevent research more than encouraging it. It seems to me that the metaphor of the black box is too readily used as a way of critiquing algorithms, without critically scrutinizing the metaphor itself. What is gained and what is lost when we draw on the metaphor of the black box to describe algorithms? To what extent does the metaphor work at all?

WAYS OF KNOWING ALGORITHMS: THREE STEPS TO CONSIDER

Just like the algorithm itself—understood in the engineering way as step-by-step procedures for solving an emerging problem—the following section provides some guiding steps that chart out *some* ways of knowing algorithms. Be warned, however: these steps are nothing like a real algorithm that meticulously needs to be followed in order to obtain a desired solution. Unlike an algorithm, methods are never just simple recipes that researchers can follow to solve a given problem. The kinds of realities that social science and humanities try to describe and make sense of, which includes software and algorithms, are 'complex, diffuse and messy' (Law 2004, p. 2). To talk about emergent methods seems somewhat of an oxymoron. It is not that there is a bucket of existing methods (for instance, interview, survey, document analysis) from which the researcher can choose and then a set of new and emerging methods that are in the process of being conceived. Methods are always emerging, or at least they should be, just as there is never a one-size-fits-all solution to approaching the complex, diffuse, and messy reality of social phenomena. As Law puts it, modes of knowing the world do not 'demand neat, definite, and well-tailored accounts. And they don't do this precisely because the realities they stand for are excessive and in flux, not themselves neat, definite, and simply organised' (Law 2004, p. 14). In a messy world, including messy methods and messy algorithms, what are some of the modes of inquiry that help systematize and produce knowledge about the sociotechnical realities of which algorithmic systems are part?

Step One: Do Not Fear the Black Box

As this discussion suggests, there has been a tendency in social science and humanities discourse on algorithms to frame the secretive nature of a proprietary algorithm as a profound epistemic problem. The first step in knowing algorithms is not to regard the 'impossibility of seeing inside the black box' as an epistemological limit that impinges any 'futile attempts at knowledge acquisition' (von Hilgers 2011, p. 43). It seems to me that focusing on the notion that algorithms are black boxes grants them a special place in the world of unknowns that perhaps is not fully deserved. As Ashby recognized: 'In our daily lives we are confronted at every turn with systems whose internal mechanisms are not fully open to inspection, and which must be treated by the methods appropriate to the Black Box' (1956, p. 86). Because opacity, secrecy, and invisibility are not epistemic anomalies, but rather a basic condition of human life, the black box is not something to be feared but something that 'corresponds to new insights' (von Hilgers 2011, p. 32).

When confronted with a black box, the appropriate task for the experimenter, as Ashby (1956) saw it, is not necessarily to know exactly what is inside the box, but to ask instead which properties can actually be discovered and which remain undiscoverable. For Ashby and the early cyberneticians, the black box was not an obstacle but a means for play and exploratory experimentation (Kaerlein 2013, p. 659). Speculative experimentation and playing around with algorithms to figure out how they work should not merely be reserved for hackers, gamers, spammers, and search engine optimizers (SEO). In the spirit of reverse engineering—'the process of extracting the knowledge or design blueprints from anything man-made' (Eilam 2005, p. 3)—media scholars might want to approach algorithms from the question of how they work and their 'operational logics' (Wardrip-Fruin 2009).

In my own research I have drawn on a mode of inquiry that I call *technography*. Broadly speaking, I approach the complex ways in which software intersects with sociality in a way that is similar to anthropological methods of ethnography. This is to say that technography, as I use the term, is a way of describing and observing technology in order to examine the interplay between a diverse set of actors (both human and non-human). In contrast to ethnography, with its focus on 'documenting people's beliefs and practices from the people's own perspectives' (Riemer 2009, p. 205), technography has technology as its perspective; specifically, the norms and values that have been delegated to and materialized in technology. While the ethnographer seeks to understand culture primarily through the meanings attached to the world by people, the technographic inquiry starts by asking of what the software itself is suggestive.

Following Ashby's cybernetic lead, what is at stake in a technographic inquiry is not to reveal some hidden truth about the exact workings of software or to unveil the precise formula of an algorithm. Instead, the aim is to develop a critical understanding of the mechanisms and operational logic of software. To borrow from Galloway, the question is 'how it works' and 'who it works for' (2004, p. xiii). Just as the ethnographer observes, takes notes, and asks people about their beliefs and values, Ashby's observer describes what he sees and what he think he sees. The researcher confronted with the black box algorithm does not necessarily need to know much about coding or programming. As Ashby points out, 'no skill is called for! We are assuming, remember, that nothing is known about the Box' (1956, p. 89).[2] Unlike the study of people, technology cannot be asked about its beliefs and values. Again, this perceived limitation should not hold us back from critically scrutinizing software. In order to explore of what software seems suggestive, 'specific tricks have to be invented to *make [it] talk*' (Latour 2005, p. 79). Both Ashby and Latour suggest paying attention to the kinds of information offered by objects as they relate to an observer. Just as people become visible and intelligible by offering information and having their stories told, objects have to enter into accounts in order to be accounted for (Latour 2005, p. 79). Algorithms enter into all kinds of account, which researchers may easily trace.

At the level of the interface, algorithms 'offer a description of themselves' by the visual output of information they deliver. The content and information we encounter as part of interfaces like the Facebook news feed have already been carefully curated and formatted. As Galloway points out, 'data have no necessary visual form' (2011, p. 88). What we see, therefore, is never raw data, but data that have been put into a form through a process of algorithmic 'in-formation'. For the technographer, the question becomes how exactly data are being put into new forms of meaningfulness. Just as ethnographers assemble notes, interviews, and observations into a new account of a cultural phenomenon, technographers build their account of algorithms by assembling information from different sources. Confronted with one's own limited understanding of an algorithm or algorithmic systems, the question is '*where* does one go to learn what one needs to know' in order to understand more confidently (Winner 1993, p. 363)? In the case of the Facebook algorithm, a researcher might want to consult the following sources and sites: patent applications and similar documents that detail and lay out technical specifications, press releases, conference papers on machine learning techniques, recorded documents from developer and engineering conferences, company briefs, media reports, blog posts, Facebook's initial public offering (IPO) filing, and so on. Such a reading of technological mechanisms 'is possible because various traces and semiotic systems cluster around technical artefacts and ensembles' (Mackenzie 2002, p. 211).

In a study on the ways in which Facebook algorithms operate to organize the regimes of visibility on the news feed, I compiled data aggregated from auto-ethnographic observations of the interface with publicly available information about the mechanics of the sites (see Bucher 2012). By systematically archiving screenshots from two Facebook feeds—one seemingly unfiltered and one that is algorithmically curated—I was able to continuously compare and contrast the two modes of making visible over the course of six months. This rather simple experiment of reverse engineering offered a useful approach to the seemingly black-boxed nature of the Facebook system, and revealed the algorithmic systems of Facebook as more gray than black. Ultimately, I see the experimental mode of inquiry as a 'trick' in the sense of Latour, in terms of making the software 'talk', or offer a description of itself. Finding means of making technology reveal itself—making it 'talk'—constitutes a way to engage in a reading that takes as its starting point the kinds of things that technology itself can be said to signify and suggest.

Step Two: Do Not Expect the Solution to Be Inside the Black Box

Letting the software speak in order to read it in the way 'one reads any text' (Galloway 2004, p. 20) is not without its problems. Claiming that software talks quickly runs the risk of anthropomorphizing technology, of attributing causality where it might not necessarily belong. As we have seen, debates about black-boxed algorithms are often susceptible to a particular brand of causal attribution better known as technological determinism by claiming that algorithms *cause* certain things to happen. While I think it is important to maintain a certain agency on behalf of algorithms—indeed, they *do* things—the critical agent is hard to identify. At a most basic level, algorithms do things by virtue of embodying a command structure (Goffey 2008, p. 17). For the programmer, algorithms solve computational problems by processing an input toward an output. For users, algorithms primarily do things like help find something, filter content, organize news, limit access, or recommend products. The doing of algorithms can also be seen in the various ways they help shape experience and make people feel, for example how they animate frustration, curiosity, or joy. As Introna suggests, algorithms do not simply express the world (Introna 2016). Rather, algorithms performatively enact a world (produce different entities) as they become incorporated in situated action (Introna 2016). When algorithms become part of people's everyday lives, incorporated into financial markets or entangled in knowledge production, they do something to those domains. However, what algorithms do in these cases cannot simply be understood by opening up the black box, as it were. Again, the metaphor of the black box becomes little more than a red herring, one that distracts from the fact that the box might just contain another black box. Thus, the second step in knowing algorithms is not to expect the solution to be inside the box.

Do not get me wrong: knowing the exact procedures the machine uses to solve a problem can be very worthwhile, especially for those who can read the code. Nevertheless, we should not expect the algorithm to look anything like the short, neat, mathematical formulas that we have become accustomed to identifying as *the* Facebook algorithm, or *the* Google algorithm. As Gillespie points out, 'what we might refer to an algorithm is often not one algorithm but many' (2014, p. 178). Take the famous PageRank algorithm. Often used as a synonym for the Google algorithm, it is but one part of a whole system of networked algorithms working on creating a neatly curated list of search results. This inevitably raises the question of how much else we need to know in order to know the algorithm. Where do the compilers, machine code, data structures, training data, databases, and hardware fit in? What about the programmers, companies, regulators, or users?

While we want to avoid 'fetishizing algorithms' (Crawford 2016) as if they hold some magical causal power, we should not be too dismissive of the fetish either. The fetish sits right at the heart of our interest in knowing algorithms.[3] Instead of simply dismissing it as a false belief, the fetish may in fact serve as a point of access to knowledge. To impute fetishism to others, as Keane suggests, 'is to set in motion a comparison, as an observer asserts that someone else is attributing false value to objects' (1997, p. 667). Fetishism is above all a charge made by someone who accuses someone else of being a naïve believer (Latour 2010). Fetishists, however, do not care whether they mistakenly see magical power in a commodity or substitute an object for their mother's 'lack'.[4] It is the anti-fetishist who cares, who seems bothered by the fact that people naïvely believe (Latour 1999). As Chun proposes in her reading of code as fetish, calling something a fetish is not simply to dismiss it. She suggests that source code is fetishized insofar as it is frequently conflated with action, sustaining 'the fantasy of the all-powerful programmer, a subject with magical powers to transform words into things' (2011, p. 9).

The notion of fetish also allows us to recognize the boundaries and limits to knowing software in the first place. As Chun writes, code as fetish underscores code as a 'dirty window pane' rather than as a window that leads us to the 'source' (2011, p. 54). Instead of a quest for an origin source, the fetish acts as 'an enabling condition' (Chun 2011, p. 54) by opening up questions about the conditions for the sensible and intelligible. The fetish, then, does not obscure vision but leads it elsewhere, sometimes even to places where we might see more clearly. For fetishists do not care what the truth is, but how the object makes them feel and relate to the world around them. As Latour (2010) suggests, the fetish does not just show the ambiguity surrounding an object that talks, it is also an object that provokes talk.

As fetish, the algorithm can be considered a 'talk-maker' (Latour 2010, p. 4), acquiring what Marres (2012) calls 'powers of engagement'. This is to say that what the algorithm does is not necessarily 'in' the algorithm as such (Introna 2016). Rather, we may begin to understand the doing of algorithms through the ways in which they are being articulated, discussed, and contested in the public domain. According to Marres and Lezaun (2011), objects not only acquire the capacity to mediate matters of concern, but through that mediation become objects of scrutiny and struggle in and of themselves. To better understand algorithms as talk-makers, I conducted a study that set out to explore their cultural imaginaries by tapping into some of the situations that made people express their perceptions about algorithms, using social media (see Bucher 2016). During a six-month period, I regularly searched Twitter for combinations of keywords relating to algorithm, including 'Facebook algorithm', 'algorithm AND Facebook', 'algorithm AND weird', 'algorithm AND creepy', and so on. The aim was to understand how people experience algorithms by taking their own accounts as a starting point. What I found scrolling through the Twitter search results were endless snippets of personal algorithm stories, amid the even more endless marketing advice of 'social media experts'. Querying Twitter every other week, I manually sifted through the stream of algorithm aphorisms and took screenshots of the ones that seemed to be more personal rather than marketing orientated. Using a research profile I had set up on Twitter, I contacted people who had recently tweeted about their experiences with and perceptions of algorithms to ask whether they would be willing to answer a couple of question related to that tweet. At the time of writing, the study contains data from twenty-five individuals who agreed to answer questions about their perceptions of algorithms and the context of the tweet they had posted. Despite the difficulty in accessing or discovering people's personal encounters with algorithms, I found that many users are in fact already aware of algorithms. They encounter algorithms in all kinds of situations, from the recently purchased Christmas gift that appears on the shared family computer as an ad ruining the surprise, through to the almost forgotten friend who suddenly reappears on the Facebook news feed after years of silence. The stories that people tell about their experiences with algorithms suggest that algorithms particularly reveal themselves in moments of disruption, surprise, and breakdown. There is the 'whoa' moment when people become aware of being tracked and followed by the machine. There are the situations in which people find themselves misplaced and wrongfully categorized by the algorithm. There is the popularity game that many media-savvy users have become accustomed to playing, trying to amend their behavior to better fit the algorithmic logic in place. For researchers interested in understanding the affective dimensions of algorithms, then, it might just be a matter of *where* they go to look for these stories. Sometimes it is not a matter of peeking inside the box, but getting behind the tweets.

Step Three: Consider the 'Boxing' of the Box

If the second step critically scrutinizes the alleged blackness of the box, the third step in knowing algorithms asks researchers to consider the 'boxing' of the box. The tentatively final step—at least in the context of this speculative pseudo code—is recognizing the networked and entangled nature of algorithms. Latour (1999) reminds us that all black boxes are black boxes because they obscure the networks and assemblages they assume and were constituted by. For Latour, all scientific and technical work is made invisible by its own success through a process of *blackboxing*. In a much-cited example of an overhead projector breaking down, Latour suggests that the black box reveals itself as what it really is—not a stable thing, but rather an assemblage of many interrelated parts (1999, p. 183). When a machine runs smoothly, nobody pays much attention, and the actors and work required to make it run smoothly disappear from view (Latour 1999, p. 34). For Latour, the black box ultimately hides its constitution and character as a network, while blackboxing refers to the process whereby practices become reified. If the metaphor of the black box is too readily used as a way of critiquing algorithms, Latour's notion of blackboxing reminds us that what we might want to critically scrutinize is the ways in which algorithms *become*. As Seaver has noted, algorithms 'are not standalone little boxes, but massive, networked ones with hundreds of hands reaching into them, tweaking and tuning, swapping out parts and experimenting with new arrangements' (2013, p. 10). For Seaver, the boxing of the box entails studying the ways in which algorithms are developed, examining 'the logic that guides the hands' (2013, p. 10). While there is much to be gained by studying the values and beliefs that go into the making of algorithmic systems, the classic laboratory study or developer ethnography is complicated by the fact that algorithms today are increasingly based on machine learning techniques, which means that algorithms themselves are continuously changing and evolving.[5] As Introna points out, the evolving nature of algorithms means that even the representatives of Google and other organisations respond that it is difficult to say exactly what it is what their algorithms actually do (2016).

While algorithms may be blackboxed in the sense described by Latour, they are far from stable configurations. Take the algorithm curating the Facebook news feed. As with algorithmic systems in general, there is never a guarantee that we will step into the same river twice, since the algorithm is regularly tweaked, personalized, and subject to A/B testing. As Gillespie suggests, 'the black box metaphor fails us here, as the workings of the algorithm are both obscured and malleable' (2014, p. 178). Indeed, if we only concentrate on opening the black box, as if simply a lid stands between the algorithm and us, we risk missing the fundamentally networked and entangled nature of algorithms. In a day and age where algorithms are no longer simply programmed once and for all (if they ever were), where they may adapt and change as a result of being exposed to particular data sets and user input, what methods can we use to understand these algorithms in becoming?

Part of the difficulty in examining algorithms as dynamic, mutable, and entangled entities is locating them in the first place. As Gillespie (2014) reminds us, algorithms are embedded in the lived world, part of information infrastructures and standards, shaped by communities of practice, trained on specific data sets, affected and driven by user data, which makes it difficult, if not impossible, to single them out. Introna (2013) therefore suggests examining algorithms as part of particular situated practices. The critical task for Introna is to study why algorithms are incorporated into specific practices and how these practices change as a result. For Latour (1999), the critic should engage in forms of reverse blackboxing, identifying the specific actors and processes that are made invisible in the process of making the box appear as a stable and static entity. As the overhead projector example suggests, the networked and entangled nature of the black box becomes particularly evident when it breaks down. A final methodological strategy in knowing algorithms, then, is to locate and examine the occasions offered by accidents, breakdowns, and controversies (Latour 2005; Marres 2012).

In my own research, the particular case of the YouTube 'reply girls' offered one such occasion through which the becoming of algorithms could be usefully studied. Around 2012 a group of female YouTube users, better known as the 'reply girls', discovered a quirk in the recommender algorithm and used it to attract an audience that could be translated into advertising revenue. These 'reply girls' essentially produced reply videos to other popular YouTube videos, using thumbnails of their cleavage-baring bodies to attract clicks. While the commentators quickly dismissed the reply girls as spammers, the case also provides a vivid example of how people respond to and create cultural forms specific to particular algorithms. Moreover, the case usefully shows how algorithms have particular histories, and that they evolve and change for many different reasons. Partly as a response to the public outcry against the reply girls, YouTube changed its recommender system. In other words, part of knowing algorithms requires being attentive to their becoming, acknowledging the fact that, like everything else, they have histories and that these histories are full of events, accidents, and breakdowns that offer a glimpse into their nature, controversies, interested parties, stakeholders, and discourse. While the changing nature of algorithms may indeed pose some methodological challenges, it also opens up questions surrounding the conditions of change and the kinds of cultural forms that emerge in the wake of specific algorithmic systems of entanglement.

CONCLUSION

Let this be the general conclusion: for every epistemological challenge the seemingly blackboxed algorithm poses, another productive methodological route may open. The complex and messy nature of social reality is not the problem. Just as algorithms constitute but one specific solution to a computational problem, we cannot expect a single answer to the problem of how to know algorithms. As has been suggested throughout this chapter, perhaps knowing algorithms is not even the solution (see also Chun 2011 and Gillespie 2014). Still, and borrowing from Law, 'one thing is sure: if we want to think about the messes of reality at all then we're going to have to teach ourselves to think, to practice, to relate, and to know in new ways' (2004, p. 2). In this chapter the black box was used as a heuristic device to deal with this mess—not by making the world less messy, but by redirecting attention to the messiness that the notion of the black box helps to hide. Not to be taken as a definitive, exhaustive list of well-meant advice, I offered three steps to consider when researching algorithms.

First, do not regard the 'impossibility of seeing inside the black box' as an epistemological limit that impinges on any 'futile attempts at knowledge acquisition' (von Hilgers 2011, p. 43). Ask instead what parts can and cannot be known and how, in each particular case, you may find ways to make the algorithm talk. Second, avoid false causal attribution, but keep the magic and sense of mystery that algorithms seem to evoke. While fetishizing algorithms as if they pose the ultimate answer to connective life may lead us astray, the notion of the fetish is not to be dismissed lightly. Instead of expecting the truth to come out behind the curtain or to lay there in the box just waiting for our hands to lift the lid, take those beliefs, values, and imaginings that the algorithm clearly solicits as a point of departure. For are we as researchers not ourselves guided by a sense of mystery and enchantment about the things that we are interested in and study? Then we should not fear the rhetoric of magic surrounding algorithms, but instead productively feed on it by examining some of the cultural imaginations that exist. Third, keep in mind that the black box is not as seamless as it may appear. Various actors and stakeholders once composed black boxes in a specific historical context for a specific purpose. Importantly, they evolve, have histories, change, affect, and are affected by what they are articulated to. While we often talk about algorithms as if they were single stable artifacts, they are *boxed* to precisely appear that way.

Knowing networked algorithms is complicated by new machine learning techniques and the proliferation of data, making it difficult to assess the question of who does what, where, and in what way. The dynamic and malleable nature of algorithms also complicates our conceptions of the black box as such. If the black box by definition is a device of which only the inputs and outputs are known, what remains of the metaphor when we can no longer even be certain about the inputs or outputs? When algorithms start adapting to the data to which they are being exposed without being explicitly programmed to do so, as the concept of machine learning suggests, it remains unclear what the inputs once were, or the exact nature of the output. Perhaps what we are left with is this: algorithms are neither black nor box, but a lot more gray, fluid, and entangled than we may think.

Notes

1. I am paraphrasing tweets that I have used in a study on people's perceptions of algorithms (Bucher 2016). The original tweets have been slightly altered to protect the participants' privacy.
2. Although the black box demands no particular skill from the observer and experimenter, there should be no doubt about the usefulness of developing some form of procedural literacy with regard to interpreting the mechanisms of software (see Montfort 2016).
3. According to Pietz (1985), fetishism historically emerged as a problem-idea in the Portuguese colonial encounter with the West African Other during the 16th and 17th centuries. Pietz (1988) remarks how the colonial Enlightenment thinkers frequently observed that pre-modern Africans were inclined to false causal reasoning about physical nature.
4. Fetishism has played a major role in Marx's theories on capitalist society as well as in Freud's psychoanalytic interventions. For both of these thinkers, the concept of the fetish takes as its starting point the phenomenon of substitution. For Marx, the commodity fetish is a substitution for people's relationships to each other. To read more about his diagnosis of capital as fetish, see Marx (1976). To read more about how Freud addresses the topic, see Freud (1961).
5. Broadly speaking, machine learning refers to 'a subfield of computer science concerned with computer programs that are able to learn from experience and thus improve their performance over time' (Surden 2014, p. 89). Machine learning algorithms challenge some deeply ingrained ideas about agency, as they are not only able to improve performance, but also 'create an internal computer model of a given phenomenon that can be generalized to apply to new, never-before-seen examples of that phenomenon' (Surden 2014, p. 93) without being explicitly programmed to do so.

References

Anderson, C. (2013) Towards a Sociology of Computational and Algorithmic Journalism. *New Media & Society* 15(7): 1005–21.

Ashby, W. (1956) *An Introduction to Cybernetics* (London: Chapman & Hall).

Beer, D. (2009) Power Through the Algorithm? Participatory Web Cultures and the Technological Unconscious. *New Media & Society* 11(6): 985–1002.

Bucher, T. (2016) The Algorithmic Imaginary: Exploring the Ordinary Affects of Facebook Algorithms. *Information, Communication & Society* 20(1): 30–44.

Bucher, T. (2012) Want to Be on the Top? Algorithmic Power and the Threat of Invisibility on Facebook. *New Media & Society* 14(7): 1164–80.

Chun, W. (2011) *Programmed Visions: Software and Memory* (Cambridge, MA: MIT Press).

Colett, S. (2007) *Cracking Google's 'Secret Sauce' Algorithm*. Available at: http://www.computerworld.com/article/2543807/networking/cracking-google-s-secret-sauce-algorithm.html (accessed 7 December 2015).

Crawford, K. (2016) Can an Algorithm be Agonistic? Ten Scenes from Life in Calculated Publics. *Science, Technology, & Human Values* 2016 41(1): 77–92.

Diakopoulos, N. (2015) Algorithmic Accountability: Journalistic Investigation of Computational Power Structures. *Digital Journalism* 3(3): 398–415.

Eilam, E. (2005) *Reversing: Secrets of Reverse Engineering* (Indianapolis: Wiley).

Freud, S. (1961) Fetishism. In J. Strachey (transl.), *The Standard Edition of the Complete Psychological Works of Sigmund Freud, Volume XXI (1927–1931)* (London: Hogarth), pp. 147–58.

Galison, P. (1994) The Ontology of the Enemy: Norbert Wiener and the Cybernetic Vision. *Critical Inquiry* 21(1): 228–66.

Galloway, A. (2011) Are Some Things Unrepresentable?, *Theory Culture & Society* 28(7–8): 85–102.

Galloway, A. (2004) *Protocol: How Control Exists After Decentralization* (Cambridge, MA: MIT Press).

Gillespie, T. (2014) The Relevance of Algorithms. In T. Gillespie, P. Boczkowski and K. Foot (Eds.), *Media Technologies* (Cambridge, MA: MIT Press), pp. 167–95.

Gillespie, T. (2016) Algorithm. In B. Peters (Ed.), *Digital Keywords* (Princeton: Princeton University Press), pp. 18–30.

Goffey, A. (2008) Algorithm. In M. Fuller (Ed.), *Software Studies: A Lexicon* (Cambridge, MA: MIT Press), pp. 15–20.

Introna, L. (2016) Algorithms, Governance, and Governmentality On Governing Academic Writing. *Science, Technology & Human Values* 41(1): 17–49.

Kaerlein, T. (2013) Playing with Personal Media: On an Epistemology of Ignorance. *Culture Unbound: Journal of Current Cultural Research* 5(4): 651–70.

Karppi, T. and Crawford, K. (2015) Social Media, Financial Algorithms and the Hack Crash. *Theory, Culture & Society* 33(1): 73–92.

Keane, W. (1997) From Fetishism to Sincerity: On Agency, the Speaking Subject, and Their Historicity in the Context of Religious Conversion. *Comparative Studies in Society and History* 39(4): 674–93.

Kincaid, J. (2010) EdgeRank: The Secret Sauce That Makes Facebook's News Feed Tick. *TechCrunch* 22 April: http://techcrunch.com/2010/04/22/facebook-edgerank (accessed 7 December 2015).

Kitchen, R. with following: Kitchin, R. (2016) Thinking Critically About and Researching Algorithms. *Information, Communication & Society* 20(1): 14–29.

Kitchin, R. and Dodge, M. (2011) *Code/Space: Software and Everyday Life* (Cambridge, MA: MIT Press).

Knuth, D. (1998) *The Art of Computer Programming: Sorting and Searching* (Boston: Addison-Wesley).

Latour, B. (1999) *Pandora's Hope: Essays on the Reality of Science Studies* (Cambridge, MA: Harvard University Press).

Latour, B. (2005) *Reassembling the Social* (New York: Oxford University Press).

Latour, B. (2010) *On the Modern Cult of the Factish Gods* (Durham: Duke University Press).

Law, J. (2004) *After Method: Mess in Social Science Research* (London: Routledge).

Lenglet, M. (2011) Conflicting Codes and Codings: How Algorithmic Trading Is Reshaping Financial Regulation. *Theory, Culture & Society* 28(6): 44–66.

Mackenzie, A. (2002) *Transductions: Bodies and Machines at Speed* (London: Continuum).

Marres, N. (2012) *Material Participation: Technology, the Environment and Everyday Publics* (London: Palgrave Macmillan).

Marres, N. and Lezaun, J. (2011) Materials and Devices of the Public: An Introduction. *Economy and Society* 40(4): 489–509.

Marx, K. (1976) *Capital: A Critique of Political Economy, Vol. 1* (London: Penguin).

McKelvey, F. (2014) Algorithmic Media Need Democratic Methods: Why Publics Matter. *Canadian Journal of Communication* 39(4): 597–613.

Montfort, N. (2016) *Exploratory Programming for the Arts and Humanities* (Cambridge, MA: MIT Press).

Napoli, P. (2014) Automated Media: An Institutional Theory Perspective on Algorithmic Media Production and Consumption. *Communication Theory* 24(3): 340–60.

Oremus, W. (2014) *Facebook's New Secret Sauce. Slate* 24 April: http://www.slate.com/articles/technology/technology/2014/04/facebook_news_feed_edgerank_facebook_algorithms_facebook_machine_learning.html (accessed 7 December 2015).

Pasquale, F. (2015) *The Black Box Society* (Cambridge, MA: Harvard University Press).

Pietz, W. (1985) The Problem of the Fetish, I. *Res: Anthropology and Aesthetics* 9(Spring): 5–17.

Pietz, W. (1988) The Problem of the Fetish, IIIa: Bosman's Guinea and the Enlightenment Theory of Fetishism. *Res: Anthropology and Aesthetics* 16(Autumn): 105–23.

Riemer, F. (2009) Ethnography Research. In: S. Lapan and M. Quartaroli (Eds.), *Research Essentials: An Introduction to Designs and Practices* (San Francisco: Jossey-Bass), pp. 203–21.

Seaver, N. (2013) Knowing Algorithms. Working Paper for *Media in Transition* 8 (Cambridge, MA). Available at: https://static1.squarespace.com/static/55eb004ee4b0518639d59d9b/t/55ece1bfe4b030b2e8302e1e/1441587647177/seaverMiT8.pdf (accessed 7 December 2015).

Striphas, T. (2010) *How to Have Culture in an Algorithmic Age*. Available at: http://www.thelateageofprint.org/2010/06/14/how-to-have-culture-in-an-algorithmic-age (accessed 7 December 2015).

Surden, H. (2014) Machine Learning and Law. *Washington Law Review* 89(1): 87–115.

Tufekci, Z. (2014) Engineering the Public: Big data, Surveillance and Computational Politics. *First Monday* 19(7): http://firstmonday.org/article/view/4901/4097 (accessed 7 December 2015).

Vanhemert, K. (2013) The Secret Sauce Behind Netflix's Hit, 'House Of Cards': Big Data. *Co.Design* 19 February: http://www.fastcodesign.com/1671893/the-secret-sauce-behind-netflixs-hit-house-of-cards-big-data (accessed 7 December 2015).

von Hilgers, P. (2011) The History of the Black Box: The Clash of a Thing and its Concept. *Cultural Politics* 7(1): 41–58.

Wardrip-Fruin, N. (2009) *Expressive Processing: Digital Fictions, Computer Games, and Software Studies* (Cambridge, MA: MIT Press).

Winner, L. (1993) Upon Opening the Black Box and Finding it Empty: Social Constructivism and the Philosophy of Technology. *Science, Technology, and Human Values* 18(3): 362–78.

CHAPTER 6

Sketching Bitcoin: Empirical Research of Digital Affordances

Pablo R. Velasco

Bitcoin was originally a protocol to avoid double spending in a decentralized and public payment system, proposed in 2008 by someone known by the pseudonym of Satoshi Nakamoto. Alongside the protocol she/he unveiled a first working version of the source code to implement the payment system. The necessary preconditions for its materialization, however, had been developed at least since the 1970s: the advancements in cryptographic techniques embodied in Bitcoin (for instance, Merkle trees, Blind signatures, Elliptic Curve Digital Signature Algorithm), both failed and successful attempts at the creation of digital cash (for example, Digicash, Mondex, B-money, Bitgold), and the 1990s cypherpunk political atmosphere contributed directly and indirectly to the emergence of cryptocurrencies. The system was slowly adopted by small cryptographic communities at first, both for its state-of-the-art design regarding security and anonymity (highly praised characteristics within the community) and for its speculative potential. It was this last attribute that attracted many people after Bitcoin achieved a somewhat more mainstream status when it achieved parity with the US dollar. The same year saw the appearance of Mt. Gox (a Bitcoin market exchange) and Silk Road (a digital black market), two of

P.R. Velasco (✉)
University of Warwick, Coventry, UK
e-mail: P.R.Velasco-Gonzalez@warwick.ac.uk

© The Author(s) 2016
S. Kubitschko, A. Kaun (eds.), *Innovative Methods in Media and Communication Research*, DOI 10.1007/978-3-319-40700-5_6

the most controversial phenomena related to Bitcoin, and the recognition of it as a solid alternative payment system by WikiLeaks and the Electronic Frontier Foundation. Media attention and government concerns grew from 2011 to the end of 2013, when the value of a bitcoin exceeded US $1000. Today, the Bitcoin market capitalization floats at around $3.5 billion. Its success is difficult to measure, in part because of its novelty and also because of its shady behavior (even though transactions are public, no names, places, or reasons are attached to them). The technology behind it is also spreading to applications where the monetary characteristics are not a goal but a means to another end (for example, smart contracts). At this point of Bitcoin's evolution it carries a huge potential to shape a significant part of the digital horizon, thus making it a suitable, if not necessary, research object to understand contemporary networked society.

While much research has been devoted to its instrumental improvements and weaknesses, only a few studies have aimed to investigate the social and political aspects of cryptocurrencies. As a first step I will therefore discuss contemporary literature on Bitcoin and distinguish between technical and social research, in an effort to provide a basis for identifying native social structures within this digital assemblage. I am particularly interested in digital research sprouting from the technical affordances of digital objects, yet directed toward socio-political enquiries. With this as guidance, I develop indicators and a method to map some of the entities of the Bitcoin network on a geographic canvas. I present this method in detail, and discuss what it is able to show and what its attached limitations are. I argue that many digital methods share unavoidable constraints for social research embedded in their own digital objects: digital grammar, framework design intentions, and epistemological clauses.

BITCOIN AND SOCIAL SCIENCE RESEARCH

Bitcoin is a metamorphous object. It is possible to provide minimal definitions of it from diverse perspectives: a digital tool for making payments (de Jong et al. 2015), computer software (Karlstrøm 2014), an informational commodity (Bergstra and Weijland 2014), an egalitarian creation (Boase 2013), or, as Yves Mersch, member of the Executive Board of the European Central Bank, has put it, 'the regional currency of the Internet' (Mersch 2014, n.p.). It can also be easily defined as a distributed public record, an anonymity tool, and a network of machines. These definitions can agglutinate, overlap, and even contrast with each other, depending on the observing field. Because Bitcoin is at the same time a protocol, a currency, a software, a network, and a cultural phenomenon, it can play the discontinuous role of instrument, method, and object of research. In this chapter, I will refer to it mostly as an object, in part following the science and technology studies (STS) literature tradition that understands objects as nodes with their own agency and social weight within networked assemblages (Latour 2007), but also to stress its materiality. Although many of its manifestations could be analyzed as instantiations without material attributes (that is, software), they depend on an array of machines, cables, routers, and many layers of hardware for their performance (Kittler 1995).

From the researcher's point of view, Bitcoin is a relatively new digital object. The 'digital' has been defined as 'composed of many different kinds of elements, ranging from computer networks, scanners, algorithms, software and applications to different actors, institutions, regulations and controversies' (Ruppert et al. 2013, p. 31). Many disciplines from the social sciences such as media and communication studies, cultural geography, digital anthropology, science and technology studies, internet studies, digital cultures, and digital sociology (Wynn 2009) are heavily involved with digital research and some have even been spawned by it (Lupton 2014, p. 13). However, as technology surrounds most of our activities, a similar fate to the online–offline division occurs to the digital and non-digital distinction (Berry 2014). Information can be produced, mediated, organized, or made digitally available to different degrees, and with that it becomes difficult to outline the fuzzy borders between the digital and the social or between the digital and its counterparts (Cramer 2013). Digital and non-digital entities can take the form of native and non-native data, subjectivities, techniques, objects, institutions, methodologies, and so on.

Bitcoin, as a digital object, is framed by its own medium-specific constraints and regimes, and also produces its own kind of data, categories, and agencies. Due to its novelty, it stands on a challenging starting position. It was designed to be an oxymoron under close observation: regarding its actual technical functioning, it is transparent and public (certainly not without complexities, since its guts require at least a little notion of how cryptology strategies are enabled in software). Observation for this side of the object is open and the working and results for every transaction made with the device are easily available (Bitcoin Block Explorer—Blockchain. info 2015). The social aspects of its use are, however, on a nicely crafted dark side. Unlike more traditional research on social networks like Twitter or Facebook, where social content, data, and metadata of how these software-enabled platforms are used are gathered and analyzed in closed spaces, or even partially available for the non-corporate researcher, the data on cryptocurrencies is democratically scarce.

It is possible to identify two broad sets of research on this digital object. On the one hand there is research on its technical capabilities, made from natively technical disciplines (such as computer science); on the other hand there is research on the social characteristics embedded in the production, usage, and effects of the device. In the first group it is common to find studies concerned mainly with flaws in its anonymization capacities, user privacy evaluations, or transaction dynamics. Biryukov and his colleagues (2014) unmasked Bitcoin users by linking pseudonyms (or wallet addresses) to the IP addresses of the origin of the transactions. In order to do so, they built their own Bitcoin client (which is feasible considering that core clients are open sourced), in which a function was implemented to send specific protocol messages and to initiate parallel connections to the same Bitcoin server (full node). Their method consisted in identifying the entry nodes of the client, to which the client initially sends its IP address as seen from the internet. A correlation was then made between identified entry nodes and the first servers to forward the transaction. This concept was successfully tested on the Bitcoin testnet. With similar concerns around the privacy of the system, Androulaki and her colleagues (2013) built a simulator of a Bitcoin network to analyze the privacy provisions of Bitcoin. Their methodology exploited existing implementations of the client: using programmed parsers (written in Pearl and C++) to extract public information on transactions in the early stages of the device. Behavior-based clustering techniques (K-Means, KMC) and Hierarchical Agglomerative Clustering (HAC) algorithms were then used to cluster generic addresses in a model that showed privacy vulnerabilities for a great part (up to 40%) of the modeled users.

The research team around Meiklejohn et al. (2013) included an analysis of the flow of payments until April 2013. This work is concerned with how often coins were expended and in which quantities. It gathered a considerable number of wallet addresses from different Bitcoin services. By manually engaging in 344 transactions with diverse mining pools, wallet services, exchanges, vendors, gambling sites, and laundry services, the researchers were able to gather data and associate addresses with services. They used two heuristics to correlate transaction data with address data, and focused on identifying 'change' addresses; that is, residues of transactions that remain with the same user, but are stored in one-time-use addresses and then may be reincorporated into a bigger amount at another address. They successfully identified interactions between major institutions (for example, between Mt. Gox, the former Bitcoin exchange that suspended trading in February 2014, and Satoshi Dice, a gambling platform). The methodology benefited from an empirical test network of transactions that took place between different university actors. Kondor and his colleagues (2014) also made use of the public transaction information displayed in the blockchain. They measured degree distribution, degree correlations, and clustering over time in the structure of the network. A thorough analysis of the Bitcoin network allowed them to identify two moments in the system, one before business accepted it as a form of payment and one after, and a correlation between accumulated wealth and number of transaction partners. Baumann et al. (2014) also provided an analysis of transactions, using descriptive statistics and network analysis. Like the former studies, they utilized algorithms to mine public data on transactions. Posterior graph analysis was conducted via NetworkX, a Python library. Descriptive statistics were further applied to the data set of transactions. Even though these are different approaches making use of different research techniques, what groups them together is their main concern with the efficiency of the system.

Examples of research within the social sciences include the theorization of Bitcoin infrastructure affordances, the political demographics of its community, and critiques of its adherents' ideology. Maurer (2015) picks up on the idea of the railroad system as the 'rails' of monetary infrastructures to think about contemporary telecom companies as the 'pipes' of the money token. He argues that Bitcoin is a phenomenon where both the token and the rail have collapsed into one in the form of the blockchain. Together with his colleagues, he also expands on the semiotics of Bitcoin and its rethinking of privacy, labor, and value debates (Maurer et al. 2013). Ongoing studies (Smyth 2014) show that there is strong diversity among the people orbiting cryptocurrencies and propose to address the whole phenomenon as a 'cryptocoin ecosystem', composed of actors with different motivations, backgrounds, and reactions, rather than a community. An elaborated critique on cryptocurrency enthusiast 'communities' is also raised by Scott (2014), who emphasizes that digital-anonymous-decentralized ledger systems are not by themselves a guarantee of good use or the community growth of societies. That is, they can be alternatives to current economic systems, as well as perfectly well suited for the endurance of a typical 'defensive individualism mediated via mathematical contractual law'

(Scott 2014, n.p.). Laszka et al. (2015) hypothesize, through a game theoretic model analysis, the incentives and outcomes of a distributed denial-of-service (DDoS) attack between Bitcoin mining rigs, and offer foreseeable outcomes like the migration of miners to other rigs. This kind of study theorizes the technical affordances of the network, as many technical disciplines do, but it is also concerned with the social elements, such as competitive behavior positions and migrations inside the network.

This last study has encapsulated in a theoretical model a specific kind of methodological stance that I intend to follow; that is, a methodology that takes as its starting point a technical affordance of the digital object, but that is interested in the social underpinnings and outcomes entangled in this technical specificity. The former examples of research concerned with the technical capabilities of Bitcoin use different techniques to observe and analyze the transactions in the network and are mostly concerned with security issues generated by the use of the system. They parse and correlate data that exist in the blockchain. Like many of them, I also take advantage of the public data generated by the network. However, the data I have chosen to gather are not stored in the blockchain, and thus another method is required to actively gather them. The work described in this chapter uses a completely different notion of what is to be understood as a node in the network. Nodes in previous work act like abstract entities of a model or as invisible users—in most cases identified with a Bitcoin wallet. I use an empirical approach in the sense that the nodes on the network I follow are physical machines, which are in most cases sensitive to geographic labeling. Since I am interested in generating a socio-political perspective from the technical affordances of a digital object, I then offer an indicator to measure the machines' dedication within the network. The result is a legible version of the location of physical nodes and their weight in the form of commitment in a defined period. Bitcoin as a device can be understood, much like apparatuses, configurations, and assemblages, as something to bring together entities, methods, and practices (Lury and Wakeford 2012). Data scraping, geographic information systems (GIS), and modeling techniques make possible the convergence of these entities and signal possible causalities, as well as previously unknown communication channels. Considering this, I start by signaling one of the most basic entities of the whole ecosystem, the network node, to approach this new assemblage via one of its particular affordances.

BUILDING A MAP OF THE BITCOIN NETWORK

Part of the promise of cryptocurrencies is to be globally available to everyone: the code is open and different clients can run on almost any contemporary computer. From an instrumental point of view, the Bitcoin network is essentially formed by its nodes, thus the mapping of these entities can provide a good image of its geography. However, not every user qualifies as a node. A node is any type of machine capable of running a piece of open-source software (for instance, Bitcoin Core), which allows it to receive, send, and store information on all the transactions. This network of machines is what makes possible the efficient running of Bitcoin transactions of information. The modification of the notion of node is also methodologically relevant as, in this work, nodes are materially conceptualized. The idea of node, and thus of edge, dwells between a physical and a logical topology. Nodes are materialized by such an approach: information flow is not depicted as an abstract diagram, but as an enactment of physical bodies—machines, in the case of the first part, and humans and other non-humans as the notion of ecosystem grows. Bitcoin's success as a distributed network and open-source protocol can enhance a blurring of the bodies associated with the production and transaction of digital tokens. From a methodological perspective, network analyses of a logical topology depict nodes and edges that easily detach from its more material representations.

Nodes in the Bitcoin network can be broadly categorized as 'full nodes' and 'lightweight nodes'. The latter are just clients that send and receive payments without storing the full blockchain, and therefore participate in the transactions but not in the maintenance of the infrastructure. A lightweight participant is the equivalent of a credit card user making a payment: information about his resources travels on a surface for which he is not responsible. The credit card has no value in it; if it disappears, nothing but a piece of plastic is lost. The card's sole function is to be a secure authorization key to make changes to a ledger. The latter is the money. When the ledger subtracts an amount and adds it in another place, money is lost or gained. But beyond giving approval, payer and payee take no part in what is completely a third-party, standardized administrative action (de Jong et al. 2015). Both the ledger and the tracks along which this information transits belong to different agencies (banks, governments, financial institutions of all kinds), not to the card user. In this sense, Bitcoin works a lot like old and ordinary finance systems: a Bitcoin user may lose her phone or laptop, but the resources are still in the ledger, and as long as she keeps a copy of her secret keys, which are a cryptographically developed form of identification, her satoshis (the smallest possible unit of a Bitcoin) can be reclaimed. The lightweight node approves transactions to be made to the ledger, but neither makes the changes nor helps in distributing the transmission of transactions. A full node, on the other hand, is responsible for the relay and validation of blocks of transactions, and its resources provide storage and bandwidth for the network's upkeep (FAQ – Bitcoin 2015). Unlike traditional registry administration, here the ledger is legion. Every full node contains a 'copy' of it (with no original) and validates its transactions. These are the structural skeleton of the network and the condition of possibility for users and transactions, therefore playing a crucial role in the endurance of the digital phenomenon of distributed cryptocurrencies. Interestingly, nodes do not need to be users of cryptocurrencies: they can help the network without ever receiving or sending Bitcoins (unlike miners, nodes receive no economic stimulus for a severely machine-demanding job). At the time of writing, the blockchain weighs over 30 gigabytes— synchronization requires significant bandwidth and energy, considering that it has an effect on the network only when it is connected. Miners are a kind of node specialized in collecting new transactions into blocks and require specific hardware and working conditions to do so; given their particular role in the Bitcoin ecosystem, I differentiate them from regular nodes. The distinctions I am making can be summarized as follows: (1) a node[1] is not necessarily a user of the Bitcoin currency; (2) a user (or lightweight node) of the Bitcoin currency is not necessarily a node; (3) a node is not necessarily a miner; but (4) every miner is a node.

It is possible to set up a Bitcoin server to act as a listener to other broadcasting nodes. The Bitnodes website, supported by the Bitcoin Foundation, provides an application programming interface (API) for a server of this kind,[2] which makes it possible to retrieve a limited amount of information about the network at any moment. With the intention of achieving an overall observation of the network's behavior, I set up a machine that continually collects and stores this information from it.

In order to keep the data as complete as possible, the scripts run on a low-cost, dedicated Raspberry Pi that is permanently connected to the internet. The retrieval of information is done by a simple script that makes a request for the hostname of the server, country code, city, latitude, longitude, time zone, internet service provider (ISP), user agent, height, last connections, and protocol version, from every node connected to the network. This simple Python script retrieves new 'snapshots' of the whole network every five minutes. New 'snapshot' data is time stamped and stored in a separated json-formatted file, for later retrieval. Every snapshot can be read as a static moment of an ever-changing map of the physical network, containing all the node locations forming the network at that moment. Gathering around 160–190 snapshots per day allows me to zoom in on how the network changes on a daily basis and over stretched durations. Through more Python scripts I generated sets from this data that were not evident or immediately retrievable through the Bitnodes API.

Using a second Python script, I queried and produced sets of 'strong', 'weak', and 'ghost' nodes, being the machines that have been part of the Bitcoin network uninterruptedly, interruptedly, and for less than one day, respectively, during a certain time span. This allows me to propose categories of commitment or interest directly related to geographic zones. Full nodes for keeping the network healthy are becoming scarcer and scarcer; support for the network has decayed since its high point at the end of 2013. There is even an incentive program that provides a monthly amount of money to nodes that accomplish certain criteria to be considered highly healthy peers. Following this thread, I observe and classify different degrees of *commitment*, as an indicator based on continuity: I consider *strong* nodes those who are connected at every moment of the sample, *ghost* nodes those who are connected in less than 10 % of the moments in the sample, and nine levels of *weak* nodes, 'weak9' being nodes present in 90–99 % of the sample, 'weak8' those present in 80–89 %, and so on. Strong and weak nodes are a minority in the sample network, which is mostly formed of ghosts (see Fig. 6.1). The broader the sample, the more predominant the ghosts become. As Fig. 6.2 shows, an extended sample considers 1317 continuous snapshots (around a week of data) from which a mere 4.3 % of nodes are strong, a small sum compared to 69.4 % of ghost nodes.

The hierarchization of nodes serves as a bedrock for an initial analysis of the geographic characteristics of the network. However, it is important to note that the mere data collection and simple categorization of the data have already created an implicit research 'contract' that defines the range of use of the data. This is not restricted to information on nodes within distributed cryptocurrencies, but encompasses the number of digital objects used in digital research. Digital devices, as objects of research and as methodological tools, not only are able to change sociality and knowledge (Ruppert et al. 2013, p. 22), but are also expressions of an epistemology developed within instrumental assemblages. The origin of the information

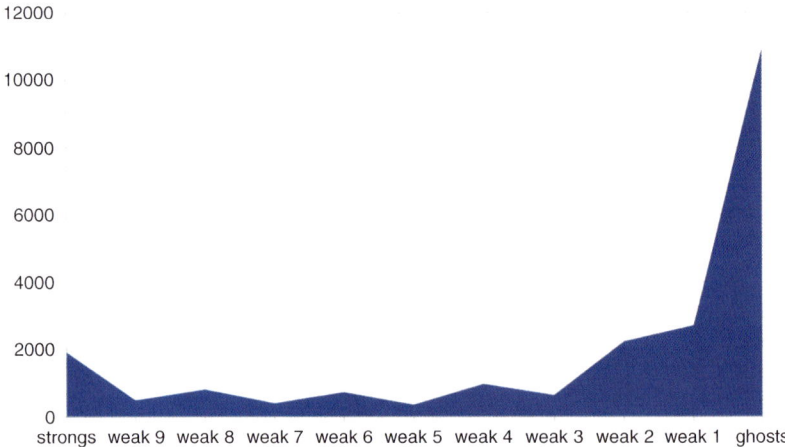

Fig. 6.1 Distribution of strong, weak, and ghost nodes from a random sample of fifteen 'snapshots' of the network between March and May 2015. © Pablo R. Velasco

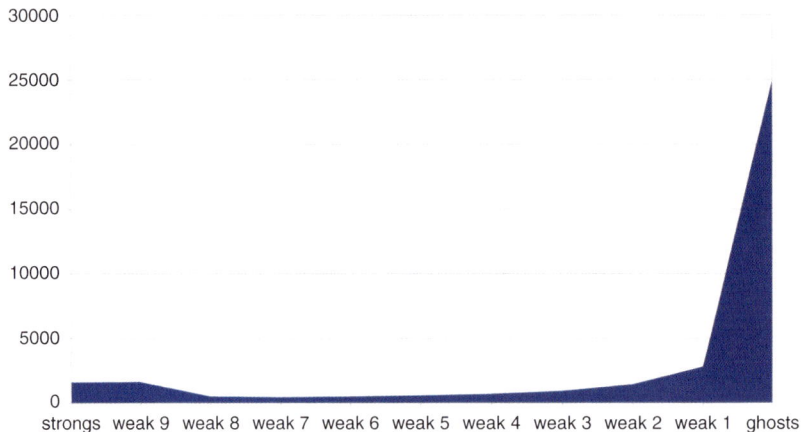

Fig. 6.2 Distribution of strong, weak, and ghost nodes from a sample of 1317 'snapshots' of the network from the last week of 2014. © Pablo R. Velasco

(the grammar), the intentions that guide the creation of the frameworks used with this grammar (the development), and the multiplication of methods in future epistemological directives are already embedded in the many manifestations of the digital objects. Both the device (the server, acting as a node), the instructions for retrieval and distillation (the scripts), and the data (the information for each node and snapshot) are considered 'natively digital' (Rogers 2009). This means that they are subject to pre-defined categories, specificities, definitions, and interactions that are implicit and may not even be evident. That is, an unavoidable computational ontology comes with the use of many digital objects, with its own rules, logic, and 'grammar'—a set of unitary actions of human activities represented in computation (Agre 1994). The researcher working with digital methods is forced, by platforms and 'medium-specific' inheritances, to become an analyzer and a distiller: data collection becomes extraction, and the making of knowledge, distillation (Marres and Weltevrede 2013). The different steps involved in the creation of the node map are soaked in this grammar.

First, API calls offer a limited set of *a priori* formatted categories and definitions for the possible data. Characteristics of the node object exist within this logic. While protocol version is an existing category of this kind of entity—it is a relevant piece of information for the effective functioning of the network—the political stance of the node owner or the general incentives for keeping this node running are not machine relevant. Traditionally important categories for social research may not appear, in part because this device was not designed for this kind of information retrieval, but also because social categories are not part of most technical grammars. Then, scraping data from the Bitcoin network involves 'medium-specific' limitations, analytic assumptions 'alien' to social research, and an inherent risk of importing 'inquiry categories' into our own (Marres and Weltevrede 2013). The same applies to the distillation process, which is also produced by code categories. While coding in general has broad and creative outcomes, it is also 'the manifestation of a system of thought—an expression on how the world can be captured, represented, processed and modeled computationally with the outcome subsequently of doing work in the world' (Kitchin and Dodge 2011, p. 26).

Permutations within digital grammar are also not neutral. They are created with deliberate intentions and goals. Digital transactional data and algorithms are not usually designed with the purposes of social researchers in mind. Although some cases are inherited from academic logics (for example, page rank and citation schemes; see Beer 2012), the mold cases for the data allocation are made to and from quite different perspectives. At this point Facebook data scientists have access to what is probably the largest ever concentration of social interaction data and metadata (contents, actors, relations), and while their methodological behavior can resemble that of the social researcher, their ends and aims are most certainly focused on another chain of intentions, and framed by specific systems of thought, political economies, and politics (Kitchin 2016). Examples might be providing a better experience for the user to enhance the business, in order to improve its marketing performance or even create new products (Gerlitz and Helmond 2013; Cusumano and Goeldi 2013), like Facebook's Messenger or Twitter's Periscope. Similar sets of digital techniques and tools for research are used with dissimilar intentions.

Digital methods are easily transformed into epistemological data; it has been argued that what defines the digital is not its new technical possibilities, but the actual transmutation and multiplication of methods (Mackenzie and McNally 2013). According to this idea, digital methods do not only display data about something in the world, but turn this production into data about how things are known, data that can get dissolved into other digital devices. Multiplied methods become data themselves. The former methodological description shows more about what we are allowed to apprehend via our own methods than about how exactly machines are distributed in the world. Even though it does shows the latter, from a methodological point of view the importance of the mapping resides in the epistemological highlighting of relations; that is to say, what the location of machines says about how a broader ecosystem is understood. The very process of localization builds on what we think we can know of this ecosystem. Methods relying on data manipulation replicate this grammar and, in doing so, influence potential epistemologies for future objects.

It is important to take this into account while observing the outcomes of these digital methodologies: a small territorial look at the Bitcoin system.

A GLIMPSE OF THE BITCOIN ECOSYSTEM

Gathered and distilled data can be visually displayed through the CartoDB platform.[3] A map of a small sample (see Fig. 6.3) shows a highly distributed ghost population, probably composed of recurrent users or curious bystanders of the network. Among the weak distribution, the majority are part of the weaker, which means that most probably are not part of dedicated servers, but eventual users of the Bitcoin Core, who, for example,

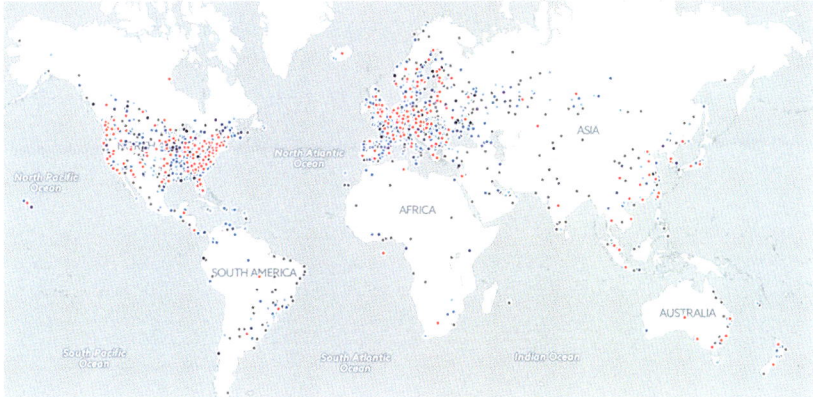

Fig. 6.3 Map of strong (*red*), weak (*blue*), and ghost (*gray*) nodes from a random sample of fifteen 'moments' of the network between March and May 2015. This map can be thoroughly explored at: https://timeknows.cartodb.com/viz/7b8e0d76-edb2-11e4-a3b1-0e43f3deba5a/embed_map (accessed 9 January 2016). Image and data: © Pablo R. Velasco. Template: © OpenStreetMap contributors © CartoDB, CartoDB attribution

connect to the network just to make a transaction but without the intention of continually preserving its infrastructure.[4] It is feasible to argue that a significant number of ghost and weak nodes are zombie machines, especially in geographic areas of low-cost bots (Huang et al. 2014). Strong nodes, on the other hand, are scarce but solid. Given the range of time and schedule of the sample, it is highly unlikely that they have unwilling operators. These nodes have been connected uninterruptedly, and thus are, for whichever reason, resolute supporters of the network. It is reasonable to assume that a great part of them can also be considered miners and benefit economically from their role.

It can be observed (see Fig. 6.3) that the weak and ghosts usually encircle the strong regions, providing a map of interest where urban areas produce stronger nodes, encircled predominantly by less interested parties in concentric rural areas. For example, London is clearly a comfortable niche for strong nodes, and its surrounding suburban areas are populated with weak and ghost nodes, therefore showing an urban and highly localized community of network upholders, and a stronger commitment to the network situated in the north of Europe. A point of departure to have a rational reading of the map must obviously consider that a great percentage of black areas (for example, Russia) are not inhabited or do not have distributed internet access. Therefore, black rural areas and high-lighted urban centers are expected.

The great majority of strong nodes inhabit the USA and the north of Europe, and on a minor scale the east coast of Asia. This proves that the global network is in reality a very localized phenomenon, with only a fistful of nodes in Latin America, Africa, and the Middle East. A closer regional look (see Figs. 6.4 and 6.5) shows that most of the strong nodes in Europe belong to the UK, Germany, France, and the Netherlands, but again, few can be considered committed in Spain, Portugal, and the whole region of the Balkans. It shows that unlike other emerging payment and value-storage systems like M-Pesa (Jack and Suri 2011), Bitcoin is a phenomenon whose network support resides in the north. It adds up to the majority of web technologies sustaining the Digital Divide Cartogram (Lovink and Zehle 2005, pp. 110–1), which depicts a map where coun-tries' sizes are inversely proportional to their internet usage, showing a world bloated in the south (with some exceptions). Updated maps that also consider the proportion of internet users show that this digital divide remains (Graham et al. 2012). It is not surprising that regions with a high

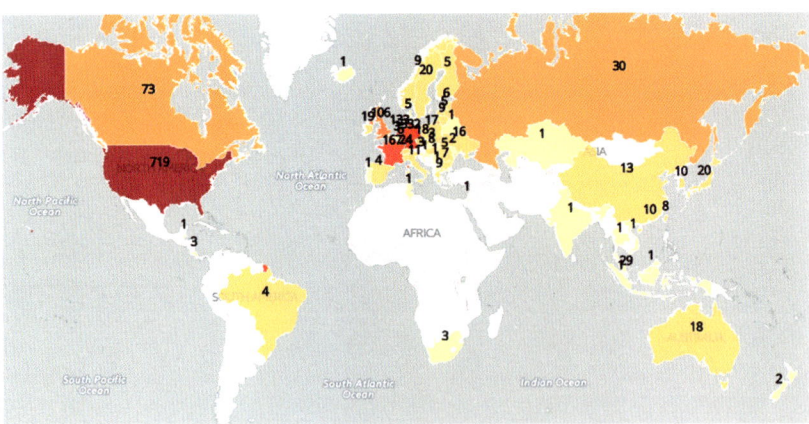

Fig. 6.4 Strong nodes in the world. Image and data: © Pablo R. Velasco. Template: © OpenStreetMap contributors © CartoDB, CartoDB attribution

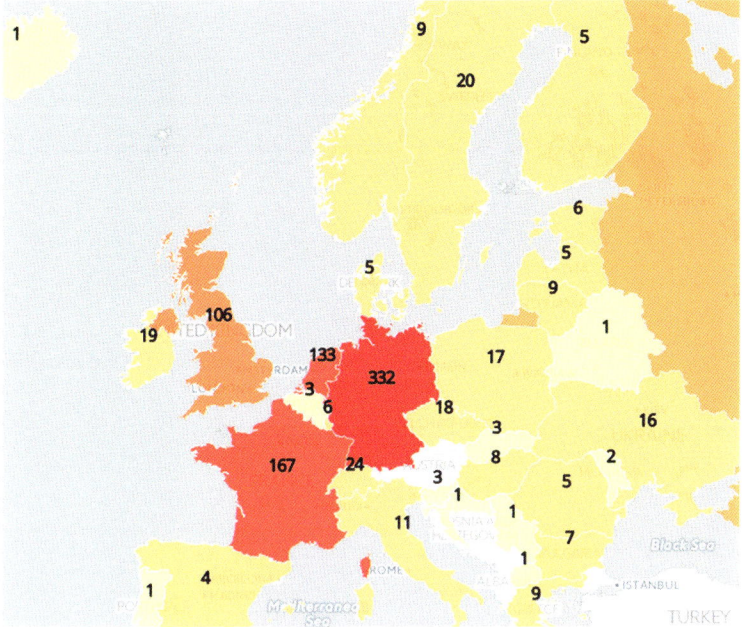

Fig. 6.5 Detail view of strong nodes in Europe. Image and data: © Pablo R. Velasco. Template: © OpenStreetMap contributors © CartoDB, CartoDB attribution

number of internet users are also hosts of many strong nodes. However, it is interesting to see that regions with a high percentage of internet users are not necessarily the ones with the biggest percentage of strong nodes (see Fig. 6.6). Canada, the Czech Republic, Australia, France, Germany, Ireland, the Netherlands, Singapore, Sweden, and Switzerland show a considerable number of network users when considering their population of internet users.

Although crucial for its functioning, the map of the network shows only a minimal part of the whole Bitcoin ecosystem. In order to obtain a more comprehensive geography, other kinds of agencies must be added: the legal position of countries, indigenous markets, and mining concentration in the network. Digital objects and digital methodologies produce new subjectivities, whether deliberately, like administrators of social sites shaping their own users (Gehl 2014), or with the mere use of computational

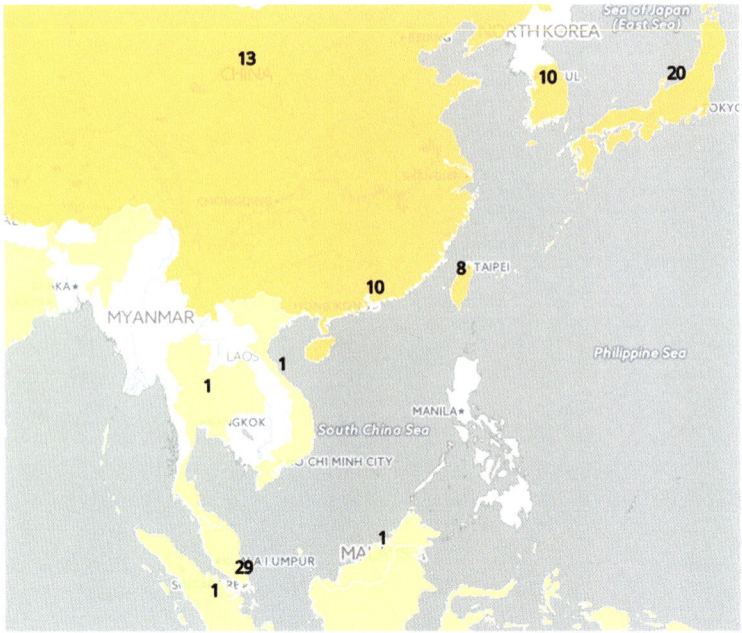

Fig. 6.6 Percentage (in *red*) of strong nodes and percentage (in *blue*) of internet users (Internet Live Statistics) by country. (Internet Live Statistics (2015) ranks the total number of internet users by country based on statistical analysis from different sources: the International Telecommunication Union's 'Measuring the Information Society Report', the World Bank Group's 'Internet Users Data', the Central Intelligence Agency's *World Factbook*, and data from the United Nations' Department of Economic and Social Affairs). © Pablo R. Velasco

grammar (Castelle 2013). The specific grammar of the network produces networked nodes, while the research methodology deliberately eases the emergence of particular strong entities. The emergence of Bitcoin as a financial device produced the figure of the miner, also by design, and of the market exchange, as an expected by-product. While the first two, the strong node and the miner, are mainly technical agencies, which can remain unnoticed as long as the infrastructure works as it is supposed to, the markets are capable, as new agencies, of reshaping relationships between individuals and states (Ruppert 2012); specifically, between users of the device as currency and states as financial regulators. These three figures intersect with each other in a variety of ways. Following the visual analysis of the nodes, I will stack the geographic attributes of two more of these entities.

A second map (see Fig. 6.7) adds tracked statements of different countries regarding digital currencies (not only Bitcoin, although this is the most used example) to the strong nodes' distribution.[5] Most reactions cluster at the end of 2013, when the phenomenon hit the mainstream media, and all have different weights regarding its legal validity. Countries in this map are color coded as permissive (green), cautious (yellow), and restrictive (red). Most states maintain a rather cautious approach, strongly advising caution in the use of digital currencies but without necessarily expressing a negative opinion or banning the use of the device. The map also shows an extract of the statement and the legal entity responsible for it. A third layer shows the location of the Bitcoin exchange headquarters, the fiat currencies that can be exchanged in it, and the size of the market for a period of six months.[6] Headquarters are a minimal indicator of these entities' geography, since most of them have registered offices outside their original territories. However, they show a historical interest in the device. For example, although ANX has offices in the USA and exchanges ten different fiat currencies, it is originally from Hong Kong, where it maintains its headquarters. The Asian coast has invested significantly in cryptocurrencies and has developed many interested parties in the last few years.

Separate retrieval and distillation processes allow me to display a visual ecosystem of Bitcoin-related agencies. The resulting map shows the expected behavior of the ecosystem, for example a high number of strong nodes and buoyant markets inside permissive/cautious legislation niches. However, it is in the discontinuities of the stacked agencies where it is possible to observe the socio-technical guts of the system. Here is an example of the multiple readings that this method allows: it enables the observation of empirical social interactions between new power structures (such as miners or cryptocurrency exchanges). In particular, China becomes an interesting location on the map: considering its huge number of internet users, it has a noticeably low percentage of strong nodes. To this can be added the outstanding share of the market that it has in relation to exchange headquarters (see Fig. 6.8). It is one of the few countries that has enacted harsh regulation of cryptocurrencies. Despite the discouraging legal environment (see Cawrey 2013; Franco 2015) and the minimal

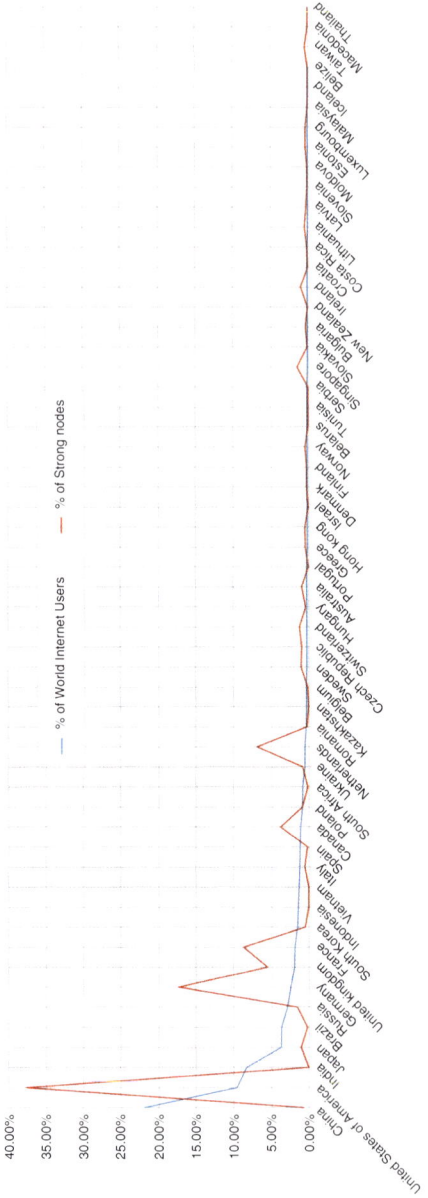

Fig. 6.7 Geography of a Bitcoin ecosystem, including country legislation status on Bitcoin (restrictive in *red*, cautious in *yellow*, and permissive *green* tones), strong nodes (*red* points), markets (*blue* points, sized by market share). (This map can be thoroughly explored at: https://timeknows.cartodb.com/viz/00ba6572-111b-11e5-b43e-0c018d66dc29/embed_map (accessed 9 January 2016)). Image and data: © Pablo R. Velasco. Template: © OpenStreetMap contributors © CartoDB, CartoDB attribution

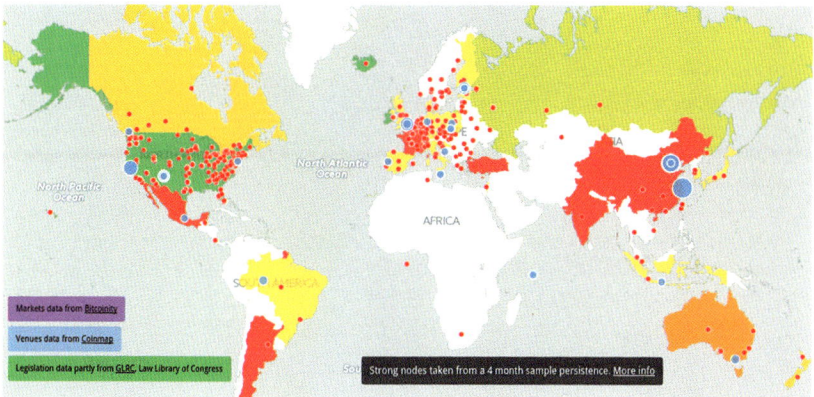

Fig. 6.8   Location of exchange headquarters by market share. © Pablo R. Velasco

number of committed nodes, China's exchanges accumulate the majority of the Bitcoin stockpile. This remarkably unbalanced situation depicts the existence of a second indicator within the network other than the sum of nodes; that is, not so much the quantity, but the node quality. In theory every node replicates transactions and works to build blocks of them, therefore producing Bitcoin units, but in practice only a few nodes have the capacity to produce Bitcoins. These nodes can be considered actual miners, who use dedicated hardware for the operation, and usually associate in pools due to the amount of computer power needed to produce new units successfully. Estimations of these pools' production capacity—or hashrate within the Blockchain—show again that a handful of pools operate the majority of the blocks (see Fig. 6.9). What is more, three of the biggest pools, BTCChina, Antpool, and F2pool, are operated from China.

The previous analysis of the map leads to a more readable image on the weight of the Chinese territory for Bitcoin. Neither nodes, nor miners, nor markets are by themselves representations of China as a nation; however, they do represent a crucial agglutination in the Bitcoin ecosystem space. Other significant findings may be obtained by zooming into other zones of the stacked map layers. The geographic distribution of nodes as digital entities, pictured via native digital methods, showed an incomplete map of an ecosystem with decisive social features. To understand the territory of the ecosystem, mixed

Fig. 6.9 Mining pools' hashrate distribution from 13–17 March 2016; screenshot from https://blockchain. info/pools (accessed 17 March 2016)

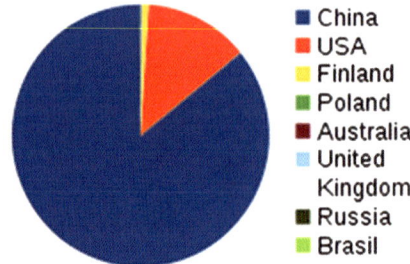

agencies—whose existence lies on the border of the digital space created by the device—must also be considered. Only after doing this is it possible to observe that the numbers and geographic distribution of the basic network entities are barely related to the actual entity's weight within the network.

Conclusions

As with many new digital objects, the emergence of Bitcoin generates an opportunity to produce new methodologies. Specific research paths can emerge from what the affordances of novel digital objects bring up and redistribute among other social science research methodologies, obeying the argued distributed nature of social research in online environments (Marres 2012). Agencies modeled by digital methods, like 'strong nodes', inherit attributes from the digital logic of their digital devices, in most cases unavoidably. Then, digital research must consider the implicit contract of working with entities derived from computational sources, especially when tied to extraction and distillation techniques.

Law and Ruppert (2013, p. 239) pose an open question on how the dynamics of methods that are shaped by the social that work to format the social, and that are used opportunistically, intersect with each other. Far from attempting to answer such an elusive interrogation, I would add to it that the awareness of current computational epistemologies and an acknowledged intention of the researcher to restructure the social are key to identifying the opportunistic shaping of society: how devices collect, communicate, and store data; how their grammar belongs inevitably to social and political institutions; and how their usage directly reinforces a kind of knowledge articulated by the devices' own logic. Consequently, methods should be used and designed taking this into consideration and highlight aspects of the device that are less constrained by computational epistemologies. This follows the suggestive path of innovative methods; that is to say, methods that 'are able to grasp the here and now in terms of somewhere else, and in doing so—if they can also change the problem, to which they are addressed—they expand the actual, inventively' (Lury and Wakeford 2012, p. 13). It also resonates with 'affirmative' approaches to 'biased' digital research methods like methods to exploit the ambiguity of digital devices, treating them as an empirical resource positively marked by bias (Marres 2015). From this perspective, 'innovative' denotes the notion of not only coming forth, but also emerging as a change in the previous state of affairs caused by the devising, use, and deployment of methods.

Notes

1. Henceforth, by nodes I will refer to full nodes unless otherwise stated.
2. The code and instructions to set up a forked server are available at https://github.com/ayeowch/bitnodes (accessed 10 January 2016). The information gathered by the API is, however, the same as that gathered by setting up a personalized version of the server.
3. © OpenStreetMap contributors © CartoDB attribution (https://cartodb.com/).
4. As far as I know, there is no way to know whether a node is the public interface of more than one machine, for example a mining rig. Also, nodes may be hijacked computers, as this is common practice both inside and outside the Bitcoin network (Litke and Stewart 2014; Huang et al. 2014), and evidently should not be considered as strong supporters. However, there is no guaranteed way to identify hijacked nodes, due to Bitcoin protocol restrictions.
5. Most of this data comes originally from a Regulation Report of 2014 (Global Legal Research Directorate 2014), which has been partly updated.
6. Market data was obtained via databitcoin.org. It shows the market volume share of Bitcoins, from 19 January to 19 June 2015.

References

Agre, P. (1994) Surveillance and Capture: Two Models of Privacy. *The Information Society* 10(2): 101–27.

Androulaki, E., Karame, G., Roeschlin, M., et al. (2013) Evaluating User Privacy in Bitcoin. In A.-R. Sadeghi (Ed.), *Financial Cryptography and Data Security* (Berlin, Heidelberg: Springer), pp. 34–51.

Baumann, A., Fabian, B. and Lischke, M. (2014) Exploring the Bitcoin Network. Proceedings of 10th International Conference on Web Information Systems and Technologies (Barcelona), pp. 369–74.

Beer, D. (2012) Using Social Media Data Aggregators to Do Social Research. *Sociological Research Online* 17(3): 10.

Bergstra, J. and Weijland, P. (2014) Bitcoin: A Money-like Informational Commodity. Working Paper (University of Amsterdam), http://arxiv.org/pdf/1402.4778.pdf (accessed 9 January 2016).

Berry, D. (2014) *Critical Theory and the Digital* (London: Bloomsbury).

Biryukov, A., Khovratovich, D. and Pustogarov, I. (2014) Deanonymisation of Clients in Bitcoin P2P Network. Proceedings of the 2014 ACM SIGSAC Conference on Computer and Communications Security (New York), pp. 15–29.

Bitcoin Block Explorer – Blockchain.info (2015) https://blockchain.info (accessed 7 January 2016).

Boase, R. (2013) Cypherpunks, Bitcoin & the Myth of Satoshi Nakamoto. Cybersalon Nov 5: http://www.cybersalon.org/cypherpunk/ (accessed 10 January 2016).

Castelle, M. (2013) Relational and Non-Relational Models in the Entextualization of Bureaucracy. *Computational Culture* 3: http://computationalculture.net/article/relational-and-non-relational-models-in-the-entextualization-of-bureaucracy (accessed 9 January 2016).

Cawrey, D. (2013) Baidu and China Telecom Stop Accepting Bitcoin, Price Slumps Again. *CoinDesk*. 7 Dec: http://www.coindesk.com/baidu-stops-bitcoin-price-slumps-again (accessed 10 January 2016).

Cramer, F. (2013) What Is 'Post-digital'? APRJA 3(1): http://www.aprja.net/?p=1318 (accessed 9 January 2016).

Cusumano, M. and Goeldi, A. (2013) New Businesses and New Business Models. In W. Dutton (Ed.), *The Oxford Handbook of Internet Studies* (Oxford: Oxford University Press), pp. 239–61.

de Jong, E., Tkacz, N. and Velasco, P. (2015) 'Live as Friends and Count as Enemies': On Digital Cash and the Media of Payment. In G. Lovink, N. Tkacz, and P. de Vries (Eds.), *Moneylab Reader: An Intervention in Digital Economy* (Amsterdam: Institute of Network Cultures), pp. 257–67.

FAQ – Bitcoin (2015) https://bitcoin.org/en/faq (accessed 9 January 2016).

Franco, E. (2015) Inside the Chinese Bitcoin Mine That's Grossing $1.5M a Month. Motherboard 6 Feb: https://motherboard.vice.com/read/chinas-biggest-secret-bitcoin-mine (accessed 10 January 2016).

Gehl, R. W. (2014) Power/Freedom on the Dark Web: A Digital Ethnography of the Dark Web Social Network. *New Media & Society* 18(7): 1219–35.

Gerlitz, C. and Helmond, A. (2013) The Like Economy: Social Buttons and the Data-Intensive Web. *New Media & Society* 15(8): 1348–65.

Global Legal Research Directorate (2014) Regulation of Bitcoin in Selected Jurisdictions. Law Library of Congress: http://www.loc.gov/law/help/bitcoin-survey/?loclr=bloglaw (accessed 9 January 2016).

Graham, M., Hale, S. and Stephens, M. (2012) Featured Graphic: Digital Divide: The Geography of Internet Access. *Environment and Planning A* 44(5): 1009–10.

Internet Live Statistics (2015) Internet Users by Country (2014). http://www. internetlivestats.com/internet-users-by-country (accessed 12 January 2016).

Jack, W. and Suri, T. (2011) Mobile Money: The Economics of M-Pesa. Working Paper 16721 (National Bureau of Economic Research, USA), http://www. nber.org/papers/w16721 (accessed 10 January 2016).

Karlstrøm, H. (2014) Do Libertarians Dream of Electric Coins? The Material Embeddedness of Bitcoin. *Distinktion: Scandinavian Journal of Social Theory* 15(1): 23–36.

Kitchin, R. (2016) Thinking Critically About and Researching Algorithms. *Information, Communication & Society* 20(1): 14–29.

Kitchin, R. and Dodge, M. (2011) *Code/Space: Software and Everyday Life* (Cambridge, MA: MIT Press).

Kittler, F. (1995) There Is No Software. *ctheory*. http://journals.uvic.ca/index. php/ctheory/article/view/14655/5522 (accessed 12 January 2016).

Kondor, D., Pósfai, M., Csabai, I. and Vattay, G. (2014) Do the Rich Get Richer? An Empirical Analysis of the Bitcoin Transaction Network. *PLoS One* 9(2): e97205.

Laszka, A., Johnson, B. and Grossklags, J. (2015) *When Bitcoin Mining Pools Run Dry: A Game-Theoretic Analysis of the Long-Term Impact of Attacks between Mining Pools. 2nd Workshop on Bitcoin Research* (San Juan: Puerto Rico).

Latour, B. (2007) *Reassembling the Social: An Introduction to Actor-Network-Theory* (Oxford: Oxford University Press).

Law, J. and Ruppert, E. (2013) The Social Life of Methods. *Journal of Cultural Economy* 6(3): 229–40.

Huang, D., Dharmdasani, H., Meiklejohn, S., et al. (2014) Botcoin: Monetizing Stolen Cycles. Paper presented at *NDSS 2014 Symposium* (San Diego, USA), http://cseweb.ucsd.edu/~snoeren/papers/botcoin-ndss14.pdf (accessed 10 March 2016).

Litke, P. and Stewart, J. (2014) BGP Hijacking for Cryptocurrency Profit. *Dell SecureWorks* R7 August: https://www.secureworks.com/research/bgp-hijacking-for-cryptocurrency-profit (accessed 6 January 2016).

Lovink, G. and Zehle, S. (2005) *Incommunicado Reader* (Amsterdam: Institute of Network Cultures).

Lupton, D. (2014) *Digital Sociology* (London: Routledge).

Lury, C. and Wakeford, N. (2012) Introduction: A Perpetual Inventory. In C. Lury and N. Wakeford (Eds.), *Inventive Methods: The Happening of the Social* (London: Routledge), pp. 1–25.

Mackenzie, A. and McNally, R. (2013) Living Multiples: How Large-Scale Scientific Data-Mining Pursues Identity and Differences. *Theory, Culture & Society* 30(4): 72–91.

Marres, N. (2012) The Redistribution of Methods: On Intervention in Digital Social Research, Broadly Conceived. *The Sociological Review* 60(S1): 139–65.

Marres, N. (2015) Why Map Issues? On Controversy Analysis as a Digital Method. *Science, Technology & Human Values* 40(5): 655–86.

Marres, N. and Weltevrede, E. (2013) Scraping the Social? Issues in Live Social Research. *Journal of Cultural Economy* 6(3): 313–35.

Maurer, B. (2015) *How Would you Like to Pay: How Technology Is Changing the Future of Money* (Durham: Duke University Press).

Maurer, B., Nelms, T. and Swartz, L. (2013) 'When Perhaps the Real Problem Is Money Itself!': The Practical Materiality of Bitcoin. *Social Semiotics* 23(2): 261–77.

Meiklejohn, S., Pomarole, M., Jordan, G., et al. (2013) A Fistful of Bitcoins: Characterizing Payments among Men with No Names. In *Proceedings of the 2013 Conference on Internet Measurement Conference* (New York, USA), 127–40.

Mersch, Y. (2014) Euro Banknotes – A Means of Payment Recognised Worldwide. Speech given at the Bergeldsymposium of the Deutsche Bank 19 May, https://www.ecb.europa.eu/press/key/date/2014/html/sp140519.en.html (accessed 15 January 2016).

Rogers, R. (2009) *The End of the Virtual: Digital Methods* (Amsterdam: University of Amsterdam Press).

Ruppert, E. (2012) Category. In C. Lury and N. Wakeford (Eds.), *Inventive Methods: The Happening of the Social* (London: Routledge), pp. 36–47.

Ruppert, E., Law, J. and Savage, M. (2013) Reassembling Social Science Methods: The Challenge of Digital Devices. *Theory, Culture & Society* 30(4): 22–46.

Scott, B. (2014) Visions of a Techno-Leviathan: The Politics of the Bitcoin Blockchain. *E-International Relations* 1 Jun: http://www.e-ir.info/2014/06/01/visions-of-a-techno-leviathan-the-politics-of-the-bitcoin-blockchain/ (accessed 10 January 2016).

Smyth, L. (2014) The Politics of Bitcoin. *Simulacrum* 7 Mar: http://simulacrum.cc/2014/03/07/the-politics-of-bitcoin (accessed 6 January 2016).

Wynn, J. R. (2009) Digital Sociology: Emergent Technologies in the Field and the Classroom. *Sociological Forum* 24(2): 448–56.

CHAPTER 7

Beyond Blobology: Using Psychophysiological Interaction Analyses to Investigate the Neural Basis of Human Communication Phenomena

Richard Huskey

Communication scholars have long investigated the relationships between communication phenomena and cognitive processes, although few have looked at the neural architecture that enables these relationships. As a consequence, many communication theories treat the brain as an unknowable black box. Rapid advances in brain-imaging technologies have allowed for the systematic investigation of the mind/brain and researchers are increasingly utilizing these methods to examine the neural basis of human communication behavior.

Early brain-imaging studies typically focused on identifying the neural substrates of a given psychological process. Today, large-scale meta-analyses now show that the same neural structures are often involved in a diverse array of cognitive processes (Yarkoni et al. 2011). If the same brain regions are involved in a variety of cognitive process, then brain-mapping studies alone can tell us only so much about the neural organization of the mind. Accordingly, researchers are increasingly investigating how connected

R. Huskey (✉)
Ohio State University, Columbus, OH, USA
e-mail: huskey.29@osu.edu

© The Author(s) 2016
S. Kubitschko, A. Kaun (eds.), *Innovative Methods in Media and Communication Research*, DOI 10.1007/978-3-319-40700-5_7

123

neural structures interact with one another in order to enable various cognitive processes (for example, Bassett and Gazzaniga 2011; Friston 2011; Weber et al. 2015a).

This chapter introduces communication scholars interested in conducting functional magnetic resonance imaging (fMRI) investigations to psychophysiological interaction analysis (PPI; Friston et al. 1997), a method for assessing task-modulated brain–network connectivity. Given that fMRI is still relatively uncommon among communication researchers, this chapter begins with a brief introduction to how the technology works and what sort of questions can be addressed with this method. With that said, readers are encouraged to consult more detailed introductions (see Weber et al. 2015b) or one of the many excellent textbooks on the topic (for example, Huettel et al. 2009). From there, this chapter provides a brief overview of the rationale for understanding the mind (and the communication phenomena it enables) as resulting from dynamic interactions between various brain structures. This includes a specific example where a higher-order cognitive process, flow experiences (Csíkszentmihályi 1990) resulting from media use, is thought to emerge as the result of a neural coupling between attentional and reward networks (Weber et al. 2009). This chapter then discusses the methodological particulars associated with using a PPI analysis to test the synchronization theory of flow, before concluding with a broader outlook on applications to communication theory and research. Specifically, it will discuss how investigations of neural connectivity can be used for theoretical falsification, conceptual refinement, and distinguishing constructs that have similar phenomenological characteristics and behavioral outcomes.

How Does fMRI Work and What Sort of Questions Can It Address?

In the most general sense, fMRI is a method for identifying the brain regions that are recruited during a given psychological process. This inference is well established and corresponds to the following logic: (1) a specific task or stimulus (2) results in localized neural activity that (3) includes changes in metabolic demands for oxygen and glucose, thereby (4) necessitating an increase in localized blood flow that (5) alters the ratio between oxygenated and deoxygenated hemoglobin (known as the blood oxygen level–dependent, or BOLD, contrast), where (6) this change is detectable by magnetic resonance techniques (DeYoe et al. 1994). Importantly, this signal is best understood as a measure of neuronal input and *not* as a measure of neuronal output (Logothetis et al. 2001; Logothetis and Pfeuffer 2004). This means that fMRI captures an indirect measure of neuronal activity, one that is characterized by a poor signal-to-noise ratio (Huettel et al. 2009).

Weber and colleagues (2015b) identify three general classes of questions that fMRI can be used to address. The first deals with localization and is focused on identifying the structures that are recruited during different communication processes. The second and third questions ask whether specific neural structures are recruited for distinct communication processes, or if activity in these structures is observable during a variety of processes. The takeaway is that fMRI is useful for addressing a narrowly constrained set of questions. This may be one of the reasons why the technique has seen limited adoption within the communication discipline. However, recent inquiries have demonstrated the utility of using fMRI for communication theory building and testing, particularly in instances where previous efforts have been stymied by the limitations inherent in more traditional measures (see Weber et al. 2015a). The remainder of this chapter details (1) a rationale for a networked theory of the mind; (2) a method for examining neural connectivity; and (3) the ways in which this can be used to advance communication theory and research.

What Is Connectivity and Why Does It Matter?

Early theorizing understood the brain as an information processing system where modular neural structures were recruited to perform unique cognitive tasks (Fodor 1983). Accordingly, the first fMRI studies set out to localize cognitive functions to specific brain regions. These brain-mapping studies provided a foundational understanding of the mind's neural organization and paved the way for modern conceptualizations of the mind/brain. Today, a growing body of research demonstrates that the brain is a complex system that (1) recruits multiple structures to perform different computational tasks; where (2) these structures work together or one exerts an influence over another in order to perform computations; and (3) the output of this computation can be characterized as greater than the sum of the individual subcomponents (Bassett and Gazzaniga 2011). This is known as emergence (Weber et al. 2015a), a phenomenon where complex higher-order cognitive functions emerge from dynamic interactions between distributed networks of neural modules (Strogatz 2003). Indeed, mounting evidence supports the view that different cognitive processes result from unique interactions between neural networks (Bullmore and Sporns 2012; Davison et al. 2015; Gu et al. 2015; Hermundstad et al. 2013, 2014; Petersen and Sporns 2015).

The relevance of neural connectivity and its application to communication research might not be immediately clear to scholars unaccustomed to thinking about psychological processes in such terms. To help overcome this lack of familiarity, let us consider a cognitive process commonly cited in the communication literature from a connectivity perspective: flow theory (Csíkszentmihályi 1990). Flow is a positively valenced subjective experience characterized by feelings of complete attentional focus, a loss of temporal awareness, diminished self-consciousness, and the sense that an activity is inherently rewarding. Weber et al. (2009) draw on the latest developments in the cognitive neuroscience literature in order to link the subjective experience of flow with well-established neuropsychological processes. Their synchronization theory of flow can be broken down into four premises. First, neural networks are capable of oscillating at the same frequency, and this shared oscillation (synchronization) indicates that networks are working together. Second, synchronization is a discrete state. Networks are either in sync or they are not. Third, the synchronization of neural networks is energetically cheap and the combined effect of synchronized networks is greater than the sum of the individual parts. The final assumption understands flow as the result of a synchronization between attentional and reward networks under conditions of a balance between task challenge and individual skill. Together, these assumptions are thought to account for the wholly absorptive and highly rewarding nature of flow experiences. The next sections discuss the practical aspects of using PPI analyses to test synchronization theory's connectivity prediction.

Neural Connectivity

Connectivity can be broken down into three subcategories: structural connectivity, functional connectivity, and effective connectivity (Friston 2011). Structural connectivity is concerned with the white-matter fiber tracts that connect different brain structures, and it is structural connectivity that enables different brain regions to work together. Cognitive processes modulate the strength of neuronal connections between brain regions. This basic observation underlies the principles of functional and effective connectivity, between which Friston (2011) is careful to distinguish. Functional connectivity describes statistical dependencies (for example, correlation) between neural activity in two or more brain regions. By comparison, effective connectivity is concerned with the influence that one structure exhibits over another.

Importantly, methods that were once useful for testing functional connectivity have since been modified to test effective connectivity. As an example, modern coherence analysis (which examines the correlation between two neural regions in the frequency domain) can be modified to assess time-shifted correlations between brain regions (Ashby 2011). In such analyses, one region is thought to exert influence on another when neural activity that has been shifted back in time correlates with temporally unaltered activity in another region. Here, a coherence analysis begins to look more like an assessment of effective connectivity. This may be one of the reasons why functional connectivity is often used as an umbrella term to describe analyses that investigate statistical relationships (including directionality and influence) between structurally connected brain regions (O'Reilly et al. 2012). For simplicity's sake, this chapter uses the term functional connectivity when referring to methods for assessing both functional and effective connectivity.

A key idea of structural connectivity is that it constrains functional connectivity, in that neural structures cannot be functionally connected if they are not also structurally connected (Friston 2011). Accordingly, structural connectivity at least partially explains individual differences in task-related neural activity (Miller et al. 2012) and even partially predicts individual differences in functional connectivity (Chu et al. 2015). However, after a critical developmental period (and barring any neurological damage), structural connectivity within an individual remains largely invariant (Seung 2012). Therefore, if we wish to understand how communication phenomena modulate brain states, then we are primarily interested in understanding how functional connectivity differs between communication processes. This chapter necessarily narrows its focus to statistical methods for assessing functional connectivity, while recognizing that it is structural connectivity that enables functional relationships in the first place.

In practice, researchers interested in assessing functional connectivity have a vast number of analytic methods at their disposal. Wang et al. (2014) identify forty-two different approaches belonging to seven different families of analysis (that is, correlation, h^2, mutual information, coherence, Granger causality, AH, and transfer entropy), and even more analyses are available (see, for example, Ashby 2011; Friston 2011). While each has utility for testing communication research questions, it is beyond the scope of this chapter to address all these methods. Instead, the chapter provides an introduction to PPI analysis, a common approach for assessing functional connectivity that builds on statistical principles with which communication scholars are already quite familiar.

PSYCHOPHYSIOLOGICAL INTERACTIONS

The primary utility of PPI analysis is an investigation into task-modulated functional connectivity. The analysis itself is based on two fundamental principles of neural activity (Friston et al. 1997). First, neural activity in two or more regions is correlated when these regions are working together. The second principle is that a task should modulate the strength of the correlation between two regions of interest (ROIs). It is this second idea that is central to PPI analysis. One benefit of PPI is that the underlying mathematical principles are relatively easy to understand for researchers who are already familiar with standard statistics and fMRI analyses based on the general linear model (GLM). There are three steps for conducting a basic PPI analysis: select a seed ROI, extract the neural time series data for that ROI, and define a GLM (O'Reilly et al. 2012).

ROI Selection

PPI analyses are highly hypothesis driven (Friston et al. 1997). The first step in any PPI analysis is to identify a seed ROI that is thought to exert task-dependent influence over target ROIs (O'Reilly et al. 2012). There are three strategies for seed selection. The first selects a seed ROI based on anatomical or theoretical models. Large-scale meta-analyses of connectivity data may be particularly useful here (see, for example, the online platform http://neurosynth.org and Richardet et al. 2015). A second approach selects a seed ROI based on a previous GLM analysis; this is known as a functionally defined ROI (fROI).[1] A final approach selects a seed ROI based on exploratory analysis, such as an independent component analysis (ICA).

Time Series Extraction

Once a seed ROI has been defined, the neural time series data must be extracted (for each subject) from that region (O'Reilly et al. 2012). This procedure can be completed using freely available brain-imaging analysis software such as the Wellcome Trust Centre for Neuroimaging Statistical Parametric Mapping software package (SPM; http://www.fil.ion.ucl.ac.uk/spm) or the Oxford Center for Functional MRI of the Brain (FMRIB) Software Library (FSL; http://www.fmrib.ox.ac.uk/fsl). Importantly, this extracted time series has already been convolved with a hemodynamic response function (HRF), which has implications for subsequent data analysis. Functional connections in the brain occur at the neuronal level and not at the multi-determined BOLD signal level (Friston et al. 1997). Therefore, any model that uses unmodified time series data extracted from a seed ROI is necessarily misspecified (Gitelman et al. 2003). One approach for dealing with this issue is to perform a deconvolution procedure[2] on the extracted time series data. While this might sound like the opposite of a convolution procedure, the multi-determined and regionally varying nature of the BOLD signal complicates the calculations, especially for resting-state fMRI data where the timing of neural events is unknown.

Unfortunately, there is no perfect way to deconvolve an unknown HRF (O'Reilly et al. 2012), and even the best deconvolution algorithms (for example, Bush and Cisler 2013) can introduce error. Accordingly, perceptions about the necessity of deconvolution often vary depending on experimental procedure and research lab. In practice, deconvolution is likely to matter most in fast event–related designs where events change rapidly in comparison to the relatively slow hemodynamic response (Gitelman et al. 2003). Block designs, by comparison, should result in a saturation of localized blood flow in response to task-related neural activity. Therefore, it is less likely that deconvolution is as crucial for experiments that employ a block design (O'Reilly et al. 2012).

Defining a GLM

The final step in a basic PPI analysis is to define a general linear model (O'Reilly et al. 2012). The simplest GLM includes three regressors (or explanatory variables, EVs): a psychological EV, a physiological EV, and an interaction term. The psychological EV (PSY) is the task sequence convolved with an HRF. The physiological EV (PHYS) is an $n \times 1$ matrix representing the extracted time series data for the seed ROI, where n is equal to the number of images captured during a scanning session. The final EV is an interaction term—the product of the psychological and physiological EVs. The model can be written out as follows:

$$B = \beta_1 PSY + \beta_2 PHYS + \beta_3 \left(PHY \times PHYS \right) + \beta_0 + \varepsilon.$$

Deconvolution decisions also have an impact on model specification. If the time series data were deconvolved, then the physiological EV should be reconvolved with an HRF (O'Reilly et al. 2012). If deconvolution was not applied to the time series, then convolution should not be applied to the physiological EV. It is also critical to model the main effects for both the psychological and physiological EVs, as the interaction term is likely confounded by the main effects (Cohen et al. 2003). The model should also include other confounded EVs that describe the data (for example, a linear drift term, motion artifacts), as this will make the model more accurate and therefore more sensitive (O'Reilly et al. 2012). This model is then applied to all subjects in a series of first-level analyses. Once all the first-level analyses have been completed, they can be combined in a higher-level analysis using standard procedures (see Weber et al. 2015b).

Other Considerations

One limitation inherent to PPI analyses is that the analysis is often lacking in statistical power (O'Reilly et al. 2012). This limits the potential for type I error, but is problematic in that a PPI analysis may be less sensitive for detecting functional connectivity. One reason for this is that, in the simple model defined earlier, the PSY and PHYS regressors may be correlated, thus making it difficult to detect the interaction due to the presence of main effects (Friston et al. 1997). The interaction term of interest can only account for variance above and beyond that which is explained by the main effects (Cohen et al. 2003). One possible solution is to design a study that utilizes a block design, as this approach has been shown to provide increased power compared to event-related designs (Chee et al. 2003; Cisler et al. 2014).

One final approach for increasing statistical power and reducing error is known as generalized PPI (gPPI; McLaren et al. 2012).[3] The main difference from a standard PPI (sPPI; the simplified procedure with just three

EVs already described) is that a gPPI models an EV for each factor in the experimental design, instead of modeling one EV that encodes all experimental factors. An interaction term is then modeled for each factor. By increasing the number of parameters in the model, the gPPI essentially allows for the decomposition of the interaction term and a more direct comparison of functional connectivity between task conditions. In simulation and real-world data, McLaren et al. (2012) demonstrate that the gPPI improves model fit and potentially reduces both type I and type II error. When compared to sPPI analyses, gPPI analyses are particularly more powerful for event-related designs, although they are comparably powerful for block designs (Cisler et al. 2014). Unfortunately, one complication of gPPI is that the higher number of terms increases the difficulty of beta-weight interpretation (McLaren et al. 2012).

The previous paragraph suggests that PPI analyses might be subject to type I error. O'Reilly et al. (2012) demonstrate how failing to include all sources of task-related variance in the model can contribute to spurious results. As an example, they describe a hypothetical experiment where subjects navigate a maze while undergoing fMRI scanning. In such an experiment, subjects might stop to strategize the next move, turn a corner, navigate a straight path, or finish the maze. In an analysis where each maze run, start to finish, was modeled in a block design, certain events, such as turning a corner or finishing the maze, might trigger a spike in neural activity, which boosts the BOLD signal, but not in the sustained manner that the block design assumes. Increasing model specificity (for example, a gPPI) might be one method for mitigating this concern, but this example also suggests that researchers should carefully consider whether a block design is an adequate fit for their assumptions about neural activity. Like any fMRI study, subject ability, attention, learning, and exhaustion might influence neural activity.

Finally, PPI analyses are typically based on a linear application of the GLM. However, it is well known that many neural processes are non-linear (Friston et al. 2000), and the presence of a non-linear relationship between seed and target ROIs might drive spurious PPI results (O'Reilly et al. 2012). There are possible solutions for dealing with non-linear relationships in a PPI analysis (for an extended discussion, see Harrison and Friston 2004). In one example, Weber et al. (2014a) add a quadratic term to account for non-linearities in the data. Their PPI model is as follows:

$$B = \beta_1 PSY + \beta_2 PHYS + \left(\beta_3 PSY + \beta_4 PSY^2 \right) \times PHYS + \beta_0 + \varepsilon.$$

One benefit of this approach is that it enables the investigation of network criticality, or the threshold values that result in synchronization within a network (for an extended discussion of network dynamics and criticality with a particular focus on their relationship to communication phenomena, see Sherry 2015).

PPI Utility

PPI analyses have a number of benefits that make them well suited for testing synchronization theory. First, unlike exploratory methods such as ICA, PPIs are highly hypothesis driven. Synchronization theory offers explicit hypotheses concerning which alerting, orientating, and reward structures are likely involved in flow (see Weber et al. 2009), and many of these predictions see preliminary support among early brain-mapping investigations of flow (Huskey et al. 2014; Klasen et al. 2012; Ulrich et al. 2014). Together, these studies provide a strong foundation for selecting relevant seed ROIs that allow for direct tests of the theory's main hypotheses.

PPIs are also useful for extending our understanding of how synchronization theory works. In their 2009 paper, Weber and colleagues theorize that flow is the emergent property of a synchronization between attentional and reward networks. However, they do not specify the direction of influence between these structures. Recent neuroscientific results indicate that the reward value of a stimulus predicts activation in structures associated with alerting attention (for example, Stanisor et al. 2013). This suggests that neural activity in reward networks might exert influence over attentional networks during flow. PPI analyses would be useful for investigating this as yet untested hypothesis. My collaborators and I are actively conducting work in this area and our initial results are proving promising. Finally, a PPI analysis paves the way for more sophisticated techniques such as those that use graph theoretical approaches for understanding whole-brain connectivity patterns between cognitive states (see Gu et al. 2015).

Concluding Remarks and Future Directions

Communication scholars are increasingly adopting brain-imaging research methods. This chapter continues in that trajectory by explaining how PPI analyses can be used to assess communication questions with fMRI data. While PPI analyses are particularly useful for testing synchronization theory, they may also be useful for investigating other communication phenomena. Specifically, they can be used for theoretical falsification, conceptual refinement, and as a means for distinguishing constructs that share similar phenomenological and behavioral outcomes. This chapter's discussion of the synchronization theory of flow (Weber et al. 2009) has demonstrated the utility of PPIs for theoretical falsification. However, what of the other two issues that connectivity analysis might address?

There are several opportunities for brain-imaging research to advance communication theory, but the growing body of research focused on the neural basis of persuasion provides a particularly salient example (for example, Chua et al. 2011; Falk et al. 2009, 2012; Ramsay et al. 2013; Seelig et al. 2014; Weber et al. 2014b). Many persuasion theories argue that attitude and behavior change results from an interaction between features of a message and audience characteristics. However, in a recent review, Vezich et al. (2016) argue that brain-imaging investigations of persuasion heavily implicate the role of socio-emotional processes in persuasive outcomes. As of now, these processes are not accounted for in many of the most prominent persuasion theories. This is an instance where brain-imaging analyses, particularly with a connectivity focus, can assist in refining existing theoretical models.

Neural connectivity analyses are also useful when traditional approaches (for example, self-report, behavioral paradigms) struggle to distinguish between different theoretical constructs. Returning again to flow during media use, the experience is characterized by a loss of temporal and self-awareness, intense concentration, and a pleasurable experience. Some researchers have argued that this might be related to losses in self-regulation associated with video game addiction (Wood and Griffiths 2007; Gentile 2009). A forthcoming review demonstrated that not only do flow and video game addiction share similar self-report and behavioral outcomes, but each construct is also associated with neural activation in similar brain regions (Weber et al. 2017). Nevertheless, if flow experiences during media use are different from video game addiction, then it should be possible to observe different neural connectivity patterns for each cognitive process. A recent review hypothesizes that video game addiction should be associated with a brain state where reward networks exert bottom-up control over attentional structures, while flow should be associated with synchronized connectivity between these networks (Craighead et al. 2015). This provides an example where connectivity analyses can be used to identify a biomarker for psychological processes that are difficult to assess using more traditional approaches.

More generally, the neural basis of many communication phenomena remains largely unexplored (for an extended discussion with examples for how to get started, see Weber et al. 2015a). While brain-mapping studies represent an important first step (Weber et al. 2015b), this chapter argues that connectivity analyses add crucial information about how neural structures, acting in a networked architecture, enable higher-order communication processes. Neuroscientific advances within the discipline will develop more rapidly if our early studies investigate not only brain mapping, but neural connectivity.

This is an exciting time for connectivity research characterized by considerable technical and analytic advances. At the same time, stronger magnetic fields in fMRI scanners are allowing for better structural connectivity imaging and, therefore, more biologically plausible specification of functional connectivity models (Lohmann et al. 2012). These are complemented by attempts to map the entire human connectome (Seung 2012). Recent developments such as multi-voxel pattern analysis (Norman et al. 2006) and hyper-graph techniques (Davison et al. 2015) move beyond assessing relationships between a few ROIs and allow for the analysis of complex, whole-brain network states that characterize cognitive tasks. In addition, there are serious attempts to combine both structural and functional connectivity data in large-scale databases, with the goal of developing a better understanding of human cognition and behavior (for example in the case of the Human Connectome Project). Communication scholars are familiar with thinking in network terms and have advanced many sophisticated models for assessing network architectures (Lazer et al. 2009). It is exciting to imagine a future where the skills of communication scholars will bolster investigation into the human brain.

NOTES

1. Importantly, fROIs should be defined independently of the task under investigation in order to prevent artificially inflated results (see Weber et al. 2015b).
2. There are several deconvolution algorithms that can be implemented in both SPM and AFNI (National Institute of Mental Health; https://afni.nimh.nih.gov/afni, accessed on 10 August 2016). By comparison, FSL does not have a built-in deconvolution algorithm.
3. An SPM toolbox for conducting gPPI analyses is available here: http://www.nitrc.org/projects/gppi. FSL is also capable of conducting gPPI analyses.

Acknowledgments The theoretical rationale and methodological procedures for assessing neural connectivity have been a hot topic of discussion within the Media Neuroscience Lab (http://medianeuroscience.org). Two collaborators deserve special recognition and thanks. René Weber at UC Santa Barbara was the first to introduce me to neural connectivity and has provided helpful guidance for conceptualizing communication phenomena from a connectivity perspective. Michael Mangus at UC Santa Barbara deserves special praise for his technical contributions, particularly the development of automation procedures that make the manipulation of large brain-imaging data sets much more manageable. I am sincerely grateful for their help.

REFERENCES

Ashby, F. (2011) *Statistical Analysis of fMRI Data* (Cambridge, MA: MIT Press).

Bullmore, E. and Sporns, O. (2012) The Economy of Brain Network Organization. *Nature Reviews Neuroscience* 13(5): 336–49.

Bassett, D. and Gazzaniga, M. (2011) Understanding Complexity in the Human Brain. *Tzrends in Cognitive Sciences* 15(5): 200–9.

Bush, K. and Cisler, J. (2013). Decoding Neural Events from fMRI BOLD Signal: A Comparison of Existing Approaches and Development of a New Algorithm. *Magnetic Resonance Imaging* 31(6): 976–89.

Chee, M., Venkatraman, V., Westphal, C., et al. (2003) Comparison of Block and Event-related fMRI Designs in Evaluating the Word-frequency Effect. *Human Brain Mapping* 18(3): 186–93.

Chu, C., Tanaka, N., Diaz, J., et al. (2015) EEG Functional Connectivity is Partially Predicted by Underlying White Matter Connectivity. *NeuroImage* 108: 23–33.

Chua, H., Ho, S., Jasinska, A., et al. (2011) Self-related Neural Response to Tailored Smoking-cessation Messages Predicts Quitting. *Nature Neuroscience* 14(4): 426–7.

Cisler, J., Bush, K. and Steele, J. (2014) A Comparison of Statistical Methods for Detecting Context-modulated Functional Connectivity in fMRI. *NeuroImage* 84:1042–52.

Cohen, J., Cohen, P., West, S., et al. (2003) *Applied Multiple Regression/Correlation Analysis for the Behavioral Sciences.* 3rd ed. (Mahwah: Lawrence Erlbaum).

Craighead, B., Huskey, R. and Weber, R. (2015) Video Game Articles addiction: What Can We Learn From a Media Neuroscience Perspective? *Argentinean Journal of Behavioral Sciences* 7(3): 119–31.

Csíkszentmihályi, M. (1990) *Flow: The Psychology of Optimal Experience* (New York: HarperCollins).

Davison, E., Schlesinger, K., Bassett, D., et al. (2015) Brain Network Adaptability Across Task States. *PLoS Computational Biology* 11(1): 1–14.

DeYoe, E., Bandettini, P., Neitz, J., et al. (1994) Functional Magnetic Resonance Imaging (FMRI) of the Human Brain. *Journal of Neuroscience Methods* 54(2): 171–87.

Falk, E., Berkman, E. and Lieberman, M. (2012) From Neural Responses to Population Behavior: Neural Focus Group Predicts Population-level Media Effects. *Psychological Science* 23(5): 439–45.

Falk, E., Rameson, L., Berkman, E., et al. (2009) The Neural Correlates of Persuasion: A Common Network Across Cultures and Media. *Journal of Cognitive Neuroscience* 22(11): 2447–59.

Fodor, J. (1983) *The Modularity of Mind: An Essay on Faculty Psychology* (Cambridge, MA: MIT Press).

Friston, K. (2011) Functional and Effective Connectivity: A Review. *Brain Connectivity* 1(1): 13–36.

Friston, K., Buechel, C., Fink, G., et al. (1997) Psychophysiological and Modulatory Interactions in Neuroimaging. *NeuroImage* 6(3): 218–29.

Friston, K., Mechelli, A., Turner, R., et al. (2000) Nonlinear Responses in fMRI: The Balloon Model, Volterra Kernels, and Other Hemodynamics. *NeuroImage* 12(5): 466–77.

Gentile, D. (2009) Pathological Video-game Use Among Youth Ages 8 to 18: A National Study. *Psychological Science* 20(5): 594–602.

Gitelman, D., Penny, W., Ashburner, J., et al. (2003) Modeling Regional and Psychophysiologic Interactions in fMRI: The Importance of Hemodynamic Deconvolution. *NeuroImage* 19(1): 200–7.

Gu, S., Pasqualetti, F., Cieslak, M., et al. (2015) Controllability of Structural Brain Networks. *Nature Communications* 6(8414): 1–10.

Harrison, L. and Friston, K. (2004) Effective Connectivity. In J. Ashburner, K. J. Friston, and W. D. Penny (Eds.), *Human Brain Function*. 2nd ed. (San Diego: Academic Press), pp. 1019–47.

Hermundstad, A., Bassett, D., Brown, K., et al. (2013) Structural Foundations of Resting-state and Task-based Functional Connectivity in the Human Brain. *Proceedings of the National Academy of Sciences of the United States of America* 110(15): 6169–74.

Hermundstad, A., Brown, K., Bassett, D., et al. (2014) Structurally-constrained Relationships Between Cognitive States in the Human brain. *PLoS Computational Biology* 10(5): 1–9.

Huettel, S., Song, A. and McCarthy, G. (2009) *Functional Magnetic Resonance Imaging*. 2nd ed. (Sunderland: Sinauer Associates).

Huskey, R., Mangus, M., Yoder, C., et al. (2014) The Neural Correlates of Flow Experiences During Video Game Play. *Paper presented at the 64th annual conference of the International Communication Association* (Seattle, USA).

Klasen, M., Weber, R., Kircher, T., et al. (2012) Neural Contributions to Flow Experience During Video Game Playing. *Social Cognitive and Affective Neuroscience* 7(4): 485–95.

Lazer, D., Pentland, A., Adamic, L., et al. (2009). Life in the Network: The Coming Age of Computational Social Science. *Science* 323(5915): 721–3.

Logothetis, N. and Pfeuffer, J. (2004) On the Nature of the BOLD fMRI Contrast Mechanism. *Magnetic Resonance Imaging* 22(10): 1517–31.

Logothetis, N., Pauls, J., Augath, M. et al. (2001) Neurophysiological Investigation of the Basis of the fMRI Signal. *Nature* 412(6843): 150–7.

Lohmann, G., Erfurth, K., Müller, K., et al. (2012) Critical Comments on Dynamic Causal Modelling. *NeuroImage* 59(3): 2322–9.

McLaren, D., Ries, M., Xu, G., et al. (2012) A Generalized Form of Context-dependent Psychophysiological Interactions (gPPI): A Comparison to Standard Approaches. *NeuroImage* 61(4): 1277–86.

Miller, M., Donovan, C.-L., Bennett, C., et al. (2012) Individual Differences in Cognitive Style and Strategy Predict Similarities in the Patterns of Brain Activity Between Individuals. *NeuroImage* 59(1): 83–93.

Norman, K., Polyn, S., Detre, G., et al. (2006) Beyond Mind-reading: Multi-voxel Pattern Analysis of fMRI Data. *Trends in Cognitive Sciences* 10(9): 424–30.

O'Reilly, J., Woolrich, M., Behrens, T., et al. (2012) Tools of the Trade: Psychophysiological Interactions and Functional Connectivity. *Social Cognitive and Affective Neuroscience* 7(5): 604–9.

Petersen, S. and Sporns, O. (2015) Brain Networks and Cognitive Architectures. *Neuron* 88(1): 207–19.

Ramsay, I., Yzer, M., Luciana, M., et al. (2013) Affective and Executive Network Processing Associated with Persuasive Antidrug Messages. *Journal of Cognitive Neuroscience* 25(7): 1136–47.

Richardet, R., Chappelier, J.-C., Telefont, M., et al. (2015) Large-scale Extraction of Brain Connectivity from the Neuroscientific Literature. *Bioinfomatics* 31(10) 1640–7.

Seelig, D., Wang, A.-L., Jaganathan, K., et al. (2014) Low Message Sensation Health Promotion Videos Are Better Remembered and Activate Areas of the Brain Associated with Memory Encoding. *PloS One* 9(11): 1–10.

Seung, S. (2012) *Connectome: How the Brain's Wiring Makes Us Who We Are* (New York: Houghton Mifflin Harcourt Trade).

Sherry, J. (2015) The Complexity Paradigm for Studying Human Communication: A Summary and Integration of Two Fields. *Review of Communication Research* 3(1): 22–54.

Stanisor, L., van der Togt, C., Pennartz, C., et al. (2013) A Unified Selection Signal for Attention and Reward in Primary Visual Cortex. *Proceedings of the National Academy of Sciences* 110(22): 9136–41.

Strogatz, S. (2003). *Sync: The Emerging Science of Spontaneous Order.* New York: Hyperion.

Ulrich, M., Keller, J., Hoenig, K., et al. (2014) Neural Correlates of Experimentally Induced Flow Experiences. *NeuroImage* 86(1): 194–202.

Vezich, S., Falk, E. and Lieberman, M. (2016) Persuasion Neuroscience: New Potential to Test Dual Process Theories. In E. Harmon-Jones and M. Inzlicht (Eds.), *Social Neuroscience: Biological Approaches to Social Psychology* (New York: Psychological Press).

Wang, H., Benar, C., Quilichini, P., et al. (2014) A Systematic Framework for Functional Connectivity Measures. *Frontiers in Neuroscience* 8(405): 1–22.

Weber, R., Tamborini, R., Westcott-Baker, A., et al. (2009) Theorizing Flow and Media Enjoyment as Cognitive Synchronization of Attentional and Reward Networks. *Communication Theory* 19(4): 397–422.

Weber, R., Alicea, B., Huskey, R., et al. (2014a) The Dynamics of Attention in Video game Environments: A Functional Magnetic Resonance Imaging Study. *Paper presented at the 64th annual conference of the International Communication Association* (Seattle, USA).

Weber, R., Huskey, R., Mangus, J., et al. (2014b) Neural Predictors of Message Effectiveness During Counterarguing in Anti-drug Campaigns. *Communication Monographs* 82(1): 4–30.

Weber, R., Eden, A., Huskey, R., et al. (2015a) Bridging Media Psychology and Cognitive Neuroscience: Challenges and Opportunities. *Journal of Media Psychology* 27(3): 146–56.

Weber, R., Mangus, J. and Huskey, R. (2015b) Brain Imaging in Communication Research: A Practical Guide to Understanding and Evaluating fMRI Studies. *Communication Methods and Measures* 9(1–2): 5–29.

Weber, R., Huskey, R., and Craighead, B. (2017) Flow Experiences and Well-being: A Media Neuroscience Perspective. In M. B. Oliver and L. Reinecke (Eds.), *Handbook of Media Use and Well-being: International Perspectives on Theory and Research on Positive Media Effects* (New York: Routledge), pp. 183–96.

Wood, R. and Griffiths, M. (2007) Time Loss Whilst Playing Video Games: Is There a Relationship to Addictive Behaviours? *International Journal of Mental Health and Addiction* 5(2): 141–9.

Yarkoni, T., Poldrack, R., Nichols, T., et al. (2011) Large-scale Automated Synthesis of Human Functional Neuroimaging Data. *Nature Methods* 8(8): 665–70.

CHAPTER 8

As We Should Think? Lifelogging as a Re-emerging Method

Alberto Frigo

'As We May Think' is the title of an article written by Vannevar Bush (1945) at the end of World War II. His article is at the center of my discussion and provocation. While lifelogging, or rather the technology enabling ordinary individuals to capture, store, and retrieve their lives, has been much criticized by both scholars and public opinion for its privacy implications, I will make use of my chapter to provide an alternative way to look at this phenomenon, and to go as far as to propose it as an indispensable method for scholars to better sense and understand the complex media-generated landscape around them. I will do so by providing a broader historical contextualization of lifelogging and deepen the contemporary discussion on an everyday life increasingly governed by sensors and algorithms. Secondly, while inviting media scholars to embrace technical complexity in an autoethnographic fashion, I will introduce a set of instructions on how to get started on lifelogging as a research method. Lastly, I will present my own manual lifelogging methodology as a concrete example of information retrieval and subsequent knowledge production.

A. Frigo (✉)
Södertörn University, Stockholm, Sweden
e-mail: alberto.frigo@sh.se

© The Author(s) 2016   139
S. Kubitschko, A. Kaun (eds.), *Innovative Methods in Media and Communication Research*, DOI 10.1007/978-3-319-40700-5_8

BUSH'S LEGACY: AN ALTERNATIVE WAY TO DEAL WITH COMPLEXITY

Coming back to the article 'As We May Think', I shall begin by mentioning that its author, Vannevar Bush, was the person in charge of directing the scientific agenda of the United States during World War II—an agenda fully dedicated to the development of weapons of mass destruction, not least its ultimate manifestation, the atomic bomb. It was in 1945 that Bush, sensing a future of peace ahead of him, started reconsidering the role of the scientist. While his intention in the article was to assign to the post–World War II scientist a philanthropic role, in the very first paragraphs he immediately recognizes a big challenge: As scientific knowledge continued to multiply, how was the new scientist going to deal with it? In this respect Bush wrote:

> There is a growing mountain of research. But there is increased evidence that we are being bogged down today as specialization extends. The investigator is staggered by the findings and conclusions of thousands of other workers—conclusions which he cannot find time to grasp, much less to remember, as they appear. Yet specialization becomes increasingly necessary for progress, and the effort to bridge between disciplines is correspondingly superficial. Professionally our methods of transmitting and reviewing the results of research are generations old and by now are totally inadequate for their purpose. (1945, p. 1)

More than half a century earlier, a young Friedrich Nietzsche (1980 [1874]) had already realized how knowledge overflow was becoming an obstacle to renewing societal constellations in Germany at that time. The fascistic answer to this, a drastic cleansing of the old for the sake of a new social integrity, had self-destructive effects. Having directly experienced such effects, namely the full course of modern warfare, it was now Bush, the leading American scientist of his time, who proposed a new way of dealing with knowledge overflow. The alternative was no longer a drastic 'bundling' of the overflow into one dogmatic view imposed by a regime. The American alternative to dealing with the increasing overflow in a non-dictatorial fashion was based on a visionary technology meant to implement the cognitive faculties of individuals. This technology, which Bush named the Memex, was supposed to assist users in their process of collecting and retrieving information, enhancing not only their working space but most particularly their head via a head-mounted camera (Fig. 8.1).

Fig. 8.1 The interplay between desktop computing and wearable computing: my failed attempts to wear cameras in order to document my life along with my mental processes such as my thoughts and my dreams. At that time, in early 2000, I was not aware of Vannevar Bush's article nor of wearable computers. Social media did not exist and sousveillance for me was simply an intellectual necessity. © Alberto Frigo

In this respect, Bush's contribution has been that of considering ways to deal with rather than neglect or subdue a world increasingly turned more complex by media technologies; after the devastating attempts of authoritarian ideologies, he proposed a more individualistic way to deal with complexity and transformation. Unwittingly, Bush suggested a stoic alternative in line with that of the Roman emperor and philosopher Marcus Aurelius (161–180 CE; see Aurelio 1980), whose meditations were often focused on his acceptance of social transformations as much as a fire taking its course. It was through thinking about complexity that Bush came to propose the Memex as a stationary and wearable device for the scientist of the future to be able to deal with knowledge overflow.

The Rise of the Wearable Computer Paradigm

Up to the present day Bush has been considered a visionary, not least because he was among the first to envision desktop computing, the digital paradigm shaping human lives since the 1980s. Yet his vision went beyond this, as he signaled a paradigm shift that will shape human lives even more pervasively—or might even be doing so already. The new paradigm I am talking about is wearable computing, or more specifically lifelogging, a wearable system that automatically and systematically captures, organizes, and retrieves the 'total' reality of a human being.

Wearable computers became possible to experiment with only in the 1990s—half a century after Bush's vision—as the decrease in size of digital technologies coincided with an increase in computing capacity. It was then that young Massachusetts Institute of Technology 'cyborgs' like Steve Mann and Thad Eugene Starner began to test on themselves the possibility of augmenting their outer reality (Mann 1997) as well as their inner memory (Rhodes and Starner 1996). Initially conceived in the spirit of Bush as devices to create super-scientists, soon the trend took a sharp turn at the beginning of the 2000s as human–computer-interaction research on wearables, particularly led by Microsoft Research, promoted these as devices to assist older people with memory impairment (Hodges et al. 2006). With the rise of smartphones and so-called social media platforms in the early 2000s, the notion of wearable computers became blurred.

Since then the idea of an embodied computer, much like that incorporated in a cyborg skin, has been replaced by the success of a wide range of handheld media accessories like tablets, smartphones, and computerized watches. Equally, the idea of personal memory augmentation has been replaced by social media. After over a decade of enthusiasm, then, the possibility offered by digital technology of building lifelogging and/or wearable devices to augment the memory of users (Bell et al. 2002; Rhodes and Starner 1996) has turned into a general stark criticism. As these devices became available to the public in the form of neck-worn (for example, Microsoft's Sense Cam) or head-mounted (for example, Google Glass) gadgets, it dawned on ever more people that these devices have the potential to turn into the ultimate apparatuses for companies to establish themselves as gatekeepers of personal data. Along the way, corporations were able to make record-breaking profits by analyzing unprecedented volumes of data and targeting people's lives with increasingly accurate commercial offers that the very lifelogging devices superimpose on their reality.

STEPPING BACK FROM CRITICISM AND NEGLECT: A LOOK AT LIFELOGGING AS AN ALTERNATIVE METHOD

The criticism that has arisen both in public opinion and in various academic fields has only vaguely addressed where the exact threat of an all-capturing and totally instrumentalizing device lies (Sellen and Whittaker 2010). It is clear to me that this threat consists not so much in the act of systematically documenting reality, but rather in delegating this task to an 'intelligent' system. Namely, the threat lies in the automation of the process of capturing, organizing, and retrieving (or, better, in the case of these lifelogging gadgets 'sharing') the reality of the user. Sensors and algorithms make up the 'artificial intelligence', turning users into a mere Pinocchio guided by a Jiminy Cricket, a lifelogging device instructing them on how to behave for the sake of contemporary capitalist culture. Therefore, in the worst yet most likely scenario—perhaps depending on whether the device was purchased or given away for free—the lifelogging device will turn into a Cat and a Fox examining the captured data and directing Pinocchio to plant his golden coins in the garden of the miracles, 'the new economy'.

At this point, scholars of the world should feel relaxed—they ought not to go around wearing clumsy devices, nor ought they to face the increasing complexity of the world as Bush had wished them to. The old canons and archaic notions that scholars keep recycling can still be perfectly applicable with a bit of tweaking. Additional notions, borrowed from other fields, can also be applied, allowing a certain set of understandings that might provide more or less predictable results and might result in a more general discourse befitting the genre of academic mannerism. Avoiding the pursuit of any criticism on pre-configured academic manners and methods and the constant battle to put more or less emphasis on one or the other, this chapter pursues Bush's idea, but from a different, more historically elaborated perspective.

What seems fallacious at this point is to consider Bush's vision in terms of automation. A scientist wearing a device configured to capture, organize, and retrieve data automatically will replace the very human scientist if not completely, at least partially. As data themselves seem to become too complex for a human brain to deal with, programs in the near future will in fact take up this role, considerably reducing the role of the scientist to some kind of data hermeneutic and black-box scavenger. Now, my idea is simple and implies the creation of a personal lifelogging framework to gather, process, and retrieve information without the aid of purposely created frameworks and automation. My belief is that any researcher processing such a self-tailored lifelogging framework will develop a body of knowledge generated from the conflict that will necessarily arise between it and the more or less automated frameworks designed by the establishment to intellectually accommodate and financially exploit them.

A manual and self-crafted lifelogging approach can therefore position researchers in a dual state of understanding. On one hand they becomes the carrier of an actual experience of re-enactment of an otherwise taken-for-granted automation of everyday life and, on the other, they enter into constant confrontation between their ever-growing self-crafted framework motivated by their desire for knowledge and the established corporate framework motivated by worldly purposes alone.

The kind of lifelogging I am talking about here is essentially different from the automated lifelogging gadgetry now for sale. It recovers some more ancient strands of scholarly discourse preceding the Enlightenment. To put it briefly, I argue that instead of conceiving of lifelogging as a tool for scholars to 'augment' their capabilities automatically, lifelogging can be conceived instead as a method to accompany the intellectual formation of any scholar or intellectual. Lifelogging, as commonly understood, may at first sight only be regarded as the process of recording one or more instances of reality through a camera or other types of sensors. What I am aiming to look into is a different form of logging that sees individuals becoming this automation, or, in other words, embedding in their own behavior a procedure that allows them to keep track of the processes characterizing their formation along with the complex transformation surrounding them.

In this respect, the method I am proposing can be reviewed as an update of already existing reflective methodologies, particularly autoethnography. If the latter is a merging of ethnography and autobiography (Adams et al. 2014) that avoids bracketing out the ways in which the life of researchers is intertwined with their research, the lifelogging element can be viewed as a more up-to-date way to collect fieldnotes, immersing researchers in the very media generating the phenomena they wish to investigate. In this line of thought, lifelogging as autoethnography attempts to accommodate the elements of mess and chaos, the overflow and complexity of our contemporary reality, while also maintaining a high level of readability, more in line with literature than with philosophical texts (Goodall 2004). To this extent, lifelogging produces the research material from which research can take place.

Beyond the prose-like text advocated by autoethnographers to reach a broader audience (Adams et al. 2014), lifelogging also brings in other popular media such as photography, video and audio recording, 3D rendering, and so on. It expands the palette with which particular contemporary phenomena are filtered; it provides not so much, as in Bush's vision, a material that can be specifically referred to by pointing at its particular elements, but rather a mass of clay from which researchers can represent their experience of being in the media.

Also, the resulting empirical work, along with the experience of lifelogging researchers processing this information in person, becomes the possibility for them to develop an autonomous framework of knowledge production. What I am aiming to suggest here, alongside the discussion of other scholars daring to look into or around the black box of our automated surroundings, is to invite researchers to come up with raw replacements for this pre-configured black box and to stick to them as much as Chinese farmers, afraid to lose their human nature, obstinately and with effort carry the water from the river to the field, refusing to use a machine.

The outcome of this effort to conduct a parallel and self-crafted lifelogging framework, avoiding the automated and pre-configured framework projected onto contemporary individuals by the establishment, may in turn be producing an extensive body of knowledge of which researchers can periodically produce a mental synthesis (Fig. 8.2). This synthesis comes close to that proposed by autoethnography, but it additionally presents the raw media traces that lifelogging researchers have systematically sampled. Even without this synthesis, however, researchers conducting a self-crafted lifelogging framework will in the end be able to provide a media archaeological artifact, a black box that reflects their time. My belief is that, being manually generated, this black box will have a better chance of being interpreted not by well-trained scientists with specific decoding machines, but rather by other humans stumbling upon it, comparing and interpreting the different flows within it like the languages of a Rosetta stone.

Rosetta Stoning

As I have so far presented it, lifelogging can be conceived not as a black box of ourselves in the context of the mega-black boxes pervading contemporary life, but rather a way to establish a combination of empathy and confrontation with the opaque mechanisms and procedures affecting our everyday, resulting in a Rosetta stone, or, as we shall shortly see, a mental architecture

Fig. 8.2 The personal museum of the humanist Ferrante Imperato—an inspiring setting to let us think about the human black box that each researcher could deliver, processing information with effort via a lifelogging framework and mapping it onto a structure like this room. Public domain work of art available at: http://www.ausgepackt.uni-erlangen.de/presse/download/museum_des_imperato.jpg (accessed 10 March 2016)

resembling combinatorial systems and mnemonic architectures. In a minor way, and to better contextualize my concept with the contemporary discussion, the Rosetta stone I mean comes close to Lev Manovich's (1999) concept of database aesthetics from a sequential type of thinking to a more spatial one. Metaphorically speaking, I am thinking here of lifelogging as not a simple decoding of the complex environment around us (Ashby 1956), but as an unofficial gearbox customized and operated by researchers themselves alongside their already pre-configured and automated activities of living (Fig. 8.3). To be more concrete, I am talking about the devising of a technique that in fact does not necessarily make use of technology; it keeps human agents both directly involved in the action of granularly

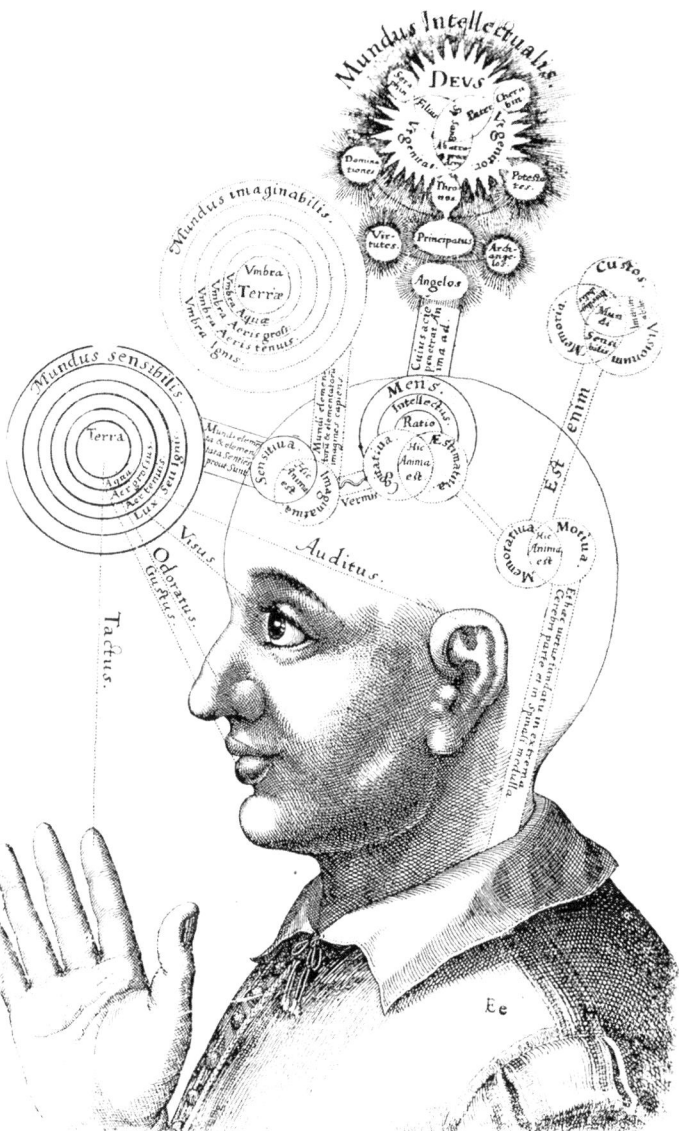

Fig. 8.3   Robert Fludd's idea of a microcosm is emblematic for me to think of personal gears that are self-crafted to operate along with gears of much bigger orders. Public domain work of art available at: https://upload.wikimedia.org/wikipedia/commons/0/0c/RobertFuddBewusstsein17Jh.png?uselang=de (accessed 10 March 2016)

processing information as well as in charge of the overall framework that at any time they are able to expand, contract, and improve.

This very simple act of noting an external and/or internal occurrence and the immediate placing of this occurrence within one or other stream of thought is *per se* sufficient to create not only ongoing fieldwork that should gain scientific credibility, but also the very method with which individuals can extensively and continually analyze the complex reality in transformation both around and within them, alongside the struggle they have to face to maintain their personal framework at a time in which corporate frameworks are becoming ever more pervasive. In this respect, I shall warn those who still wish to attempt to match this active and full-encompassing practice with that of an archivist, a collector, or any hoarder: there is no slight interest here in creating artificial memory and adding more retroactivity in the process of the researcher; rather, it is a methodology with which the present surroundings are taken care of in a proactive fashion.

What I am talking about here is a more discreet kind of logging than the one that arose from Bush's idea and generally from the American technological debate. I am referring instead to a lifelogging dedicated to the creation of a framework for personal use designed by the researcher to manually accommodate everyday complexity. Therefore, rather than blanking out this complexity or automatically capturing it, researchers develop a place to become aware as well as empathic with their everyday. This framework should not be perceived as obstructive—contemporary humans are already trained to undertake additional procedures such as sliding the card on a door reader before actually opening the door. Annotation of our own process of observation and reflection can be easily customized by any subject in relation to the process of observing and reflecting. There is nothing new in all of this. To some extent, as I will clarify below, I can claim that this manual process of observation only finds a precursor in the southern European scholarly tradition (Rossi 1983) criticized and finally dismissed in the 16th and 17th centuries in the north of Europe.

An Earlier History of Lifelogging

The art of 'allocating' different memories in the human mind and being able to retrieve them is generally known as *ars mnemonica* (Yates 1966). From Cicero onward, several prominent figures have utilized it, or at least praised it through extensive essays speculating on such an art rather than testing it out, with the exception of Peter of Ravenna. Looking at these essays now, I can see a strong resemblance with many contemporary writings published within the field of human–computer interaction, praising the benefits of automated lifelogging. Equally, the criticism that characterizes lifelogging articles now characterized *ars mnemonica* essays then. From René Descartes to Erasmus of Rotterdam, from Heinrich Cornelius Agrippa to Francis Bacon, as if in preparation for the Enlightenment, rising northern scholars ridiculed the southern European Ciceronian trend.

It is in the lines of the criticism brought forward by Bacon (1962 [1623]), however, that we can read the striving for a new science and realize that something of the old tradition was kept. Rather than thinking of a scholar utilizing mnemonic techniques as a 'unambulist', even Bacon saw the necessity for a new instrument with which a new science could be developed. I might be the first to compare Bush's Memex to Bacon's ideas of perfect tables, and doing so can be hazardous and anachronistic. Having said that, I will further explicate this somewhat unusual comparison. Bacon thought of the new scientist as in need of perfectly designed tables to be completed in order to 'generate' new knowledge. I highlight the word 'generate', since what became evident also to Bacon is that by developing a framework in which knowledge should be seized, one is also generating new possibilities in the attempt to complete what is missing.

Now, having looked into criticism of Bacon, I like to depict a different image of the new scholar, no longer as the cyborg and scary-looking as well as threatening super-human. The criticism I have presented in the previous section is in fact mostly based on the rise of technological devices and the fetishism as well as the phobia growing around them. If we are to shift our attention instead onto the imaginary techniques that sporadic individuals have elaborated with every new paradigm, we can think of lifelogging not only as a symptom of our digital age, but also as a more meaningful source of understanding it. With this, my thought is in line with that of Marshall McLuhan, who wrote:

> In the history of human culture there is no example of a conscious adjustment of the various factors of personal and social life to new extensions except in the puny and peripheral efforts of artists. The artist picks up the message of cultural and technological challenge decades before its transforming impact occurs. He, then, builds models of Noah's arks for facing the change that is at hand. (1964, p. 77)

I thus imagine pre-Enlightenment humanists attempting to create universal systems of knowledge production, like Raymond Lull, Giordano Bruno, John Amos Comenius, and Giulio Camillo, as humanists engaged in devising imaginative media or simply as shamans, as Jacques Ellul (1964) would define them to distinguish them from *homo faber*. These shamans adhere to rituals and formulas creating a much-denigrated technology of magic that has the quality of not only reflecting the human condition affected by the technology of the *homo faber*, but also providing a remedy to heal its consequences, as also prophesied by McLuhan (1964). This concept is slightly in line with that proposed by media archaeologists (Kluitenberg 2006). Contrary to the latter, however, I am not seeking to argue for a look into the 'deep time' of the media searching for these techniques, but rather into a new kind of humanist creating these magical techniques today as we speak.

I therefore think of engaged humanists as always on the look-out for new elements to depict from the reality around them, much like the traditional figure of a poet roaming cities and landscapes with a notebook always at hand, or that of transcendentalist philosophers. I am writing this bearing in mind the criticism that followed the attempt to put into practice the very tables that Bacon's followers had developed for knowledge production (Wilkins 1668). My point here is the same as that Augustine of Hippo made in regard to the development of the *ars mnemonica*. We should not expect to develop universal methods or frameworks for others to utilize; they would simply be too rigid and arbitrary. Nonetheless, I like to stress the potential to allow, as pointed out by Augustine in regard to the *ars mnemonica* (see Yates 1966), personal frameworks of operation that are tailored by that very humanist and become meaningful to him. What I wish to say is that, if on one side scientists in the 17th century had a hard time trying to constrain their knowledge within tables developed by Baconian followers, it could have been a totally different matter if it had been suggested to these scientists to develop their own framework, or, as Paolo Rossi (1983) puts it, their own *clavis universalis*, one to access all doors of knowledge and to develop a personal understanding of all matters. As knowledge becomes increasingly relative and theoretical frameworks arbitrary over time in any case, why not allow this form of subjective knowledge to develop further?

Stepping down from the Enlightenment tradition to know beyond, and sticking to the motto '*noli altum sapere*', translatable as 'be not high-minded', subjective understandings resulting from a framework in which the observing and thinking of humanists are traced within a structure that they have developed might give rise to a different type of knowledge production, a production bringing fresh and new insights to the very transforming landscape of which the documenting subject becomes the testimony. While a recollection in tranquility is certainly always required, the repertoire of this ongoing and constant fieldwork should not be conceived as some form of art. Rather, I argue, it is a step out of a certain academic comfort; it is a step based on which a humanist decides to accept the complexity of the object of study and deals with it, producing a knowledge that is not inconsistent but 'transformative'. This knowledge does not crystallize in particular blocks setting up an ivory tower. I am aware that this could be its main weakness, as it may not be able to survive as an entity within a social, political, cultural, and economic landscape. However, it can be argued that it could better befit the new digital technology paradigm given its ubiquity and versatility. In fact, as Bush also noted, the creation of a personal referential system can allow a freer way to discuss matters more associatively, bringing the documenting subject closer to a Ciceronian; a much criticized eclectic, who is however more in line to withstand the ever-transforming complexity of modern time. This figure stands apart from that of the cyborg and that of the artist, apart then from enthusiasm for the future and adherence to past traditions. It is the figure of the now that can encompass all others.

How to Conduct Lifelogging Research

In the previous sections I have thus far attempted to justify and make space for manual lifelogging as a research method. Prior to giving a concrete example of my own lifelogging method, I will now provide a few guidelines for how to get this method to work.

Step 1: Get Aware

Take a notebook or, better, look in the print room of your university department. There should be plenty of paper printed on one side in the garbage. Pick a big enough clump and cut it in half if you can, then staple one of the shorter sides. You will have a notebook. Carry it always with you together with a pen and try to develop a certain awareness around and about yourself. Be attentive and annotate the various manifestations occurring not only during your time at work, but especially your personal life, on the metro, at home, and with friends or even better while traveling. By doing so, slowly this awareness will move into the background, allowing you to become more natural in your tracking.

By doing so, after only a month it will also be clear what streams of information befit your nature. Try to identify them clearly; work out a possible system that allows you to log the reality within and around you, sticking to the main streams of recurrences that you have identified. Try to express also the most subconscious aspects of yourself, like your dreams and imagination, and find ways to represent them in an ongoing manner. Allow a good deal of serendipity in the overall process of documentation and simplify what seems too awkward and time consuming to document. Let time design and embed lifelogging in your behavior!

Step 2: Get Digital

At this point you might feel you want to embark on another challenge and attempt to experiment with the various media offered to you by, for example, your smartphone. Besides the possibility of being able to keep up your annotation in text there via a note editor, you have a camera, a dictaphone, and other media to explore. Keep up the manual logging of your everyday life and start thinking of a system with which you can coherently bring it all together. Start to think of a virtual or physical architecture, for example, in which you can bring together your work and in which you can sit and reflect about it. You might want to print things out and order them in space, or simply compact them sequentially in various boxes, or you can use folders on your computer or create a dedicated website. In this respect, do learn how to code some basic HTML. Most importantly, do not fall for a pre-configured system arranging things for you—you will regret it and the lifelogging experience will not only diminish, but you will be doomed to a technology that will in any case shortly become obsolete.

Step 3: Get Out

You are now becoming not so much one of these much in vogue makers, you are now becoming a professional stower, sampling reality and carefully stowing it away within a pre-configured architecture that you have designed. At this point you can start sitting down and contemplating your outcomes. It is indeed not necessary to look into it in detail; the very experience of sampling and stowing has enriched you and that alone can allow you to reflect on it. You capture therefore you are! Soon enough, however, you will experience the fact that the ever more established frameworks projected onto society by corporations and institutions are constantly trying to attract you into their caves. Interestingly, now you have created an alternative place from which you can anchor one of your feet while immersing yourself with your logging device into such engulfing systems. Attempt to introduce your system within these other systems and analyze the black-out or black hole that you can potentially create.

Introducing My Personal *Clavis Universalis*

As I do not wish this chapter simply to bring forward arguments without presenting their source or any practical examples, it is time now to reveal in more concrete terms from which perspective I am talking. My perspective is an ambiguous one and I wish readers to avoid attempting any categorization while reading the description that is to come. I invite them instead to think in terms of the scattered historical background that I have thus far provided, which deals with self-crafted lifelogging as a scientific method. I am about to introduce *a sommi capi* my own method and to discuss its reception within academic contexts in more detail. I can shortly summarize that, when growing up, I kept many a journal about my thoughts, my dreams, my days, and my trips. It was my way of transcribing what I experienced by my own hand and with pen to paper. At this time I also experimented with clumsy analog equipment to interlink this journaling with filming the various processes of my daily life. In the summer of 2000—feeling fed up with carrying around and editing with 18 mm equipment—I sewed all my journals into a poncho and left Vancouver, where I was studying, to reach a remote place where I could go over my journals and at last make something out of them. I had a book in mind and months later, when I finally reached a remote peninsula in the tropics, I attempted to set up a little office space by the beach, turning my poncho into a hammock and going through my journals. It was the most depressing period of my life. I realized then how depressing it was to be retroactive, pausing life to go back to previous data.

At this point I made it back to Canada. It was the time in which the first digital devices appeared on the market and right then, unaware of any scientific discussion, I set out to develop a system to proactively deal with the rich reality around and within me (Fig. 8.4). I was about to pursue my scheme when the first academic counter came from my university

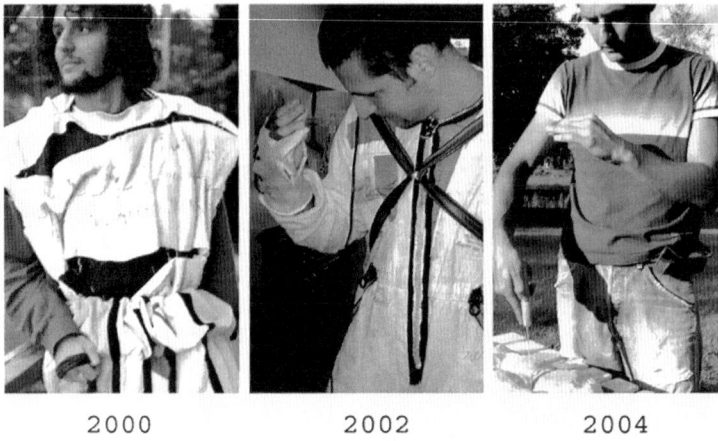

2000   2002   2004

Fig. 8.4 Showing my development from retroactive to proactive ways of capturing my life. © Alberto Frigo

professor at that time. On presenting my scheme, the old man took out his pen and crossed it through. During this early period I kept experimenting with various technologies to allow me to continuously record and annotate my life. Not only was I too clumsy in setting up a proper system, it also became too overwhelming to constantly have to deal with always-on devices recording long chunks of, for example, video. It was out of this frustration that I decided to go light and developed a system to symbolize certain thoughts and events rather than to describe them in full (see the resulting online archive at http://2004-2040.com). Rather than slaughtering technologies literally to customize them on myself, I therefore started a more successful practice of using off-the-shelf devices and being very basic, capturing only specific things at specific times.

Now, twelve years later, I have my scheme up and running. My basic tactic was to start with myself, creating a record of all my activities by photographing every object that my right hand uses (I started this on 24 September 2003, a few months before lifelogging pioneer Gordon Bell started wearing his automatic camera). From myself, I slowly developed a framework gradually embracing the reality around me. At this point in time I am conducting thirty-six projects simultaneously and I will do so until 2040, when a 12 × 12 meter calendar depicting 1,000,000 activities will have been accomplished.

The framework I have developed could potentially embrace and extend to other forms of production, such as artistic production, commercial production, and particularly academic production. Parts of the project have been branching in these directions in an escalation that has gradually attempted to map out my own productivity toward a significant palette of representative outputs with which I could engage as a humanist. Time (over ten years) as well as my involvement in the process gave me such directions. I am now able to utilize this framework of mine to deal with reality and to process it, even though it does not befit the official methods established by cultural and academic institutions. Interestingly enough, this approach is defined as art by scientists and as science by artists; either way too subjective or objective. Nonetheless, it has become a method through which I can on the one hand relate to my experience of living not so much with technology and/or through technology, but *as* technology, re-enacting procedures that devices are more and more capable of automating; and on the other confront the establishment and the faulty conventions it undertakes to uphold its economic and political power, against the natural flow and constant transformation that I experience in becoming technology.

Conclusion

In this chapter I wish to bring forward lifelogging as a possible way in which scholars should start thinking about knowledge production, stepping back from the industrialized way of patenting academic methods. I encourage new scholars to attempt to deal individually with the crafting of their own framework to capture, organize, and retrieve (or better, elaborate) their personal realities. Such crafted frameworks become particularly relevant at a time in which other digital frameworks such as those of social media have taken the upper hand. I claim these frameworks to be augmenting not the intelligentsia, but rather the dementia of a population no longer able to decide for itself, instead constantly having to check on its quantifying gadget as a new sort of confessionary priest at hand, whose only purpose is monetary. While at first glance self-crafted frameworks might seem narcissistic and/or asocial, in my experience they actually develop a strong empathy for the world surrounding the active observer, enforcing on them a common sense that gets altered in more openly philanthropic enterprises.

In this context, it is important to stress that what I have elaborated throughout this chapter is particularly relevant in the field of media studies. If we are not to believe that crafting and practicing a personal lifelogging framework can in fact create an awareness to sustain an objective reflection of reality, I am now to position another advantage of promoting these personal frameworks in an academic context. Generally speaking, the usual critique is that if we are both to create and practice these frameworks, we are not going to achieve an objective and detached point of view. Yet, applied in more concrete terms to media studies, as social media also become more invasive and embedded in media scholars' day-to-day life, making them too blended in to understand the phenomenon (at least according to the previous reasoning), the options get smaller. At this point a media scholar can look nostalgically at the past, creating an anti-environment that makes only implicit sense of contemporary transformations. Or, as I would argue instead, the very personal media framework I have been talking about so far can create the same anti-environment in the present. In other words, it creates not really an anti-environment in which to take shelter, but rather an alternative in which one can take the necessary distance from the current social media transformation. It does not escape from it nor does it promote it. Instead, it experiences it, equipped with the critical distance of an inner eye ready to impress and express what the surrounding transformation reveals to it.

Such a process, as I have already said, not only enables a more associative way of thinking, but even a more tolerant one: moving beyond the *ars mnemonica* tradition or any memory study approach, we should think of lifelogging as a method more in *ars combinatorial* terms. In the 13th century BCE the Majorcan Franciscan Raymond Lull borrowed the *zaijria*, a system of combinatorial wheels coming from the Arabs to generate new knowledge (Rossi 1983), as a way to integrate religious knowledge in the increasingly multi-cultural society of Spain. Consequently, he attempted to create a universal system not only for Christians and Muslims, but also Jews already keen on esoteric methods like the kabbalah. Now, if monotheism as well as canonical dogmatism can be conceived as the issue for integration in the world's increasingly multi-cultural landscape, perhaps lifelogging can be rethought as a mean for generating knowledge beyond any fixed framework or dogma, but crafted by any humanist for tracking purposes. Briefly, I can summarize this knowledge in six parts:

1. *Technical.* Researchers are not only asked to craft their own lifelogging framework, but to maintain it through time and along with progress that quickly makes hardware and software obsolete.

2. *Empirical.* Once the lifelogging framework is in place, researchers will necessarily come to have a better knowledge of themselves, being able to measure as well as curate their life in a balanced manner, therefore also curating aspects that modern intellectuals might not take care of, such as physical training and outdoor exposure in general, for example gardening, and generally unveiling the processes of autonomous survival.

3. *Maieutic.* Via a dedicated curation of their lifelogging framework, researchers will develop a feeling for certain threads of knowledge that might have already being developed elsewhere. Nonetheless, through their willingness to develop or maintain their framework, they will be keen to intuitively reinvestigate these threads.

4. *Ethnographic.* In order to develop and disseminate the outcome of their lifelogging framework, researchers are pushed to live in different places in which they will necessarily perfect their framework against new circumstances, but also they will annotate and filter these new circumstances on themselves.

5. *Historical.* With time, the researcher will keep registering not only the content of their framework but also examples that relate to it and to its outcome, developing a sort of personal encyclopedic universe, a culture shaped also through what they serendipitously come into contact with.

6. *Critical.* By a constant confrontation with the cultural, political, and economic establishments, researchers with their framework will necessarily develop an underlying criticism against their artificial and conventional structures.

The result is not an answer to a problem, but a system that can provide a myriad of hints from which a problem can be analyzed. It is thus producing a basis for open interpretations that are able to provide dynamic truths about reality. In this respect, lifelogging as a method can be thought of as a way to deal with constantly increasing complexity and transforming surroundings by proactively involving the researcher. It should not be misunderstood as or diminished to an artistic methodology, but rather be a meta-scientific effort going far beyond the temporal and spatial boundaries set by institutionalized academic environments. It is a quest for truth coming close to the concept of auto-ethnography, but going beyond it in that media researchers do not reject but completely embrace with their own body and mind the algorithm and automation dictating the social, political, cultural, and economic transformations at hand. It is a manual and engaged ethnography that I am advocating.

REFERENCES

Adams, T., Holman Jones, S. and Ellis, C. (2014) *Autoethnography, Understanding Qualitative Research* (Oxford: Oxford University Press).

Aurelio, M. (1980) *Pensieri* (Milan: Mondadori).

Ashby, W. (1956) *An Introduction to Cybernetics* (London: Chapman & Hall).

Bell, G., Gemmell, J. Lueder, R., et al. (2002) MyLifeBits: Fulfilling the Memex Vision. *Proceedings of the 10th ACM conference on Multimedia* (New York, USA), pp. 235–8.

Bush, V. (1945) As We May Think. *Atlantic Monthly* 176(July): 101–8.

Hodges, S., Williams, L., Berry, E., et al. (2006) SenseCam: A Retrospective Memory Aid. In P. Dourish and A. Friday (Eds.), *UbiComp 2006: Ubiquitous Computing* (Berlin: Springer), pp. 177–93.

Goodall, H. L. (2004) Narrative Ethnography as Applied Communication Research. *Journal of Applied Communication Research* 32(3): 185–94.

Kluitenberg, E. (2006) *Book of Imaginary Media: Excavating the Dream of the Ultimate Communication Medium* (Rotterdam: NAI Publishers).

Rossi, P. (1983) *Clavis Universalis: Arti della Memoria e Logica Combinatoria da Lullo a Leibniz* (Bologna: Mulino).

Bacon, F. (1962 [1623]) *The Advancement of Learning* [De augmentis scientiarum] (London and New York: Dent).

McLuhan, M. (1964) *Understanding Media: The Extensions of Man* (Cambridge, MA: MIT Press).

Mann, S. (1997) Wearable Computing: A First Step Toward Personal Imaging Cybersquare. *Computer* 30(2): 25–32.

Manovich, L. (1999) Database as Symbolic Form. *Convergence* 5(2): 80–90.

Nietzsche, F. (1980 [1874]) *On the Advantage and Disadvantage of History for Life* (Cambridge: Hackett Classics).

Rhodes, B. and Starner, T. (1996) Remembrance Agent: A Continuously Running Automated Information Retrieval System. *Proceedings of the 1st International Conference on the Practical Application of Intelligent Agents and Multi Agent Technology (PAAM '96)*, pp. 487–95.

Sellen, A. and Whittaker, S. (2010) Beyond Total Capture: A Constructive Critique of Lifelogging. *Communications of the ACM* 53(5): 70–7.

Wilkins, J. (1668) *An Essay Towards a Real Character and a Philosophical Language* (London: Gellibrand). Available at: http://quod.lib.umich.edu/cgi/t/text/text-idx?c=eebo;idno=A66045 (accessed 15 January 2016).

Yates, F. (1966) *The Art of Memory* (Chicago: University of Chicago Press).

PART III

Experience

Sarah Pink

DIGITAL ETHNOGRAPHY

Ethnography is one of the most established research approaches for doing research with and about people, their experiences, everyday activities, relationships, material cultures, social environments, and more spectacular events or performances. Ethnographers have long since worked with media, both as a research method, as a research topic, and perhaps most importantly as something that we acknowledge is an almost inevitable and universal element of everyday life. As digital technologies are increasingly ubiquitous in everyday life, as well as in the more extraordinary events and activities in which people become involved, then it becomes important to do research in a way that accounts for this, even if it does not necessarily put 'the digital' at the center of the study. While the three chapters in this part show how ethnographic methods can be fruitfully employed on film, multi-media political practices, and mobile technologies, this short introduction focuses on digital ethnography as an emerging and influential subfield.

As my colleagues from the Digital Ethnography Research Centre and I have noted in *Digital Ethnography: Principles and Practice* (Pink et al. 2016), there is no single definition of ethnography, therefore it would

S. Pink (✉)
RMIT, Melbourne, VIC, Australia
e-mail: sarah.pink@rmit.edu.au

be difficult to advance a simple statement about or guide to what digital ethnography involves. For example, ethnographic methods and processes are played out differently when they are inflected with disciplinary theories and approaches, such as in anthropology, sociology, and design research, although advocates for all fields claim to be doing ethnography. Moreover, ethnography is used across a range of interdisciplinary fields, including cultural studies and, of particular relevance to the digital, media and communication studies.

Our approach has been to focus on 'digital ethnography practice that takes as its starting point the idea that digital media and technologies are part of the everyday and more spectacular worlds that people inhabit'. This has meant taking what we have called a non-digital-centric approach to the digital, which also acknowledges the 'digital intangible'—those elements of digital environments or worlds that we can sense but not necessarily see, as well as those aspects that researchers cannot see or sense until they are made aware of them by research participants. As such, we are interested in 'the relationship between digital, sensory, atmospheric and material elements of our environments'. Therefore, digital ethnography is not a 'tool box' method that can be applied directly in an already existing format to a research problem or question. Instead, it is an approach to ethnography that involves being concerned with how the 'digital has become part of the material, sensory and social worlds we inhabit, and what the implications are for ethnographic research practice' (Pink et al. 2016, p. 7).

As I have already noted, digital ethnography will always be inflected by the theoretical and practice stances of particular disciplines and fields of study. For example, the field of 'digital anthropology' (Horst and Miller 2012) would inflect digital ethnography practice in particular ways, sometimes toward a material culture approach to understanding digital technologies as part of our worlds and environments. Other approaches, which might be more rooted in media phenomenology or phenomenological anthropology, might put human experience and perception at the center of their ways of doing digital ethnography (Pink and Leder Mackley 2013). Other related but different approaches can be found in a series of other volumes that likewise seek to develop ways of doing ethnography that engage with digital environments and the human relationships that are implicated through them, such as in the work of the sociologist Christine Hine (2015), the anthropologist Tom Boellstorff (2008), and others.

Nevertheless, the important point to keep in mind is that throughout these different renderings of the relationship between the digital and ethnography is the consistent recognition that we need to engage with the digital as part of the way in which we operate as ethnographers. I do not go into detail here about the different methods used, but the chapters in this book will provide some examples. However, I would emphasize that just as digital ethnography can be shaded and directed by disciplinary theory, it is also always developed as part of specific projects. Digital ethnography methods have included doing ethnography online and as such participating with people online as part of the research process; interviewing people with their technologies; accompanying people as they use digital technologies in everyday life; asking people to make images that they post online and working with them to understand their meanings; or video-recording people as they use technologies or demonstrate their uses of technologies in everyday life, and asking them to reflect on these activities.

These research methods are, however, not a set of pre-determined techniques that are subsequently applied, but are always evolved as part of a specific research project, question design, and practice. Methods can vary depending on circumstance, because they need to be responsive. What is more important to keep in mind as a constant influence in any ethnographic process is the need to consider some of the core principles that have become embedded in most approaches to ethnographic practice. These include the need to be reflexive about the ways in which we produce knowledge, the status of that knowledge, and subsequently what this tells us about what that knowledge can mean academically, and if disseminated in non-academic contexts. It also brings to the fore the idea of ethnography, particularly in anthropology, as involving doing research *with* rather than *about* people. That is, it is always a collaborative exercise.

This means that digital media are part of the worlds in which we live and research, they are part of the lives of our research participants, they are part of the tools and techniques that we use to do ethnographic research, and they are equally implicated in the ways in which we and others represent and disseminate our work. Digital technologies also form alliances with particular ways of doing ethnography, enabling us to enhance that practice in new ways. For instance, the possibilities for participatory ethnographic techniques increase as online collaboration with research participants becomes possible. Other examples include the parallel or linked possibility of doing ethnography *in public* to different degrees and extents (see Pink and Abram 2015). For example, John Postill's ethnographic research with groups of internet activists whom he calls 'freedom technologists' involves him writing up fieldnotes and blog entries as he goes along, in ways that are in correspondence with the people who participate in his projects (Postill 2015). His *media/anthropology* blog therefore creates a kind of public digital ethnography, beyond public scholarship as it has been conceived in the past.[1] Another example is the *Mobilizing Media for Sustainable Outcomes in the Pacific Region* project, led by Heather Horst, Jo Tacchi, and Dominic Friguglietti. This project uses the 'Research from the Field' section of its blog to bring together the on-the-ground research with the design of a tool kit in conversation with the project's industry organization, ABC International Development, and the Pacific Media Assistance Scheme. The blog posts range from insights and trends emerging through research on mobile phones, social media, and the internet to development practitioners and filmmakers using media in Communication for Development initiatives.

Indeed, the possibility of making digital ethnography projects come alive online as they emerge and develop creates new ways to engage research participants, other academics, and students with research in progress. A good example of this is the *Locating the Mobile* website, where the research team has posted examples of the work that the collaborative team spanning Australia, Japan, and China produced during the fieldwork process. The website shows ongoing work on mobile locative media and privacy in families through accessible written and photographic texts, as well as news updates and other materials. The *Energy and Digital Living* website is an example of a different way of engaging with the possibilities of digital media in relation to research and design that involved the study of people's relationships with digital technologies and the making of digital design interventions for energy demand reduction. In the research process digital video methods were used extensively, and digital technologies were also important for the wider project team's work, involving energy monitoring and measurement. However, part of our ethnography work in this project was also to research how people used digital technologies in their everyday lives. In this project, differently to the two discussed earlier, the website was constructed after the project was completed. This was because it was conceived partly as a site through which we could tell the stories of the project once we had gained certain insights and understandings, and because we wanted participants to be able to make informed decisions, over time, about how or if they wanted to be depicted on video on the website. The site also has different aims in terms of its potential audiences, seeking to be accessible yet also an introduction to a digital research and design theme, methodology and project, and set of materials, which can be viewed by people interested in the issues, students, and researchers.

To conclude, digital ethnography is not just one method or research strategy. It is based in an acknowledgment that we need to theorize and understand how the digital has become part of the world in which we live and research. It is not simply about studying how people use digital media, or using digital media to study people. Instead, it is concerned with a wider vision of how everything we do as ethnographic researchers is happening in ways that might be more or less relational to digital media, and an acknowledgment that we will continue to change with them as we move on into the future.

NOTES

1. For this and the websites mentioned subsequently, see: http://johnpostill. com, https://sites.google.com/site/mobilisingmediainthepacific/research-from-the-field, http://locatingthemobile.net, and http://energyanddigi-talliving.com (all accessed 10 March 2016).

REFERENCES

Boellstorff, T. (2008) *Coming of Age in Second Life: An Anthropologist Explores the Virtually Human* (Princeton: Princeton University Press).

Hine, C. (2015) *Ethnography for the Internet: Embedded, Embodied and Everyday* (London: Bloomsbury).

Horst, H. and Miller, D. (Eds.) (2012) *Digital Anthropology* (London: Berg).

Pink, S., Horst, H., Postill, J., et al. (2016) *Digital Ethnography: Principles and Practice* (London: Sage).

Pink, S. and Leder Mackley, K. (2013) Saturated and Situated: Rethinking Media in Everyday Life. *Media, Culture and Society* 35(6): 677–91.

Pink, S. and Abram, S. (Eds.) (2015) *Media, Anthropology and Public Engagement*, (Oxford: Berghahn).

Postill, J. (2015) Public Anthropology in Times of Media Hybridity and Global Upheaval. In S. Pink and S. Abram (Eds.), *Media, Anthropology and Public Engagement* (Oxford: Berghahn), pp. 164–81.

CHAPTER 9

Visual Ethnography and the City: On the Dead Ends of Reflexivity and Gentrification

Emily LaDue

Ethnography can be understood as an accumulation of knowledge and information, and visual ethnography as an accumulation of images. Urban development can be understood as an accumulation of property, rent, and finance capital. Reflexivity and gentrification, two ways of looking at these processes of accumulation, represent an actual desire for actual resistance to anti-colonial methods of research and anti-capitalist methods of organizing our world. However, they fall short by design. The discursive work of both the reflexive turn and the gentrification critique allows for a personal reflection or orientation to stand in for what may be considered politics—an engaged and organized strategy of resistance to the structural institutions creating inequalities and toward building better institutions. An examination of the reflexive turn and the gentrification critique may offer visual ethnographers and urban ethnographers insight into the dead ends of these fixes when used as a politics in and of themselves, and the dangers in the reception of work that relies on researcher reflexivity and a critique of gentrification alone. Our scholarly research

E. LaDue (✉)
University of Pennsylvania, Philadelphia, PA, USA
e-mail: eladue@asc.upenn.edu

© The Author(s) 2016
S. Kubitschko, A. Kaun (eds.), *Innovative Methods in Media and Communication Research*, DOI 10.1007/978-3-319-40700-5_9

may be contributing to an ever-expanding knowledge base, but it is as urgent a time for productive and meaningful work toward a restructuring of our lives as ever, as we experience an increase in income gaps, precarity of jobs, prison populations, state violence, and health and environmental inequalities, along the same race- and class-based lines as since the beginning of the history of capitalism.

The political dead end of these 'critical' methodologies proves useful: it can reveal to us the structure of disorientation, and take the emphasis away from our individual mis- or disorientation. Thinking of fixing gentrification or making it better, or even deploying a 'development for all' model, like a reflexive addition to our ethnographic methodology, reaffirms a colonial apologetic position, that those who have been historically recognized by civil society as subjects are the ones who can change this relationship. In critiquing gentrification, those considering themselves as partaking in, furthering, and benefitting from gentrification maintain their position as actors capable of change—they are part of why gentrification is happening, and therefore their actions can improve it. While populations moving back to cities are indeed acting, they are acting according to a logic of capital, and to act antagonistically to gentrification would require more than adjusting behaviors. Thus, to challenge this logic, we must reorientate the tools for analysis. Both gentrification and self-reflexivity have perhaps become such ubiquitous topics in gentrifying cities and in ethnographic research because they stop short of a critique of the organization and trajectory of capital.

In this chapter, I examine two critical methodological turns: the reflexive turn in ethnographic methods as an attempted methodological fix for colonialist relationships in anthropology, and the gentrification critique of urban development as an attempted discursive and theoretical fix for pro-growth development. I first give a brief overview of the reflexive turn and argue its limitations. Next, I describe how the critical lens of gentrification is analogous to reflexivity and why it is productive to understand this mirrored relationship as part of a structural positionality of power and whiteness. Taking off from here, I present a possible methodological approach to break with this orientation. The clarity in understanding about these processes and these propositions is based on the work and research I have done with El Kilombo Intergalactico, a community organization in Durham, NC, USA, dedicated to bringing together people of color, migrants, students, and low-income residents building to determine their shared future.

Throughout my research of the city, I have benefitted from learning from El Kilombo and its members' ten years of collective intellectual production of information and analysis about Durham and, more generally, the working of capitalism in the city. My methods for studying the city in my current research project have evolved from seminars and discussions with them. In order to appropriately credit El Kilombo's thinking, provide useful research, and ultimately write this chapter, one methodological conclusion that we have reached that we believe is fair and appropriate to the work of their community assembly is to position their thinking in my research as another theoretical apparatus to understand the city. By my use of information from seminars, discussions, and literature they have produced, they will appear in this study as another source of knowledge and theory.[1]

REFLEXIVITY

As the history of anthropology coincides with the history of colonialism, and through the work of many of those cited here, ethnography as a method has been working to reinvent itself as subversive to these tendencies. Michael Taussig provokes the idea that when race, gender, and other signifiers were social constructions, 'the brilliance of the pronouncement was blinding' so that 'the beginnings of knowledge were made to pass for actual knowing' (1993, p. xvi). Reflexivity had this affect on anthropology—it was a first step toward decolonizing the discipline, but it was taken as an end; and then arguably served to curtail efforts at decolonizing anthropology from radical Black and Brown movements and scholarship across the world (Harrison 1997). James Clifford and George Marcus (1986) are usually credited with bringing in the reflexive turn, although this can be seen as part of the problem in the crediting of the movement toward reflexivity. Perhaps it was the struggles of decolonization and within that refusing to be objectified by the West that led anthropologists to have to put their structural positioning into question.[2] The reflexive turn is often discussed as a product of the post-modern turn, but both are symptomatic reactions of the institutionalized West to the political struggles of the mid-20th century (see Reyes 2012). The direction of knowledge is from struggle to researcher, regardless of whether there is a reflexive account built in of how that process is taking place (Buck-Morss 2009). This is the point where an intervention must be made on two levels if we are to be politically engaged: where we position ourselves as researchers in relation to political struggle, and who and what our research is serving. I return to this in the final section of the chapter.

The reflexive turn in anthropology came as a corrective to the colonial apparatus that anthropology was built to support, but is constantly falling short because the basis of its research is acceptance of the other—even the self as other—at times perhaps putting into question why and how we are othered from each other and ourselves, but never actually able to struggle against that global structure and condition. Since Clifford and Marcus's *Writing Culture* in 1986, the debate over thick description and thin description made a turn to a particular style and poetics that can be used to communicate effectively what it is that we study ethnographically. This attention to style has been at the center of these anthropological debates—not the act of research itself, but the ways on which anthropologists are presenting their work. But as Mascia-Lees et al. warn, 'Anthropologists influenced by postmodernism have recognized the need to claim a politics in order to appeal to an anthropological audience' that is thirsty for inclusion and knowledge about the world-changing movements of the colonized and ghettoized populations of the world (1989, p. 14). Yet in arguing that the reflexive turn is another demonstration of the power of the male ethnographer and serves only to reinforce the power and direction of the male ethnographic gaze, a move made by feminist theory decades earlier, they too fail to consider the struggles for life and liberation of indigenous and colonized people for the past five hundred years, with the struggle of women fitting into that history as well. Their argument falls short as equating the relationship of anthropologist to native to the relationship of man to woman—because, for one, what of native women, a discussion more fully wrought by Trinh Minh-Ha that same year, and what of the world structure built on the relationship of colonizer to colonized (Trinh 1989; Mies 1986)?

Reflexive, distinct from only reflective, does not merely imply peering at ourselves, but taking ourselves into account as we work and making adjustments. Clifford and Marcus's *Writing Culture* culminates in this idea and brings to light the importance of Geertz's 'thick description' and the researcher's positioning as a vessel for observation and analysis (Clifford and Marcus 1986; Geertz 1973). John Jackson's intervention calling for 'thin description' asks researchers instead to take seriously the notion that we do not know everything, we cannot observe everything, and that the move to make claims to know everything is subscribing to a belief in a purity of culture that just is not sincere (Jackson 2013). Thin description becomes a critique of reflexivity where, Jackson writes, 'Ethnography at its best is a small attempt to create this alternative magic, to provide various paths along a variegated and mystical roadway, alternative tactics for breaking death's ironclad chokehold' (Jackson 2013, p. 13). In other words, it can help us understand the actual living world of which we are a part and parse out our 'zombified notions' that both haunt us and feed us—but when we kill the zombies, what remains in their place? The iron chokehold of death is likely more related to the inability for another world that we desire to be built within these structures.

We engage in reflexive practices when we realize that we get to do this work from a comfortable position, when it feels like we are part of the problem, and when our subjects make it clear to us directly or through the knowledge they impart that we are only mediators between the power of social science and the lives and social, political, and economic conditions of those we study. Jackson has nudged us: 'Actively capturing our own demise (in images, sounds, and words) might be one way to negotiate such disciplinary death and dying, just one more way to make a case for what the future of ethnography is and ain't' (Jackson 2012, p. 495). In other words, to recognize instead that we are indeed part of this structure, but are just as disempowered or empowered as those we study in challenging it, may be a good starting point to move past this dead end.

Filming Ourselves

Not least because digital media and ways to play digital media are in the hands of more people, and books and journals from academic presses are not, video offers a possible intervention if produced for these purposes. Faye Harrison noted both Zora Neale Hurston's and Katherine Dunham's use of literature and dance to share knowledge more broadly beyond the academy before it was in vogue to do so (Harrison 1997, p. 6). Just as the current call for body cameras on police officers is limited because it keeps the power of the camera in the hands of the powerful, and because discussions of gentrification are being used to fill in for actual structural antagonism (or being used to prevent it), calling on anthropologists to record what they are doing through video does not disrupt the flow and direction of vision. Margaret Mead (2003) called on anthropologists to use the filmic and photographic technology available to them to record people and their behavior in order more clearly—in other words, more scientifically—to understand and represent them, because of the additional knowledge and observation available in an image. Instead, we can think about flipping and critically examine why we are relying on the visual to wipe our hands and eyes clear of our own role in perpetuating what we intend on critiquing.

Films can present us with ways to understand our own positioning as researchers, and as actors, in building the city. We are left in a position where the real, and the sincere, have been gentrified as well. As Sarah Pink summarizes, reflexivity does not mean that 'subjectivity could (or should) be avoided or eradicated [...]. Ethnographic knowledge and text can only ever be a subjective construction, a "fiction" that represents only the ethnographer's version of a reality, rather than an empirical truth' (Pink 2013, p. 23). So why do ethnography? And does ethnography have any way to move beyond an individual's interpretation of a subject? In the face of cultural debates about ethnographic authenticity, and a profound emphasis on what is real and authentic, Jackson has called for ethnographic sincerity, rather than authenticity. Yet this too begs for more, if the ends being pursued are beyond the research and toward a liberatory politics.

When we refer to gentrification, the acknowledgment that it is happening begins to be the critique and to pass for actual understanding of how gentrification is a particular manifestation of capitalism operating at this time. Much like the idea of reflexivity in film, the concept of gentrification implies a discourse of critique, but only requires an observation that there is something or even just a notion that something uncomfortable is happening. Documentaries about gentrification demonstrate this reflexivity as politics most visibly and offer a productive way to understand the dead ends of discourses of gentrification and reflexivity; the intersection of the two demonstrates the impossibility of moving beyond the terrain of the reflexive. This occurs in Kelly Anderson's film *My Brooklyn*, which provides well-researched data about rent-intensifying development in Brooklyn, and offers one way to think through these abstracted analyses of capital and politics, by positioning corporations and the city officials who back them as the cause of gentrification. The film is being screened in gentrifying cities across the country, attended by various audiences, and offers useful information about how major corporations and developers are working with politicians and profiting from the historical disinvestment of the inner cities.

The film studies gentrification through the eyes of a self-critical gentrifier. In the end, she is left thinking alone about her role in all of this, a dead end to the struggle that is actually where it leaves many of us; without a strategy or political project to which it relates, where does it leave us but as isolated individuals with little power to act and only power to reflect and critique, a valuable but ancillary function? The film does not have to offer solutions, but by positing that if better policies to prevent massive development and the self-reflection of gentrifiers may offer a way out, it leaves power in the hands of those same people. When an ethnographer or filmmaker includes their own role in perpetuating a process that they are critiquing, it reveals to us not their 'ethnographic sincerity', but their lack of ability to be both 'in and out'—revealing this position reveals a definitive in, perhaps because of the ability of the academy to accommodate critique without any change (Jackson 2005; Harrison 2008). The cause of gentrification is placed on corporations and city officials supporting corporate development, which then allows a false sense of unity and community to appear among the characters in the film, including Anderson. Anderson's making of the film is equated with her taking responsibility for these actions. This film does offer us a chance to do ethnography on a text categorized as documentary but presenting itself as a reflexive study, with the filmmaker giving the audience a narrative of herself and her positionality in relation to her subject, in this case gentrification. Arguably, the film presents a collective voice of Brooklyn rooted in a structural position of black and brown communities as represented through interviews and footage of organized attempts to stop certain developments. However, it does not articulate this as such, but instead operates from a reflexive position, Anderson a gentrifier looking not to be, and realizing that may not be an option without dramatic change. The vague horizon of change ends without a politics, and with an individual consumer-based view of gentrification that leaves the viewer being asked to be sympathetic to Anderson and to blame other structures of capitalist power for this process.

The Empty Political Orientation of Gentrification

Neil Smith (1996), theorizing on the limits of studying gentrification as a consumer-driven process, offered a critique of what in anthropology we know as the reflexive turn. He observed how post-modern and post-structuralist theory offered a way to view gentrification as culturally driven and a form of 'emancipatory politics' for the gentrifier, with resources from a family history of being white and being offered state resources, but now rejecting that suburban life created by her parents' generation, now able to create whatever life she imagines in the state-abandoned spaces of inner cities. The freedom to reject suburban life, posed as racist, judgmental, and old, gives both the gentrifier and the researcher the image of political intent and action through whatever individual action may be undertaken (Smith 1996, p. 41). Observed in cities across the world, gentrifying neighborhoods are marked by defining features of individualism, consumerism, and humanitarian discourses and actions that are manifest in businesses such as CrossFit gyms, yoga studios, cafés, jazz clubs, and breweries. In sociology, Sharon Zukin (1982, 2014) and David Grazian (2003) have offered extensive research on the consumption cultures of gentrification and the desire of white middle-class populations to get close to what they see as authentic culture—through consuming blackness in the form of historically black cultural production (jazz, blues, soul, and hip hop music; soul food) and in cultures centered around the consumption of a product able to contain various levels of dedication and erudition (coffee, beer, and various food trends). The prevalence of individual improvement and focus on the self in the form of body sculpting, meditation, extreme athletics, and health food demonstrates a crossover between individualism and humanitarianism, such as with yoga studios offering various retreats involving community service and donations to various aid groups, charity races, and free 'community days' at CrossFit gyms.

The focus on the individual and their place in the world and responsibility as a 'global citizen' has given ample reasoning and justification for socially responsible consumerism, popularly represented by companies such as Whole Foods—which took over many spaces that were previously run by local cooperatives in cities; now, in cities such as Durham, NC, cooperatives opened as anchors in gentrifying neighborhoods are reopening and positioning themselves as the local alternative to Whole Foods. In these spaces a working critique of gentrification is now operating. In Durham, at the grand opening of the new co-op, representatives from its non-profit landlord raised the issue of whether what they are doing is gentrification, during a conversation about the role of the co-op in attracting wealthier populations into the black working-class neighborhood within which it sits. Duke University, a major actor in the redevelopment of Durham for the past two decades, sponsored and hosted a talk in one of its redeveloped warehouse spaces about gentrification in the city. The talk, by a former city planner and homeowner in one of the most rent-intensifying districts in the city, offered a brief history of unequal development in cities, detailed research on the levels of rent intensification in gentrifying neighborhoods, and a discussion about what to do about it. The discussion centered on solutions such as being a good neighbor, supporting land trusts, and voting for compassionate representatives—all of whom have supported pro-growth policies or 'development for all' policies. These solutions all share a common focus on the gentrifier being able to continue operating as such, but with concerted efforts toward vague aspirations of community and responsibility. I do not doubt that many people are concerned about inequalities in cities and their role in perpetuating them, but the turn toward individual actions as solutions, even when done by many individuals, continues to fall short of an actual organized critique or resistance to the decline of social welfare and housing, the displacement of communities, and the inequality of resource availability. Moreover, the university, once perhaps a place for sustained critique, is performing as such while acting as the political and economic backbone of rent-intensifying (Reed 1999) development in the city (El Kilombo seminar 2014). The university hosts its own spaces of critique, and as researchers interested in political and social justice, we must actually grapple with this contradiction.

Grittiness: The Popular Reflexivity of Gentrification

Gentrification has become a ubiquitous term in cities undergoing the process that the concept attempts to capture. Disinvested areas of cities are gradually inhabited by and developed according to the tastes of the new population, who have economic and mobile flexibility and, as the common understanding goes, are looking for a lifestyle and situation that is more diverse, stylish, and matched to their tastes. These populations are moving to and building in previously disinvested post-industrial cities, but they are reflecting on and discussing the changes in our urban landscapes across various media platforms. Blogs, magazines, and newspapers have been covering recent waves of gentrification, and some are exclusively focused on covering news on the gentrification front, such as the *Atlantic Cities* subpublication and local blogs and features in newspapers (in Durham, for example, at least a dozen blogs have come, and some gone, covering that city as a subject). Place-based lifestyle magazines promote cities and focus on shaping identities and highlighting new restaurants, event spaces, and shops while shaping historical narratives (Greenberg 2000; Jenkins 2016; and my own research on publications in North Carolina). A significant number of these publications are explicitly engaging with the concept of gentrification and critically encountering changes in the city, for an audience of readers who are taking part in these processes. The field of action and subjecthood is consistent.

As Smith outlined, the idea of gentrification was useful, but perhaps now it does not work as a way to describe the situation happening in cities. As he notes, the term gentrification emerged in the mid-1960s with sociologist Ruth Glass, in the midst of a 'nascent counterculture' in Greenwich Village and other middle-class relocations to the city throughout Europe, North America, and Australia (Smith 1996, p. 35). This counterculture relied on the cheaper urban spaces that had been disinvested for a place to live. Now, in addition to the cheaper rent, the counterculture relies on the critique of gentrification itself for a place to live. Durham-based writer Matt Hartman alludes to this in a recent article entitled 'Branding the Commons' in *Jacobin Magazine*: 'Yet development is now not only targeting public land, but the public itself, the very culture that ties a community together' (Hartman 2015, n.p.). He makes a distinction between a past development that did not include 'cultural capitalism' to a development that now capitalizes on the 'grittiness' that used to be a source of pride for the 'people of Durham' (Hartman 2015). Two questions arise: Who are the people who 'developed a pride in the "grittiness"' and what is contained in a term like grittiness? It is this pride in grittiness that is exactly the methodological, and political, challenge that I am attempting to (compassionately) critique. In other words, productive research is neither about our feelings toward those with fewer rights or resources who are the subjects of our research or our new neighbors on their way out; nor is it about how to improve gentrification/capitalism or return to liberalism because it has gone bad (it has always been this way)—the issue is that our current economic and political structural organization is not working for any of us, not for those for whom it has never worked, who we can clearly see are abandoned and criminalized now as the surplus, or for those of us who are relying on their dispossession to flourish, but need constant mirages of politics and critique in order to just barely live with ourselves (Wacquant 2009, 2012; El Kilombo 2015).

Nearly a decade ago, a now displaced community of mostly Latino and African American residents, in the neighborhood that has now become the alt-downtown bar scene, led a struggle to fulfill a standing public resolution and retain a full-sized soccer field in a park that was the center of community life, in the face of a behind-the-scenes proposal to transform the park into a place that suited the desires of a selective, majority-white charter school next door. Ultimately, the city drafted a resolution that left the park closed for a year, a critical year in which nearly the entire community was priced out of the neighborhood as houses and apartments flipped and the area filled with eight bars and restaurants.

During this struggle, the community center in the neighborhood that was working to save the field, El Kilombo Intergalactico, began flagging up the resulting inequalities of Durham's wave of development and relating it to the recent historical wave of gentrification across the world. They have written a thorough account of this struggle (see El Kilombo 2011). Hundreds of low-income residents and their supporters filled city council and other quasi-public meetings about the park, and a handful of their opponents would turn out as well. It was during the park struggle that I began filming gentrification and its resistance in Durham, and studying with El Kilombo. However, outside of those being displaced in the neighborhood, El Kilombo, and several community supporters, no one wanted to hear that gentrification was happening in Durham. Even supporters of the community viewed this as an isolated struggle, and in my interviews and in local media, Durham was being conceived and discussed as successfully avoiding gentrification, and as doing development better than other cities such as Brooklyn, NY, Portland, OR, Austin, TX, and San Francisco, CA. In fact, several of the supporters were new to Durham from these other cities, leaving in part to escape gentrification. In Durham, they said, people were aware that this *could* happen, but were taking steps to provide opportunities to poor people, preserve low-income housing, and include several voices in this development.

Since then, six new hotels have been built, dozens of restaurants and bars have opened, and major neighborhoods have shifted. According to census reports, the quickest-changing neighborhoods near downtown have changed by over 40 % from low to high income. Durham Innovation District built in old warehouse spaces to attract biotech research and development companies. Suddenly, discussions of gentrification are brimming. Articles have circulated in news and social media (Cook 2014; Lilly 2013; Hartman 2015). An art exhibit in a downtown gallery entitled Durham Under Development went on view in February 2016, and includes several 'community events' including community forums, artist receptions, and a spoken word and dance performance. Two hotels are sponsors of the show, and proudly boast about their own local space and community development work, while carefully recognizing that there is a long way to go for equality in the city.

The currency of this show is the issue of Durham's development and its effects, and at each event there is a spoken-in-earnest desire to engage with broader populations while acknowledging the work to be done to get to this point. This call for inclusivity and to get a more diverse population at this constructed platform marks a power of language in constructing and regulating value. Without stating this, these events would not be considered progressive, or perhaps not even considered art. This expressed desire goes a long way in garnering positive responses from the crowds at the events; the currency of poverty, and the currency of blackness, goes a long way in discussions of gentrification by those considered to be part of the gentrifying populations. Those participating in the gentrification of cities, like ethnographers, are obsessed with what they are doing. Images of resistance to development, and resistance to structural power relations, are officially trending. Now the neighborhood around the park and downtown has become a space for middle-class consumption, and the stakes are one's own image of oneself, which looks decidedly better when drinking in a new café and critiquing gentrification, perhaps an affect of 'cruel optimism' about the sustainability of our world (Berlant 2011).

Historically, these rhetorical nods to change have been recorded as ineffective and as perpetuating racial structures. This is a notably distinct moment from the fight led by organized black communities for inclusivity in housing and development in the post-Depression and post-war United States. At that time, the Underwriting Manual of the Federal Housing Administration (FHA) and neighborhood racial covenants made it legal to discriminate on mortgages based on race until 1950, and the practice continued long after. Organized black resistance pressured the FHA to change the language of its Underwriting Manuals that listed the requirements to receive government-backed mortgages for banks in the 1930s and 1940s: a change from excluding black populations explicitly in 1944, to a language of protecting against 'adverse influences' (Freund 2010, p. 209). Now, white revanchist populations are asking for the voices of those being displaced and not benefitting from expensive hotels and restaurants to be part of the conversation—to come to the newly developed downtown spaces built largely in part to the historical racism and government neglect and devaluation of these properties in the past. Thus, when the organizer of the exhibit asks 'How do we reach into other communities?', the coded other is the same coded other as the devalued populations of the government-backed building of the white suburbs that so many are now escaping. This is the rhetoric that is at work in what I am studying as development media, an ethnographic approach grounded in communications that I am attempting in place of a reflexive ethnography.

STUDYING UP, PRODUCING KNOWLEDGE

How to 'study up' then, and interview the developers, planners, and officials who view the poor in the city as 'cockroaches', as one executive remarked in an interview, in need of scattering via lights being turned on? This is where researching from a position of political grounding is the most sincere and productive—how else to produce a useful ethnography if not from the honest position of a critique of the powerful interests at work? John Jackson writes of his ethnography of the 'racioscape,' in which 'to think' it is to:

> Imagine an engagement with what is usually left over from (and left out of) academic theories of racial essentialism and social constructedness. It is ethnography of the fake, the simulated, the counterfeit, if only insofar as such a predilection helps us peek through reality's opened back doors. (Jackson 2005, p. 59)

If my work is an ethnography of the 'gentrification-scape', the field of discourse around development in Durham, through a study of a particular non-profit institution involved in development in the city, studying the discourses that give rise to actual value production requires a study of the discourses at work, including the reflexive discussions of gentrification.

In ethnographic practices, the focus on this decentering of the subject has led to a dramatic inward, individual focus of the researcher and her role in the research process. In this way, socially responsible consumerism is akin to socially responsible research. In politically oriented and social justice research, a potential for research appears when we are earnestly trying to address a lack of knowledge or understanding on a subject and shed light on or fix inequalities that we see around us. As researchers, at best, we can offer useful information and analysis about the world in which we live and where it may be going. To push the cynical view, our work is dependent on the existence of suffering and inequality, and the academy allows us to study and critique this without an organized response to it. This may not be the world for which we asked, but since it is the world in which we live, we are also complicity partaking in a form of extractivism. The reflexive turn in ethnography provided, and provides, a way for ethnographers to account for inequalities in power, much like gentrification allows us to account for inequality without compromising the structure that keeps it in place. I am not calling for a return to positivistic anthropology, nor am I calling for researchers to ignore their own positionality in their work. I am urging that instead of flagging their own position and its influence on the work, a more productive politics may be to incorporate a resulting analysis of this position into the research conducted in the first place.

Examining whether the work we do is being produced in common and for a community in resistance, or is being produced in common and used for academic debate, is key. In 2012, Mara Kaufman, writing as part of the organized community El Kilombo in Durham, urged for a reorientation toward knowledge production and organization and away from the idea of bridging a gap between academia and activism regarding social change (Kaufman). As Kaufman notes, producing ourselves for the market as academics 'risks becoming the management function of this […] self-managed human capital driven by cultural more than wage capital' (2012, p. 824), and in the activist sphere, the various activities undertaken by an individual become resume assets of how well one manages oneself. Now, these activities and relationships with community organizations can be traded in as assets toward an academic future as well—working with community organizations, showing dedication to the political cause of the research, and declaring authentic intentions. As Kaufman writes: 'The myth of leading one's own life […] is built on a refusal of a process of subjectivation beyond our control, leading us back again to the illusion that holding progressive policy positions or making ourselves visible as participants in particular activities constitutes doing politics' (Kaufman 2012, p. 826).

Moreover, it is far too easy to 'mine' the communities we study: 'individually extracting that great wealth of intelligence and innovation that serious, ongoing collective organization generates' (Kaufman 2012, p. 825). Reflexivity in our work risks allowing for this mining while acknowledging that it may be happening, and may turn back and even distract us from recognizing that it is happening at all. The ethnographer is a person who finds almost any experience interesting because any experience can be studied. Unfortunately, with the university behind that person, that drive can have consequences of dispossession and destruction for a community or a neighborhood. Or, the ethnographer can take and leave without much of a trace, and continue a career taking material and immaterial artifacts in the name of elite knowledge.

Beginning in the mid-1990s, universities participated in reflexivity on a large scale. They began spending thousands of dollars and committing faculty and student time to social entrepreneurship and community engagement, while encouraging and rewarding it in admissions and other promotions. Community service centers, service learning, and documentary projects abound at top research universities. At the two universities I have attended, for example, Duke University in Durham, NC and the University of Pennsylvania in Philadelphia, PA, the community service centers were developed as part of an effort to improve the public image of the universities and the cities in which they were situated. A required component of these experiential programs is student reflection, often in the form of blog posts and 'letters home', discussing what they are learning and how what they are learning is changing them. These programs add authenticity, intention, and value to the lives of university students and researchers, while making claims to benefit surrounding communities deemed in need of such services. Services such as tutoring, ESL (English as a second language) assistance, and skills sharing can of course be of some benefit to those giving and receiving; however, in the larger context of the role of universities and their wide-ranging corporate and non-profit collaborators, these programs may very likely do more work for the university than for those on the receiving end.

As these shifts coincide directly with the retrenchment of state-provided welfare and education services, they can be viewed as integral to the generalized global move toward non-profit management of citizen welfare, a precarious level of care that is rooted in and dependent on unequal development. Current and former public relations officers and administrators at these institutions credit the reason for their development as improving the image of the university in the eyes of students and parents, as well as in the eyes of the cities where these universities operate (Author Interviews 2014). The value of the positive image making, the mined knowledge for the students' erudition and meaningful lines on a résumé, and the spaces of capital investment and securitization of property for the university is incomparable to hours of tutoring.

These efforts keep knowledge and power moving in one direction—from those lacking in basic services to the university itself and the students, who are moving to increasingly the only available jobs, in non-governmental organization (NGO) and development work. Susan Buck-Morss wrote of the influence of the Haitian revolution on Hegel's master–slave dialectic and his lack of acknowledgment of this influence (Buck-Morss 2000).

The Enlightenment ideals of freedom and self-determination stem from slave rebellions, although they were put to use to violently distinguish white men from black men in terms of what made a human, and the Enlightenment thinkers are credited with these concepts. Buck-Morss notes that 'this glaring discrepancy between thought and practice marked the period of the transformation of global capitalism from its mercantile to its protoindustrial form' (2000, p. 821), which is key to understanding the role that the self-critical researcher is playing in this transformational moment of late capitalism. The discourse of community engagement and social justice is pervasive in the university as poverty worsens, ghettos are reinscribed, and a liberal elite grows.

Thus, to claim a political orientation, and to transform these relationships, we must position ourselves and act with communities in struggle, as well as studying the world as it is to understand what we are up against. Nader (1972) called on researchers to look at power with as discerning an eye as we look at those we see as having less power. In 'Up the Anthropologist: Perspectives Gained from *Studying Up*', she speaks to researchers who are wrestling with why we study what we do and where this information goes, with an assumed worldview that there are gross human inequalities that should be addressed and amended. There have been several stunning ethnographies about bureaucracies, governments, and Wall Street, for example the work of Karen Ho, Melissa Fisher, and Caitlin Zaloom (Ho 2009; Fisher 2012; Zaloom 2010). Nader's method of studying up forces us to reframe our questions about inequalities and shift the blame and burden to those wielding power, instead of those surviving in the face of disempowerment. It seems that we need also to figure out what that process of education can be in order to be effective, and what worlds we are a part of and trusted by. In order to do something with this knowledge, there must be a certain existing level of organization and strategy regarding those we imagine to be receiving this knowledge. Kaufman's (2012) insistence on orientating ourselves toward knowledge production and organization rather than academia and activism is one step out.

A Study of Development Media

In order to understand how economic and cultural processes are causing extreme poverty to worsen and inequality gaps to widen, and maybe begin to organize 'our way out of this mess' (El Kilombo 2015), we do need to conduct serious research about what is happening in the world. Thus, without attempting to theorize my individual role and what I could ever possibly do as an individual to stop/improve/change the gentrification process, I instead seek to uncover and explicate the current and historical conditions of possibility of rent-intensifying development and its ideological sustenance in Durham through an ethnographic research project of studying up. One method of interrogating this vast history and discursive field is through studying what I call the 'development media' that are produced to support pro-growth, rent-intensifying development: policy documents, news media, federal applications, planning literature, master plans, bureaucratic documents, human actors, oral histories, social media, building design and structure, the interactions of these media with one another, and discourses that circulate with a critique of gentrification built in. The criteria for these development media are that which is producing and reproducing ideologies about how and why development can and should occur in the city. This allows me to interrogate the premise that rent-intensifying development is needed, how and why the present public and private reinvestment in Durham is happening, and what information is circulated and how.

Part of these development media are the discourses critiquing gentrification, and spying on those discourses to understand why and how we have arrived here, when our individual political positioning and expression of that positioning have become more important than an understanding of the politics themselves. Or perhaps, we do understand and are left with nowhere to go. Other studies have used media to analyze aspects of urban development, reading the media that are circulated during urban redevelopment and using them as evidence to make a larger point, and to showcase the media's role in promoting a pro-growth development agenda (Gotham and Greenberg 2014). Other studies attempt to look at media itself as an agent of development (McCann 2004, 2002; Beauregard 2003; Spigel 2001). McCann's (2002) concept of 'meaning-making discourses' is relevant to my concept of 'development media' in that he is arguing that these discourses are inextricably linked to actual economic development and is seeking a way to determine how different actors construct and express meaning. These studies are particularly relevant to this emerging method of development media. However, they differ in where they actually place the value of discourse. Discourse has exchange value itself, used to attract money and capital, as well as to appease and persuade critics. In a simple form, grant writing, political elections, and city council meetings are direct practices in value-producing discourse. McCann uses the term 'meaning-making discourses' to refer to the discourses that are central to cultural politics but 'fundamentally intertwined with the place-making politics of local economic development' (McCann 2002, p. 387 and p. 397) in order to demonstrate that the politics of culture and economy are one and the same and are used strategically to effect political economic changes. The methodological concept of development media encompasses this idea and takes it a step further, to argue that the media of development are doing value-producing work toward a pro-growth agenda in the city. The media have been mobilized to support images of inner-city crime as linked to certain populations. Timothy Gibson and Mark Lowes's (2007) edited volume *Urban Communication: Production, Text, Context* offers multiple case studies that work to understand the role of discourse in producing abstract urban space. They look at how governments, developers, and business representatives use media to effectively change urban landscapes and alter the perceptions and lived realities of communities.

Similar to academic and popular discourses about gentrification, the issue raised of reflexivity in visual ethnography, and ethnography more broadly, risks taking the place of a politics rooted in an analysis of structural power. Perhaps it is too little, too late at this point, in that raising the issue of gentrification after gentrification has become the norm, in my field site of Durham[3] and also in cities across the world, and raising the issue of reflexivity while already in the position of researcher are both positions that render a proposed different way and different orientation of power utterly impossible. Yet maybe, that could lead us to the dead end of research and political practice where we want to find ourselves, with the only method an impossible one[4]—a method whose intention is much wider in scope than our own positionality.

NOTES

1. El Kilombo Intergalactico's writings can be found at http://www.elkilombo.org/our-word.
2. I owe this thinking to Alvaro Reyes's lectures from his Geography course at the University of Chapel Hill, North Carolina, 'Racialized Spaces and Proper Places: Frantz Fanon', Fall 2015.
3. Except that the issue of gentrification was raised almost a decade ago by a local community facing displacement and El Kilombo Intergalactico's articulation.
4. The term 'impossible' has been used by El Kilombo and by the EZLN to refer to the impossibility of the project of politics ahead of us, but that this impossible choice is the only actual choice (El Kilombo 2012; EZLN 2014).

References

Beauregard, R. (2003) *Voices of Decline: The Postwar Fate of U.S. Cities.* 2nd ed. (New York: Routledge).

Berlant, L. (2011) *Cruel Optimism* (Durham: Duke University Press).

Buck-Morss, S. (2009) *Hegel, Haiti and Universal History.* Illuminations (Pittsburgh: University of Pittsburgh Press).

Buck-Morss, S. (2000) Hegel and Haiti. *Critical Inquiry* 26(4): 821–65.

Clifford, J. and Marcus, G. (Eds.) (1986) *Writing Culture: The Poetics and Politics of Ethnography: A School of American Research Advanced Seminar* (Berkeley: University of California Press).

Cook, J. (2014) Made in Durham. *The Bitter Southerner.* http://bittersoutherner.com/made-in-durham (accessed 10 March 2016).

El Kilombo Intergalactico (2015) The Beginning of the End? Or the End of the Beginning? http://www.elkilombo.org/the-beginning-of-the-end-or-the-end-of-the-beginning (accessed 10 December 2015).

El Kilombo Intergalactico (2011) What's at Stake in Old North Durham Park? 8 December: http://www.elkilombo.org/whats-at-stake-in-old-north-durham-park-2 (accessed 10 December 2015).

El Kilombo Intergalactico (2012) *The Impossible Choice* 8 September: http://www.elkilombo.org/the-impossible-choice/ (accessed 10 March 2016).

EZLN (2014) *Fragments of La Realidad I* 4 May: http://www.elkilombo.org/fragments-of-la-realidad-i (accessed 8 August 2015).

Fisher, M. (2012) *Wall Street Women* (Durham: Duke University Press).

Freund, D. (2010) *Colored Property: State Policy and White Racial Politics in Suburban America* (Chicago: University of Chicago Press).

Geertz, C. (1973) *The Interpretation of Cultures: Selected Essays* (New York: Basic Books).

Gibson, T. and Lowes, M. (Eds.) (2007) *Urban Communication: Production, Text, Context.* Critical Media Studies (Lanham: Rowman & Littlefield).

Gotham, K. and Greenberg, M. (2014) *Crisis Cities: Disaster and Redevelopment in New York and New Orleans* (Oxford: Oxford University Press).

Grazian, D. (2003) *Blue Chicago: The Search for Authenticity in Urban Blues Clubs* (Chicago: University of Chicago Press).

Greenberg, M. (2000) Branding Cities: A Social History of the Urban Lifestyle Magazine. *Urban Affairs Review* 36(2): 228–63.

Harrison, F. (2008) *Outsider within: Reworking Anthropology in the Global Age* (Urbana: University of Illinois Press).

Harrison, F. (Ed.) (1997) *Decolonizing Anthropology: Moving Further toward an Anthropology of Liberation.* 2nd ed. (Arlington: Association of Black Anthropologists and American Anthropological Association).

Hartman, M. (2015) Branding the Commons. *Jacobin Magazine* 16 June: https://www.jacobinmag.com/2015/06/gentrification-cultural-capitalism (accessed 10 March 2016).

Ho, K. (2009) *Liquidated: An Ethnography of Wall Street* (Durham: Duke University Press).

Jackson, J. L. (2005) *Real Black: Adventures in Racial Sincerity* (Chicago: University of Chicago Press).

Jackson, J. L. (2012) Ethnography is, Ethnography ain't. *Cultural Anthropology* 27(3): 480–97.

Jackson, J. L. (2013) *Thin Description: Ethnography and the African Hebrew Israelites of Jerusalem* (Cambridge, MA: Harvard University Press).

Jenkins, J. (2016) Public Roles and Private Negotiations: Considering City Magazines' Public Service and Market Functions. *Journalism* 17(5): 619–635.

Kaufman, M. (2012) A Politics of Encounter: Knowledge and Organizing in Common. *American Quarterly* 64(4): 823–26.

Lilly, L. (2013) Gentrification Rocks North Carolina's Working Class. *Workers World* 27 October: http://www.workers.org/articles/2013/10/27/gentrification-rocks-north-carolina-working-class (accessed 10 March 2016).

Mascia-Lees, F., Sharpe, P. and Cohen, C. (1989) The Postmodernist Turn in Anthropology: Cautions from a Feminist Perspective. *Signs: Journal of Women in Culture and Society* 15(1): 7–33.

McCann, E. (2004) 'Best Places': Interurban Competition, Quality of Life and Popular Media Discourse. *Urban Studies* 41(10): 1909–29.

McCann, E. (2002) The Cultural Politics of Local Economic Development: Meaning-Making, Place-Making, and the Urban Policy Process. *Geoforum* 33(3): 385–98.

Mead, M. (2003) Visual Anthropology as a Discipline of Words. In P. Hockings (Ed.), *Principles of Visual Anthropology*. 3rd ed. (Berlin: Mouton de Gruyter), pp. 3–12.

Mies, M. (1986) *Patriarchy and Accumulation on a World Scale: Women in the International Division of Labour* (London: Third World Books).

Nader, L. (1972) Up the Anthropologist: Perspectives Gained From Studying Up. In D. Hymes (Ed.), *Reinventing Anthropology* (New York: Vintage), pp. 284–311.

Pink, S. (2013) *Doing Visual Ethnography*. 3rd ed. (London: Sage).

Reed, A. (1999) *Stirrings in the Jug: Black Politics in the Post-Segregation Era* (Minneapolis: University of Minnesota Press).

Reyes, A. (2012) On Fanon's Manichean Delirium. *The Black Scholar* 42(3–4): 13–20.

Smith, N. (1996) *The New Urban Frontier: Gentrification and the Revanchist City* (London: Routledge).

Spigel, L. (2001) *Welcome to the Dreamhouse: Popular Media and Postwar Suburbs.* Console-Ing Passions (Durham: Duke University Press).

Taussig, M. (1993) *Mimesis and Alterity: A Particular History of the Senses* (New York: Routledge).

Trinh, T. (1989) *Woman, Native, Other: Writing Postcoloniality and Feminism* (Bloomington: Indiana University Press).

Wacquant, L. (2012) Three Steps to a Historical Anthropology of Actually Existing Neoliberalism. *Social Anthropology* 20(1): 66–79.

Wacquant, L. (2009) *Punishing the Poor: The Neoliberal Government of Social Insecurity* (Durham: Duke University Press).

Zukin, S. (1982) *Loft Living: Culture and Capital in Urban Change* (Baltimore: Johns Hopkins University Press).

Zukin, S. (2014) Restaurants as 'Post Racial' Spaces. Soul Food and Symbolic Eviction in Bedford- Stuyvesant (Brooklyn). *Ethnologie française* 44(1): 135–47.

CHAPTER 10

Exploring Inclusive Ethnography as a Methodology to Account for Multiple Experiences

Paola Sartoretto

Studies of the relation between media and social or political action, particularly those looking into activism and mobilization, usually focus on one medium, configuring what Alice Mattoni and Emilano Treré (2014) have called a one-medium bias. This trend has become stronger in recent years, when certain devices such as mobile phones, or popular online platforms such as Facebook and Twitter, have received almost unfettered attention from media researchers exploring activism and social movements. Recent studies of social action, political activism, and social movements have tended to focus heavily on new digital media (see, for example, Castells 2012; Bennett and Segerberg 2012) and analyze activist action from the perspective of media usage. Interviews, netnography, and content analysis are commonly utilized methods, which undeniably provide an in-depth view of patterns of social action related to these particular media. However, what such methods tend to overlook is the complex array of practices and processes that occur in the interplay between mediated and direct communication.

P. Sartoretto (✉)
Stockholm University, Stockholm, Sweden
e-mail: paola.sartoretto@lai.su.se

© The Author(s) 2016
S. Kubitschko, A. Kaun (eds.), *Innovative Methods in Media and Communication Research*, DOI 10.1007/978-3-319-40700-5_10

On a different dimension, too strong a focus on new technologies that are unequally available across different groups tends to give an skewed view of the democratizing potentials of these technologies; a view that is predominantly Western and based on the habits of the middle classes in the Euro-American context. Such a strong focus on technologies that are not widely available ignores the experiences of the have-nots, or the have-less (Qiu 2009). In order to tackle this imbalance, I argue for the relevance of a more holistic approach that is attentive to communicative processes and transcends the materiality of media. By focusing on the experiences of marginalized groups that are geographically isolated and do not have access to the most advanced technologies, it is possible to broaden the horizons of analysis of the interplay between social action and media. A socially situated analysis of communicative processes can thus benefit from an ethnographic outlook strongly anchored on social theory.

As Jack Qiu (2009) notes, as soon as we start talking about developments in information and communication technologies (ICT), there is a tendency to 'immediately think about the digital divide' (Qiu 2009, p. 1) between the information haves and have-nots. This binary thinking, Qiu argues, is over-simplifying, because not having gadgets or skills does not mean that people will not find strategies and ways to overcome social exclusion and participate in communicative processes using the resources they have at their disposal. It is understood that research methodologies alone cannot solve a problem that is epistemological in its essence—how we categorize and analyze media-related experiences. Research methodologies that are a result of reflexive efforts can, however, help elucidate epistemological problems in a way that addresses their complexity. When it comes to our relation to media, both as individuals and as groups, we must acknowledge the social and political structures in which this relation unfolds and the variety of media with which we interact.

Due to its reflexive nature, ethnography is especially suited to exploring the full depth and breadth of our relation to media (see, for example, analysis of social movements by Costanza-Chock 2014; Kavada 2015). However, in order for it not to make exclusions based on access to media, or fall on the binary understanding of the digital divide about which Qiu warns us, ethnography must also account for a multiplicity of media, or what Sasha Costanza-Chock (2014) calls multi-media organizing. My purpose here is exactly to explore the possibilities and challenges of multi-media ethnography, hoping that the development of new technologies that create textured spaces (Jansson 2009) will push us to in-depth inquiries about the nature of social change and its relation to media.

ETHNOGRAPHY IN MEDIA AND COMMUNICATION RESEARCH

Ethnography or ethnographic research is a term used to define varying research methodologies—participant observation, fieldwork, action research, to name but a few (for an in-depth discussion see Hammersley and Atkinson 2007). What these methodologies have in common are the presence and participation—at different levels—of the researcher in the environment where the phenomena that are researched take place. These research methodologies and the strategies that stem from them are open-ended and usually non-systematic; that is to say, the researcher enters the field 'as it is' rather than constructing artificial research situations. According to Clifford Geertz (1973), ethnographic studies are characterized by a specific mindset—the researcher's endeavor is to identify systems of meanings, social structures, and rationales that lie deeper than what is observed at the surface. Such research strategies will be the basis for a descriptive analysis, or, as Geertz calls it, 'thick description'. This is a description that goes beyond the face value of what is observed and provides analytic insights usually anchored in theoretical conceptualizations. So, when I use the term ethnography I do not mean a particular method, but a set of research strategies and the kind of research endeavor that informs them.

On a meta level, by focusing on studies of social movements, political action, mobilization, and protest, I wish to highlight and discuss the consequences of a recent emphasis on the use of technologies. My aim is to present alternatives for research that are methodologically inclusive and account for social, economic, and political diversity. I start by discussing how the questions we pose and the ways we empirically explore them can exclude certain kinds of experience. Next, I will discuss how ethnography can become an inclusive methodology by accounting for life experiences that are not made visible through other research methods. The understanding of ethnography proposed here speaks to both the feminist and radical strands of ethnographic research, in the sense that it seeks to make visible the experiences of marginal and dominated subjects and endeavors to speak with (instead of speaking about) the subjects of research. Finally, I discuss these questions in relation to my own fieldwork experience, reflecting on my attempt to perform multi-media ethnography.

INCLUSION, EXCLUSION, AND DIVERSITY
IN COMMUNICATION RESEARCH

Research on the intersection between so-called new media and different kinds of political agency has had an upsurge in recent years. This is possibly due to a conjunction of factors such as a rise in discontent with politics on the one hand and rapid technological developments on the other. From 2000 onward a move can be noted from studies of web pages, use of email lists and forums, and the interplay between protest action and media to investigations of communicative processes facilitated by digital social media and mobile devices.

Studies carried out and published during the last five years show a clear bias toward new technologies, which causes a geographic imbalance that favors technology-rich Western countries. A bias toward new technologies can also easily become a class or geographic bias when research focuses on the habits and activities of the middle classes in developed countries.

On the particular question of political participation, action, and mobilization, and their relation to technology, certain methodological strategies will tend to favor young and educated subjects who have access to the internet and disposable time to be active in forums and online discussions. Studies using interviews and survey methods tend to end up with a sample of mostly young and highly educated individuals (see, for instance, Gustafsson 2012; Wojcieszak and Smith 2014). As a result, the corpus of knowledge will be skewed toward experiences that might be prominent but are certainly not inclusive. This is a particular problem with surveys in which most respondents tend to have a higher level of education.

When it comes to methodological choices, qualitative and exploratory methodologies have become more common. Also, methodologies based on the analysis of big data in order to identify trends and patterns in media use and content creation are becoming more popular as the technologies that allow this kind of data collection and gathering become more accessible (Hindman 2008; Bennett and Segerberg 2013; for a critical analysis of big data research in media and communication, see boyd and Crawford 2012). Although surveys have been largely used to map out protest action and digital social network use (recent studies using survey methodologies are Tufekci and Wilson 2012; Enjolras et al. 2013; Zúñiga et al. 2014), ethnography-informed studies have also been carried out. Many of these studies use ethnography or ethnography-inspired methods in order to explain how technological development plays a role in different sorts of political agency. In such cases, the balance between analysis and description that can be achieved through ethnography is particularly suited to exploring the nature of social change and its interplay with technological development.

Ethnography has evolved from being the study of the 'others' and their habits and costumes to the contemporary attempts of social sciences to understand processes, which include people, artifacts, texts, and relations. Thus, as media (as channels, artifacts, or arenas of communication) came to occupy a significant place in people's lives, media ethnography emerged as a methodological approach to understand the ways in which people relate to media. However, when it comes to the study of political agency, mobilization, activism, and related phenomena, there seems to be somewhat of a divide between an understanding of the conscious citizen who possesses the skills and resources to voice her dissent through the media and the beneficiary of projects that aim to empower those who do not possess skills or resources and create opportunities and arenas for self-representation and expression. It is the epistemological representation of the binary distinction between haves and have-nots (Qiu 2009). In this context, my argument is that this distinction stems from a media-centric focus that guides research to those who are already using technologies or lack them. With its descriptive character and its focus on processes and relations, ethnography allows us not only to analyze the social uses of technologies, but also gives visibility to an array of experiences and realities that are made invisible by binary categorizations such as those that Qiu identified.

When technologies become agents capable of enabling or modifying social phenomena, it is easy to accept the idea that the presence or lack of material resources and skills will be a defining factor for these social phenomena in which technologies are embedded. Of course this is an epistemological problem, not a methodological one; at the same time, the knowledge we have of social phenomena derives to a great extent from research that may have departed from an exclusive understanding of phenomena. This tandem relationship between epistemology and methodology leads to the question of whether and to what extent methodological choices can lead to less reductionist understandings of social phenomena. The answer is that while the way in which a problem or phenomenon with its different aspects is understood guides the production of knowledge, methodologies that have an exploratory character permit an open view of research problems. In addition, exploratory methods such as ethnography are better suited to tackling the one-medium bias (Mattoni and Treré 2014) and the reductionist categorization between the haves and have-nots (Pieterse 2009) that Qiu (2009) identified.

In a recent article on de-Westernizing communication studies, Waisbord and Mellado (2014) highlight a number of aspects that have made media and communication studies a field that has been constructed on Western ideas and problems. This has led to theory building that explains phenomena that are typical of Western–Northern societies. If research has as a starting point concepts and theories that are not easily transferable to non-Western realities, it will probably not use methodologies that allow for new theory building. In this sense, ethnographic methodologies that depart from open ontological premises can be a way to address the Western bias in media and communication studies.

In this sense, this methodological effort resonates with Boaventura de Sousa Santos's (2007) argument that Western social sciences create absences by not properly accounting for and recognizing the experiences that fall outside the Western–Northern context. It follows that those who lack material resources in the form of technologies and the skills to use these technologies are put in the condition of helpless victims for whom the only goal is modernization. The linear views on modernization and reductionist ideas on technological skills are examples of ontological premises that guide methodological choices, which in turn make certain experiences invisible. Methodological choices are thus one way to address the dichotomy between the haves and the have-nots, addressing in this way the invisibility of certain groups and practices. As an outcome, we can reach a more nuanced understanding of the intersection between social action and media. Because it is an open-ended method that looks deep into lived experiences, ethnography allows for a more multi-faceted consideration of media practices. Instead of departing from media usage and concentrating on the medium, an ethnographic study will depart from the group in question and make visible not only the media practices, but also how certain struggles develop and how communicative processes are a constitutive element in social struggles. Furthermore, the abundance of technological artifacts and easy access to the latest technologies that we enjoy in the West can blind us to the fact that the majority of people live with scarce access to technologies. It is equally important to understand how these people deal with scarcity than it is to delve into our technology-saturated lives. The key here is the fact that there are no pre-determined assumptions about roles and uses of technologies that guide ethnographic work, different from other methodologies. This means that practices and realities that might not be accounted for or addressed by theory will be made visible through empirical efforts (Waisbord and Mellado 2014).

Of course, it is not possible to solve these problems just by choosing certain methodologies. It is also necessary to be aware of exclusion and invisibility dynamics that may play a role in designing research strategies and choosing empirical cases. Recent studies that analyze the interplay between media and social action and protest can illustrate this argument. Many of these studies have particularly looked into so-called new media practices, focusing on a specific medium or platform (Kavada 2010; Kropczynski and Nah 2011; Bennett and Segerberg 2012; Harlow 2012; Lester and Hutchins 2012; Meraz and Paparachissi 2013; Penney and Dadas 2013). When the medium strictly guides methodological and empirical choices, we run two different risks. The first is the exclusion of groups who are not active—or not active enough—users of technologies. The second is the exclusion of practices that are in essence communicative but that are not mediated by new technologies. As discussed in the previous section, the creation of absences can be particularly noticed in the discussion about the interplay between media and political participation and action. These exclusions have so far led to a technological-deterministic bias in the understanding of the interplay between media and political and social action. The idea that wherever and whenever there is media there will be communication—and that the more media there are, the more communication there will be—is insidiously gaining a stake in the discipline as a quasi-paradigm. One way to problematize and challenge this idea is by using methodological strategies that allow for the inclusion of groups and practices that are less visible and act outside the global hubs of action.

Such groups and practices have to be approached not as residuals of modernization processes—which is usually the case when we depart from technological-determinist premises—but as constitutive parts of a reality that needs to be analyzed in its own terms. The first step to designing inclusive methodologies is to avoid two different biases: the technological bias and the one-medium bias (Mattoni and Treré 2014). Taking this first step requires an ethnographic mindset (Geertz 1973) in order to see beyond the appearances. Different from other methods that isolate the empirical object that is being studied from its context, ethnography is a context-based method. This means that the researcher accesses technologies, cultural products, and the practices related to them in a holistic and relational way.

Socially Situated Multi-media Ethnography

In the last decades research in media and communication has become more attentive to spatial and social aspects (see Bräuchler and Postill 2010; Couldry 2004) related to media and communication. This can be particularly noticed in the studies and discussions that address media practices in their complexity, as opposed to a more dichotomist view of production and reception. Brigitte Bräuchler and John Postill note that the analysis of media practices connects the discipline of media and communication studies and anthropology. In attempting to incorporate practice theory in media studies, the authors pose questions that open up ethnographic methodologies: 'In what ways do different media practices overlap with one another and with non-media practices? How can we begin to map and theorize the bewildering diversification of media practices in recent years?' (Bräuchler and Postill 2010, p. xi). These questions are explicitly contextual and relational: they place media practices in a social context in which they will be related to non-media practices, to one another, and to socio-political contexts. Postill notes that practice theory is 'centered on "practices" rather than structures, systems, individuals or interactions', and further argues that 'theories should not be divorced from empirical research' (2010, p. 1).

For media and communication studies, this will mean a move away from positivist and functionalist paradigms that many times inform and guide more systematic methodologies such as surveys and experiments. Moreover, practice-based research will focus on activities, interrelations, and interactions, which means that it is not the medium that guides the different data-collection strategies but the embodied activities related to media. Particularly when it comes to social and political action and mobilization, instead of planning data-collection strategies toward certain media—social media platforms, mobile phones, video—they will seek to observe activities such as production, interaction, and, in this case, mobilization and action. These strategies will facilitate and enable investigation of the questions that Bräuchler and Postill (2010) raise: namely, the relation between media and non-media practices, overlapping of media practices, and the diversification of media practices. Such kinds of socially situated multi-media ethnography have been performed, for example, by Clemencia Rodríguez (2011), Paulo Gerbaudo (2012), Stefania Milan (2013), and Costanza-Chock (2014), who have studied forms of social action such as protest, mobilization, and media activism. Gerbaudo (2012) investigates media practices among activists in Spain, Egypt, and New York with an open view to media, observing how different mediated and non-mediated practices play a role in the organization and performance of protest. Following the same methodological path, Milan (2013) has analyzed different forms of media activism; her point of departure is the enactment of emancipatory practices and not the kinds of media that are used. Costanza-Chock (2014) used a variety of methods from participatory research action to interviews to analyze and discuss media practices among immigrant organizations on the USA–Mexico border. By using methodologies and data-collection strategies that are strongly grounded in social practices, these studies provide analytic descriptions of recent phenomena. The socially situated outlook grants that the analysis will include a variety of experiences and media practices.

So in practical terms of research design, what does socially situated multi-media ethnography look like? Of course, it would be an anachronism to attempt to systematize ethnography, which is *per se* an unsystematic research methodology guided by the empirical object on the first hand. What we can do is to define certain principles that will grant that media practices will be explored in their complexity, multiplicity, and depth. Starting from the epistemological standpoint, the view on practice must be open—as in Nick Couldry's question 'what types of things do people do in relation to media?' (2004, p. 121). These practices and activities will always be connected and related to social and individual conditions and will be performed according to varying levels of rationality and socialization. Therefore, looking into media practices allows us also to access the social and individual contexts in which these practices take place. At the empirical level, this same openness should be transferred to the outlook on media—media practices are diverse because media themselves are diverse, and because societies and people are diverse. It is not possible to grasp this diversity if we try to isolate one medium from its relational place in the media ecology (Tacchi 2006). Finally, perhaps the most obvious principle is that the object of inquiry should be a social relation and not a particular medium. These principles are summarized in Fig. 10.1, which illustrates the tandem relation between epistemology and methodology.

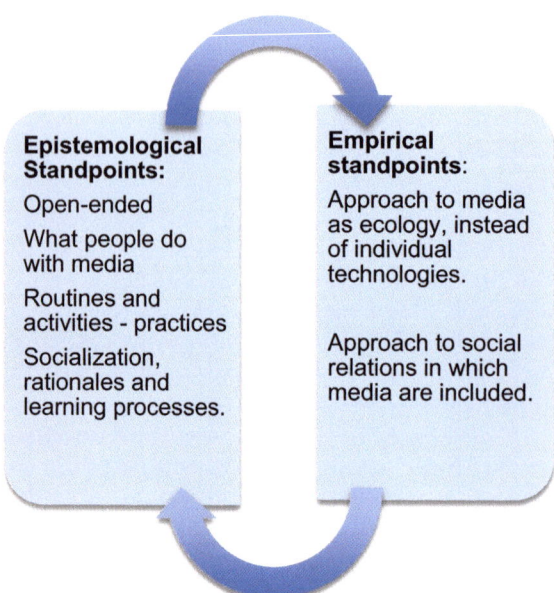

Epistemological Standpoints:

Open-ended

What people do with media

Routines and activities - practices

Socialization, rationales and learning processes.

Empirical standpoints:

Approach to media as ecology, instead of individual technologies.

Approach to social relations in which media are included.

Fig. 10.1   Relation between epistemological and empirical standpoints

EXPLORING QUESTIONS OF PARTICIPATION AND EMPOWERMENT THROUGH ETHNOGRAPHY

In my fieldwork with the Landless Workers Movement in Brazil (MST), I have explored how a subaltern social movement, formed by rural workers, relates to and uses media in order to achieve symbolic cohesion, facilitate mobilization, and participate in a dialogue with society. From the outset my aim was to provide a Southern perspective (Santos 2007) to the current discussions on the interplay between media and social mobilization. I used an ethnography-inspired approach to fieldwork. Due to time and funding constraints it was not possible to spend prolonged periods of time with MST, so the fieldwork was carried out in two fieldtrips, over a total of five months. Also, the fact that the movement is active over almost the entire country makes more difficult the work of trying to observe and understand its communicative processes. Therefore, the analysis relied heavily on interviews, even though I performed participant observation and kept a fieldwork diary during the trips. MST has press offices in Brasília and São Paulo staffed by what I refer to as professional militant journalists: professional journalists, many of them employed by MST, who are also active in the movement as militants, which means that their professional position as journalists is extrapolated from their activities in the movement. In addition, MTS runs a few radio stations in the rural communities where its members live—these were the sites where fieldwork was carried out.

By approaching the fieldwork with an open outlook toward practices, I was able to include in the analyses communicative and interactional processes that do not necessarily involve media, but play a role in how media are incorporated in routines and rituals. An example is what movement members refer to as *organicity* (see Sartoretto 2015), which means the processes through which decisions are made and daily activities are carried out in the movement. MST members see this as a democratic process because it is organic to the movement—they have created mechanisms and spaces that favor discussion and exchange of ideas. In this context, technologies have a contentious role, because the immediacy that characterizes many new media such as email and mobile phones is seen as a threat to the organic interaction dynamics that the organization has achieved. The differences here are encountered more in the orientations toward technologies—that is, the ways in which people relate to technologies—than in the technologies themselves. Although technologies have their affordances (Williams 2003), people and groups will appropriate (Sartoretto 2015) technologies in different ways, following diverse dynamics, which can only be grasped through non-media-centric approaches. Such contextual analysis would not be possible with methods that systematically isolate media as variables in an equation.

Departing from an empirically based question—what do people do with media?—and observing the situations and processes in which media are present, I was able to address analytically rationales and processes of socialization in which media play a central role. These processes proved to be a crucial element in the generational transition from older movement members who founded the organization to younger ones. Through observation of meetings, daily routines, and events, it was possible to grasp the conflicts that are brought by new media, learning processes, and the socialization of practices associated with new media, as well as how practices related to different media overlap—for instance, theatre and video production, visual arts, and digital social media.

In this case, ethnography-informed methodologies helped to avoid an unbalanced focus on those who have access to technologies or are technologically savvy, which can impair the analysis of an organization the majority of whose members live in rural areas with scarce access to technologies. They are what many call have-nots, on the dispossessed side of the digital divide. However, supporting Qiu's (2009) argument that there is more complexity than the dichotomy between haves and have-nots, these people, with structural support from the movement through training and the constitution of spaces for knowledge sharing, find ways to use media and remain politically active and mobilized. This is where the empirical, concrete, and non-systematic character of ethnography comes into play, because when we isolate media from the natural environment where media practices occur, the risk is that we will exclude those on the wrong side of the technology gap or even place them in pre-determined roles that do not reflect reality. The work that MST militants carry out with radio, theatre, and print is an example of such media practices enacted with a great level of protagonism by those who have limited access to technological resources. The fact that these people do not have access to or the knowledge to use new technologies does not mean, in this case, that they cannot proficiently use media to learn, construct an identity, maintain cohesion among the group, and, of course, communicate their struggle to those outside the group.

During fieldwork I assessed and experienced at first hand the realities of those who participated in the social movement. By being present at different places where media practices were enacted, I could describe and analyze their relational character. My presence in the press offices, rural communities, schools, events, and protests helped me to understand how media practices are intertwined with spatial aspects. An example is the radio station in one rural community outside São Paulo, which serves not only as a broadcaster but also as a meeting point for both MST members and non-members. In this situation, the radio is not just a communication technology, but also a physical space where people meet and develop a relation to the movement. The most popular program is the music show broadcast on Sundays, where local artists from the region play live. After the show ends, there is a social gathering with lunch at the same place where the radio is located.

Using research methodologies and data-collection strategies that include a variety of media, instead of focusing on one medium, helps us understand the correlations between different media practices. When individuals mobilize collectively and perform political and social action, they use a variety of media in varied ways that are many times interconnected. That is why a multi-media approach is ideal to grasp this complexity and variety. This interrelation and overlapping between different media practices have been acknowledged in recent studies (Tufekci and Wilson 2012; Harlow 2012) but not extensively explored, because these studies only investigate practices related to one medium. While surveys can identify the relation between media practices (Enjolras et al. 2013), it would be difficult to perform an analytic description of this relation through a non-contextual methodology such as survey or experiment.

At the empirical level, an approach to media as an ecology of different technologies and platforms (Tacchi 2006) facilitates the inclusion of a variety of groups in society. Considering the inequality in access and skills that is found in peripheral countries such as Brazil, research that isolates digital media from older technologies excludes a large part of the population who have limited access to technologies. This exclusion contributes to the narrative that technologies and skills are necessary to social and political mobilization, which is far from reality. In this sense, approaching media as an ecology can help us understand the mechanisms through which those who do not have access to technologies and the disposable time and skills to use them find ways to mobilize.

Using this approach in my fieldwork meant that I was able to assess the contentions in using technologies and the rationales for deliberately slowing down the process of adoption when there is a wide gap in access and when there are already other channels of communication in place. In the case of MST, the communication sector in the organization deliberately chooses not to use digital social networks for organizing protests and demonstrations, only using its Facebook profile to broadcast these events when they have already happened. The demonstrations at squares, different government buildings, and agribusiness companies research facilities, blocking of motorways, and so on are organized solely through internal channels of communication constructed through time. MST is a social movement whose mobilization depends on face-to-face communication, because this is a mode of communication whose public and access to content can be controlled more easily than digital platforms. Moreover, it has developed media practices that differ from those of Western urban middle-class formations in order to adapt to its particular profile as an organization that is vilified by some sectors of society, and to the profile of a membership that does not have the resources to make profuse use of technologies. In this case, a non-media-centric ethnography helps to understand how the construction of arenas for communication prevails over the use of media.

These processes that lead to the formation, socialization, and reproduction of media practices involve multiple technologies, platforms, and devices. They are also deeply embedded in social relations beyond the use of media. Such social relations precede the use of media and are key to understanding the rationales that guide media practices. This is the reason why inclusive media ethnographies should strive to be socially situated, as well as having a holistic outlook on media. In practice, the social relations that structure media practices must also become part of the analytic description that is the outcome of ethnography. Contemporary protests and social mobilization do not happen solely because individuals have access to media, but are the outcome of myriad factors situated in the individual, collective, and political realms. However, different media may modify social and interpersonal interactions, and it is exactly this kind of process that can only be grasped through multi-media ethnography.

CONCLUSION

In this chapter I have argued for non-media-centric multi-media ethnography as a way to include experiences outside the Western context in the process of theory and knowledge building. Non-media-centric ethnography is particularly needed to explain the interplay between communication and mobilization in unequal societies where access to information technologies is not widespread. Because it has social relations—in which media are included —as a starting point, the method allows us to grasp a wide range of communicative processes in which technologies are not the central element, or are used in ways that contradict dominant narratives of technology abundance.

This kind of ethnographic study can contribute to developing more diverse conceptualizations of communication in social movements that account for realities outside Western industrialized nations and regions. The emergence of new media technologies and their rapid spread in developed countries over the last decade has created a dominant narrative about the abundance and omnipresence of media. In this sense, non-media-centric ethnographic studies can help develop more diverse explanations of the relation between media and social mobilization that account for experiences outside the hegemonic West.

References

Bennett, W. L. and Segerberg, A. (2012) The Logic of Connective Action: Digital Media and the Personalization of Contentious Politics. *Information, Communication & Society* 15(5): 739–68.

boyd, d. and Crawford, K. (2012) Critical Questions for Big Data: Provocations for a Cultural, Technological, and Scholarly Phenomenon. *Information, Communication & Society* 15(5): 662–79.

Bräuchler, B. and Postill, J. (2010) Preface. In B. Bräuchler and J. Postill (Eds.), *Theorising Media and Practice* (New York: Berghahn), pp. xi–xii.

Castells, M. (2012) *Networks of Outrage and Hope: Social Movements in the Age of the Internet* (Cambridge: Polity).

Costanza-Chock, S. (2014) *Out of the Shadows, Into the Streets! Transmedia Organizing and the Immigrant Rights Movement* (Cambridge, MA: MIT Press).

Couldry, N. (2004) Theorising Media as Practice. *Social Semiotics* 14(2): 115–32.

Enjolras, B., Steen-Johnsen, K. and Wollebæk, D. (2013) Social Media and Mobilization to Offline Demonstrations: Transcending Participatory Divides? *New Media & Society* 15(6): 890–908.

Geertz, C. (1973) *The Interpretation of Cultures: Selected Essays* (New York: Basic Books).

Gerbaudo, P. (2012) *Tweets and the Streets: Social Media and Comtemporary Activsim* (London: Pluto).

Gustafsson, N. (2012) The Subtle Nature of Facebook Politics: Swedish Social Network Site Users and Political Participation. *New Media & Society* 14(7): 1111–27.

Hammersley, M. and Atkinson, P. (2007) *Ethnography: Principles in Practices*. 3rd ed. (London: Routledge).

Harlow, S. (2012) Social Media and Social Movements: Facebook and an Online Guatemalan Justice Movement that Moved Offline. *New Media & Society* 14(2): 225–43.

Hindman, M. (2008) *The Myth of Digital Democracy* (Princeton: Princeton University Press).

Jansson, A. (2009) Mobile Belongings: Texturation and Stratification in Mediatization Processes. In K. Lundby (Ed.), *Mediatization. Concept, Changes, Consequences* (New York: Peter Lang), pp. 243–62.

Kavada, A. (2010) Email Lists and Participatory Democracy in the European Social Forum. *Media, Culture & Society* 32(3): 355–72.

Kavada, A. (2015) Creating the Collective: Social Media, the Occupy Movement and its Constitution as a Collective Actor. *Information, Communication & Society* 18(8): 872–86.

Kropczynski, J. and Nah, S. (2011) Virtually Networked Housing Movement: Hyperlink Network Structure of Housing Social Movement Organizations. *New Media & Society* 13(5): 689–703.

Lester, L. and Hutchins, B. (2012) The Power of the Unseen: Environmental Conflict, the Media and Invisibility. *Media, Culture & Society* 34(7): 847–63.

Mattoni, A. and Treré, E. (2014) Media Practices, Mediation Processes, and Mediatization in the Study of Social Movements. *Communication Theory* 24(3): 252–71.

Meraz, S. and Papacharissi, Z. (2013) Networked Gatekeeping and Networked Framing on #Egypt. *The International Journal of Press/Politics* 18(2): 138–66.

Milan, S. (2013) *Social Movements and Their Technologies: Wiring Social Change* (London: Palgrave Macmillan).

Penney, J. and Dadas, C. (2013) (Re)Tweeting in the Service of Protest: Digital Composition and Circulation in the Occupy Wall Street Movement. *New Media & Society* 16(1): 74–90.

Pieterse, J. N. (2009) Representing the Rise of the Rest as Threat Media and Global Divides. *Global Media and Communication* 5(2): 221–37.

Postill, J. (2010) Introduction: Theorising media and practice. In B. Bräuchler and J. Postill (Eds.), *Theorising Media and Practice* (New York: Berghahn), pp. 1–32.

Qiu, J. (2009) *Working-class Network Society: Communication Technology and the Information Have-less in Urban China* (Cambridge, MA: MIT Press).

Rodríguez, C. (2011) *Citizens' Media Against Armed Conflict: Disrupting Violence in Colombia* (Minneapolis: University of Minnesota Press).

Santos, B. de S. (2007) *Renovar a Teoria Crítica e Reiventar a Emancipação Social* (São Paulo: Boitempo Editorial).

Sartoretto, P. (2015) *Voices from the Margins – People, Media, and the Struggle for Land in Brazil.* Doctoral dissertation (Karlstad: Universitetstryckeriet).

Tacchi, J. (2006) Studying Communicative Ecologies: An Ethnographic Approach to Information and Communication Technologies. *Paper presented at the 56th annual conference of the International Communication Association* (Dresden, Germany).

Tufekci, Z. and Wilson, C. (2012) Social Media and the Decision to Participate in Political Protest: Observations from Tahrir Square. *Journal of Communication* 62(2): 363–79.

Waisbord, S. and Mellado, C. (2014) De-westernizing Communication Studies: Reassessment. *Communication Theory* 24(4): 361–72.

Williams, R. (2003) *Television – Technology and Cultural Form* (London: Routledge).

Wojcieszak, M. and Smith, B. (2014) Will Politics be Tweeted? New Media Use by Iranian Youth in 2011. *New Media & Society* 16(1): 91–109.

Zúñiga, H. G. d., Molyneux, L. and Zheng, P. (2014) Social Media, Political Expression, and Political Participation: Panel Analysis of Lagged and Concurrent Relationships. *Journal of Communication* 64(4): 612–34.

CHAPTER 11

Interviewing Against the Odds

Neha Kumar

As more and more of our lives penetrates the digital sphere and 'big data'–driven approaches to understanding the world grow increasingly pervasive, it becomes relevant to reflect on whether there is still a need for alternative, more traditional forms of data gathering in media and communications research. Mark Andrejevic (2013) discusses the relatively recent epistemological turn that draws greater attention to big data, circumventing and displacing representation. We must note, however, that although there is an abundance of digital data now increasingly available to fuel this research, it remains highly provincialized—equipped to tell us much more about the West than about the rest of the world, particularly the global South, which still lacks representation in our increasingly digital media landscape (Kluver et al. 2013). In this chapter I discuss some of the challenges that arise when we set out to collect data from communities that are under-served, under-resourced, and under-represented. The challenges that researchers in these contexts encounter are not merely logistical or physical, such that the mere processes of getting to and from remote locations and overcoming linguistic barriers are difficult. The greater challenge becomes discerning the questions to ask that are relevant

N. Kumar (✉)
Georgia Institute of Technology, Atlanta, GA, USA
e-mail: neha.kumar@cc.gatech.edu

© The Author(s) 2016
S. Kubitschko, A. Kaun (eds.), *Innovative Methods in Media and Communication Research*, DOI 10.1007/978-3-319-40700-5_11

and understanding how the hidden or less obvious socially constructed lenses such as gender, class, and caste, among others, influence the data that are to be collected. Without this understanding, I argue, it would be difficult to take a 'big data'–oriented approach: How would one choose what questions to ask? And, further, how would one know how the findings are to be interpreted and what implications they might have for media and communications research?

There are differences in economic infrastructures, technology practices, cultural norms, and other dimensions, unique to the settings I consider in this chapter, that cannot all be captured by data-driven approaches. Moreover, even if we did have the ability to record varieties of data in these settings, I argue based on this that they may not necessarily bring us closer to the information we seek. In this chapter, I demonstrate the relevance of ethnographically orientated approaches and good old-fashioned, in-person interviews in light of the increasing preponderance of quantitative, data-driven methodologies. I highlight also that conducting interviews is not always straightforward and can bring unforeseeable challenges when the researcher(s) and field sites are separated by differences based on geography, culture, gender, or class. I present my field experiences—from non-Western and relatively under-studied contexts—of grappling with some of these challenges. I also emphasize the need to think deeply about the choice of methodology, and to consider the impact this choice can have on the quality of the data collected as well as that of the resulting research. I reflect on my fieldwork to suggest considerations for interviews conducted in field sites that are similarly different, with the aim of informing future research endeavors that bring forth like challenges, equipping researchers with tools and approaches to adopt in the course of their fieldwork.

The field experiences I draw on and discuss in this chapter come from two disparate research studies that I undertook. In the first, I conducted interviews of male youths in rural and small-town settings across India as part of a long-term ethnographic engagement to understand their adoption and use of mobile devices and their consumption of mobile entertainment media (Kumar 2015; Kumar and Parikh 2013). In the second, I conducted interviews of rural Indian women in the Indian state of Uttar Pradesh, also with the goal of understanding their mobile media practices (Kumar and Anderson 2015). In this chapter, I will focus not on the differences that emerged in terms of technology use and practices, but on the processes of identifying and recruiting participants to interview and how these unfolded differently. Although I focus primarily on gender-based differences in this chapter, I will stress that gender is only one of many socially constructed lenses that, when looked through, can allow us to appreciate the considerations that must be made for effective field research in culturally disparate environments. I also discuss others, such as caste and class. I aim for self-reflexivity in my consideration of these differences, since my identity as a female, US-based researcher of higher-caste and higher-class Indian origin, among other things, inevitably influences the nature and substance of the research I conduct.

Prior Work

Before I proceed, I must clarify that I am, of course, by no means the first to conduct interviews or qualitative research. Excellent precedents exist in the works of Kvale (1996), Bryman and Burgess (1999), Chase (2011), and Bryman (2016), among others. Nor am I the first to highlight that interviews (and other qualitative inquiry) can reveal truths that quantitative approaches might obscure (Becker 1996; Rubin and Rubin 2011). My goal is to draw on my own interviewing experiences in particular contexts in order to emphasize how these interviews retain a position of methodological relevance in an increasingly data-driven world. These contexts allude to the constraints in which the field of information and communication technology and development (ICTD) is enveloped.

ICTD is a fairly new and rapidly growing research domain that examines the applicability of information and communication technologies (ICTs) to development goals—those that were put forward by the United Nations in 2000 as the Millennium Development Goals (MDGs) and then in 2015 as the Sustainable Development Goals (SDGs; see Sachs 2012). Researching the design, deployment, adoption, and use of ICTs in the context of under-represented, under-served, and/or under-resourced communities—particularly in developing parts of the world—is ridden with methodological challenges. A preliminary discussion of these appeared in Brewer et al.'s (2005) and Anokwa et al.'s (2009) works in the early days of ICTD. Burrell and Toyama (2009) took this discussion further by addressing the challenges that arise when there are disparities in epistemological approaches. The field has since expanded considerably, embracing varied epistemologies and allowing for an increasingly cohesive co-existence of researchers from different disciplines keen to grow ICTD further as a field of research, a body of literature, and an established and recognized research community (Dell and Kumar 2016). This is the community I address in particular with this chapter, with the objective of enriching our ability—as a field—first to recognize and then to grapple with the methodological challenges that ICTD engenders as we proceed to develop a more nuanced understanding of the socio-cultural dimensions that affect our research.

There is also a second audience that I target—those who conduct media and communications research and pursue (or stumble into, as I did) contexts such as mine that are under-studied, but also abundant with less-understood social and cultural nuances that might interfere with appropriate interpretation of the data that are collected (Keats 2009; Bamberger 2000). And finally, I add to the active, ongoing conversation that challenges the role that 'big data' can play overall in media and communications research (boyd and Crawford 2012).

THE STUDY OF MOBILE MEDIA PRACTICES

I now present a brief overview of the two research studies I mention before discussing the methodological lessons I gleaned from these exercises. First, as mobile coverage and penetration began and grew rapidly across India in the last five to seven years (Narayana 2011), I took on the task of studying the adoption and appropriation of the increasingly ubiquitous mobile phone, sampling the population of male youth across a variety of demographics—these were the new adopters who had never before had access to their own technology device. To date these communities continue to be offline for the most part, with a flourishing ecosystem surrounding the illegal download and subsequent distribution of entertainment media. I was conducting a multi-sited ethnography that took me to rural parts of Madhya Pradesh and Rajasthan and small towns such as Bikaner and Indore, in addition to urban metropolises such as New Delhi and Bangalore. Here I obtained access to young people who came from diverse, marginalized backgrounds. Access to women was frequently a challenge, however, since that required a significant amount of trust building with the family elders (especially the men). Moreover, at the time that this ethnography took place, mobile phones were yet to be widely adopted by the women in these communities. Men were the first to adopt these devices, as I found. The creative use of these devices (for transacting in mobile media) was further limited to male youth, since they were generally the ones with time *and* access. I asked my study participants questions regarding what drove them to adopt the mobile phone, what costs and benefits they saw to owning this device, and what sustained their use of it.

This included looking into the nature of the mobile media they consumed and shared and the socio-technical configurations that emerged to support this new demand for mobile media.

My second study took place in the context of a maternal health intervention called Projecting Health (for more details on the project, see Kumar et al. 2015) across three blocks of the Raebareli district in the state of Uttar Pradesh. The team of researchers involved included health and technology experts. In this project, globally approved health norms were translated into locally crafted videos with the guidance of global health professionals and by community actors, including non-governmental organizations with several years of experience in the field and frontline health workers, among others. Although the project was operated largely by male members of these communities, this intervention brought me face to face with a diverse group of women coming from different caste/class backgrounds—both young and old, those who were relatively educated and employed by the government to perform the tasks of a frontline health worker, as well as women who were less educated (often illiterate) and unemployed. The health workers were responsible for organizing monthly meetings of the new and pregnant mothers in their neighborhoods and screening here the videos that had been created locally. This screening would allow the attendees some time with the health worker to pose their questions. It also gave them a space in which to interact with each other and share an experience that they could later discuss. Since the intervention aimed to inform the mother as well as other older women in the household, mothers-in-law and aunts of the new mothers were also welcome to attend these meetings. When I did have a chance to meet the women face to face, I was also able to ask them about their technology practices and observe them interact with their mobile phones. In the remaining part of this chapter, I will compare these experiences and discuss the differences between them.

Gaining Access

As mentioned earlier, my research found male youths to be the lead adopters of mobile phones across the Indian field sites I studied, engaging with their devices for various forms of media consumption and sharing. Their practices also gain more visibility because they are themselves more visible, as discussed in prior work (Kumar 2015). Accordingly, in the range of the urban and rural locales I explored, access to male youths was significantly easier to obtain than access to women. Not only are men more readily found in public places, they are willing and uninhibited when it comes to conversations with an outsider, and interested in learning about their lives. Being a woman was frequently influential in this regard as well. By contrast, both young and old women were harder to reach. As a research contact mentioned, 'If you want to talk to women, you will have to spend more time. You will have to go into their homes. You will have to get to know them.' In the course of my doctoral research, given the novelty of the findings obtained from talking to the men alone, I chose to focus on the latter at that time, instead of investing the time to study women, which would have involved visiting one home after another for hours on end. An additional complication was that obtaining female research contacts was a challenge in several of my field sites, since this task required the women to have a fundamentally outgoing nature—not as socially acceptable a way of being for rural Indian women overall.

I first chose to do what came more easily—reaching out to the most accessible participants and slowly snowball sampling (Goodman 1961) deeper and wider into the community. However, this led to talking only to more male youths. Were I merely to present these findings, my research would serve to generate the general impression that it was only men who engaged with mobile phones. With several of these men also being of the view that women did not *know* how to use mobile devices, in addition to the fact that several of the women do not *own* mobile devices, sampling techniques that relied on these inputs would lead to skewed findings. For an accurate picture to emerge that does justice to the complexities around women's ownership and use of mobile phones, data about their engagement with mobile phones must be collected using more qualitative approaches. Data-driven approaches that have a quantitative basis lack the sensitivity required to uncover the existing power structures that dictate technological interactions.

For an accurate picture to emerge, the researcher must jump over methodological hurdles, charting the paths for data to emerge. In the case of my research, a degree of reflexivity was essential in order to explain the focus on male participants. This also helped to highlight the fact that what one *does not see* can be as crucial as what one does observe. For example, by focusing on male youths, I was unable to discern the contribution that their relative social freedom made to their technology-adoption curves. The fact that there were physical spaces to which these youths had access and the women did not was something I overlooked in the initial phases of my fieldwork. I discuss this further later.

WHY INTERVIEW?

Before continuing to discuss interviewing, I return to the question of whether interviews can offer us insights that an abundance of data cannot. My field experiences offered me a suitable counterexample in this record. With the start of our health intervention Projecting Health, we made sure diligently to capture data regarding meetings among stakeholders and the disseminations that took place in the meetings of Accredited Social Health Activists (ASHAs) with the mothers. We knew who attended which dissemination, where it was organized, and whether there were any problems that arose because of which the dissemination was disturbed. We had access to all the kinds of numbers that we could possibly collect. In one of my initial field visits to rural Uttar Pradesh, I was keen to meet with women who had attended these disseminations and interacted with our intervention to ask them about their experience. To create a list of women to meet, I went through 'success stories', transcripts of short conversations that our ground staff had organized in order to hear from community members.

One such woman was Rani, from the village of Bhitargaon, who had indicated in her story that everyone at home, including her husband and father-in-law, had viewed the film on 'Danger Signs' and knew what to look out for when she went into labor if there were complications. This seemed unusual to me, since it was generally unheard of for men to attend these disseminations—they are organized for women and it goes against social norms for men to participate in a roomful of women. I asked if I could interview Rani and the project staff first introduced me to the ASHA who was responsible for the area in which Rani lived. This ASHA took me to Rani's house, where I found that it was not okay for me to enter her house and she was not permitted to leave it because her father-in-law would disapprove. The interview took place with the two of us seated on either side of the threshold of the house. During this interview, I found that Rani had been pregnant but unable to leave the confines of her house because she had married into an upper-caste family where, I was told, it was customary for daughters-in-law to stay at home until 'they had had a couple of children'. As a result, the ASHA had taken it upon herself to borrow the pico projector and conduct a dissemination *inside* Rani's house. That is why the men in the household had been able to watch the film as well. This was a critical finding—that some daughters-in-law could not be reached through meetings organized by ASHAs and the ASHAs had resorted to conducting 'unofficial' disseminations that they considered to be outside the scope of their duties. Although we had diligently been collecting data at the disseminations, what we discerned from this interview with Rani was that *we did not know what we did not know.* It was due to probing during the interview that we discovered the socio-cultural factors that were limiting the reach of our project. Moreover, we were able to explore additional avenues for the success of our project now that we knew about the 'unofficial' disseminations.

ONE-TO-ONE VERSUS ONE-TO-MANY

The decision of when to interview one versus many participants at the same time has been an important learning process, and one that has an impact on the quality of data collected. Through the course of my ethnographic fieldwork, I found conducting one-on-one interviews with young male participants to be reasonably straightforward. Some interviews were rich, others were not as rich, but the process of data gathering was uncomplicated. However, when I tried to meet a male participant outside of a pre-specified location, I found that it was challenging to remove the participant from his context. Whether this was at a local village concert or a mobile shop in the village market, requesting a one-on-one conversation was seen as inappropriate. When I attempted to have conversations that included large groups of men, the participants were more inclined to look at each other and either laugh or stay silent instead of addressing any questions. Interviewing several male youths at once led to greater diversions and subsequently less authentic data. I was frequently asked why I was asking the questions I posed to them, and whether I was married, 'because me and my friends were looking at you and wondering whether you were married or not'. At mobile shops, when I tried to ask the owners questions about their customers' practices, a large group of men would invariably collect beside me, eager to witness the process. Wanting to speak with one participant meant I had to be prepared to handle several others whom I had not recruited.

In the case of my interviews with women, however, the opposite was true, for the women appeared to be less inhibited in sharing their experiences when they were around other women, even if these experiences were occasionally of a private nature, or ones I might have considered private based on my own cultural background, which was both similar and different. These women would be shy and reluctant to engage in conversations with me until more women became available. In group settings, they found it easier to build on each other's accounts rather than volunteer their own. These group interviews would frequently evolve into brainstorming sessions since the women would discuss topics such as how the films could be disseminated more widely within their communities, among others. If some women were relatively quiet, the others would goad them into voicing their views, saying 'speak, don't be shy', thus helping my cause. Had I been a male researcher this kind of access would have been out of the question, which brings me to the question of how the quality of research might be affected by the gender of the researcher in such settings, influencing the larger body of work overall.

GENDER, CASTE, CLASS

Interviewing men about women and women about men can yield findings different from the reverse (Kumar 2015). For instance, the men I interviewed were inclined to believe that the women they knew were much less likely to engage with their technology devices since they simply did not know how to. This was due in part to the fact that the women, particularly those who were married, interacted with technologies largely in their own time and not generally in front of the men. Another factor that contributed to this misguided perception was the fact that women did not venture out to mobile shops as the men did. A few men who were part of our study, however, did point out that these women would hand over their mobile phones to the men in their family, and have them run their mobile-related errands instead. Again, it is not socially acceptable for women to go out into the marketplace on their own. These limitations that stem from the patriarchal values perpetuated in and by these households and societies are wont to color the perceptions of the interviewer as well. Seeing through the eyes of our participants also means understanding what is or is not visible to them.

The identity of the researcher is known to play a role in the way in which interviews (and other data-collection exercises) unfold. Although I speak Hindi and could communicate with my interview participants, I remained an 'outsider' for them (Song and Parker 1995). I have mentioned how my being a woman played out when I spoke to male youths versus married women. In a market in Bikaner, I saw a young man chatting on his laptop in three different windows simultaneously. In one window he typed 'Hi Sexy', in another 'R you there?', and in the third 'Want 2 chat?'. Intrigued, I approached him and asked if I could ask him some questions. He appeared not to have heard. I asked again, but could not get him to engage with me. When my research contact spoke to him, however, he responded. I learned that he did not wish to engage because I was a woman. His online activity would have revealed a different persona altogether, where socio-cultural boundaries seemed only to dissolve.

Conversations around caste also made their way into my interviews. Raja, a mobile shop assistant in Bikaner, asked me what caste I belonged to. In an effort to stress my progressive stand, I said that it did not matter. He persisted, saying that I made no sense—that the government recorded castes in census data, so who was I to say they did not matter? His conclusion was that I came from a lower, backward caste because I was unwilling to reveal it. Gradually I learned that my participants in Bikaner would openly converse with me only once they had satisfied themselves that I belonged to a 'respectable' caste. This became apparent when one mobile shop owner asked my research contact his full (including family) name. My contact left out his family name and only mentioned his middle name—from which his caste could not be determined. The shop owner then asked for the neighborhood where my contact lived. I was told later that he had done so to ascertain whether the neighborhood housed respectable families from upper castes. As the conversation progressed, I learned that speaking style was also a clear indicator of caste. The differential treatment meted out to members of different castes was unknown to me at first because I had nothing to which to compare.

Although caste helped me get easier access, class was not always on my side. I was seen as privileged by most groups and individuals I interviewed. Not only were my physical traits—my height or my short hair—anomalous, being city bred meant (to them) that I was weaker and less experienced. When I was offered water by a group of women in rural Rajasthan, I said yes—only to be laughed at minutes later because I could not drink directly from a pitcher without spilling the water. The men were unwilling to believe that I was doing research—they thought I was likely to be the 'police' or a 'reporter' because I carried a camera and asked too many (seemingly irrelevant) questions. One mobile shop owner thought I was asking questions because I wanted to start an illegal downloads business of my own, and proceeded to explain where I should invest and what would be less lucrative. This was when I was carefully transparent about my identity.

Gender, caste, and class are the boundaries that I encountered repeatedly in my work. There are others, such as religion, race, or region, which could have just as easily played a role. These have impacts on both the nature and quality of data collected as well as how the researcher is seen by the participants. These boundaries can sometimes be circumvented to advantage. For example, I leveraged the occasional presence of my American (Caucasian) colleagues to make the data collection proceed more smoothly. Elimination of these boundaries is not possible; they are inherently part of the socio-technical system being studied. Being aware of and reflexive about them, however, is essential to ensure that the data are analyzed appropriately.

The fact that access to research data depends so significantly on the researcher's own identity, among other factors, tells us that there are several unknowns involved. Qualitative approaches (and ethnographic ones in particular) allow us to get a better sense of the factors that might influence the nature and quality of data collected so that we can account for them when we analyze these data. Quantitative approaches would not give us this 'hidden' knowledge that is so essential to the process of sense-making.

MOBILE DATA

In this chapter, I have discussed research that was aimed at understanding the mobile media practices of men and women. Could studying mobile devices help in achieving this research outcome, circumventing the need for interviews? One of my early research attempts was indeed to obtain mobile phone data from devices by looking at memory cards and the content on them. Since the devices used were *feature phones* (those equipped with memory cards but not internet enabled) and data plans were still unaffordable, the content on these devices was controlled largely by the mobile shop owners and not the individuals, based on the frequency of visits to their shops. Thus, most devices had similar-looking repositories of mobile media. Interviews were necessary to understand where this content came from, who it was shared with, and how. Yet those interviews could not tell me, without self-reporting bias, *what* media my participants were consuming on their devices. A major confounding factor was the shared technology access model that was prevalent among my participants. Frequently, multiple individuals accessed one mobile device, as against a one-to-one device-ownership model. This is starkly different from the modes of use prevalent in the global North. Although I had expected that privacy would be a concern—because what individuals have on their mobile phones could be of an entirely personal nature—it turned out to be less so than I had anticipated. Mobile shop owners talked openly about the content on their customers' phones, although offensive content was labeled 'family content' and not discussed (likely because of my gender). Women, on the other hand, were comfortable sharing everything on their devices with me. Once again, without the use of qualitative and/or ethnographic methods, we may be likely to make inaccurate assumptions regarding privacy concerns.

CONCLUSION

The objective of this chapter was to do two things. The first was to argue that even though we are living in an increasingly data-driven world, there are research contexts (such as the study of the mobile media practices of marginalized communities) where 'big data' may not be relevant. The second was to demonstrate how careful interviewing, ethnographically motivated, can lead to reliable data, particularly when there is awareness regarding how socio-cultural differences between the researcher and the researched can unfold and influence the processes of data collection and analysis. In addition to gender, class, and caste, as discussed here, various other socially constructed realities can similarly influence data-collection processes, as well as the authenticity of the data collected. Experimenting with these different lenses can aid the researcher in becoming cognizant of the socio-cultural forces at play. Paying attention to these differences is only a recent trend in ICTD research (Dell and Kumar 2016), as the field matures and is better able to understand ICT use and adoption. I reiterate that not only would quantitative, data-driven approaches be unable to capture the essence of these differences, they would prevent us from even uncovering what differences might exist. In my field experiences, I found that widening the net to include different dimensions in my purposive sampling process gave me a richer understanding of the socio-technical context I was in, leading to greater confidence in my findings (Burrell and Toyama 2009): for example, working through the difference between perception and reality as far as women's mobile practices were concerned. Not only must these differences be duly acknowledged, the researcher needs also to be attentive to their potential impact on the quality of the resulting research.

REFERENCES

Andrejevic, M. (2013) *Infoglut: How Too Much Information is Changing the Way We Think and Know* (New York: Routledge).

Anokwa, Y., Smyth, T., Ramachandran, D., et al. (2009) Stories From the Field: Reflections on HCI4D Experiences. *Information Technologies & International Development* 5(4): 101–15.

Bamberger, M. (Ed.) (2000) *Integrating Quantitative and Qualitative Research in Development Projects* (Washington, DC: The World Bank).

Becker, H. (1996) The Epistemology of Qualitative Research. In R. Jessor, A. Colby and R. Shweder (Eds.), *Ethnography and Human Development: Context and Meaning in Social Inquiry* (Chicago: University of Chicago Press), pp. 53–71.

boyd, d. and Crawford, K. (2012) Critical Questions for Big Data: Provocations for a Cultural, Technological, and Scholarly Phenomenon. *Information, Communication & Society* 15(5): 662–79.

Brewer, E., Demmer, M., Du, B., et al. (2005) The Case for Technology in Developing Regions. *Computer* 38(6): 25–38.

Burrell, J. and Toyama, K. (2009) What Constitutes Good ICTD Research? *Information Technologies & International Development* 5(3): 82–94.

Bryman, A. (2016) *Social Research Methods*. 5th ed. (Oxford: Oxford University Press).

Bryman, A. and Burgess, R. (1999) *Qualitative Research. Vol. 2. Methods of Qualitative Research* (London: Sage).

Chase, S. (2011) Narrative Inquiry. Still a Field in the Making. In N. Denzin and Y. Lincoln (Eds.), *The Sage Handbook of Qualitative Research* (London, New Delhi, Singapore: Sage), pp. 421–34.

Dell, N. and Kumar, N. (2016) The Ins and Outs of HCI for Development. In *Proceedings of the ACM Conference on Human Factors in Computing Systems (CHI '16)*.

Goodman, L. (1961) Snowball Sampling. *The Annals of Mathematical Statistics* 32(1): 148–70.

Keats, P. (2009) Multiple Text Analysis in Narrative Research: Visual, Written, and Spoken Stories of Experience. *Qualitative Research* 9(2): 181–95.

Kluver, R., Campbell, H. A. and Balfour, S. (2013) Language and the Boundaries of Research: Media Monitoring Technologies in International Media Research. *Journal of Broadcasting & Electronic Media* 57(1): 4–19.

Kumar, N. and Parikh, T. S. (2013) Mobiles, Music, and Materiality. In *Proceedings of the SIGCHI conference on human factors in computing systems* (New York: ACM), pp. 2863–72.

Kumar, N. and Anderson, R. J. (2015) Mobile Phones for Maternal Health in Rural India. In *Proceedings of the 33rd Annual ACM Conference on Human Factors in Computing Systems* (New York: ACM), pp. 427–36.

Kumar, N. (2015) The Gender-Technology Divide or Perceptions of Non-Use? *First Monday* 20(11): http://firstmonday.org/ojs/index.php/fm/article/view/6300 (accessed 20 March 2016).

Kumar, N., Perrier, T., Desmond, M., et al. (2015) *Projecting Health: Community-Led Video Education for Maternal Health*. Proceedings of the Seventh Conference on Information and Communications Technology and Development (Singapore: ACM).

Kvale, S. (1996) *Interviews: An Introduction to Qualitative Research Interviewing* (London: Sage).

Narayana, M. (2011) Telecommunications Services and Economic Growth: Evidence from India. *Telecommunications Policy* 35(2): 115–27.

Rubin, H. and Rubin, I. (2011) *Qualitative Interviewing: The Art of Hearing Data*. 3rd ed. (London: Sage).

Sachs, J. (2012) From Millennium Development Goals to Sustainable Development Goals. *The Lancet* 379(9832): 2206–11.

Song, M. and Parker, D. (1995) Commonality, Difference and the Dynamics of Discourse in In-depth Interviewing. *Sociology* 29(2): 241–56.

PART IV

Visualization

Lev Manovich

VISUALIZING MEDIA

Early 21st-century media researchers have access to unprecedented amounts of media—more than they can possibly study, let alone search or even simply watch. A number of interconnected developments that took place between 1990 and 2010—digitization of analog media collections, decrease in prices and expansion in capacities of portable computer-based media devices, the rise of user-generated content and social media, and globalization that increased the number of agents and institutions producing media around the world—led to an exponential increase in the quantity of media while simultaneously making it much easier to find, share, teach with, and research. Many millions of hours of television programs already digitized by various national libraries and media museums, digitized library photo collections, billions of videos on YouTube and photos on Instagram, and numerous other media sources are waiting to be explored by researchers. The chapters following this short introduction address potential ways of managing and making inspiring use of the vast amount of visual data.

How do we take advantage of this new scale of media in practice? For instance, let us say that we are interested in studying how presentations and interviews by political leaders are reused and contextualized by television

L. Manovich (✉)
CUNY, New York City, NY, USA
e-mail: manovich.lev@gmail.com

programs in different countries. When I was working on a grant application designed to address this question a few years ago, we wanted to use video collections that contained tens of thousands of hours of video. We wanted to describe the rhetorical, editing, and cinematographic strategies specific to each video set, understand how different stations may be using the video of political leaders in different ways, identify outliers, and find clusters of programs that share similar patterns. But how could we simply watch all this material to begin pursuing these and other questions?

Yet even when we are dealing with large digital collections of still images—for instance, 175,000 digitized photos of life in America taken in 1935 and 1944 by photographers who were hired by Farm Security Administration—such tasks are no easier to accomplish.[1] The most basic method that always worked when numbers of media objects were small—look at all images or video, notice patterns, and interpret them—no longer works. And if we want to tag media objects manually, this also does not scale for the size of contemporary media collections of user-generated content.

Given the size of many digital media collections, simply seeing what is inside them is impossible (even before we begin formulating questions and hypotheses and selecting samples for closer analysis). Popular interfaces for massive digital media collections such as text search, and list, gallery, grid, and slide views, do now allow us to see the contents of a whole collection. These interfaces usually only display a few items at a time. Such access methods do not allow us to understand the 'shape' of the overall collection and notice interesting patterns.

We can, of course, use data analysis and visualization techniques to analyze media metadata, such as author names, production dates, program titles, image formats, or, in the case of social media services, upload dates, user-assigned tags, geo coordinates, and other user- or machine-created data. Over the years, as more 'big metadata' for media become available, we will see more scholars in communication and media studies using visualization tools to explore these metadata, and using visualizations in their publications.

In many cases, the metadata function as the data. That is to say, their analysis is the main subject of research. For example, we may use visualization to show patterns in numbers of movies from various countries shown in a set of countries over a number of years, or television programs in every country. Or we can use computer vision technologies to detect type content in millions of YouTube videos and visualize patterns in this content, and so on.

However, even the richest metadata available today for media collections do not capture many patterns that we can easily notice when we directly watch video, look at photographs, or view websites—for example, when we study the media itself as opposed to metadata about it. So when we use bar plots, scatter plots, networks, maps, and other standard visualization techniques to show patterns in (for example) distributions of television subjects, or the sentiment of user posts about the shows, this is not sufficient. So what is the solution? I think that rather than only thinking of media and communication scholars as users of existing visualization techniques and tools, we need to encourage them to develop new techniques that can allow them to study media artifacts themselves at any scale.

The popular media-access technologies of the 19th and 20th centuries, such as slide lanterns, film projectors, microforms, Moviola and Steenbeck, record players, audio- and video-tape recorders, and video-cassette recorders, were designed to access a single media item at a time at a limited range of speeds. This went hand in hand with the organization of media distribution: television channels, movie theaters, radio, record, and video stores, and libraries would all only make available a few items at a time. For instance, you could not watch more than a few television channels at the same time, or borrow more than a few videotapes from a library.

At the same time, hierarchical classification systems such as library catalogs made it difficult to browse a larger collection or explore it in ways outside of existing classifications. When you walked from shelf to shelf in a library, you were typically following a classification based on subjects, with books organized by author names inside each category. Together, these distribution and classification systems encouraged 20th century media researchers to decide beforehand what media items to see, hear, or read. A researcher usually started with some subject in mind—films by a particular author, works by a particular photographer, or categories such as '1950s experimental American films' and 'early 20th century Paris postcards'. It was impossible to imagine navigating through all films ever made or all postcards ever printed. One of the first media projects to organize its narrative around navigation of a large media archive is Jean-Luc Godard's *Histoire(s) du cinema*, which draws samples from hundreds of films. The popular method for describing a larger media set—content analysis, such as tagging of semantics in a media collection by several people using a pre-defined vocabulary of terms—also requires that a researcher decide beforehand what information would be relevant to tag. In other words, as opposed to exploring a media collection without any pre-conceived expectations or hypotheses—just to 'see what is there'—a researcher has to postulate 'what was there'; that is, what are the important types of information worth seeking out.

The current standard in online media access—computer search—does not take us out of this paradigm. Search interface is a blank frame waiting for you to type something. Before you click on the search button, you have to decide what keywords and phrases to search for. So while search brings a dramatic increase in speed of access, its deep assumption (which we may be able to trace back to the origins of search in the 1950s when most scientists did not think about how huge massive digital collections could become) is that you know beforehand something about the collection that is worth exploring further.

My informal review of the largest online institutional media collections available today suggests that the typical interfaces they offer combine 19th century technologies of hierarchical categories and mid-20th century technology of information retrieval (such as search using metadata recorded for media items). Sometimes collections also have subject tags. In all cases, the categories, metadata, and tags were input by the archivists. This process imposes particular orders on the data. As a result, when users access institutional media collections via these websites, they can only move along a fixed number of trajectories defined by the taxonomy of the collection and types of metadata.

In contrast, when you observe a physical scene directly with your eyes, you can look anywhere in any order. This allows you quickly to notice a variety of patterns, structures, and relations. Imagine, for example, turning the corner on a city street and taking in the view of the open square, with passersby, cafés, cars, trees, advertising, store windows, and all the other elements. You can quickly detect and follow a multitude of dynamically changing patterns based on visual and semantic information: cars moving in parallel lines, houses painted in similar colors, people who move along their own trajectories and people talking to each other, unusual faces, shop windows that stand out from the rest, and so on.

We need similar 'media visualization' techniques that would allow us to observe vast media universes and quickly detect interesting patterns. These techniques have to operate at speeds many times faster than the normally intended playback speed (in the case of time-based media). Or, to use an example of still images, we should be able to see important information in one million images in the same time as it takes us to see it in a single image. These techniques have to compress massive media universes into smaller observable media 'landscapes' compatible with human information-processing rates. At the same time, they have to keep enough of the details from the original images, video, audio, or interactive experiences to enable the study of subtle patterns in the data.

A number of experimental projects have already started to move in this direction. For example, in 2016 NYPL (New York Public Library) Lab created an online interactive visual interface that combines visualization and media browsing to allow visitors to navigate across hundreds of thousands of public domain images.[2] In 2014, archive.org released its own innovative interface that allows exploration of video clips from over one million television programs. Such projects give us a preview of how media and communication studies scholars may use visualization in the future—that is, rather than only being its 'users', they would also become inventors of new methods and interfaces for researching media.

NOTES

1. See http://www.loc.gov/pictures/collection/fsa (accessed 10 March 2016).
2. For this and the following website, see http://publicdomain.nypl.org/pd-visualization and https://archive.org/details/tv (both accessed 10 March 2016).

CHAPTER 12

Ways of Seeing Data: Toward a Critical Literacy for Data Visualizations as Research Objects and Research Devices

Jonathan Gray, Liliana Bounegru, Stefania Milan, and Paolo Ciuccarelli

'Every image embodies a way of seeing' wrote the British art critic John Berger in his 1972 classic *Ways of Seeing* (Berger 1972, p. 10). Through the book and accompanying television series, he proposed elements of a critical literacy for making sense of the visual landscapes that we inhabit—from reproductions of art historical masterpieces to the advertising that adorns our cities and media environments. As well as guiding the attention of his viewers and readers around specific images, he also sought to examine the way in which images are reproduced and mediated (drawing on the

J. Gray (✉) • S. Milan
University of Amsterdam, Amsterdam, Netherlands
e-mail: contact@jonathangray.org; Stefania.Milan@eui.eu

L. Bounegru
University of Groningen, Groningen, Netherlands
e-mail: liliana.bounegru@gmail.com

P. Ciuccarelli
Politecnico di Milan, Milan, Italy
e-mail: paolo.ciuccarelli@polimi.it

© The Author(s) 2016
S. Kubitschko, A. Kaun (eds.), *Innovative Methods in Media and Communication Research*, DOI 10.1007/978-3-319-40700-5_12

227

work of the German philosopher and critic Walter Benjamin), as well as the broader social, cultural, economic, and political contexts around them.

In the digital age, data visualizations are becoming an increasingly prominent genre for the visual representation and mediation of collective life—from digital analytics dashboards to interactive news graphics. Similarly, data visualizations are becoming more and more popular in media and communications studies, and in the humanities and social sciences more broadly. According to Stephen Few, 'data visualization is the graphical display of abstract information for two purposes: sense-making (also called data analysis) and communication' (2014, n.p.). This might include, for example, the representation of information about numbers, words, relations, times, or locations. But why have data visualizations become so prevalent? And what does it mean to approach data visualization as a research device? What might it offer media and communications scholars? Data visualizations promise to assist us in making sense of complex data and complex phenomena, allowing us to simplify and bring order to dense information, for explanatory and communicative purposes. They may help us to analyze, filter, browse, and explore complex information. Paraphrasing Marshall McLuhan (1962), data visualizations are said to amplify our senses and our abilities to make sense of the world around us. Yet data visualizations are not a neutral tool. They come with particular 'ways of seeing', particular analytic, mediation, and narrative regimes regarding which we ought to be attentive as we use data visualizations to do research and tell stories.

Taking inspiration from Berger's agenda, in this chapter we argue that the use of data visualizations as both instruments and objects of study requires commensurate forms of critical literacy. We also draw on Philip Agre's (1997) notion of 'critical technical practice' for the social study of artificial intelligence and from Bernhard Rieder and Theo Röhle's (2012) notion of 'methodological reflexivity' in relation to digital methods in the humanities and social sciences, both of which gesture toward forms of engagement with new research methods and technologies that are accompanied by critical reflection on their uses. We seek to extend Rieder and Röhle's proposition that research practices ought to 'oscillate [...] between concrete technical work and methodological reflexivity' (2012, p. 80) to the practice of working with data visualizations.

We argue that data visualizations are not only bright adornments to our 21st-century information environments. They embody and engender not only particular ways of *seeing* (as Berger comments), but also ways of *knowing* and ways of *organizing* collective life in our digital age. In other words, data visualizations reflect and articulate their own particular modes of rationality, epistemology, politics, culture, and experience. It is precisely to emphasize these 'world-making' capacities that in this chapter we prefer the term 'device' to the more commonly utilized term 'tool' to refer to data visualization. While the term 'tool' establishes the object as possessing coherence and connotes an instrumental relationship between user and object, this chapter proposes to develop an account of data visualization as device in order to draw attention to its capacity to 'assemble and arrange the world in specific social and material patterns' (Law and Ruppert 2013, p. 230). While arriving at media and communication studies with particular inscriptions as already described, following Law and Ruppert (2013) we argue that data visualization as a device is at the same time indeterminate and open to multiple and diverse forms of usage. For this reason, to follow Marres and Gerlitz (2015), deploying data visualization in media and communication research may be thought of as a process of developing mechanisms to align its affordances (and limitations) with the discipline-specific conventions of our fields. Given the growing role of data visualizations in our information environments, we think it is vital to develop a critical literacy to read, understand, and work with them.

We propose a three-part heuristic framework for what should be taken into account when reading, working with, and conducting research about data visualization. In doing so, this chapter does not aim to develop a practical guide for the effective use of visualization in media and communication research *per se*. Instead, we propose a framework to sensitize researchers to forms of mediation embedded in data visualization as a research device in order to support its critical and reflexive use.

This framework is organized around three forms of mediation that can be studied in relation to data visualization: (1) the mediation from *world to data* of the sources of information that underpin visualizations; (2) the mediation from *data to image* of the graphical representations of this information; and (3) the mediation from *image to eye* and the mind in the socially, culturally, and historically specific 'ways of seeing' engendered in the data visualization. Each of these three forms of mediation can be studied with a broad range of methods—from more familiar qualitative and quantitative approaches (such as visual and textual analysis, interviews, or surveys) to emerging digital and computational methods. We describe and illustrate these different forms of mediation, and ways of studying them, with reference to a collection of over two hundred data visualizations about public finances.

While for heuristic purposes our framework proposes the study of mediations between 'world', 'data', 'image', and 'eye', our intention is to provide a starting point to inform and broaden inquiry rather than to propose a neat and rigid distinction between these different elements. They are in fact mutually constitutive, such that data constitute as much as they represent the societal dynamics that they measure (Espeland and Stevens 2008) and regimes of measurement and visualization are generative of specific publics, practices, and cultures (Ruppert 2015). The forms of mediation we propose are also not exhaustive. For example, drawing on research on the reactivity of metrics (Espeland and Sauder 2007; Gerlitz and Lury 2014), a fourth layer of mediation could be formulated, concerned with the study of actions to intervene, respond to, and modify the dynamics that data visualizations capture. In addition to this, as the following sections will show, each of the three forms of mediation is actually constituted by multiple sublayers of mediation or inscription. These will vary according to the nature of the 'research apparatus' in which visualizations are embedded, in that different types of data and methods are accompanied by different types of inscription (Ruppert et al. 2013). We also do not hold a strict order with regard to the proposed layers of mediation.

The past few decades have seen the development of a body of literature dedicated to data visualization and information graphics. In particular, there is a growing body of books and articles offering practical guidance as well as showcasing different examples, techniques, and approaches.[1] This literature is itself interesting not only from a practical perspective, but also as a way to understand the forms of mediation involved in the composition of data visualizations—both those that receive attention and those that remain neglected—as well as the aesthetics, cultures, values, ideals, and practices associated with their production. These resources can be useful as a source for disassembling and understanding the making of data visualization projects.

While many of these works focus on a single layer of mediation—that of data to the image, looking at how information is translated into graphical form—we suggest that in using and studying data visualizations it is essential to grasp not just the production of images from data, but also the data sets and data infrastructures on which data visualizations draw, as well as the cultural practices and ideals implicated in the composition of visualizations that invite a particular way of seeing. There have been a number of very informative works on this latter topic (for example Drucker 2014; Halpern 2015), which we will explore further later. Here our focus is less on data visualization as a field, but rather on developing the elements of a critical reflexivity that would accompany and inform the practice of data visualization in research and other contexts. This critical reflexivity is important not only in the study of data visualizations as objects, but also in improving our abilities to deploy them as research devices. We outline research outlooks and methods for studying all three forms of mediation, as well as pointing to further resources that may be useful for each one.

AN EXAMPLE: VISUALIZING INFORMATION ABOUT PUBLIC FINANCES

To illustrate our proposed framework, we have chosen to work with a collection of data visualization projects about public finances. These include data visualization projects from media organizations, journalists, civil society organizations, and public institutions. This collection has been gathered in the context of research to map empirically how information about public finances is used in the service of democratic engagement with fiscal policy (Gray 2015a).[2]

There are two main reasons why we consider this thematic focus suitable to make our case. First, there is a long tradition of work exploring public finances with information graphics. Edward Tufte uses public finances to illustrate discussion of different techniques in his classic *The Visual Display of Quantitative Information*, citing a venerable tradition of information graphics that 'nearly always create the impression that spending and debt are rapidly increasing' (Tufte 2001, p. 65). He alludes to the fiscal information graphics of the Scottish engineer, economist, and pioneer of statistical graphics William Playfair, such as the one in Fig. 12.1.

The second reason is that there is a heterogeneous constellation of different issues and concerns that are associated with public finances and fiscal policy. As well as political and economic questions, from who in society pays how much tax and how public resources are allocated, many policy areas are underpinned by discussions about public finances, from international development to climate change. The complexity and competing narratives around this topic make it well suited to illustrate different approaches for studying data visualizations.

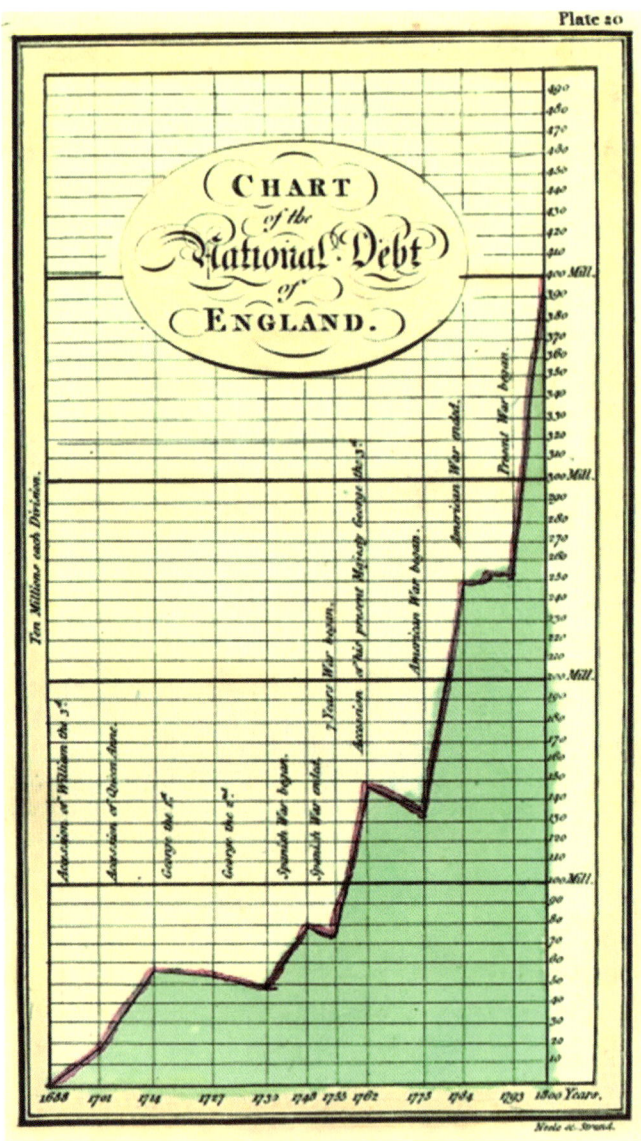

Fig. 12.1 'Chart of the national debt of England' from William Playfair's *The Commercial and Political Atlas* (Playfair 1801)

THREE FORMS OF MEDIATION AND HOW TO STUDY THEM

In this section we will propose a research outlook and methods for studying each of the three forms of mediation implicated in the creation of data visualizations that we have outlined. This may serve as a checklist of questions and a menu of different methods that can be used.

From World to Data

As we shall see in the next section, many classic works on information visualization focus on the mediation of data to image—in particular focusing on the avoidance of misrepresentation. For example, Tufte suggests that 'graphical excellence requires telling the truth about data' (Tufte 2001, p. 51) and that data visualization designers should 'let the data speak for itself' (1997a, p. 45), championing an aesthetic program of 'graphical integrity' that we shall challenge and explore further. But what about the data themselves? How does the making of data shape the making of knowledge through visualizations?

Our first form of mediation to be studied is how the data used in the visualization are generated and how this process inscribes itself in the knowledge produced through data visualizations. This might include asking questions such as:

- What information and data are being represented in the visualization?
- What are the sources for this information? Where do the data come from?
- How are the data generated? What are the rationales, methods, and standards inscribed in the data infrastructures through which the data are generated?
- How are the data transformed or prepared?
- Which data sources are combined and how?
- How do the data selectively prioritize certain things over others?

The first step will often be establishing the data sources. In some cases details about the sources of the information will be explicitly referenced or linked to. In other cases additional work might be needed in order to identify these sources. This might be matching the precise tables or data sets that are used from a number of possible contenders (for example in cases where the institution or database is given, but not the exact table or data set); looking in the software source code or documentation of the visualization to look for data sources; or conducting interviews with the creators of a data visualization to establish what data were used.

Once data sets are established for a given visualization, there are different approaches to studying and analyzing them. For example, the study of data sources might draw on literature about 'sourcing practices' from media studies and journalism studies (Cottle 2003; Manning 2001; Hall et al. 1978; Berkowitz 2009). Research can also be undertaken on the 'data infrastructures' implicated in the production of the data sets that are used in the visualizations. Drawing on previous work in this area, we take the phrase 'data infrastructure' to designate socio-technical systems implicated in the creation, processing, and distribution of data (see, for example, Akrich 1992). This might include elements such as standards bodies, software systems, administrative procedures, committees, consultancy processes, and many other things (Gray and Davies 2015).[3] Here it may be useful to draw on approaches from science and technology studies (STS) to trace the politics embedded in these systems—for instance through what has been called 'infrastructure ethnography' (see, for example, Star and Ruhleder 1996; Star 1999; Bowker and Star 1999). The composition of data infrastructures will lead to the production of different types of data, from statistical data to transactional 'digital traces' extracted from digital platforms.

How might we operationalize these approaches in relation to our collection of data visualizations about public money? First, can we *identify* the data sets that are used in the visualizations? The different ways of citing or linking to data sources are themselves something that can be studied, as they may reflect different kinds of ideals, norms, or practices of knowledge production. A cursory look at different data-sourcing practices reveals a wide range of ways in which data are obtained and prepared, as well as varying approaches to publishing details about data sets, software, and methodology.

In our collection, some of the projects simply cite the name of the department from which the data were derived. One example from the *New York Times* simply says 'Source: Office of Management and Budget', with no further details.[4] Many others give much more detail—including directly linking to data sets, or even providing documentation on methodology about how the data were sourced and transformed, what assumptions were made, and so on. For example, a piece from the US investigative news outlet *ProPublica* on 'The Millions New York Counties Coulda Got' is accompanied by a short methodological walkthrough titled 'How We Analyzed New York County Tobacco Bonds', explaining how the writers obtained the data, which cash flow models they used and why, and the rationales behind other assumptions they made in the application.[5]

Publishing data sources has become *de rigueur* among some data journalism outlets. A piece from the *South China Morning Post* explains how data were extracted from PDF files and provides links to the 'raw data' used in the visualizations.[6] One data visualization from the *Guardian Datablog* gives an accompanying spreadsheet that lists a separate source URL (uniform resource locator) for every figure used.[7] If visualization projects publish the source code of their software, this can be studied in order to see the data files that have been used. For example, the Budget Key project by Israeli non-profit Public Knowledge Workshop links to the source code on the social software-sharing platform GitHub, which makes visible the changes and transformations that have been made on the data.[8]

As well as looking at the sourcing and transformation of the data, we might also look at the selection of particular data sets and tables to highlight or narrate certain aspects of public finances, such as spending, revenue, or debt. Rather than simply 'telling the truth' about public finances, these selections emphasize and de-emphasize different aspects of fiscal policy. We shall further examine the affordances of different visual forms in the next section. Suffice to say here that the selection of different data sets and tables is an important step that should be taken into account in the study of data visualizations, prior to their translation into graphical form. We can compare the data mediated in the visualization to the other data that are made available. Which indicators, subtables, or items of data have been selected, which have been left out, and how does this guide our attention toward some things and not others?

An interactive news application from *The Times* (UK) called 'The Wall of Debt' shows a dominant wall of red bricks depicting 'national debt', and a comparatively small green wall called 'cuts'.[9] The visual editorial decision to select these two items is an important one in reading this interactive graphic, engaging with a particular political economic narrative about tackling public debt through spending cuts. Another short video clip called 'Debtris' by David McCandless presents a wide variety of other fiscal data points, ultimately highlighting how the global cost of the credit crisis dwarfs other sums such as the Organization of the Petroleum Exporting Countries' climate change fund, the budget of the United Nations (UN), African debt to the West, and the funds needed to 'save the Amazon rainforest'.[10] As well as looking at the selection of data on a case-by-case basis for individual visualizations, comparative analysis may be undertaken across a larger collection.

We might also study the composition of the data themselves. We could study the headers, categories, and classifications within the data sets to understand which variables and indicators are selected and prioritized. Content analysis of documentation and associated materials may provide further details about the units, forms of analysis, methodology, software, standards, and other details about how the data were generated. This might also be supplemented by interviews with those involved in the creation of the data about their decisions. It may be that data sets are generated from other, more complex database systems that may be of interest to study. In the case of public financial data, we might look into politics, rationales, and ways of knowing inscribed into the financial management information systems through which data sets about public finance are generated. These may be studied as socio-technical systems through, for example, document analysis and interviews. Sometimes there may be documentation manuals that explain how these systems function. In the case of public-sector data infrastructures, if details are not already published, then there may be routes for formally requesting them through access to information laws. Researchers and civil society groups interested in studying what was the most detailed source of information about public spending in the UK (the Combined Online Information System, or COINS) submitted official 'freedom of information' requests about the database. While their requests for its contents were initially turned down, they submitted follow-up requests asking about the database and training materials for it, which were successful.[11]

It may also be fruitful to study the categories and classification systems articulated by the data. For example, any of the data visualizations about public money uses different categories to describe different areas of expenditure. Where do these categories come from? How did they become the way they are? On the one hand we can look at the administrative contexts in which the data sets are generated, such as the organization of public-sector bodies. We might also look at which kinds of data standards shape public-sector data systems. For example, the UN COFOG (Classifications of Functions of Government) standard is widely used as a reference in order to facilitate comparability between different national budgeting processes.[12] This is particularly relevant when it comes to looking at visualizations including multiple countries, such as in international development or climate finance. The genesis of these data standards can also be studied through analysis of (historical) document collections, the study of information systems (for example, using approaches from software or platform studies), interviews, and ethnographic studies.

From Data to Image

The second form of mediation in our heuristic framework is how visualizations mediate the data sources on which they draw into graphical form. This might include addressing questions such as:

- How are the data mediated into graphical form?
- What kinds of graphical techniques, methods, and technologies have been used?
- What are their affordances? How do they guide our attention toward different aspects of the data?
- What design decisions have been taken? What are their consequences?

These concerns are prominent in both research and practical literature around data visualizations. Edward Tufte talks of 'graphical methods that *organize and order the flow of graphical information* presented to the eye' (Tufte 2001, p. 154). He places a significant premium on the 'graphical integrity' of information visualizations such that they 'defeat graphical distortion and ambiguity' (Tufte 2001, p. 77). While this is one important way of looking at how data are mediated into graphical form, there are many other important aspects to study. Rather than just looking at accuracy, fidelity, and how graphics may be truthful or untruthful about data, we can also step back and look at their affordances—such as how they articulate structures and relationships or how they organize space, time, quantity, and categories in relation to the data.

In order to study these things, we may learn a great deal from contemporary literature about the creation of data visualizations, as well as classic literature on information graphics. These can be used in order to understand the composition of data visualizations, or to 'reverse engineer' them, which helps us to develop a critical and reflexive approach to the use of data visualization as a research device. Jacques Bertin's 1967 *Semiology of Graphics* proposes a series of 'retinal variables' (1983, p. 9) including size, value, texture, color, orientation, and shape as a starting point for analyzing and working with different types of information graphics. This work provides an extensive and richly illustrated overview of how different 'components' of information can be mapped onto different visual forms. In a similar vein, Tufte's *The Visual Display of Quantitative Information* contends that 'data graphics visually display measured quantities by means of the combined use of points, lines, a coordinate system, numbers, symbols, words, shading and color' (2001, p. 9).

While Bertin's work is explicitly limited to print graphics that fit on a 'sheet of white paper' (1983, p. 42) and many of Tufte's seminal works also focus on print graphics, many of the elements they discuss have been adopted and developed in relation to digital and interactive data visualizations. Thus we may read these influential works alongside other, more recent works that cover digital tools and methods in order to understand how different visual forms are implicated in the visualizations under study—including table graphics, maps, time lines, sparklines, networks, graphs, flow diagrams, small multiples, motion charts, bubble charts, and treemaps. These different forms can also be combined to highlight different aspects of the data. We may also look at the affordances of the software or the platforms that were used to create data visualizations (see, for example, Wright 2008; Manovich 2002, 2011, 2014). As well as desktop software applications, there is a growing number of visualization tools that enable visualizations to be generated and embedded. There is also a growing number of software libraries and components that are widely used to translate data into different graphical forms.

How might we use these approaches to study our collection of data visualizations about public money? We could look at the different graphical forms used in data visualizations to organize attention around different aspects of public finances. For our collection, this could include examining how different graphical elements are used in order to:

• Show a 'bigger picture' of breakdowns of totals into different categories.
• Put different figures into context.
• Show the geographic distribution of funds.
• Show trends or developments over time.
• Show breakdown of funds by sector or recipient.
• Show networks of financial flows.
• Compare different parts of the budgeting cycle (for example, commitments and actual expenditure).
• Compare revenues, expenditures, and debts.
• Show allocations per capita.

The formal characteristics of different visualizations in a collection can be studied with reference to either a pre-defined vocabulary of elements or through an 'open coding' or 'emergent coding' process (see Strauss and Corbin 1998). As similar visual elements can play different roles in different contexts, it is crucial to note not only their presence or absence, but their *relations* with other elements in the visualization as a whole. For example, compare the use of bubbles in the visualizations in Figs. 12.2, 12.3, 12.4, 12.5, and 12.6).

With these examples we can see how the bubbles are arranged, scaled, and colored in order to draw out different characteristics of public finances—from representing hierarchical relationships in national budgets, to the locations of development funds, to health spending per capita over time, to spending per department over time, to relationships between recipients of public contracts, to the differences between commitments and spending. In each case, the bubbles are used in different ways to represent different things—with the position, size, and color having varying significance for each graphic. These different ways of organizing visual phenomena thus articulate and emphasize different ways of organizing knowledge about public finances.

As well as studying the characteristics of visualizations, their creators could be interviewed regarding their techniques, methods, software tools, and design choices. Where software repositories are available,

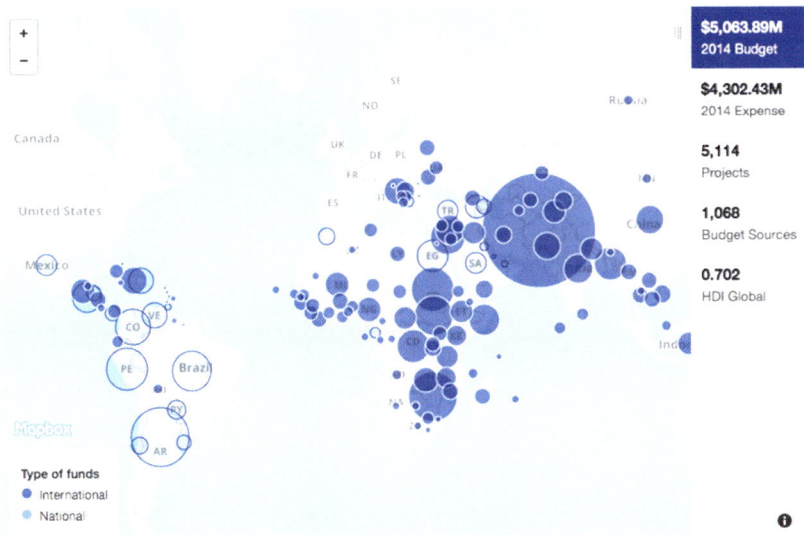

Fig. 12.2 Geographic distribution of international development spending (UNDP); http://open.undp.org/#2014 (accessed 10 March 2016)

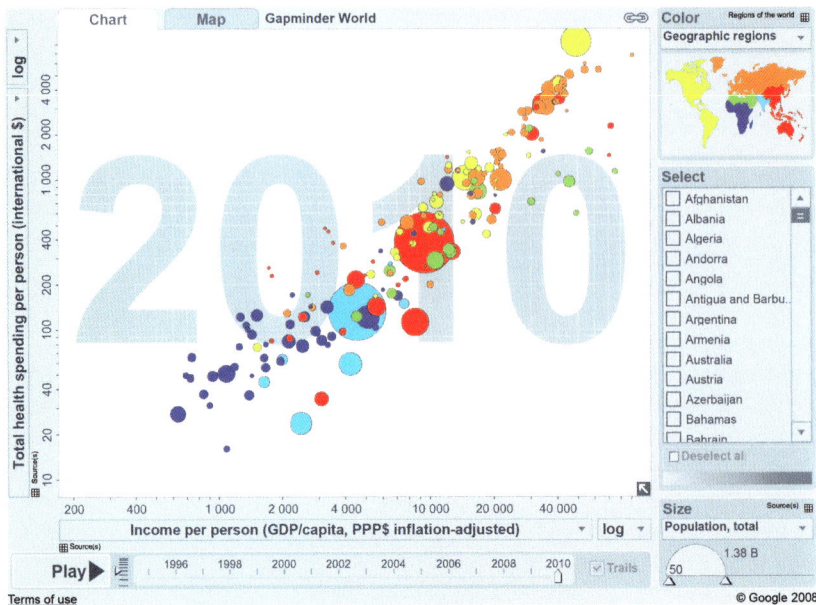

Fig. 12.3 Health spending per person compared with income per person over time; free material from http://www.gapminder.org/world (accessed 10 March 2016)

PODER EJECUTIVO

| | Enero | Febrero | Marzo | Abril | Mayo | Junio | Julio | Agosto | Septiembre | Octubre | Noviembre | Diciembre |

MIN. DE AGRICULTURA Y GANADERÍA

MIN. DE DEFENSA NACIONAL

MIN. DE EDUCACIÓN Y CULTURA

MIN. DE HACIENDA

MIN. DE INDUSTRIA Y COMERCIO

MIN. DE JUSTICIA Y TRABAJO

MIN. DE LA MUJER

MIN. DEL INTERIOR

MIN. DE OBRAS PÚBLICAS Y COMUNICACIONES

MIN. DE RELACIONES EXTERIORES

MIN. DE SALUD PÚBLICA Y BIENESTAR SOCIAL

MIN. DE TRABAJO, EMPLEO Y SEGURIDAD SOCIAL

PRESIDENCIA DE LA REPÚBLICA

VICEPRESIDENCIA DE LA REPÚBLICA

Fig. 12.4 Spending by different government departments over time (Government of Paraguay); https://www.contrataciones.gov.py/datos/visualizaciones/contratos (accessed 10 March 2016)

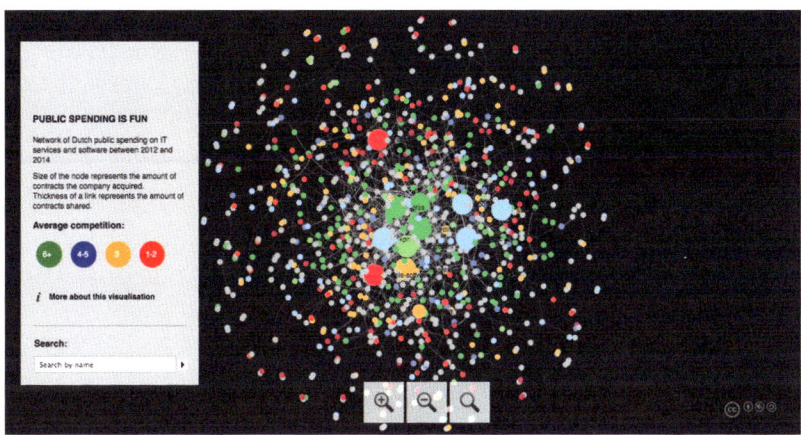

Fig. 12.5 Network of Dutch public spending on IT services and software (Adriana Homolova); http://www.homolova.sk/dh/it/# (accessed 10 March 2016)

תקציב המדינה לשנת 2016 הוא 464 מיליארד ₪
כיצד ניתן להבין אותו ביחס לתקציב 2015?

203 התחומים שגדלו מופיעים בצבעים חמים, 92 אלה שקטנו מופיעים בצבעים קרים

⊙

הכל ביחד

Fig. 12.6 Comparing commitments and spending in Israeli budget (Budget Key); http://www.obudget.org (accessed 10 March 2016)

these can also be analyzed in order to understand how data sources are being mediated into graphics, whether for individual repositories or for collections. We might, for example, study repositories associated with fiscal data visualization projects on GitHub.[13]

From Image to Eye

The third and final form of mediation in our heuristic framework is how the image appears to the eye and to the mind. As we saw in the last section, visualizations emphasize different aspects of data through design choices, techniques, and software that organize data into graphical form. However, these graphical forms also engender and depend on different socially, culturally, and historically contingent *ways of seeing data*. Hence we might ask:

- What kinds of visual cultures and practices are implicated or reflected in the data visualization? Where do these come from?
- What forms of usage are inscribed in the visualization? Who are the publics of the data visualization? How is it circulated, cited, and shared?

Rather than seeing the visual forms as neutral instruments for making evidence visible—or, as Tufte puts it, 'instruments for reasoning about quantitative information' (Tufte 2001, p. 9)—we can study their genealogies, aesthetics, and epistemological affordances to situate them in relation to other ideals, values, and practices. For example, visualizations can be read against the background of histories of science, technology, and modernity that explore the relationship between vision, knowledge, and image-making practices, from accounts of occidental 'ocularcentricism' (see Jay 1988) to the role of visual cultures in the development of conceptions of objectivity (see Daston and Galison 2010).

There have been several recent works that make the case for drawing on hermeneutic approaches from the humanities to enhance the study of data visualizations. For example, in her book *Graphesis*, Johanna Drucker advocates 'critical study of visuality from a humanistic perspective' in order to 'de-naturalize the increasingly familiar interface that has become so habitual in daily use' (Drucker 2014, p. 9–10). She explores the emergence of contemporary 'visual epistemology' with reference to a broad range of developments in art, architecture, design, industry, philosophy, and computer science—from the emergence of graphical design to interdisciplinary deliberations about visual abstraction between artists and designers associated with the Bauhaus school in Weimar Germany. In her *Beautiful Data*, Orit Halpern also similarly aims to 'denaturalize and historically situate' ideals and practices of data visualization (Halpern 2015). She traces the genesis of what she calls 'communicative objectivity' that has come to be associated with data visualizations, drawing on a different disciplinary constellation focusing on cybernetics, communication science, behavioral science, engineering, management studies, urban planning, and military research. There is also a growing body of literature focusing on the aesthetics of data visualization (see Manovich 2002; Jevbratt 2004; Lau and Vande Moere 2007; Whitelaw 2008; Sack 2011; Cubitt 2015) as well as on the development of different visual forms such as the time line (see Rosenberg and Grafton 2013) or those associated with network analysis (see Freeman 2004). The narrative dimension of data visualizations can also be studied (see Segel and Heer 2010; Venturini et al. 2016).

How might these kinds of approaches be adopted to study specific data visualizations, such as our collection about public finances? We could study the aesthetics of these visualizations—for example, the clean, minimalistic style adorned with primary-color palettes and icons that has become so widely adopted in many contemporary information graphics (Fig. 12.7).

This is similar to the aesthetic that Tufte advocates: championing efficiency and parsimony, maximizing the 'data–ink' ratio, and eliminating 'chartjunk'. He proposes that 'the design of statistical graphics is a universal matter [...] like mathematics' and that insight into the design of visualizations may be obtained through the study of 'excellence in art, architecture and prose' (Tufte 2001, p. 10). Peter Galison (1990) has previously studied the links between architectural modernism and the universal aspirations of logic, mathematics, and philosophy in the first few decades of the 20th century. Many of the fiscal data visualizations in our collection look to share this aesthetic. Several of them incorporate icons or pictograms reminiscent of those associated with the Isotype Institute of Marie and Otto Neurath, which has exercised an important influence on the contemporary aesthetics of data visualization (Zambrano and Engelhardt 2008; Mayr and Schreder 2014; Headrick 2000; Rayward 2008; Fig. 12.8).

Fig. 12.7 Openaid.se (Swedish International Development Cooperation Agency); http://www.openaid.se/aid/2014 (accessed 10 March 2016)

Genealogical study may help to enrich research about what has given rise to the contingent forms that data visualizations may take, identifying a range of different influences and origins of different visual forms. Starting points may be provided through interviews with designers as well as content analysis of relevant design materials—which may be complemented with historical texts and archival research.

We might also study the specific visual forms that are transposed to mediate public money. Many visualizations are described and/or organized as dashboards, giving users an overview of multiple key indicators and trends over time in a single viewing pane, inviting narratives of oversight, optimization, balance, and control (see Tkacz 2015).

As well as studying data visualizations as cultural forms from a humanistic perspective, we can also trace their circulation, reception, and how they are used and viewed by different publics (see Kennedy et al. 2016). In addition to interviews and workshops, digital methods could be utilized to extract and analyze traces from digital platforms and online spaces in order to review the contexts in which visualizations are being used and shared (Rogers 2013). For example, we could query for names or URLs of projects on social media, search engine results, news media, or collections of documents. This may also help to chart the particular publics and context of usage of the visualizations—which can assist with their study as social and cultural forms.

Home and Factory Weaving in England

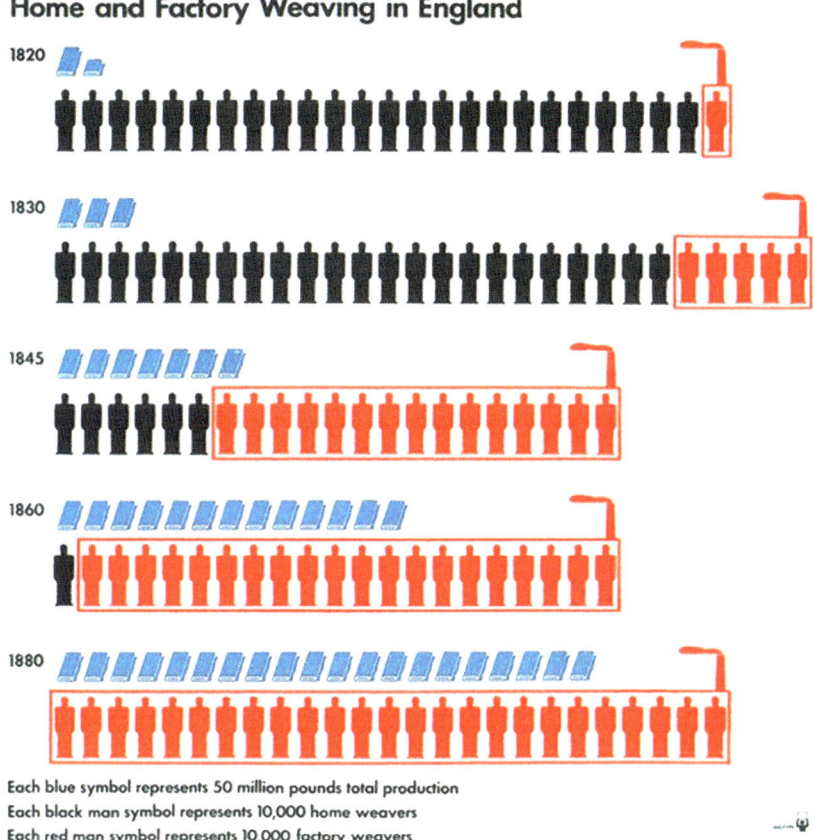

Each blue symbol represents 50 million pounds total production
Each black man symbol represents 10,000 home weavers
Each red man symbol represents 10,000 factory weavers

Fig. 12.8 'Home and Factory Weaving in England' (Neurath 1939)

CONCLUSION

In this chapter we have proposed a heuristic framework that may be used to develop critical reflexivity around the use of data visualization as an object of research or a communicative or analytic device in research. We have illustrated this framework with reference to a collection of data visualizations about public money, and suggested some methods and approaches that could be used to study them.

First, we looked at the study of data sources, focusing on research approaches to examine how they selectively articulate and mediate different aspects of the world—including how to identify sources, tracing how they have been transformed, and studying data infrastructures. Secondly, we looked at ways to study how the data sources are mediated into graphical form—including through the analysis of their visual properties, software, and design choices. Thirdly and finally, we looked at ways of studying graphical forms as socially, culturally, and historically contingent forms engendering different ways of seeing—including by tracing their diverse influences, and by analyzing their circulation and contexts of usage.

We hope that the study of these three forms of mediation through some of the approaches that we have discussed in this chapter may provide a useful starting point for researchers who wish to use data visualization as a research object or device. As data visualizations become more and more central, prominent, and familiar as ways of knowing and organizing phenomena, we think it becomes imperative to develop a richer understanding of the ways of seeing and ways of knowing that they engender. Just as Berger's *Ways of Seeing* helped to advance broader awareness of the critical study of images and visual culture, so we hope that further research in this area will advance literacy around ways of seeing data and ways of seeing with and through data visualizations. As visualization tools and practices become more and more ubiquitous, this might include not only the development of a critical *hermeneutics*, but also new kinds of self-reflexive *praxis* for the creation and reconfiguration of visualizations that are attentive to the forms of mediation that we have outlined. Experimentation in this direction might be informed by calls for non-reductive visualization (Manovich 2002), humanistic interfaces (Drucker 2014), feminist data visualization (D'Ignazio 2015), inventive methods (Lury and Wakeford 2012), rethinking dashboards (Tkacz 2015), and critical analytics (Rogers 2015).

NOTES

1. See, for example: Cairo, 2012; Card et al., 1999; Cleveland, 1993, 1994; Few, 2009, 2012, 2013; Heller and Landers, 2014; Katz, 2012; Krum, 2013; Lima, 2011; McCandless, 2012, 2014; Meirelles, 2013; Munzner, 2014; Murray, 2013; Rendgen, 2014; Spence, 2014; Steele and Iliinsky, 2010; Tactical Technology Collective, 2014; Tufte, 1990, 1997a, 1997b, 2001; Yau, 2011, 2013.
2. For an extensive collection of examples of fiscal data visualizations see Gray (2015b).

3. Gray and Bounegru are currently working on another project on 'data infrastructure literacy', which includes further suggestions on approaches to studying and working with data infrastructures.
4. http://www.nytimes.com/interactive/2010/02/02/us/politics/20100201 -budget-porcupine-graphic.html?_r=0 (accessed 10 March 2016).
5. See https://projects.propublica.org/graphics/ny-millions and https:// www.propublica.org/article/how-we-analyzed-new-york-county-tobacco-bonds (accessed 10 March 2016).
6. http://widgets.scmp.com/infographic/20140304/budget2014/data (accessed 10 March 2016).
7. http://www.theguardian.com/news/datablog/2010/sep/22/tax-gap-information-beautiful (accessed 10 March 2016).
8. https://github.com/OpenBudget (accessed 10 March 2016).
9. http://appliedworks.co.uk/work/the-times-defining-a-new-era-of-data-journalism (accessed 10 March 2016).
10. https://www.youtube.com/watch?v=K7Pahd2X-eE (accessed 10 March 2016).
11. https://www.whatdotheyknow.com/request/schema_for_coins_database (accessed 10 March 2016).
12. http://unstats.un.org/unsd/cr/registry/regcst.asp?Cl=4 (accessed 10 March 2016).
13. Bounegru and Gray are currently involved in developing tools and methods for working with metadata from GitHub as part of other research projects.

REFERENCES

Agre, P. E. (1997) Toward a Critical Technical Practice: Lessons Learned in Trying to Reform AI. In G. C. Bowker, S. Star, L. Gasser, et al. (Eds.), *Social Science, Technical Systems, and Cooperative Work: Beyond the Great Divide* (Mahwah: Lawrence Erlbaum), pp. 131–58.

Akrich, M. (1992) The De-Scription of Technical Objects. In W. Bijker and J. Law (Eds.), *Shaping Technology/Building Society: Studies in Sociotechnical Change* (Cambridge, MA: MIT Press), pp. 205–24.

Berger, J. (1972) *Ways of Seeing* (London: Penguin).

Berkowitz, D. (2009) Reporters and Their Sources. In K. Wahl-Jorgensen and T. Hanitzsch (Eds.), *The Handbook of Journalism Studies* (New York: Routledge), pp. 102–15.

Bertin, J. (1983) *Semiology of Graphics: Diagrams, Networks, Maps* (Madison: University of Wisconsin Press).

Bowker, G., and Star, S. (1999) *Sorting Things Out: Classification and its Consequences* (Cambridge, MA: MIT Press).

Cairo, A. (2012) *The Functional Art: An Introduction to Information Graphics and Visualization* (Berkeley: New Riders).

Card, S. K., Mackinlay, J., and Schneiderman, B. (Eds) (1999) *Readings in Information Visualization: Using Vision to Think* (San Francisco: Morgan Kaufmann).

Cleveland, W. S. (1993) *Visualizing Data* (Murray Hill: Hobart Press).

Cleveland, W. S. (1994) *The Elements of Graphing Data* (Murray Hill: Hobart Press).

Cottle, S. (2003) News, Public Relations and Power: Mapping the Field. In S. Cottle (Ed.), *News, Public relations and Power* (London: Sage), pp. 3–24.

Cubitt, S. (2015) Data Visualization and the Subject of Political Aesthetics. In D. Berry and M. Dieter (Eds.), *Postdigital Aesthetics: Art, Computation And Design* (London: Palgrave Macmillan), pp. 179–90.

D'Ignazio, C. (2015) What Would Feminist Data Visualization Look Like? MIT Center for Civic Media 20 December: https://civic.mit.edu/feminist-data-visualization (accessed 10 March 2016).

Daston, L. and Galison, P. (2010) *Objectivity* (Cambridge, MA: MIT Press).

Drucker, J. (2014) *Graphesis: Visual Forms of Knowledge Production* (Cambridge, MA: Harvard University Press).

Espeland, W. N. and Stevens, M. L. (2008) A Sociology of Quantification. *European Journal of Sociology* 49(3): 401–36.

Espeland, W. N. and Sauder, M. L. (2007) Rankings And Reactivity: How Public Measures Recreate Social Worlds. *American Journal of Sociology* 113(1): 1–40.

Few, S. (2009) *Now You See It: Simple Visualization Techniques for Quantitative Analysis* (Oakland: Analytics Press).

Few, S. (2012) *Show Me the Numbers: Designing Tables and Graphs to Enlighten.* 2nd ed. (Burlingame: Analytics Press).

Few, S. (2013) *Information Dashboard Design: Displaying Data for At-a-Glance Monitoring* (Burlingame: Analytics Press).

Few, S. (2014) Data Visualization for Human Perception. In M. Soegaard and R. Dam (Eds.), *The Encyclopedia of Human-Computer Interaction.* 2nd ed. (Aarhus: The Interaction Design Foundation), available at: https://www.interaction-design.org/literature/book/the-encyclopedia-of-human-computer-interaction-2nd-ed/data-visualization-for-human-perception (accessed 20 March 2016).

Freeman, L. C. (2004) *The Development of Social Network Analysis* (Vancouver: Booksurge).

Galison, P. (1990) Aufbau/Bauhaus: Logical Positivism and Architectural Modernism. *Critical Inquiry* 16(4): 709–52.

Gerlitz, C and Lury, C. (2014) Social Media and Self-Evaluating Assemblages: On Numbers, Orderings and Values. *Distinktion* 15(2): 174–88.

Gray, J. (2015a) Open Budget Data: Mapping the Landscape. Available at: http://papers.ssrn.com/sol3/papers.cfm?abstract_id=2654878 (accessed 15 March 2016).

Gray, J. (2015b) Examples of Fiscal Data Visualisations. *figshare*. Available at: https://figshare.com/articles/Examples_of_Fiscal_Data_Visualisations/1548331 (accessed 15 March 2016).

Gray, J. and Davies, T. (2015) Fighting Phantom Firms in the UK: From Opening Up Datasets to Reshaping Data Infrastructures? Working paper presented at the Open Data Research Symposium at the 3rd International Open Government Data Conference (Ottawa). Available at: http://papers.ssrn.com/sol3/papers.cfm?abstract_id=2610937 (accessed 10 March 2016).

Hall, S., Critcher, C., Jefferson, T., et al. (1978) *Policing the Crisis: Mugging, the State, and Law and Order* (London: Macmillan).

Halpern, O. (2015) *Beautiful Data: A History of Vision and Reason Since 1945* (Durham: Duke University Press).

Headrick, D. R. (2000) *When Information Came of Age: Technologies of Knowledge in the Age of Reason and Revolution, 1700–1850* (Oxford: Oxford University Press).

Heller, S. and Landers, R. (2014) *Raw Data: Infographic Designers' Sketchbooks* (London: Thames and Hudson).

Jay, M. (1988). The Rise of Hermeneutics and the Crisis of Ocularcentrism. *Poetics Today* 9(2): 307–26.

Jevbratt, L. (2004) The Prospect of the Sublime in Data Visualizations.

Katz, J. (2012) *Designing Information: Human Factors and Common Sense in Information Design* (Hoboken: Wiley).

Kennedy, H., Hill, L., Aiello, G., et al. (2016) The Work that Visualisation Conventions Do. *Information, Communication & Society* 19(6): 715–35.

Krum, R. (2013) *Cool Infographics: Effective Communication with Data Visualization and Design* (Indianapolis: Wiley).

Lau, A. and Vande Moere, A. (2007) Towards a Model of Information Aesthetics in Information Visualization. In *Proceedings of the 11th International Conference Information Visualization* (Washington, DC: IEEE Computer Society), pp. 87–92.

Law, J. and Ruppert, E. (2013) The Social Life of Methods: Devices. *Journal of Cultural Economy* 6(3): 229–40.

Lima, M. (2011) *Visual Complexity: Mapping Patterns of Information* (New York: Princeton Architectural Press).

Lury, C. and Wakeford, N. (Eds.) (2012) *Inventive Methods: The Happening of the Social* (London: Routledge).

Manning, P. (2001) *News and News Sources: A Critical Introduction* (London: Sage).

Manovich, L. (2002). Data Visualisation as New Abstraction and Anti-sublime. In B. Hawk, D. Rieder and O. Oviedo (Eds.), *Small Tech: The Culture of Digital Tools, Electronic Mediations* (Minneapolis: University of Minnesota Press), pp. 3–9.

Manovich, L. (2011) What is Visualisation? *Visual Studies* 26(1): 36–49.

Manovich, L. (2014) Visualization Methods for Media Studies. In C. Vernallis, A. Herzog and J. Richardson (Eds.), *Oxford Handbook of Sound and Image in Digital Media* (Oxford: Oxford University Press), pp. 253–78.

Marres, N. and Gerlitz, C. (2015) Interface Methods: Renegotiating Relations Between Digital Social Research, STS and Sociology. *The Sociological Review* 64(1): 21–46.

Mayr, E. and Schreder, G. (2014) Isotype Visualizations. A Chance for Participation & Civic Education. *JeDEM – eJournal of eDemocracy and Open Government* 6(2), 136–50.

McCandless, D. (2012) *Information is Beautiful* (New York: Collins).

McCandless, D. (2014) *Knowledge is Beautiful* (New York: Collins).

McLuhan, M. (1962) *The Gutenberg Galaxy: The Making of Typographic Man* (Toronto: University of Toronto Press).

Meirelles, I. (2013) *Design for Information: An Introduction to the Histories, Theories, and Best Practices Behind Effective Information Visualizations.* (Beverly: Rockport Publishers).

Munzner, T. (2014) *Visualization Analysis and Design* (Boca Raton: CRC Press).

Murray, S. (2013) *Interactive Data Visualization for the Web* (Sebastopol: O'Reilly).

Neurath, O. (1939) *Modern Man in the Making* (New York: Knopf).

Playfair, W. (1801) *The Commercial and Political Atlas, Representing, by Means of Stained Copper-Plates, the Progress of the Commerce, Revenues, Expenditure, and Debt of England during the Whole of the Eighteenth Century.* 3rd ed. (London: Wallis).

Rayward, W. B. (Ed.). (2008) *European Modernism and the Information Society: Informing the Present, Understanding the Past* (Aldershot: Ashgate).

Rendgen, S. (2014) *Understanding the World: The Atlas of Infographics* (Köln: Taschen).

Rieder, B. and Röhle, T. (2012) Digital Methods: Five Challenges. In D. M. Berry (Ed.), *Understanding Digital Humanities* (London: Palgrave Macmillan), pp. 67–84.

Rogers, R. (2013) *Digital Methods* (Cambridge, MA: MIT Press).

Rogers, R. (2015) From Dashboards to Critical Analytics. Paper presented at Data Power Conference (University of Sheffield).

Rosenberg, D. and Grafton, A. (2013) *Cartographies of Time: A History of the Timeline* (New York: Princeton Architectural Press).

Ruppert, E. (2015) Doing the Transparent State: Open Government Data as Performance Indicators. In: R. Rottenburg, S. E. Merry, S.-J. Park and J. Mugler (Eds.), *A World of Indicators: The Making of Governmental Knowledge through Quantification.* (Cambridge: Cambridge University Press), pp. 1–18.

Ruppert, E., Law, J. and Savage, M. (2013) Reassembling Social Science Methods: The Challenge of Digital Devices. *Theory, Culture & Society* 30(4): 22–46.

Sack, W. (2011) Aesthetics of Information Visualization. In M. Lovejoy, C. Paul and V. Vesna (Eds.), *Context Providers: Conditions of Meaning in Media Arts* (Bristol: Intellect), pp. 123–50.

Segel, E. and Heer, J. (2010) Narrative Visualization: Telling Stories with Data. *IEEE Transactions on Visualization and Computer Graphics* 16(6): 1139–48.

Spence, R. (2014) *Information Visualization: An Introduction* (New York: Springer).

Star, S. (1999) The Ethnography of Infrastructure. *American Behavioral Scientist* 43(3): 377–91.

Star, S. and Ruhleder, K. (1996) Steps Toward an Ecology of Infrastructure: Design and Access for Large Information Spaces. *Information Systems Research* 7(1): 111–34.

Steele, J. and Iliinsky, N. (Eds.) (2010) *Beautiful Visualization: Looking at Data through the Eyes of Experts* (Sebastopol: O'Reilly).

Strauss, A. and Corbin, J. (1998) Basics of Qualitative Research. Techniques and Procedures for Developing Grounded Theory. 2nd ed. (London: Sage).

Tactical Technology Collective (2014) *Visualising Information for Advocacy.*

Tkacz, N. (2015) Connection Perfected: What the Dashboard Reveals. Keynote Address at Digital Methods Winter School 2015 (University of Amsterdam).

Tufte, E. R. (1990) *Envisioning Information* (Cheshire: Graphics Press).

Tufte, E. R. (1997a) *Visual Explanations: Images and Quantities, Evidence and Narrative* (Cheshire: Graphics Press).

Tufte, E. R. (1997b) *Visual and Statistical Thinking: Displays of Evidence for Making Decisions* (Cheshire: Graphics Press).

Tufte, E. R. (2001) *The Visual Display of Quantitative Information.* 2nd ed. (Cheshire: Graphics Press).

Venturini, T., Bounegru, L., Jacomy, M. and Gray, J. (2016) How to Tell Stories with Networks: Exploring the Narrative Affordances of Network Graphs with the Iliad. In M. T. Schaefer and K. van Es (Eds.), *The Datafied Society: Social Research in the Age of Big Data* (Amsterdam: University of Amsterdam Press).

Whitelaw, M. (2008) Art Against Information: Case Studies in Data Practice. *Fibreculture* 11: http://eleven.fibreculturejournal.org/fcj-067-art-against-information-case-studies-in-data-practice (accessed 10 March 2016).

Wright, R. (2008) Data Visualization. In M. Fuller (Ed.), *Software Studies: A Lexicon.* Cambridge, MA: MIT Press), pp. 78–87.

Yau, N. (2011) *Visualize This: The FlowingData Guide to Design, Visualization, and Statistics* (Indianapolis: Wiley).

Yau, N. (2013) *Data Points: Visualization That Means Something* (Indianapolis: Wiley).

Zambrano, R. N. and Engelhardt, Y. (2008) Diagrams for the Masses: Raising Public Awareness – From Neurath to Gapminder and Google Earth. In G. Stapleton, J. Howse and J. Lee (Eds.), *Diagrammatic Representation and Inference* (Berlin: Springer), pp. 282–92.

CHAPTER 13

Urban Sensing: Potential and Limitations of Social Network Analysis and Data Visualization as Research Methods in Urban Studies

Luca Simeone and Paolo Patelli

Across contemporary cities of the so-called developed world we are witnessing the convergence of three trends: an increase in the urban population, which—despite its substantial diversity—has been reported since 2008 as the majority of the world population (UNFPA 2011; Brenner and Schmid 2013); a peak in the number of mobile broadband subscribers, which results in an increasingly mobile access to the internet (ITU 2014); and a rise in the numbers of autonomous objects and physical devices connected to the network (Townsend 2013). These trends describe the intersection of global urbanization and the spread of ubiquitous information and communication technologies (ICT). One consequence of such concurrent

L. Simeone (✉)
Malmö University, Sweden, Malmö
e-mail: me@luca.simeone.name

P. Patelli
Designer and Researcher, Milan, Italy and
Amsterdam, The Netherlands
e-mail: paolo.patelli@me.com

© The Author(s) 2016
S. Kubitschko, A. Kaun (eds.), *Innovative Methods in Media and Communication Research*, DOI 10.1007/978-3-319-40700-5_13

253

phenomena is the multiplication of traces left in the digital layer of the city by its inhabitants and by the devices with which they interact.

Nowadays, a massive amount of user-generated content is created daily through Facebook, Twitter, Foursquare, and similar online social networking services (see Schroeder 2014). Thanks to the proliferation of digital devices, such as smartphones and tablets, and ubiquitous connectivity, city inhabitants and visitors are able to, for example, use online social networks while on the move, share images and videos in real time, 'live tweet' from a concert, or 'check in' at their favorite locations.[1] Most of these social networks associate geographic markers with posts, tweets, and pictures, and this allows for the creation of a significant amount of geo-located information, which is continuously updated, liked, and commented on by social media users. This informational layer affects the way in which cities are perceived or lived in by their inhabitants as well as by visitors, in place and remotely, in close-up interactions and at a distance. Think, for example, of first-time city visitors who browse through online social networks to get recommendations on places to visit, events, restaurants, and bars, or of local inhabitants who use Twitter to report on the quality of the local bus transportation system. These examples clearly indicate how the way in which people experience urban environments can be affected by their interaction with the informational landscape across social media, both locally and globally. Variously labeled by geographers and social scientists the geoweb, spatial-social media, user-generated content, and volunteered geographic information (VGI), such layers and applications could easily be ascribed to the domain of neogeography (Graham and Zook 2013), traditionally defined by the use of geographic techniques and tools by a non-expert group of users, for personal and community activities.

Users can be—at different times or even the same time—both consumers and producers of content. In this context, different kinds of software arise to add a curatorial affordance, cutting across cyberspace as much as the physical space of the city. Graham and Zook (2013) note that never before have so many representations of the meaning of places—either deliberate commentaries or offhand byproducts of daily life—been so readily available for consumption and contestation. Such an overwhelming wealth of depictions results from and at the same time encourages the simultaneous emergence of software and social systems that sort and present vertical selections of layered representations of places (Graham 2005; Zook and Graham 2007c). Places and their experiences are increasingly defined by dense and complex layers of representation that are created, accessed, and filtered via algorithms and a variety of digital technologies. Geo-coded references tracing economic, social, cultural, and political experiences of the city form a digital dimension to place that is embedded within urban landscapes (Graham and Zook 2013) and is easily available for interpretation to software and users. The powerful analytic techniques that strive to make sense of the large amounts of data continuously produced in the city, however, often operate in the background and are themselves difficult to see and to comprehend (Greenfield 2013).

In earlier works (Simeone et al. 2012; Lupi et al. 2012; Ciuccarelli et al. 2014), we documented several experiments that aimed at creating software that gathers and analyzes geo-located information posted on social networks. The common idea behind these experiments was to use the massive amount of information daily published as geo-located user-generated content in order to distill insights on how the city is experienced and lived, thus supporting urban studies. Within the overall framework of this book on *innovative methods in media and communication research*, this chapter offers further remarks and reflections on experiments conducted within Urban Sensing, a research project funded by the European Commission. Urban Sensing was orientated toward creating a custom-made software platform to investigate user-generated content coming from selected social networks (Facebook, Twitter, Foursquare, Flickr, Instagram). The platform was conceived in order to be:

- connected to multiple data streams related to various cities (experiments were carried out for Milan, New York, Barcelona, and the Randstad region);
- configurable, so that various indicators could be taken into consideration, according to the partners' and stakeholders' areas of interests and the geographic areas of investigation.

Overall, the project tried to provide insights into the perceived attractiveness and characterization of neighborhoods, informing answers to related questions: Which are the most frequently mentioned places of a given city across social networks? Which are the places that are never mentioned? Why? What is it that makes people talk about a geographic area? Is it theaters or the food scene? What are the recurring keywords in tweets from specific locations? Can these sets of keywords offer a characterization of these geographic areas? Urban Sensing as a software platform tried to answer these and similar questions by directly collecting and examining what city inhabitants and visitors publish on social media channels.

The Urban Sensing project refers in its title to the possibility of building new methods, relevant within urban studies, starting from the harvest and visualization of big urban data. Representations of the urban environment and of the urban experience can be constructed—in this example cartographically—starting from information produced and shared by citizens and visitors across social networking services. Citizens are in fact co-producing big urban data, along with the physical and 'sentient' infrastructures of the city, and performing as sensors when they witness phenomena and report about them, or just transmit sensations, relative to their subjective experience of urban space, making them part of the spatial social web. This chapter builds on the authors' experience as designers and researchers within Urban Sensing and provides materials for scholars and researchers to reflect on the potential and limitations of social network analysis and data visualization as research methods in urban studies. The chapter starts with a few fundamental considerations on the limitations and distortions inherent in any measurement and technical mediation, considering the particular context of evaluations stemming from quantitative analyses of big data. The chapter then moves to mapping out precursory initiatives and projects that made use of the spatial web to study the contemporary city. Subsequently, Urban Sensing is introduced as a project through some of the experiments it allowed. Its methodologies are explained in their limitations and potentialities, which lead to the concluding reflections on the relevance in the field of urban studies of sensing the urban through the social web.

MEASURING AMPLIFIES AND REDUCES

The promise most often associated with the phenomenon of big data in the urban context is to make the city knowable and manageable in real time, sentient in some way. This makes an appealing prospect for urban management and studies. Indeed, in both fields the act of data collection and the production of large data sets have a long tradition, under a supposedly neutral and scientific objectivity, as in the national census or the land register. Urban sensing, a set of analytic practices related to the phenomenon of big urban data, is aimed at a further transformation in the processes of knowing—and hence possibly controlling, and actuating—the city.

On the definition of big data itself, however, there is no agreement, in academia and in industry alike. Lev Manovich (2011) notes that the term 'big data' was first used in science in reference to an amount of information so great as to require supercomputers to process it (but that now can be analyzed on a laptop). Moreover, related data sets, such as the collections of tweets shared from a particular location, are not even comparable in size to the traditional census data. The amount hence cannot be the only characteristic of a new ecosystem of information. Big urban data are extremely heterogeneous, of an extemporaneous character, detailed, and of a relational nature; they bring multi-dimensional and rich contextual information, or metadata. The term big data in this sense is not so much a reference to the size of the data set, but rather to the ability to search, aggregate, and cross information. More broadly, boyd and Crawford (2012) define big data as a cultural, technological, and academic phenomenon, based on the relations between the possibilities and technical accuracy in collecting, analyzing, and comparing data; the analytic ability to identify patterns and advance theses and social, legal, economic, or technical claims; and the widespread myth that large data sets provide a higher form of intelligence and knowledge that it is otherwise impossible to reach. Specifically, Rob Kitchin (2014) indicates the sources of big urban data in three categories: data generated from traditional forms of surveillance, such as the steps of a turnstile; data generated automatically as an intrinsic function of a device or system, such as the traceability of the activities of mobile phones; and information produced and voluntarily shared by users, including interactions on social media, crowdsourcing, and activities such as Open Street Map.

The city and its population become part of a constellation of instruments that cross different scales, all connected through multiple networks, which provide continuous data on the movements of people and materials (Farinelli 2003). While the data collected directly from volunteer production can represent an important resource, it is especially forms of data that are automatically generated that have captured the imagination of a new understanding and management of the urban. These forms of instrumentation provide abundant data in systematic and dynamic, well-defined, and resolute ways on the activities and processes of the city, making it possible to perform real-time analysis and imagine adaptive forms of intervention. In what is called the 'real-time city', people have visual and tangible access to real-time information about their city, which enables them to make decisions more in sync with their environment, with what is actually happening around them (Calabrese et al. 2006); this applies in various ways to different users: policymakers, managers, citizens. As shown by Carlo Ratti (2014), along with others, scenarios and concepts of application of the 'real-time city' are located exactly at the intersection of the domains of the built environment, people, and information. The ways in which they unfold, however, are not solely definable as technical matters.

Don Ihde (1979, 2009), a philosopher of science and technology, has developed a phenomenological analysis of technologically mediated relations, defining structures of amplification and reduction wherein the implementation of technological systems has amplifying and reducing effects on the interactions among members of a community. The thesis that more data, supported by appropriate systems of visualization, can improve the quality of decisions, both technical and democratic, therefore improving the efficiency of services and systems, might prove weak when considering that in every measurement only what is quantifiable of a phenomenon would be visible. Following Ihde, it can be argued that the use of sensors—and really of any kind of digital information—necessarily amplifies the phenomena of the city that can actually be measured, with a necessary reduction in the total field of vision or interest, consequently obscuring what is not measurable. Sensors and instruments themselves become central in this structure, as anything that is mediated through them then appears necessarily different. In other words, analyzing relations and interactions between citizens and urban places—a building, a public space, infrastructure— using sensor technology and digital data amplifies the measurable phenomena and reduces embodied human experience. Ihde contrasts the fully sensual mundane experience of everyday life with that of a mono-sensory world mediated by technological tools. The so-called multi-sensory experience of ubiquitous sensors of the 'smart city' can provide only a partial and limited image.

EXISTING WORK

Starting from the mid-2000s, several initiatives and projects, either conducted by research institutions (for example, CASA at University College London, Spatial Information Design Lab at Columbia University, or Senseable City Lab at the Massachusetts Institute of Technology) or independent designers and design firms (for example, Christian Nold, Art is Open Source, or Stamen Design), began to explore possibilities in the spatial social web for description of the urban environment and the experience of the city.

The work in this field has been influenced equally by artists, such as the Situationists—who pioneered the cartographic representation of a subjective space—and by the work of scholars coming from different disciplines, from geography, to urban studies, to computer science (Zook and Graham 2007a; Girardin et al. 2008; Kotov et al. 2011; Liu et al. 2011; Shi and Barker 2011). A significant part of these studies also stems from the earlier work of Manuel Castells (1996), who reflects on the relation between structured technical information and the global expansion of capital, as well as from the work of Arjun Appadurai (1990), who introduces the concept of mediascape to look at how media such as television, radio, newspapers, and the narratives and images they produce shape the world we inhabit.

Exploring similar issues but in specific relation to digital and interactive information technologies, authors such as Stephen Graham, Mark Graham, and Matthew Zook examine how digital data and information coming from multiple sources (sensing technologies, ubiquitous computing, and user-generated content) play an important role in shaping urban experiences (Graham 1998; Graham 2011; Zook and Graham 2007b, 2007a). Zook and Graham also note how the analysis of digital data produced by users can offer valuable insights into how inhabitants and visitors perceive and live cities (Graham and Zook 2011). If used as a research method, social media analysis can complement traditional methods for analyzing users' perceptions and activities in cities, such as surveys, interviews, or ethnographic observations. These methods generally require significant economic resources and, as such, are generally limited to a specific sample of city users, a specific geographic area, and a specific period of investigation. Social media analysis can offer a complementary method for this kind of study, especially if conducted through software platforms, which allows the examination of a large number of data sets in real time and in a semi-automatic way.

A key element for Urban Sensing has been how best to visualize the information and the insights emerging from the social media analysis. On the one hand, the software platform would generally deal with massive data sets, which were analyzed in real time, continuously producing information. How best to render this real-time analysis through clear and easy-to-understand visualizations was a paramount challenge of the project. In this sense, Urban Sensing's visualization strategies built on the suggestions of a good number of authors and experts in visual design (Bevington 2008; Heer and Shneiderman 2012; Bertin 1983; Tufte 2006;

Harris 2000; Segel and Heer 2010; Yau 2013). On the other hand, the insights that Urban Sensing produced had a geo-located dimension and it was therefore important to visualize these results on a set of maps. The work of authors such as Mike Crang, Richard Schein, Denis Cosgrove, and James and Nancy Duncan on emerging and collaborative carto-graphic practices has provided a good grounding (Crang 1996; Schein 1997; Cosgrove 1999; Duncan and Duncan 2005). In Urban Sensing, novel geographies are built out of heterogeneous content produced by city users; real-time data are processed to produce knowledge that is visu-ally explorable, in order to formulate new understandings of the city and implement programs in the real world.

Urban Sensing and Its Experiments

Urban Sensing is a research project funded by the European Commission (2012–2014). Over the course of three years, three research centers (T-Connect from Italy, IT4All from France, and the Technical University of Kosice from Slovakia) and four companies (Accurat from Italy, Mobivery and SISU Labs from Spain, and LUST from the Netherlands) worked together in order to create a software platform for social media analysis and visualization. The software platform is articulated in four components:

- An acquisition engine that gathers multiple data streams from user-generated content platforms and other sources and integrates them into a single knowledge base.
- An interpretation layer, where data are analyzed according to various techniques, including text mining, and grouped in clusters.
- A web-based component that allows end users to perform specific searches within pre-defined domains through an easy-to-use interface.
- A visualization layer that plots the information on a set of maps, using multiple visual representations.

Regarding the data flows, the system architecture is articulated in two processes:

- A process that fetches data from multiple sources (Facebook, Twitter, Foursquare, Flickr, Instagram) and integrates them using several techniques (including crawling) into a common data model and indexes the information in the knowledge base.
- Another process that queries, filters, and aggregates the data.

The platform has been tested in a set of twelve experiments (Simeone et al. 2012; Ciuccarelli et al. 2014; Simeone in print), conducted in collaboration with potential end users (such as scholars in urban studies or architects and urban planners, from both private companies and public offices). These experiments wanted to check whether these end users considered meaningful the results of the social media analyses as performed and visualized by Urban Sensing.

In the following, we present one of the experiments conducted in 2013 for the city of Milan (Italy). In this experiment, we wanted to study the Bovisa district, a specific area located north of the city center. Bovisa is an old industrial area, which lost its economic centrality when, starting in the 1950s, most of its factories were dismantled and moved farther from the center. Today it is experiencing a period of renewal: many activities have relocated into this area, including several departments of the schools of Design, Architecture and Engineering of the Polytechnic University. Bovisa is still undergoing a profound transformation and a wide array of stakeholders—from the municipality, to service providers, private companies, and real estate developers—are interested in understanding how inhabitants, commuters, and visitors perceive and live in this area of the city. In this case, Urban Sensing was configured to track the number of photos and contributions related to a specific geographic location and shared over Flickr and Twitter, and the number of check-ins in Foursquare for each venue in a pre-defined time lapse. The idea was to gather geo-located information on the most crowded areas of Bovisa, on working days and at weekends, and at different times of the day.

Figure 13.1 shows how the Urban Sensing platform plots the geographic locations associated with Twitter contributions (blue dots) on a map of Milan, also displaying temporal trends (for instance, the number of contributions per day in the time span). It presents the geographic distribution of tweets in Bovisa and in the neighboring districts, as collected between 24 June and 24 September 2013.[2] The resulting map clearly displays the areas where a higher concentration of tweets was published. The same trends emerge even more clearly in Fig. 13.2, zooming in over the premises of the Polytechnic University. In Fig. 13.2 a further element is introduced: while the blue dots represent the initial position of users, the green and red dots show the positions of the same users immediately before and after. By connecting the dots, users' movements can be traced over time, to provide insights not only on the most crowded areas of Bovisa, but also

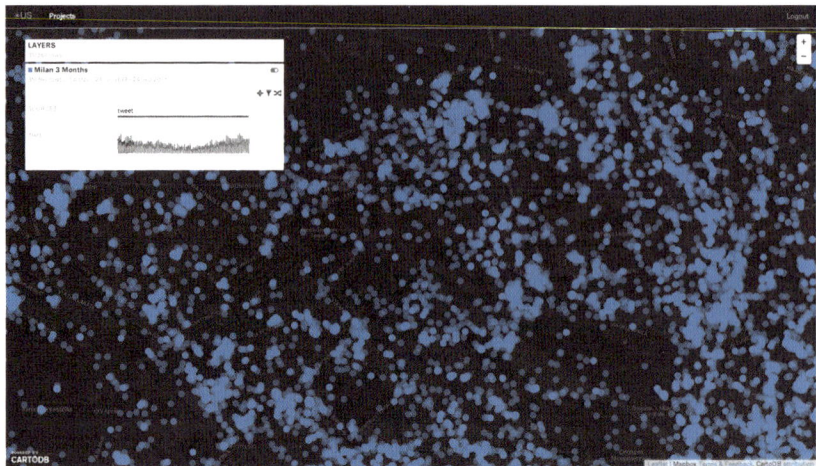

Fig. 13.1 Urban Sensing, visual representation of tweets in Bovisa, Milan (August–September 2013); elaborated by Marco Vettorello and Alex Piacentini

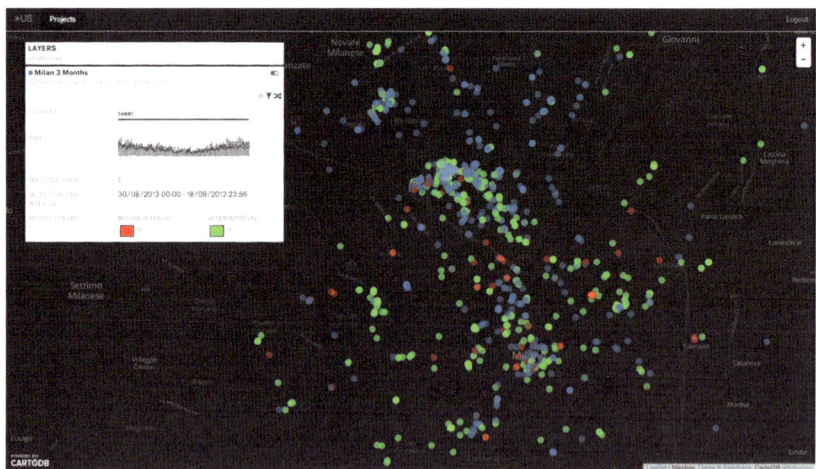

Fig. 13.2 Urban Sensing, zoom over the area of Bovisa, in Milan (August–September 2013); elaborated by Marco Vettorello and Alex Piacentini

on the trajectories among them, on the locations from which students, researchers, and other personnel come before getting to the Polytechnic campus, and where they go after.

Some of the insights emerging from the analysis simply confirm already well-known local dynamics, such as the peaks of social media activity on weekday evenings from Brera, where people tend to go for the 'aperitivo', a traditional buffet-style dinner that many cafés, pubs, and bars typically offer from 6 pm to 9 pm. Other insights reveal less visible patterns. Some areas, such as via Cenisio, showed unpredicted behaviors in terms of spikes of contributions at night, which gave the researchers the opportunity to observe the area and discover the unexpected presence of trendy night spots.

The methodological approach behind this experiment was developed into a five-step process:

(1) Samples of geo-located user-generated content, produced and shared through a selection of social media channels, were collected and studied. Flickr, Twitter, and Foursquare offered a sufficient number of contributions for Milan and, in particular, for the specific area of Bovisa.

(2) Topics to be investigated in an urban context were chosen, in this case the location of landmarks, points of interest, patterns of mobility, and the ways in which public spaces are used in the area of Bovisa and greater Milan.

(3) In order to analyze the selected topics, a number of central questions were identified: Which are the areas in Bovisa where people contribute the most? Where do the students of the Polytechnic University go after they leave the campus? From which areas of the city do they daily commute? Where do they go after school?

(4) Data were collected and interpreted. For example, in order to highlight the areas with the greatest amount of contributions, the Urban Sensing platform had to be configured to take into consideration the following dimensions of social media data:

Flickr

– Number of published images in a given geographic area in a pre-defined time lapse.
– Natural-language analysis of the textual description of the image shared.

– Comparative analysis between geo-tagged contents and the users' profile information.
– User profiling according to the actual spatial distribution of the content produced.

Twitter

– Number of geo-located contributions in a given geographic area in a pre-defined time lapse.
– Number and frequency of mentions of a place by unique users (as analyzed through natural-language analysis).
– User profiling according to language or place of residence.
– User profiling according to number of tweets and followers.

Foursquare

– Number of check-ins for each venue in a pre-defined time lapse.
– Spatial distribution of venue categories in a given area.
– Comparative analysis between geo-tagged contents and the users' profile information.

While dimensions related directly to users and their profiling were collected in order to provide the analysis with contextual information, individual contributors were systematically anonymized, to preserve their privacy. Such dimensions include a user's country of origin and the language used in their contributions, but also tracking of social media activity over time, from which the platform was able to trace past movements and guess future interactions in the city. As we shall see in the next paragraph, we consider this latter process problematic in relation to issues of privacy and control.

(5) A visual representation of the results was designed and developed. In this case, CartoDB was chosen as an initial versatile mapping tool. CartoDB is a cloud-based geo-spatial database that allows users with a basic understanding of web programming to create and customize maps based on uploaded data (for example, tables, KLM, and Shapefile) in an easy and intuitive way. CartoBD has been integrated with a custom-made web interface where the user can perform activities such as importing, selecting, filtering, sorting, and inquiring. A second layer of interaction allows users to analyze content (for example, keyword-based queries, place-related

queries, and sentiment analysis of data), to perform statistical analysis, to aggregate data, and to overlap data (for example, to integrate and compare data analysis with other data sources).

REFLECTIONS ON THE POTENTIAL AND LIMITATIONS OF URBAN SENSING IN URBAN STUDIES

Urban Sensing unfolded through a series of experiments, according to an approach that is quite established in design research (Gaver 2012; Frankel and Racine 2010; Frayling 1993). The term 'experiment' is used here to designate the procedure tentatively adopted to try out some of the ideas and methods illustrated in the preceding paragraphs. William Gaver points out how in research through design, 'design practice is brought to bear on situations chosen for their topical and theoretical potential' (Gaver 2012, p. 937). In these situations, design practice—such as the design and implementation of the Urban Sensing platform and its visualizations—plays a fundamental role in shaping the way in which the research project is framed and carried out, and continual reflection on the results of the design practice allows for articulating and re-elaborating conceptual insights (Ciuccarelli et al. 2014). In our strategy, design experiments—such as the one presented in the previous section—were the cornerstone of a research through design approach.[3]

Within Urban Sensing, multiple experiments have been conducted in collaboration with a wide array of stakeholders, also external to the research and development team.[4] Architects, urban planners, and managers working for public or private organizations, scholars, and companies potentially interested in the insights produced by the platform participated at various stages, from the initial brainstorming sessions aimed at defining the requirements of the technological platform, up to the usability testing aimed at evaluating the user experience design. Most importantly, these stakeholders offered their view on the insights emerging from the platform. From the perspective of our research, urban studies were therefore seen not just as an academic field, but as closely linked to city design, planning, and management activities.

Drawing on the feedback received, Urban Sensing seems to yield some potential in terms of studying how city inhabitants and visitors perceive and use the urban space. More specifically, the research project can support urban studies by providing data and insights that can complement traditional research methods, both qualitative and quantitative. Our experience with Urban Sensing showed that in some cases data just confirmed well-known city dynamics; in others, the social media analyses and visualizations highlighted less usual patterns, which then directed more traditional urban investigations. At the same time, the experiments also showed several serious limitations in the use of social media analyses and visualization as a research method in urban studies.

First, the production of media content and mobile access to social networking services, both necessary to share geo-located contributions, is still limited to a segment of city inhabitants and visitors. Second, while Urban Sensing fully respected the privacy policies of each social networking and media platform, and even applied additional anonymization techniques (Naor and Yung 1989), it showed that serious issues in terms of privacy need to be tackled. In particular, even within the stricter limits of the Urban Sensing platform, it would be possible to track the contributions of individual users over time and to infer patterns in their use and experience of the city.

Third, the accuracy of geo-located social media analyses is affected by the distribution of free Wi-Fi networks. In particular, tourists visiting foreign countries might not have data plans that allow a constant internet connection. The chances are that in these situations, they use free Wi-Fi at hotels, restaurants, or other public spaces to upload their pictures on Facebook or to tweet. The spatial distribution of these Wi-Fi spots can affect the geographic markers of any user-generated content. Peaks of contributions might therefore emerge in correspondence with the distribution of Wi-Fi spots. Fourth and finally, Urban Sensing cannot discern between—and therefore collects both—users' contributions related to their spatial context, and comments or conversations completely unrelated to urban issues. In most of the collected contributions, there is no clear intentionality from users to influence urban planning and management processes. Can this lack of intentionality undermine the potential of this kind of platform as a tool for more participatory processes? This is an important issue further explored in another publication (see Simeone 2016).

The main effect of Urban Sensing consists in the revelation of existing conditions and configurations of society and urban space. Potentially, by revealing conditions and relations, this project could identify new paths for action. Making public previously opaque configurations in the cycles of urban activity and expression renders them available for debate. However, the citizens as well as the related urban areas portrayed within the platform were not directly affected by the project itself, in the sense that the artifacts generated through Urban Sensing (for example, data visualizations) never reached the actual spaces and the citizens it studied. In most of our experiments, city inhabitants and visitors—whose social media contributions were being monitored and studied—were not even aware of the existence of the software platform.

What if we introduced materials, objects, and designed artifacts into the concrete field of urban perception? What if we tried to engage city inhabitants and visitors in a more deliberate way? Interventions attempting to close the loop in the urban space could activate an involvement, an interaction, and possibly offer new ways of inhabiting the city (DiSalvo 2012). In doing so, a project such as Urban Sensing, brought out and into the messy realm of street life, could alter the conditions of the urban experience. Its objects and artifacts, when experienced in their aesthetic dimension as well as in their political potential, could produce new conditions and urban experiences.

The aesthetic activity of the project could be extended to include other spaces, times, and forms of activity. As argued by Jacques Rancière (2010), what characterizes the aesthetic act in particular is that it introduces new subjects and heterogeneous objects in a field of perception. The deployment and distribution of informational and aesthetic artifacts in the urban realm would enable alternative ways to participate and take part in a common environment. This last point highlights a common limitation in the ways in which Urban Sensing and big urban data analyses and data visualizations can actually affect everyday life. In fact, if it is increasingly common to see such tools in the hands of managers and decision makers, only more rarely do they allow the same legibility of urban phenomena to the persons who are part of the depicted conditions. We see this as a serious shortcoming in using approaches such Urban Sensing as a research method in urban studies.

Conclusions

In the specific perspective carried out in our project, urban studies were closely linked to processes and practices of urban planning, design, and management. Analyses emerging from Urban Sensing were providing city administrators, urban planners, and architects with insights to be put into action. Although this clearly offered some benefits, the reflections presented in this chapter show first, the need to consider carefully the effects of amplification and reduction in big urban data analyses—the fact that the tools we choose to measure reality affect the working image resulting from the process—and second, the need to engage city inhabitants and visitors, to make them aware of the use of such tools as research methods, and of the visual and physical outputs of the research itself. Data appear to offer a truth inherent to social and economic relations, and robust empirical evidence for urban practice and political management; they are often seen as the source of neutral and objective measurements of what is happening in the city, free from any political ideology. At the same time, it is argued that data can only portray a constrained reality, through specific narratives.

As part of his critical inquiry into the reality of the 'smart city'—intended as a managerial and pragmatic culture of the city mostly proposed by technology companies and embraced as a service by decision makers—Adam Greenfield (2013) shows how some easily measured value can only be used as a proxy for a reality that is harder to quantify. Moreover, distortions of ostensibly neutral results are inevitably entangled with the choices made by an algorithm's designers. Data are never 'just' the data, and even asserting this condition or otherwise is inherently political, an interested decision. The emphasis, moreover, is very often put on the visual outputs of contemporary imaging technologies, where a capacity to transform data into image and its reversibility to transform image into data produce a new set of possibilities. Such imaging technologies have a degree of 'constructibility' built into them. Through computational processes one can at one level 'dial in' different sets of data—as in tomography. Data are turned into complex visualizations, and the latter move from scientific imaging to the parallel burgeoning of similar imaging in the arts, communications, contemporary media, and entertainment (Ihde 2009). In the enthusiasm for the possibilities of knowledge that may emerge from the large amounts of urban data finally available, the risk is producing a form of instrumental realism, where what is made through these instruments would become the real world. If cities can hardly be reduced to measurable phenomena, Urban Sensing and technologies of big urban data can still provide useful knowledge of urban systems and urban life, but a proper implementation requires a critical understanding of what is being amplified and reduced.

In conclusion, we believe that social media analyses and visualizations such as those that Urban Sensing produces can offer some value as a research method in urban studies, in terms of highlighting particular city dynamics, which can be further investigated using more traditional research methods.

Platforms such as Urban Sensing can be easily configured, plugged into various social media streams, and put into operation in just a few days. Various stakeholders such as urban scholars, designers, planners, managers, and other interested actors can use social media analyses and visualization as a quick-and-dirty research method. It is important to consider, however, that using platforms such as Urban Sensing as a research method in urban studies does not provide definite answers, but instead ignites questions for further debate and experimentation, especially with regard to the following issues. There is a risk that the knowledge that emerges from the large amounts of urban data may produce a form of instrumental realism, where what is made through these instruments can be mistaken for the real world. The project, by revealing conditions and relations, could identify new paths for action. Revealing previously opaque configurations in the cycles of urban activity and expression makes them available for debate. The projects' artifacts themselves could enter the domain of real life, directly affecting the city's inhabitants and visitors, as well as the related urban areas. Interventions in the urban space could activate involvement among actors, and possibly offer new ways of inhabiting the city.

NOTES

1. In 2015, 52.7 % of the global online population accessed the internet from their mobile phone (http://www.statista.com/statistics/284202/mobile-phone-internet-user-penetration-worldwide, all accessed 5 February 2016). In 2015 there were around 1.96 billion social network users worldwide (http://www.statista.com/statistics/278414/number-of-worldwide-social-network-users, all accessed 5 February 2016). According to Nielsen's *2014 Digital Consumer Report* (more specifically focused on the US market), the monthly social media time spent per person on smartphone apps is around 20 hours (http://www.nielsen.com/content/dam/corporate/us/en/reports-downloads/2014%20Reports/the-digital-consumer-report-feb-2014.pdf, accessed 5 February 2016).
2. In Milan, the number of geo-localized tweets per day varies, but generally ranges between 5000 and 9000. At the time of writing (February 2015), the average number of tweets per day is 6.846.
3. Koskinen et al. define design experiments as 'pieces of design carried out as a part of a research effort' (2008, p. 47).
4. We use the term stakeholder in a broad sense (Freeman 2010), to include all the actors that affect or are affected by a specific process, project, or organization.

REFERENCES

Appadurai, A. (1990) Disjuncture and Difference in the Global Cultural Economy. *Theory, Culture and Society* 7(2–3): 295–310.

Bertin, J. (1983) *Semiology of Graphics: Diagrams, Networks, Maps.* 2nd ed. (Madison: University of Wisconsin Press).

Bevington, W. (2008) A Visualization-based Taxonomy for Information Representation: Identifying Images with Icon Schematics. *Parsons Journal for Information Mapping* 1(3).

boyd, d. and Crawford, K. (2012) Critical Questions for Big Data: Provocations for a Cultural, Technological, and Scholarly Phenomenon. *Information, Communication and Society* 15(5): 662–79.

Brenner, N. and Schmid, C. (2013) The 'Urban Age' in Question. *International Journal of Urban and Regional Research* 38(3): 731–55.

Calabrese, F. and Ratti C. (2006) Real Time Rome. *Networks and Communication Studies* 20(3–4): 247–58.

Castells, M. (1996) *The Rise of the Network Society. The Information Age: Economy, Society and Culture. Vol. 1* (Oxford: Blackwell).

Ciuccarelli, P., Lupi, G. and Simeone, L. (2014) *Visualizing the Data City – Social Media as a Source of Knowledge for Urban Planning and Management* (New York: Springer).

Cosgrove, D. (1999) *Mappings* (London: Reaktion Books).

Crang, M. (1996) Envisioning Urban Histories: Bristol as Palimpsest, Postcards, and Snapshots. *Environment and Planning A* 28(3): 429–52.

DiSalvo, C. (2012) *Adversarial Design* (Cambridge, MA: MIT Press).

Duncan, J. and Duncan, N. (2005) *Landscapes of Privilege: The Politics of the Aesthetic in an American Suburb* (New York: Routledge).

Farinelli, F. (2003) *Geografia: Un'introduzione ai modelli del mondo* (Turin: Einaudi).

Frankel, L. and Racine, M. (2010) The Complex Field of Research: For Design, through Design, and about Design. *Proceedings of DRS2010* (Montréal).

Frayling, C. (1993) Research in Art and Design. *Royal College of Art Research Papers* 1(1): 1–5.

Freeman, R. (2010) *Strategic Management: A Stakeholder Approach* (Cambridge: Cambridge University Press).

Gaver, W. (2012) What Should We Expect from Research Through Design? *Proceedings of the 12th SIGCHI Conference on Human Factors in Computing Systems* (New York, USA), 937–46.

Girardin, F., Calabrese, F., dal Fiore, F., et al. (2008) Digital Footprinting: Uncovering Tourists with User-Generated Content. *IEEE Pervasive Computing* 7(4): 36–43.

Graham, M. (2011) Time Machines and Virtual Portals The Spatialities of the Digital Divide. *Progress in Development Studies* 11(3): 211–27.

Graham, M. and Zook, M. (2011) Visualizing Global Cyberscapes: Mapping User-Generated Placemarks. *Journal of Urban Technology* 18(1): 115–32.

Graham, M. and Zook, M. (2013) Augmented Realities and Uneven Geographies: Exploring the Geolinguistic Contours of the Web. *Environment and Planning A* 45(1): 77–99

Graham, S. (1998) The End of Geography or the Explosion of Place? Conceptualizing Space, Place and Information Technology. *Progress in Human Geography* 22(2): 165–85.

Graham, S. (2005) Software-sorted Geographies. *Progress in Human Geography* 29(5): 562–80

Greenfield, A. (2013) *Against the Smart City* (New York: Do projects).

Harris, R. (2000) *Information Graphics: A Comprehensive Illustrated Reference* (New York: Oxford University Press).

Heer, J. and Shneiderman, B. (2012) Interactive Dynamics for Visual Analysis. *Communications of the ACM* 55(4): 45–54.

Ihde, D. (1979) *Technics and Praxis: A Philosophy of Technology* (Dordrecht: Reidel).

Ihde, D. (2009) Imaging Technologies. In J. Olsen, S. Pedersen and V. Hendricks (Eds.), *A Companion to the Philosophy of Technology* (Malden: Blackwell), pp. 205–9.

ITU (International Telecommunication Union) (2014). *World Telecommunication/ ICT Indicators Database.*

Kitchin, R. (2014) The Real–Time City? 'Big Data' and Smart Urbanism. *GeoJournal* 79(1): 1–14.

Koskinen, I., Binder, T. and Redström, J. (2008) Lab, Field, Gallery, and Beyond. *Artifact* 2(1): 46–57.

Kotov, A., Zhai, C. and Sproat, R. (2011) Mining Named Entities with Temporally Correlated Bursts from Multilingual Web News Streams. *Proceeding of WSDM '11, ACM International Conference on Web Search and Data Mining* (New York, USA), 237–46.

Liu, X., Jiang, L., Wei F., et al. (2011) QuickView: Advanced Search of Tweets. *SIGIR '11 Proceedings of the 34th International ACM SIGIR Conference on Research and Development in Information Retrieval* (New York, USA), 1275–6.

Lupi, G., Patelli, P., Simeone, P., et al. (2012) Maps of Babel. Urban Sensing through User Generated Content. *Proceedings of Human Cities Symposium* (Brussels).

Manovich, L. (2011) Trending: The Promises and the Challenges of Big Social Data. In M. Gold (Ed.), *Debates in the Digital Humanities* (Minneapolis: The University of Minnesota Press), pp. 460–75.

Naor, M. and Yung, M. (1989) Universal One-Way Hash Functions and Their Cryptographic Applications. Proceedings of 21st ACM Symposium on Theory of Computing (New York, USA), pp. 33–43.

Rancière, J. (2010) *Dissensus: On Politics and Aesthetics* (London, New York: Continuum).

Ratti, C. (2014) *Architettura Open Source: Verso una progettazione aperta* (Turin: Einaudi).

Schein, R. (1997) The Place of Landscape: A Conceptual Framework for Interpreting an American Scene. *Annals of the Association of American Geographers* 87(4): 660–80.

Schroeder, R. (2014) Big Data and the Brave New World of Social Media Research. *Big Data & Society* 1(2).

Segel, E. and Heer, J. (2010) Narrative Visualization: Telling Stories with Data. *IEEE Transactions on Visualization and Computer Graphics* 16(6): 1139–48.

Shi, G. and Barker, K. (2011) Thematic Data Extraction from Web for GIS and Application. *Proceedings of IEEE International Conference on Spatial Data Mining and Geographical Knowledge Services* (Fuzhou, China), pp. 273–78.

Simeone, L., Lupi, G., Patelli, P. et al. (2012) DIY GIS. *Proceedings of 12th IEEE ICALT* (Rome), pp. 253–7.

Simeone, L. (2016) Missing intentionality: the limitations of social media analysis for participatory urban design. In E. Gordon and P. Mihailidis (Eds.), *Civic Media: Technology, Design, Practice* (Cambridge, MA: MIT Press).

Townsend, A. (2013) *Smart Cities: Big Data, Civic Hackers, and the Quest for a New Utopia* (New York: Norton).

Tufte, E. (2006) *Beautiful Evidence* (Cheshire: Graphics Press).

UNFPA (United Nations Population Fund) (2011) *State of World Population 2011* (New York: United Nations Population Fund).

Yau, N. (2013) *Data Points: Visualization that Means Something* (Indianapolis: Wiley).

Zook, M. and Graham, M. (2007a) Mapping DigiPlace: Geocoded Internet Data and the Representation of Place. *Environment and Planning B* 34(3): 466–82.

Zook, M. and Graham, M. (2007b) From Cyberspace to DigiPlace: Visibility in an Age of Information and Mobility. In H. Miller (Ed.), *Societies and Cities in the Age of Instant Access* (Dordrecht: Springer), pp. 241–54.

Zook, M. and Graham, M. (2007c) The Creative Reconstruction of the Internet: Google and the Privatization of Cyberspace and DigiPlace. *Geoforum* 38(6): 1322–43.

CHAPTER 14

Mapping Topics in International Climate Negotiations: A Computer-Assisted Semantic Network Approach

Nicolas Baya-Laffite and Jean-Philippe Cointet

In the light of increasing scientific evidence about global human-caused climate change in the 1980s, an international instrument to address the emerging problem was established: the United Nations Framework Convention on Climate Change (UNFCCC). Adopted on the eve of the Rio Summit on Environment and Development in 1992, the Climate Convention has functioned since its establishment in 1994 as both the main legal instrument and the political arena of global climate governance, with the Intergovernmental Panel on Climate Change (IPCC), created in 1988, operating as the international expertise arena informing the policy process. It is during the sessions of its highest governing body, the Conference of the Parties (COP), held annually since 1995 in a different city, that the delegations representing the now 196 Parties meet. Alongside a wide variety of non-governmental actors seeking to influence the process,

N. Baya-Laffite (✉)
Université Paris-Est, Paris, France
e-mail: nicolas.bayalaffite@sciencespo.fr

J.-P. Cointet
INRA, Paris, France
e-mail: jphcoi@gmail.com

© The Author(s) 2016   273
S. Kubitschko, A. Kaun (eds.), *Innovative Methods in Media and Communication Research*, DOI 10.1007/978-3-319-40700-5_14

the Parties, grouped in various coalitions of diverse, variable, and intertwined interests, negotiate the decisions to be adopted by the COP on the ways to achieve the Convention's objective: the stabilization of greenhouse gas concentrations in the atmosphere at a level that would prevent dangerous anthropogenic interference with the climate system. Ongoing since 1995, these negotiations have been characterized by different topical conversations on a large number of complex issues corresponding to the different parties' often conflicting interests and problem framings. Mapping the climate negotiations topic structure and evolution over twenty years using a digital corpus built from the most renowned internal journal of the negotiations available on the internet, the *Earth Negotiations Bulletin*, constitutes the methodological challenge that we address in this chapter.

From the ground of local, particular, and material negotiations themselves to their representation in the form of abstract maps that can support visual exploration of the topics in the negotiations, the path we propose and explore in this chapter is a translation involving several forms of data processing, analyses, and visualizations, allowing a change of scale, while ensuring the consistency of the chain of representation (Latour 1986, 1995).

Our methodological strategy to do this translation is based on a corpus of texts reporting on the negotiations on a daily basis that we process using innovative computer-assisted tools and techniques of text mining, semantic network analysis, and data visualization that allow both quantitative and qualitative insights to be obtained into the negotiation topics. Specifically, a semantic network analysis of co-occurring terms extracted from the corpus of reports using natural language processing (NLP) techniques makes it possible, through qualitative analysis, to identify the issues that define the content of topical conversations in climate negotiations. Drawing on the data produced through the semantic network analysis, then, we are able to produce two original graphical representations that allow visual exploration of the topics addressed in the COP meetings between 1995 and 2013: first, a force-vector layout network diagram that affords a synchronic view of the topic structure of the negotiations (Fig. 14.1); and second, a tubes layout diagram that affords a diachronic view of the different topics ranked in terms of their importance over successive COPs (Fig. 14.2). Narrating the visualizations, then, allows the production of distant readings of topics' semantic structure and topic trajectories and, thereby, testing of the robustness of the maps, and the tools and methods used to produce them, in the light of the history so far of the UNFCCC negotiations.

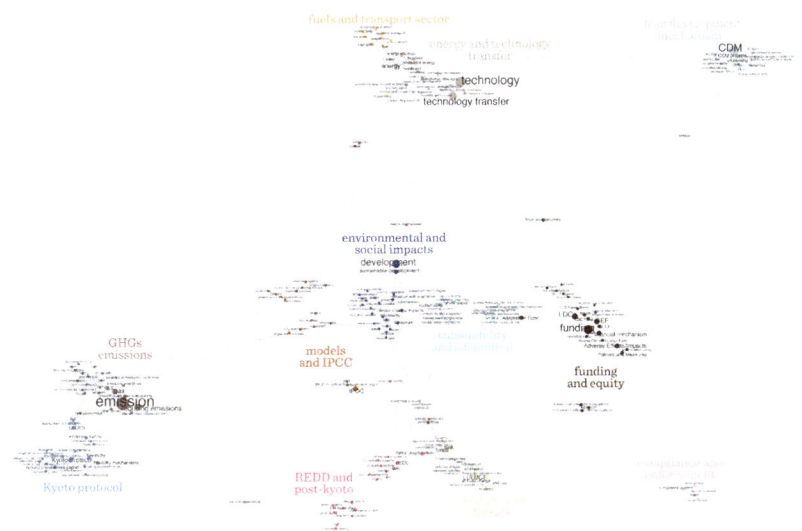

Fig. 14.1 The semantic network configuring twelve topics of COP negotiations as elicited from the *Earth Negotiations Bulletin* (ENB). © Nicolas Baya-Laffite and Jean-Philippe Cointet

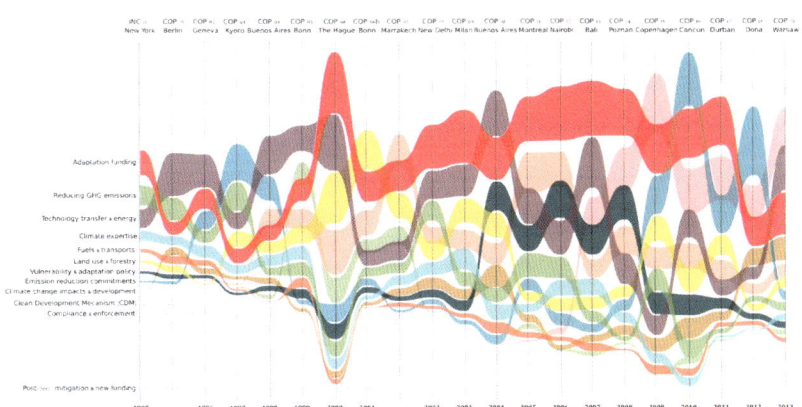

Fig. 14.2 Absolute and relative presence of the twelve framework topics within the COPs, 1995–2013. © Nicolas Baya-Laffite and Jean-Philippe Cointet

FROM NEGOTIATIONS TO TEXTS: IDENTIFYING A SOURCE FOR BUILDING A TEXTUAL CORPUS PROVIDING PROXY ACCESS TO THE NEGOTIATIONS

The first challenge we faced in undertaking our mapping of topics in climate negotiations was identifying a reliable, representative, and digitally exploitable source of textual data from which to build a corpus of text that can work as a proxy for the field where the discursive action occurs.

In our case that field of discourse is the annual meetings of the COP. While academic literature, traditional media, and social media are sources that can be, and have been, used to build proxy corpora to study climate change debates in scientific arenas (Anderegg et al. 2010; Bjurström and Polk 2011; Li et al. 2011; Stanhill 2001) and online settings (Rogers and Marres 2000; Niederer 2013; Marres 2015), these sources were of no use for us, as the aim was mapping in a systematic manner conversations *inside* the COP. The most evident source of text for such a mapping, we thought, would then be the online document repository of the Secretariat to the Convention, so as to constitute a corpus of text made of a selection of documents produced in the process. However, these documents, linked to the discussions, are very heterogeneous and unstructured and we were not able easily to use them as a proxy for what was in fact discussed on each day of negotiation. Thus, instead, we decided to use a hybrid source, informative, specialized, and based on the field, which offers a more interesting alternative proxy from which to draw a more digitally workable corpus for topic mapping: the web archive of the *Earth Negotiations Bulletin* (ENB).[1]

Edited and published by the Reporting Service of the International Institute of Sustainable Development (IISD), the ENB provides the most complete and reliable daily reports informing about thirty-three international negotiations processes on development and the environment. The twelfth volume of the ENB covers the UNFCCC negotiations. As a textual source, ENB vol. 12 is complete, homogeneous, and structured, three characteristics that make it an ideal source to be used as a proxy for digital mapping of negotiation topics. First of all, the reporting is complete. The coverage of the UNFCCC process has been continuous since 1995, with a newsletter ('daily issue') per negotiation day, offering the concerned public, starting with the negotiators themselves, an overview of topic discussions. Secondly, the reporting is trustworthy. The collective reporting process of the ENB, involving some sixty hired consultants from over thirty countries who are in the field of each meeting and four permanent IISD editors, is governed by a set of strict common standards and rules, compiled in the ENB publishing style manual, that help neutralize, as much as possible, any overt author biases. And thirdly, the reporting is structured. By virtue of the writing rules, the daily reports are always presented in the same template and using very formal language: there is a maximum length of 1800–1900 words; each issue reports—after an introduction and a brief history of the negotiations—on the official acts of the negotiations, following them by theme or daily session; each paragraph addresses specific conversations by paraphrasing, point by point, the arguments exchanged between the participants; finally, a small section called 'in corridors' reports what is happening or being related outside the framework of the official meeting. The result is a very structured, regulated presentation of contents with topically coherent paragraphs.

Drawing on this source of text, we included in our corpus all available daily texts on negotiations taking place at the annual COP. Our corpus starts in 1995, with the last session of the International Negotiating Committee of the Convention (INC) and COP1, held that same year in Berlin, and ends in 2013, with COP19 in Warsaw. Other vol. 12 issues, such as COP synthesis issues and issues from meetings other than the COP, were excluded. Also, the corpus only kept the text strictly concerning the reporting of the daily negotiations, removing all other text from the bulletins, for example the introductory part where a summary of the state of the negotiation process is presented or the credit part. The result of this is a very structured but also relatively small corpus of text, which can be kept under human control when processing using automated analysis tools.

From Texts to Diagrams: The Definition of a Text Analysis Strategy to Map Topics in the Negotiations

The choice of adequate textual processing tools and strategy is the next challenge that researchers have to face. In this kind of work there are hardly ever 'one size fits all' formulas. Creativity plays an essential role. For our mapping of negotiation topics using the ENB, we worked with the CorText Manager text analysis software developed by the researchers of the CorText Digital Platform, including one of us (Jean-Philippe Cointet). Created in 2012 with the aim of equipping scholars in the humanities with tools for empirical research that requires the processing of large textual corpora and data sets, the CorText Digital Platform functions as a hub of expertise in different relevant scientific and technical domains, ranging from natural language processing, information retrieval, and knowledge management to complex network analysis, scientometrics, and data visualization. The software solutions designed and developed at CorText are made available through a web application, the CorText Manager. Through a single user-friendly interface, the application allows users to create and manage their projects, upload and import textual corpuses and/or data sets from different sources, run a wide range of analysis tools (scripts), and get the results, including data visualizations, online.

Using this software, our methodological strategy for processing the ENB corpus is twofold: first automatic text analysis and then semantic network mapping of extracted terms.

Linguistic Processing and Lexical Extraction: Building a List of Terms Referring to Issues in the Negotiations

In order to map topics using semantic network analysis, the first step in our protocol consists of identifying relevant issue-terms in the corpus. The identification of issues draws on a combination of computer and human analyses.

The first substep is automated and consists of lexical extraction. The CorText lexical extraction tool makes use of well-established natural language processing (NLP) and information-retrieval techniques to automatically identify and extract, from a given corpus, a list of pertinent and recurring terms. First, every term is tagged according to its grammatical type: noun, adjective, verb, adverb, and so on. Then noun phrases—that is, combinations of multiple nouns and adjectives—are identified to build the set of possible multi-terms. Those that are semantically coherent (for example, 'transfer of technologies' and 'technology transfer') or whose stemmed version is identical (for example, 'adaptation technology' and 'adaptation technologies') are gathered under a single class. Multi-terms belonging to a given stemmed class in the whole corpus are then counted to obtain their frequency. Finally, the less frequent multi-stems, as well as those frequent multi-terms that are considered not lexically salient, are removed, drawing on linguistic criteria that are extensively described in Omodei et al. (2014). The result of this automatic process of lexical analysis is finally compiled in a CSV (comma-separated values) file.

The extracted list of noun phrases (also called n-grams) can include terms made of one word (monograms). Excluding them is common practice, as single words tend to be neutral and therefore less informative. However, in the climate negotiations many monograms (for example, 'funding'), as well as acronyms, initials, or abbreviations (for example, CDM, for 'clean development mechanism'), which are also monograms, refer to important issues. Thus, when parameterizing the script, we decided not to exclude monograms. While it is possible to limit the number of terms to be extracted, we decided not to, thus letting the script extract as many relevant terms as it found. In our case the automatic processing resulted in a list containing 1178 noun phrases and monograms.

The identification of terms referring to issues in the negotiations, however, cannot solely rely on automatized analyses. While automatic multi-terms extraction is a classic task in NLP, the algorithms used in this kind of processing, where the analyst does not pre-define the categories to be used, cannot provide totally satisfying results as regards the selection of terms and the automatic normalization, stemming, and classification. Thus, the second substep consists in a qualitative analysis and review of the list of terms drawing on domain-specific knowledge, and in the light of the specific criteria guiding the semantic analysis. As we will see next, producing draft semantic network visualizations on the basis of draft lists is necessary to support visual, qualitative analysis and exploration of the co-word structure variations resulting from the exclusion or inclusion of certain terms. This editing can be done online using the CorText CSV file viewer and editor, or using a spreadsheet editor like Open Office to work on the downloaded CSV file.

Thus, drawing on our own knowledge of climate negotiations and on insights gained through traditional methods, including interviews and literature reviews, we reviewed, cleaned, and normalized the list. First, from the 1178 automatically extracted terms, we eliminated all terms that appeared fewer than seven times in the corpus, as well as all terms that were not referring to identifiable matters of discussion. Thus, we did not keep countries or terms that were too vague or ambiguous. For example, 'contact group' and 'ad hoc working group', both recurrent terms referring to spaces of negotiation, were considered relevant by the algorithm, but we eliminated them as we were only interested in the issues that these groups address. Finally, we manually collated many acronyms, initials, or abbreviations with their corresponding full forms (for instance, 'CDM' and 'clean development mechanism'). Table 14.1 illustrates the extraction and gathering of

Table 14.1 Example of most frequent multi-terms in the list, with their main form, multiple forms, and frequency

Main form	Forms	Frequency
Emission	emission, emissions	990
Technology	technology	816
Funding	funds, fund, funding	790
CDM	cdm, clean development mechanism	681
Technology Transfer	technology transfer, transfer of technology, sharing technology, transfer of technologies	564
Development	development	530

forms under a main form. This time-consuming but important review of terms allowed us to enhance the quality of automatically grouped noun phrases and reduce the list to those most relevant for our analysis.

Thus, the final result, a list of 200 terms referring to issues in the negotiations, is the product of a semi-automated process, where the algorithm and human understanding of meaning in context are combined in the light of the research question guiding the mapping.

Semantic Network Analysis: Eliciting, Visualizing, and Interpreting the Topic Structure of the Negotiations

On the basis of these 200 terms, we were able to proceed to the second step in our protocol: semantic network analysis in the spirit of co-occurrence analysis (Callon et al. 1991). Specifically, we are interested in inducing categories (the number of which is not pre-specified) on the basis of the frequent joint presence of noun terms over a given unit of text (Ferrer i Cancho and Solé 2001; Mohr et al. 2013; Rule et al. 2015). In our case, the categories to be induced were the topics of negotiation; the unit of text was each paragraph of the ENB daily issues' text included in our corpus.

First, we built a co-occurrence matrix that provided the count of joint appearances of the extracted terms in the same paragraph of a dated ENB daily issue, and we summed it to build an aggregated co-occurrence matrix. Secondly, we computed a proximity score to measure the relatedness of each pair of terms. This yielded a weighted semantic network with terms as nodes and edge weights indexing similarity scores. The resulting network, where terms are linked with a strength proportional to a co-occurrence-based measure of similarity (Weeds and Weir 2005), features a very large number of edges. Therefore, as the third substep it was necessary to filter them. So, on the basis of an automatically defined threshold, we progressively increased this so as to produce a readable but still informative visualization of the network. Finally, we applied a classic *community detection* algorithm to identify clusters of terms, which we identified as topics in the negotiations (Blondel et al. 2008).

Throughout the process of analysis it was necessary to print a series of draft network mappings displaying the semantic network with a force-directed layout. This served as a visual aid for making manual term selection, adjusting the software parameters for the semantic network, and interpreting the resulting cluster configurations. Of course, all this work implied relying on available knowledge of climate negotiation. It would not have been possible to produce such analysis without a good pre-existing knowledge of the subject matter. Other than literature reviews and interviews, various workshops were organized with climate specialists and expert negotiators in various fields at several stages of the process where key decisions had to be made. The whole process required much iteration until a visually robust result was obtained.

The final network diagram is presented in Fig. 14.1. It shows the topic structure of negotiations as it emerges from our semantic network analysis of 200 'issue-terms' extracted from the ENB. We used the GePhi Forced Atlas 2 algorithm to spatialize the resulting network, as it provides several parameters for customizing the final visualization and thus allows for a good representation of the overall structure (Jacomy et al. 2014). The issue-terms are represented as nodes. The size of the nodes scales with the term's frequency in the corpus. The force vector algorithm defines the nodes' positions. The thickness of edges between nodes is a function of the co-occurrence score of the terms: terms that co-occur are linked more intensely. The nodes' colors are attributed automatically owing to their inscription in a cluster as resulting from the community detection algorithm. By defining a strong threshold of edges, noise was eliminated to bring forward significant signals in our visualization of the overall structure. The circle area over the clusters scales with the number of paragraphs assigned to each cluster. The resulting visualization affords a view of the co-occurring terms that form twelve topic clusters, which have been manually labeled, the connections defining the structure of each cluster, and connections between clusters through specific bridge terms that define the overall topic structure of the corpus.

On this basis, we applied a *paragraph projection* procedure to attribute these twelve topics to each paragraph of the ENB corpus. This enabled us, finally, to link paragraphs and topic clusters and count out the number of paragraphs per topic at each session of the COP, so as to measure the absolute size of each topic at each COP. The count was then sorted decreasingly so as to measure the relative position of each topic at each COP. This is visualized in a diachronic stream graph, presented in Fig. 14.2. We visualized them as a bump graph produced with Raw, a visualization tool developed by the Density Design of the Politecnico di Milano, Italy.

The graph shows the evolution between 1995 and 2013 of the twelve topics per session and their relative position and absolute weight. The thickness of the stream represents the topic's absolute visibility (number of paragraphs where it appears), whereas the rank of the stream at each COP represents each topic's relative presence (as compared with one another). The map affords a view of how each of the twelve topics evolved, when it emerged, became predominant, or was marginalized.

FROM DIAGRAMS TO NARRATIVE ACCOUNTS: VISUALLY EXPLORING THE NEGOTIATIONS' TOPIC STRUCTURING AND DEPLOYMENT

What can these visualizations teach us about the life of topics in the negotiations? The digital mapping process is based on what is available elsewhere in textual form, in the ENB. This does not, however, mean that visualizations bring nothing new: they bring new comprehensive visual syntheses of the COP negotiations. And if the maps do not speak by themselves, they have an affordance: they invite the reader to say what is seen. Between interpretative potentiation and constraint, the maps induce reflection on what they translate and mobilize: they trigger discussions by an effect of surprise resulting from the confrontation with something known, or something unusual, unexpected, or difficult to explain in the images. One can identify on the graph a number of moments in the case of the diachronic view, or terms in the case of a synchronic view, whose meaning is well documented in the literature. One can also wonder at many aspects of the graph (flow peaks, variations, links between nodes, size of nodes, clustering of some terms) that require additional explanation. Thus, the confrontation with the maps generates a productive feeling of perplexity that can trigger, in various 'map-user' arrangements, reflexive attitudes, both political and epistemic, toward the map and what it represents.

The first confrontation with the map is the one that takes place with the researchers producing it. And then comes a further challenge, that of the experimenter's regress (Collins 1992). Since methods and tools used to produce the visualizations are experimental, we need to confront the resulting maps with available knowledge on the mapped subject matter to test their robustness.

We propose now to briefly illustrate this with a short narrative account of the place and trajectories of topics pertaining to adaptation. Mitigation and adaptation are the two main over-arching strategies of action defining a controversial topic divide in the negotiations, whose form and evolution constitute one of the main objectives of the research discussed in this chapter. As we and our colleagues have shown in detail elsewhere (Venturini et al. 2014; Baya-Laffite and Cointet 2015), the maps demonstrate the pre-eminence of mitigation-related topic conversations. As we can see in Table 14.2, from the twelve topics identified in our semantic network mapping, eight concern issues related to mitigation, three concern issues related to adaptation, and one concerns issues relative to the scientific foundations.

In the semantic network map (Fig. 14.1), all three clusters of expressions linked to adaptation challenges are grouped at the center of the semantic network, compared to other themes relating to mitigation that are scattered around that center. Its centrality suggests its importance and its connection to all the other negotiation topics. Our mapping, on the other hand, confirms that the topic of 'vulnerability and adaptation' (Fig. 14.3) has been a long-standing taboo in the UNFCCC process. Indeed, such discussions arrived only in the 2000s. However, it also clearly shows that debates on 'adaptation funding' (Fig. 14.4) have been high on the agenda from the very beginning.

This is consistent with the most recent literature review on the topic (Khan and Roberts 2013). The fact that the issue of adaptation funding consistently figures, with some exceptions, in the top positions throughout the twenty years of negotiation is owed to pressure from the Alliance of Small Island States (AOSIS) and Least Developed Countries (LDC) to obtain the financial resources necessary to meet their adaptation needs.[2] Yet, despite such efforts, the definition of policies to address the full costs of adaptation to climate change impacts in the light of countries' vulnerabilities remained relatively marginal until the early 2000s, as the issue was put on hold after the first COP in Berlin (Yamin 2005). The reason is to be found, as documented in the literature, in the ambiguity that surrounded the concept, both on the practical and normative levels (Schipper 2006).

Table 14.2   Topic clusters and terms configuring them

Climate expertise topic and terms	
Climate expertise	Stabilization, greenhouse gas concentrations, 350 ppm, political will; mitigation options, emission scenarios, models, sea level rise, precipitation, social costs; observing systems, adaptation options, adaptive capacity; uncertainties, scientific uncertainty, IPPC, Summary for policy makers (SPM)
Mitigation-related topics and terms	
GHG emissions reductions	Greenhouse gas emissions, dangerous anthropogenic interference, reducing emissions, 1990 levels, (common but) differentiated responsibilities, commitments for non-Annex I, emissions inventories, gas, CO2, CH4, N2O, HFC, ozone, Montreal Protocol, gas-by-bas, bubble, all gasses
Emission-reduction commitments	Kyoto Protocol, Berlin Mandate, Economies in transition, Quantified emission limitation or reduction commitments (QELROs), pledges into QELROs, assigned amount units (AAU), surplus AAU, emissions trading, flexibility mechanisms, accounting rules, binding commitments, base year, future commitments, length of the commitment period, second commitment period, gap between commitment periods, Durban Platform
Compliance and enforcement	Compliance system, enforcement, expert review, facilitative branch, trigger
Energy and technology transfer	Technology, technology transfer, technology transfer mechanism, performance indicators, private sector, enabling environment, intellectual property rights, technology development, research and development, south-south, know-how, international cooperation, technology fund, environmentally sound technology, carbon sequestration, innovation, investments, public-private, business, industry, renewable energy, energy, energy efficiency
Fuels and transports	Fuel, bunker fuels, energy security, transport, maritime transport, international aviation, transportation
Land use and forests	Forest, sink, carbon stocks, forest management, sustainable forest management, forest conservation, option C, definition of forest, biome, additional activities, afforestation, reforestation, small scale afforestation and reforestation; land use, land use change, and forestry (LULUCF), harvested wood products, biodiversity, desertification, development strategies
Clean development mechanism (CDM)	Clean Development Mechanism (CDM), CDM projects, supplementarity, additionality, certified emission reductions (CERs), domestic action, cost effectiveness, prompt start, impact assessments, baselines, biomass, non-renewable biomass, distribution of CDM projects, equitable geographic distribution, leakage

(*continued*)

Table 14.2   (continued)

Post-2012 and REDD	Bali Action Plan, building blocks, shared vision, long-term cooperative action, post 2012, historical responsibility, green climate fund (GCF), fast-start financing, climate finance; mitigation actions, nationally appropriate mitigation actions (NAMAs), measuring reporting and verification (MRV), forest degradation, reducing emissions from deforestation and forest degradation (REDD); REDD and the role of conservation, sustainable management of forests and enhancement of forest carbon stocks in developing countries (REDD+); methodological guidance, international consultations and analysis (ICA), sectoral approaches, non-market approaches, market approaches
Adaptation-related topics and terms	
Impacts	Climate change impacts, development, sustainable development, poverty, poverty eradication, food, food security, agriculture, water, water resources, ocean, ecosystem, financial flows, traditional knowledge, human rights, climate justice, women, gender, indigenous peoples, local governments, local communities
Vulnerability and adaptation	Vulnerable, vulnerable countries, most vulnerable, small island, extreme event, vulnerability and adaptation, adaptation actions, mitigation and adaptation, adaptation technologies, Nairobi work programme on vulnerability and adaptation; long term action, Buenos Aires adaptation work programme, article 9, adaptation and response measures, privileges and immunities, international transaction log
Adaptation funding	Funding, financial mechanism, operating entity, financing adaptation, full costs, adaptation needs, importance of adaptation, National adaptation programmes of action (NAPA), lack of progress, new technologies, financial resources, Adaptation Fund, adverse effects/impacts, adverse effect policy, policies and measures, special climate change fund (SCCF), Global environmental facility (GEF), Least developed countries (LCDs), LCDs Fund, LCD expert group, Annex I national communications, non-annex I national communications, education

On the one hand, impacts, vulnerability, and adaptation concern local government and therefore are hard to place as objects of collective action on the global stage of the Convention. Besides, knowledge on these issues was limited. On the other, the focus on impacts, vulnerability, and adaptation appeared to many actors as an unacceptable excuse to avoid, and ultimately renounce, ambitious mitigation objectives. The stream graph confirms that in the period 2000–2004, following the rejection of the Kyoto Protocol by the United States, the publication of the third IPCC report, and new

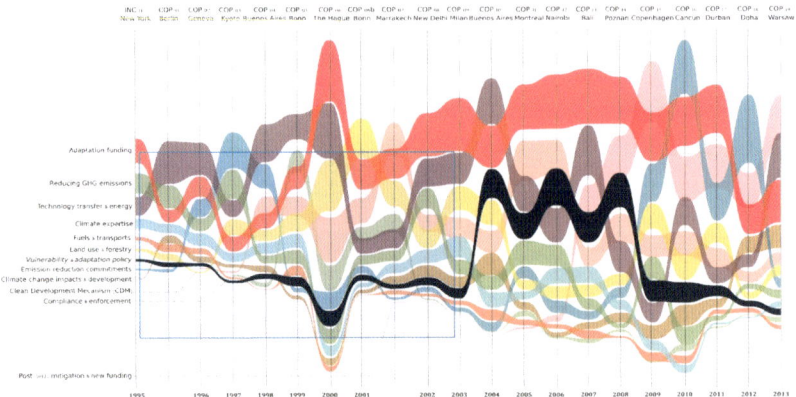

Fig. 14.3   Vulnerability and adaptation policy before 2004. © Nicolas Baya-Laffite and Jean-Philippe Cointet

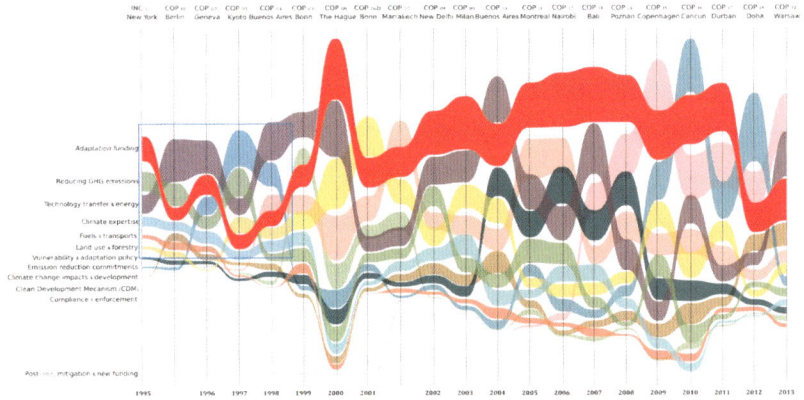

Fig. 14.4   Adaptation funding before 2000. © Nicolas Baya-Laffite and Jean-Philippe Cointet

evidence that the efforts to reduce GHG emissions would not suffice to avoid impacts in time so that systems would naturally adapt, there was an 'adaptation turn' in negotiations. The result is the predominance of the adaptation funding topic over the whole 2000–2008 period (Fig. 14.5) and an increase in the topic of vulnerability and adaptation between New Dehli (COP8, 2002) and Poznan (COP14, 2008; Fig. 14.6).

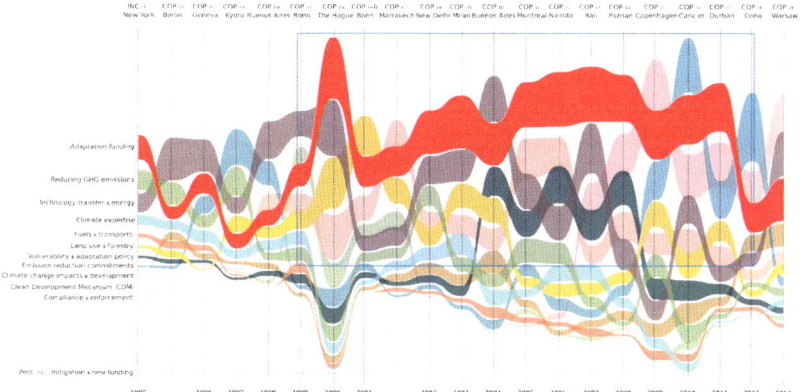

Fig. 14.5 Adaptation funding 2000–2013. © Nicolas Baya-Laffite and Jean-Philippe Cointet

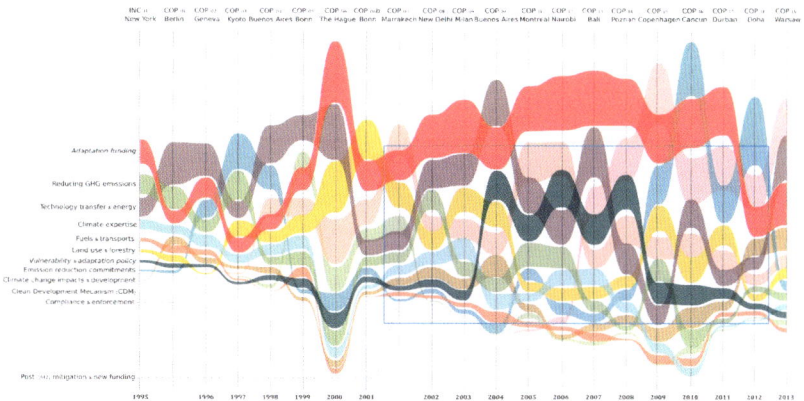

Fig. 14.6 The 'high plateau' of vulnerability and adaptation policy. © Nicolas Baya-Laffite and Jean-Philippe Cointet

Since the Delhi Ministerial Declaration on Climate Change and Sustainable Development in 2002, adaptation to the impacts of climate change became an issue in the light of development needs. The next year, in Milan (COP9, 2003), focus is put on the need to address the scientific, technical, and socio-economic aspects of vulnerability and adaptation to climate change. The result of such conversations was the Buenos Aires work program on adaptation and response measures (COP10, 2004), with a two-track approach: one addressing the scientific, technical, and socio-economic aspects, the other the improvement of information and methodologies, concrete adaptation actions, transfer of technologies for adaptation, and capacity building. The discussion continued the next year in Montreal (COP11, 2005) in the aftermath of Hurricane Katrina and other extreme weather events, showing the 'non-invulnerability' of industrialized countries. The organization of COP12 in Nairobi, Kenya provided a new opportunity to call for urgent action on adaptation for the most vulnerable countries. Results became visible both in terms of funding, with the governance structure of the Adaptation Fund almost finalized at that time, and in terms of policies, with the adoption of the Nairobi work program for the implementation of adaptation. Yet, in spite of much progress on the policy aspects, the definition of an official approach to implementing adaptation funding came only after Bali (COP13, 2007), with the end of a long-standing controversy spurred by the demand of the oil-exporting countries for compensation for the reduced oil sales linked to mitigation actions. Since the Bali COP, Parties were able to negotiate in Poznań (COP14, 2008) the governance of adaptation funding and policy mechanisms without such ambiguity. In 2009, adaptation issues lost ground again. This can be explained by two factors. First, after the failure of the Copenhagen Conference to impose new binding objectives, the priority was on mitigation. Second, this topic seems to have gained worldwide recognition in the discussions, as shown by the creation of a mitigation committee and an adaptation framework between Cancun and Warsaw. Its defenders complained less and started concentrating more specifically on financing to make the necessary actions operational.

CONCLUSION

To conclude, the maps discussed here are a product of the combination of the tools and materials used and the decisions made when using them. They are far from being a mechanical, automatic output of the tool box. Far from being replaced by the machine, the researcher is constantly interacting with its corpus and the outputs of the algorithms used to produce and visualize the data. The resulting maps create a need to redeploy the complexity by creating narrative accounts. A major asset of this representation of complex and, in some ways, stern political processes is that it calls on users to talk about these images, to engage in reflection, and to produce new interpretative hypotheses, new narrations on the evolution of negotiation themes. We did so by using them to account for the adaptation/mitigation divide in the negotiations. Yet this is simply one example among many others of narrative accounts that can be produced on the basis of the negotiations' topic maps.

Beyond these methodological challenges, a final issue that we would like to point out pertains to the life of the maps outside the academic setting where they were produced. Two websites make the maps available along with a series of narratives about the rise of adaptation: the MEDEA project website and the EMAPS' Climaps project website.[3] In this sense, one of the expectations of the researchers who took part in this mapping is that an online interface to explore the maps could help to disseminate the maps so as, hopefully, to raise interest in their use in multiple settings including academia, journalism, or advocacy. These visualizations have the potential to function as a boundary object, in different user arrangements, for discussing the past, present, or future implications with regard to the process. However, success in this sense is beyond our control and depends on how the maps are taken up by concerned actors.

Acknowledgments Nicolas Baya-Laffite acted as the main author of the manuscript and Jean-Philippe Cointet contributed his methodological expertise to the chapter. Research presented in this chapter was done to contribute to the objectives of two research projects led by médialab Sciences Po on the use of digital methods for controversy mapping: MEDEA (for Mapping Environmental Debates on Adaptation) funded by the French National Research Agency (ANR) (ANR-11-CEPL-0004) (http://medea.medialab.sciences-po.fr/#/) and EMAPS (for Electronic Maps to Assist Public Science) funded by the 7th European Framework Program (http://www.emapsproject.com/blog/). Participants in the specific research discussed in this chapter also included Tommaso Venturini (project coordinator), Ian Gray, and Kari de Pryck (médialab Sciences Po), and Vinciane Zabban (Université Paris 13). Visual design was done in collaboration with Martina Cecchi and Paolo Ciuccarelli (Density Design) in the framework of the EMAPS project. We particularly thank the participants in the data sprints organized within the EMAPS project. We also thank participants of the conferences where we presented this work, particularly to participants of the international conference on 'New Perspectives on Global Environmental Images' in Paris in October 2014.

NOTES

1. See http://www.iisd.ca/vol12 (accessed 10 March 2016).
2. It is, for example, on its demand that article 4.4 was added to the final text of the 1992 Convention, stipulating: 'The developed country Parties and other developed Parties included in Annex II shall also assist the developing country Parties that are particularly vulnerable to the adverse effects of climate change in meeting costs of adaptation to those adverse effects.'
3. See http://medea.medialab.sciences-po.fr/#/#unfccc and http://climaps.eu/#!/narrative/mitigation-and-adaptation-in-the-unfccc-debates (accessed 10 March 2016).

REFERENCES

Anderegg, W., Prall, J., Harold, J., et al. (2010) Expert Credibility in Climate Change. *Proceedings of the National Academy of Sciences* 107(27): 12107–9.

Baya-Laffite, N. and Cointet, J.-P. (2015) Cartographier la trajectoire de l'adaptation dans l'espace des négociations sur le climat. *Réseaux* 188(6): 159–98.

Bjurström, A. and Polk, M. (2011) Physical and Economic Bias in Climate Change Research: A Scientometric Sstudy of IPCC Third Assessment Report. *Climatic Change* 108(1–2): 1–22.

Blondel, V., Guillame, J.-P., Lambiotte, R., et al. (2008) Fast Unfolding of Communities in Large Networks. *Journal of Statistical Mechanics: Theory and Experiment* 2008(10): 10008.

Callon, M., Courtial, J. and Laville, F. (1991) Co-word Analysis as a Tool for Describing the Network of Interactions Between Basic and Technological Research: The Case of Polymer Chemsitry. *Scientometrics* 22(1): 155–205.

Collins, H. (1992) *Changing Order: Replication and Induction in Scientific Practice* (Chicago: University of Chicago Press).

Ferrer i Cancho, R. and Solé, R. (2001) The Small World of Human Language. *Proceedings of the Royal Society B* 268(1482): 2261–5.

Jacomy, M., Venturini, T., Heymann, S., et al. (2014) ForceAtlas2, a Continuous Graph Layout Algorithm for Handy Network Visualization Designed for the Gephi Software. *PLoS ONE* 9(6): e98679.

Khan, M. and Roberts, J. (2013) Adaptation and International Climate Policy. *Wiley Interdisciplinary Reviews: Climate Change* 4(3): 171–89.

Latour, B. (1995) The 'Pédofil' of Boa Vista. *Common Knowledge* 4(1): 144–87.

Latour, B. (1986) Visualisation and Cognition: Drawing Things Together. In H. Kuklick (Ed.), *Knowledge and Society Studies in the Sociology of Culture Past and Present* (Greenwich, CT: Jai Press), pp. 1–40.

Li, J., Wang, M.-H. and Ho, Y.-S. (2011) Trends in Research on Global Climate Change: A Science Citation Index Expanded-based analysis. *Global and Planetary Change* 77(1–2): 13–20.

Marres, N. (2015) Why Map Issues? On Controversy Analysis as a Digital Method. *Science, Technology & Human Values* 40(5): 655–86.

Mohr, J., Wagner-Pacifici, R., Breiger, R., et al. (2013) Graphing the Grammar of Motives in National Security Strategies: Cultural Interpretation, Automated Text Analysis and the Drama of Global Politics. *Poetics* 41(6): 670–700.

Niederer, S. (2013) 'Global Warming is Not a Crisis!' Studying Climate Change Skepticism on the Web. *NECSUS. European Journal of Media Studies* 2(1): 83–112.

Omodei, E., Guo, Y., Cointet, J.-P., et al. (2014) Social and Semantic Diversity: Socio-semantic Representation of a Scientific Corpus. *Proceedings of the 8th Workshop on Language Technology for Cultural Heritage, Social Sciences, and Humanities (LaTeCH)*, pp. 71–9.

Rogers, R. and Marres, N. (2000) Landscaping Climate Change: A Mapping Technique for Understanding Science and Technology Debates on the World Wide Web. *Public Understanding of Science* 9(2): 141–63.

Rule, A., Cointet, J.-P. and Bearman, P. (2015) Lexical Shifts, Substantive Changes, and Continuity in State of the Union Discourse, 1790–2014. *Proceedings of the National Academy of Sciences of the United States of America* 112(35): 10837–44.

Schipper, E. (2006) Conceptual History of Adaptation in the UNFCCC Process. *Review of European Community & International Environmental Law* 15(1): 82–92.

Stanhill, G. (2001) The Growth of Climate Change Science: A Scientometric Study. *Climatic Change* 48(2–3): 515–24.

Venturini, T., Baya-Lafitte, N., Cointet, J.-P., et al. (2014) Three Maps and Three Misunderstandings: A Digital Mapping of Climate Diplomacy. *Big Data & Society* 1(2).

Weeds, J. and Weir, D. (2005) Co-occurrence Retrieval: A Flexible Framework for Lexical Distributional Similarity. *Computational Linguistics* 31(4): 439–75.

Yamin, F. (2005) The European Union and Future Climate Policy: Is Mainstreaming Adaptation a Distraction or Part of the Solution? *Climate Policy* 5(3): 349–61.

CHAPTER 15

'Creative' and Participatory Visual Approaches in Audience Research

Katharina Lobinger

It has almost become a cliché to open chapters and articles with the diagnosis that visuals permeate our everyday environments not least due to the digitalization of media and communication technologies, which has enabled a neat integration of mobile communication, online communication, and practices in consumer photography. Recently, the fact that photography has become 'networked' has caused a paradigmatic shift in the debate about photography (Hand 2012), after an era in which scholars were concerned with the crisis of reproduction and digital photography. With photographs becoming 'networked', we witness a proliferation of images not only in the mass media but also in our everyday life-worlds. Hence, more than ever the field of visual communication needs to develop theoretical and analytic tools for coping with the challenges of the visual mode of communication. However, one contribution of visual research has widely been neglected so far: visual communication research is not only concerned with the analysis *of* visual material and the related processes of production, reception, use, and effects. It also focuses on the ways in which visuals can be used *for* research purposes.

K. Lobinger (✉)
University of Lugano, Lugano, Switzerland
e-mail: katharina.lobinger@usi.ch

© The Author(s) 2016   293
S. Kubitschko, A. Kaun (eds.), *Innovative Methods in Media and Communication Research*, DOI 10.1007/978-3-319-40700-5_15

Those methods that use visuals for research purposes are often referred to as visual methods, creative methods, or enabling methods. This is not to say that such things as 'non-creative' methods do exist. Of course, all methods have to be insightfully and creatively designed in order to yield new, fascinating, and, no less important, valid results. However, the term 'enabling methods' or 'creative methods' specifically describes a broad range of techniques that facilitate particularly deep and clear reflections and discussion of research topics by providing participants with often non-verbal opportunities to express themselves and to reflect on the issues of interest (Arthur et al. 2014, p. 160). 'Creative' methodological approaches, for example, rely on photo or video diaries, on digital story-telling, on drawing-based exercises (for example, maps, networks, time lines, thematic and non-thematic drawings), photo elicitation, or partici-patory video production, or they work with prompts or sorting tasks and many further techniques (Awan and Gauntlett 2011).

In this chapter a particular subgroup of enabling and creative tech-niques is discussed: creative *visual* methods; that is, methods in which visual material is used or produced during the research process. Originally, visual methods were developed in visual sociology (Harper 1986) and visual anthropology (Collier and Collier 1986; Collier 1957; Schwartz 1989). Recently they have also gained importance in visual communication research (Lobinger forthcoming). As will be shown in this chapter, they are particularly suited for audience studies in media and communication research (see O'Neill et al. 2013).

Visual methods can be used as stand-alone approaches. However, it has been found very useful to combine them with open-ended interviews, focus groups, or observations, where visual techniques can be 'very pow-erful aids to interviewing […] helping to access views and behaviours that are, for whatever reason, more difficult to verbalise, and bringing more creative insight to the research topic' (Arthur et al. 2014, p. 169). They can also be used in mixed-method approaches, combining qualitative and quantitative research (see the example of Q-sort discussed later).

Since the verbal and the visual modes of communication hold very differ-ent potentials, they also enable different forms of expression and reflection during research processes. For example, images are particularly suited for the representation of spatial relationships, while temporal information can be better explained by the sequential verbal mode. This is why visual methods can be efficiently used to create maps and drawings of relational structures, such as social networks. Network research especially is taking advantage of this particular strength of the visual mode (see Gamper et al. 2011). It is often argued that while 'textual communication is based on argumentation, visual communication is based on association' (Müller 2007, p. 13), and particularly this associative nature of images makes them closer related to feelings and emotions. While the grammar of the verbal mode presents the pieces of information of a narration sequentially, pictures are perceived holistically, even though their producers usually use (less formalized) representational techniques for creating visual arguments (Hawhee and Messaris 2009, p. 213). Also during the perception and reception of images we use what can be called 'reading paths'. However, these paths through the picture are less structured compared to the paths pre-defined by the verbal mode: 'Communication by association means that certain patterns and memorized visual precursors ("Vor-Bilder") are more or less spontaneously "popping up" in the beholders' minds, and that the rules that apply to visual meaning creation are less standardized and more context-dependent than meaning created and communicated in the textual mode' (Müller 2007, p. 13). These associations and visual precursors increase the polysemy of images. While, as will be argued in this chapter, visual polysemy represents a challenge for the analysis of the visual, it is a true treasure for analysis with visuals. Encouraging people to talk about pictures and letting them elaborate on subjective meanings is a very productive technique in visual elicitation studies. In general, creative visual methods often prove enjoyable and more engaging (Buckingham 2009, p. 648), even though this does not apply to all participants in all situations.

There is some controversy over the question of how to examine the 'visual data' produced by the use of visual methods. While Arthur et al. (2014) argue that visual outputs produced by participants serve the purpose of eliciting verbal discussions rather than being primary data on their own, Buckingham (2009) explicitly criticizes visual researchers for undervaluing the insights that can be gained from examining the visual material produced during research. Accordingly, he demands the development of methods to deal analytically with the visual dimensions of this material, instead of only 'falling back on participants' verbal accounts' (Buckingham 2009, p. 648).

In the following, selected creative visual methods are discussed, with particular emphasis on visual elicitation following different forms of participatory approaches, on visual Q-sort studies and card sorting procedures, and on creative drawing-based exercises. Each section starts with an overview of the basic principles and the methodological scope of the approaches. Case studies of the author's own research projects illustrate how the approaches can be employed, indicating their genuine potentials and pitfalls. Moreover, there is discussion of how the visual methods presented can be used beyond the image-centered scope of visual communication research. As will be shown, they represent particularly fruitful approaches for audience research in general.

VISUAL ELICITATION

Visual elicitation, the use of visuals during the interview process in qualitative research, was first used and described by anthropologist John Collier (1957). Collier originally used the terms 'photo elicitation' and 'photo-interviewing' to describe a particular variation of open-ended interviews in which photographs are used as an aid to interviewing, with the scope of facilitating vivid, 'deep and interesting talk' (Harper 2002). In recent applications the term 'visual elicitation' is preferred to 'photo elicitation', because the visual material used for the elicitation of verbal response is not limited to photographs but can include visual material of all kinds, such as paintings, cartoons, advertisements, diagrams, or videos (Pauwels 2012). Overall, visual elicitation refers to the use of visual stimuli with the scope of eliciting—usually verbal—response (Harper 2002; Lapenta 2012; Lobinger forthcoming).

In his groundbreaking work on the use of photographs in anthropological research, Collier identified several advantages of photo-interviewing that were later confirmed by multiple follow-up studies in the tradition of his work. For example, interviews using photo elicitation are often longer than purely verbal interviews without photographs. In this regard, Collier also found that 'photographs can be stimulating and can help to overcome the fatigue and repetition often encountered in verbal interviews' (1957, p. 857). Visual elicitation does not only produce longer and more vivid discussion. Due to the specific affordances of the different modalities, images also elicit different kinds of information compared to verbal questions (Harper 2002, p. 13). Collier (1957), for example, believed that photographs give access to latent memory. Finally, photo elicitation favors collaboration between researcher and respondent and can create a non-directive discourse (Lapenta 2012, p. 201; Collier and Collier 1986, p. 105). Particularly when respondents explore the meanings of the visual material together with the researcher, the traditional question–answer discourse structure of interviews is broken up, which reduces the hierarchy in researcher–respondent relationships.

My enthusiasm for photo elicitation also comes from the collaboration it inspires. When two or more people discuss the meaning of photographs, they try to figure out something together. This is, I believe, an ideal model for research (Harper 2002, p. 23).

While the polysemy of images represents one of the major challenges of visual content analysis, it holds methodological potential for visual interviews. Especially because there is not one fixed meaning of a picture and its elements, respondents can be encouraged to freely explore and explain what the pictures mean to them for which reasons, without fearing to give a 'wrong' answer. The semantic openness of the images thus represents a particularly valuable discursive resource for visual elicitation (Lobinger forthcoming) and 'the multiple meanings negotiated by viewers can be mined for the rich data they yield' (Schwartz 1989, p. 122).

Which images are to be used for visual elicitation depends on the research interest. Often the images are selected or produced by the researchers prior to the interview (*researcher-produced images*, non-participatory visual elicitation) with respect to the topic of investigation. In other cases, respondents are asked to take or select their own images prior to the interview or to produce them during the course of the interview (*participant-produced images*, participatory or collaborative visual elicitation; Lapenta 2012, p. 204–9; Pauwels 2012, p. 6–10).[1] However, in either case the researchers have to make sure that the selected images are related to the life-worlds of the participants. Visual elicitation is based on the circumstance that people like to talk about images if they can relate to them. But the contrary also holds true: respondents have a great deal of difficulty if they are asked to talk about images that are not related to their life-worlds. Hence, the selection of the visual material is a crucial step that merits close attention and preparation.

In a study that focused on the role and relevance of pictures and of visual communication within the complex communicative repertoires of couples, pair interviews conducted with the couples were followed by individual open-ended interviews with the partners separately.[2] In both forms of interview multiple visual and creative methods were used. In order to examine the role and meaning of visual communication in the everyday life of couples, we asked them to bring three to five photographs with them that were characteristic of or meaningful for their relationship, in order to discuss them in the initial pair interview. This represents a participatory approach that uses respondent-produced visuals that are selected from an existing collection of photographs. In semi-structured pair interviews, we asked them to explain the meaning those visuals had for them. Hence, the narration about the pictures was the main source of information, not the pictures themselves. However, we agree with Buckingham (2009) that it is also important to examine the sequence of the visual material itself. Therefore, we also conducted a picture-type analysis in which similar photographs of all interviewed couples were grouped into image types, which were then interpreted with the help of iconographic-iconological analysis (Grittmann and Ammann 2011). This procedure enabled us to identify visual techniques of performing the social relationship that were then related to the verbal narration of the couple.

The use of respondent-selected photographs had several advantages for the study. As already noted by previous visual elicitation studies, the photographs discussed proved to be ideal icebreakers within the interview. The respondents used their photographs (see Fig. 15.1) as 'anchors for storytelling' (Van House 2009, p. 1082), embedding them in their verbal narration and expanding on them where appropriate.[3] In this way, instead of merely explaining the contents of the photographs, the couple

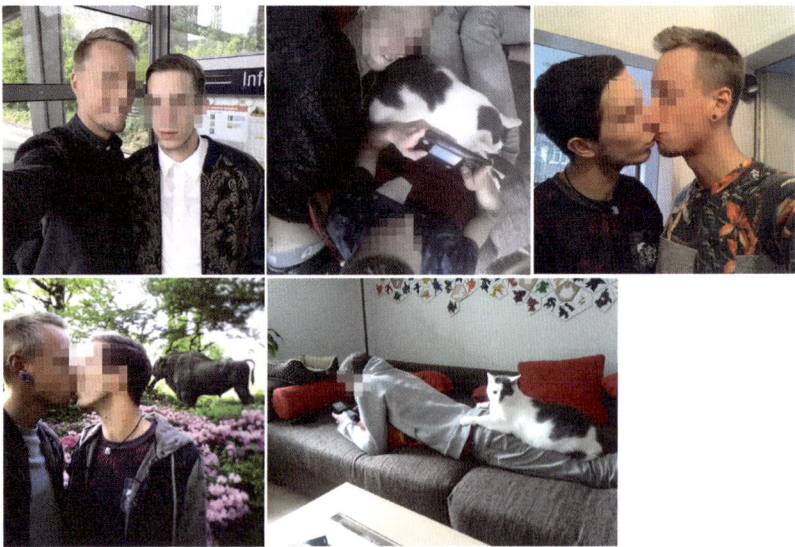

Fig. 15.1   Respondent-selected photographs used for visual elicitation in a pair interview with a homosexual couple

gave additional detailed accounts of the situational context, the reasons for taking the photographs, and the feelings involved at the moment of capture and in moments of looking at them. This information and the way in which the participants talked about the photographs helped us get a detailed impression of the meaning of visual communication and photographs for the overall relationship that we would not have obtained in purely verbal interviews. The visuals themselves and the verbal narration created around the photographs of this couple indicate that for them, photographs of everyday situations experienced together are very important in the construction of their pair identity and for the visual narration of 'being a couple'. Other couples, in contrast, instead brought with them photographs of important, special events and celebrations. Moreover, the practices of image capture are quite autonomous: all of the photographs were taken by one of the partners, either one of them taking a picture of the other, or one of them taking selfies showing both of them. Overall, the selected photographs strongly differed from couple to couple regarding their content and uses, and they are also related to different roles of visual communication in the couples' communication repertoires, an aspect that was further investigated in the verbal interviews.

CARD SORTING TECHNIQUES AND Q-SORT STUDIES

Card sorting is a knowledge elicitation technique that is characterized by particular simplicity for both researcher and participant. Various items, such as photographs, cards, and statements, are given to a participant, who is then asked to sort them into groups, to rank them, or to draw out relationships between different items or categories. It is assumed 'that the way in which participants categorize entities *externally* reflects their *internal*, mental representation of these concepts' (Fincher and Tenenberg 2005, p. 90). Regarding the sorting exercise, various forms of card sorting can be differentiated. In *open card sorting* procedures, people can freely create categories of their own choice when grouping the single items. In sorts of this kind, participants are usually additionally asked to name the categories they built and explain them to the researcher in subsequent interviews. *Closed card sorting* tasks ask participants to sort single items into pre-defined sorting categories, piles, or ranking patterns. Sorting tasks can be performed only *once* or in *repeated* sorts. Usually the sorting result obtained is not the main source of data. Rather, card sorting studies are interested in revealing the often hidden and highly subjective mental models and considerations underlying the categorization process. Particular emphasis is thus to be put on the discussion of the sorting result, which needs to be given enough time in the course of the interview (Arthur et al. 2014, p. 168). However, the sorting results obtained can also be examined qualitatively or quantitatively (see the overview in Fincher and Tenenberg 2005; Rugg and McGeorge 1997).

Visual card sorting—that is, a sorting study in which participants sort visual items in relation to each other—is considered by participants to be particularly enjoyable, which then again leads to very detailed and vivid narratives during and after the sorting process. Moreover, sorting procedures are ideally suited for intuitively handling visual items. While verbal text is perceived in a sequential, linear form, images are characterized by non-linearity and holism, fostering meaning-making processes that are based on associations and feelings (Müller 2007). These associations can often not be directly or adequately translated into the verbal code. Instead of demanding verbalizations, card sorting procedures foreground the intuitive aspects. Indeed, in our own card sorting studies (Lobinger and Brantner 2015a, b; Lobinger and Brantner 2016) we found that participants enjoyed the sorting task and were able to complete it rather quickly. However, they encountered considerable difficulties when asked to explain their sorting decisions (Lobinger and Brantner 2015b, p. 33).

In our sorting studies, Cornelia Brantner and I used a particular form of card sorting: *visual Q-sort*. Q-sort is a research technique that combines qualitative and quantitative elements in the tradition of Q methodology, founded by psychologist and physicist William Stephenson (1935, 1953). Q methodology, the study of human subjectivity, 'combines the strengths of both qualitative and quantitative research traditions by enabling the dimensions of subjective phenomena to emerge from the data in a manner that reflects a perspective intrinsic to the individuals' (Dennis and Goldberg 1996, p. 104). In visual Q-sort studies, participants intuitively sort visual items in a usually pre-defined distribution (see the example below). The results are then analyzed using statistical Q-factor analysis. Q-factor analysis is used for the identification of different factors. A factor is constituted by a group of participants who share a common perspective, a common way of thinking regarding the sorted items. Hence, Q-factor analysis correlates people, not items (Stephenson 1935). A very good and detailed overview of how to conduct Q-sort studies is provided by Watts and Stenner (2012). Visual Q-sort is an approach well suited to audience studies, allowing for insight into audience subjectivities in a rich and holistic way while at the same time providing replicability and a clear structure (O'Neill et al. 2013; Robinson et al. 2008; Stephen 1985; Davis and Michelle 2011; Lobinger and Brantner 2015c).

For example, in order to explore what represents 'favorable' visual depictions of politicians in the view of media audiences, we conducted a Q-sort study with forty participants. We used a *forced-choice Q-sort*, asking the participants to sort a fixed number of items (thirty-three photographs of a high-ranking European politician) into a fixed number of categories, using a nine-point ranking scale from totally unfavorable (−4) to very favorable (+4) with a 'neutral' middle category. Free Q-sorts, on the other hand, do not limit the number of items per category (Hess and Hink 1959). Moreover, our ranking scheme demanded a quasi-normal distribution of items, which is characteristic of Q-sort studies. Participants were thus allowed to place more items in the middle categories than in the tails (see Fig. 15.2).

Fig. 15.2 Finished exemplary Q-sort in a study on the favorability of depictions of politicians

With the study we identified different subjective perspectives on favorable depictions; in other words, we explored 'different ways of seeing' visual representations that involve different expectations of the role of politicians (Lobinger and Brantner 2016). The sorting was performed in an intensive analysis setting, combining the sorting procedure with short open-ended post-sorting interviews. This allowed us to combine the data gathered from both verbal explanations and the visual sorting results. Even though the visual sorting results represent fascinating data on their own, we found the interviews to be very helpful, since the dense visual material represents a huge analytic challenge. We thus agree with Buckingham (2009) that creative methods should not fall back on participants' verbal accounts alone. Rather, they should seek to integrate the information gathered from verbal and visual data and consider them complementary data sources (see also Awan and Gauntlett 2011). Q-sort allows for this integration in an ideal manner. While the Q-factors themselves are created based on the visual data (the sorts) produced by the respondents, the verbal interviews are used for a further dense factor interpretation.

In our study the sorting scheme was printed on a large sheet of paper, a research setting that can be described as a paper-based Q-sort study. Q-sort studies can also be conducted in eResearch settings using sorting programs and applications.[4] However, most research tools were developed for the sorting of verbal statements and cannot be easily adapted to the research needs in visual studies. In collaboration with the author, students in media informatics at the University of Bremen recently developed a tablet-based research application for the performance of smooth and intuitive visual Q-sorts.[5]

DRAWING-BASED EXERCISES IN INTERVIEWS

As already mentioned, participant-produced visuals created during the interview process can be used for visual elicitation. Recently, drawing-based exercises have gained importance in audience research (Hepp et al. 2014), and in qualitative visual network research (Schönhuth and Gamper 2013) in particular. While in quantitative network analysis visualizations are predominantly used to display the complex network structures prior to analysis, qualitative network research also uses visualizations as participatory or collaborative tools to identify and explore the social networks and their meanings for individuals in open-ended interviews

(Gamper et al. 2011). The most frequently used visual approaches, such as network maps, network drawings, or network cards, can be created with different degrees of standardization, from completely free drawings to (semi-)standardized templates to be used by the participants. On the continuum from openness to standardization, network drawings represent the most free and open approach. Respondents are asked to draw their social environment and the people involved on an empty sheet of paper according to their own ideas. Network cards, on the other hand, use different degrees of standardization. For example, concentric circles around the center, which represents the respondent, suggest different degrees of relevance of the individuals within the network. Depending on the degree of standardization, different analytic procedures are facilitated (Gamper and Schönhuth in print). Similar to Q-sorts, these participatory visualizations can be realized as paper-and-pencil, as 'paper-pen-and-tokens', and as 'digital' network maps or drawings (Gamper et al. 2011).

In the research project on visual communication in the couples' everyday communication (see earlier), the pair interview was opened with a participatory task: the couples were asked to draw their 'communication universe'. We provided them with a scheme similar to network cards (see Fig. 15.3) and asked them to position the media technologies and contents that they used within this universe. The scheme allowed them to highlight the individual relevance of the media for the partners and to differentiate media that were important for their relationship from media that were less important. With this task we wanted to find out how important visual communication and 'visual' media technologies were in the couple's 'ongoing conversation' (Berger and Kellner 1964). The drawing the participants created was very helpful during the interview. The visual–spatial representation of their 'communication universe' facilitated a focus on and explanation of their use of certain media contents and technologies, while at the same time keeping an overview of the broader repertoire of communication. In a similar approach, Hepp and colleagues used open network cards in their media-ethnographic research exploring the communicative social networks of young people. This visual approach offered them deeper insights into the subjective representations of the structural dimensions of media connectivity than verbal interviews alone would have allowed. In this regard, Hepp and colleagues found that, due to the drawing task, more aspects of media appropriation became accessible to the respondents (Hepp et al. 2014, p. 181).

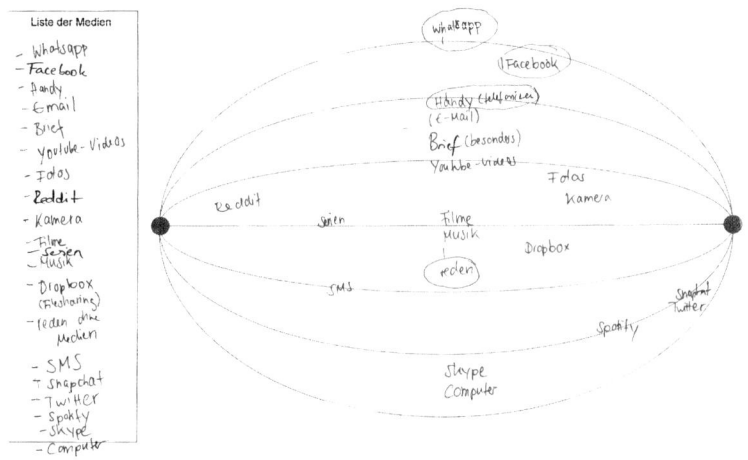

Fig. 15.3 The 'communication universe' of a couple, both partners aged twenty-six. The names of the interviewees have been removed as well as the description of the drawing task in German, originally located above the 'universe'

Conclusion

As was shown in this chapter, the use of creative visual methods, if employed adequately, has many advantages regarding the research situation as well as the results gained. Creative visual methods can be used to reduce the hierarchy in researcher–respondent relationships. Verbal interviews usually take the form of question–answer settings in which the researcher, asking questions, and the respondent, giving answers, interact. Metaphorically, visual material can be described as a third interlocutor in this regard. Both respondent and researcher look at and refer to the photographs, ideally exploring them together. Visual material can thus create a less structured atmosphere and reduced power hierarchies, leading to longer, more open interviews that are also more enjoyable to participants.

Regarding the results of creative visual methods, there is wide agreement that due to the idiosyncrasies of the visual mode, visual approaches can carve out information that is often difficult to verbalize and thus not accessible with verbal interviews alone. However, following Awan and

Gauntlett (2011), it is argued that visual methods have to be understood as complementary approaches, not as an attempt to abandon verbal data in favor of visual data. Preferably, creative visual methods should be designed in a way that enables merging of the information gathered by verbal interviews and visual methods. Moreover, it is essential to consider, for example, the visual representations created in visual research as social constructions influenced by many aspects, the situational context of the interview being only one of them. Hence, of course, visuals do not represent reality in a neutral way. However, creative visual methods have been harshly criticized for sometimes having naïve expectations and falling victim to naïve empiricism. Buckingham thus re-emphasizes: 'Data from visual research cannot be seen as transparent evidence of inner mental processes, any more than language can' (Buckingham 2009, p. 648).

Apart from acknowledging the character of images as constructs, there are some further prerequisites for successful visual research that merit close attention. The visual material used in creative methods must be carefully selected. If participants cannot relate to the visual material or do not understand the visual task they are asked to perform, the advantages of the creative approach are gambled away. Moreover, visual methods necessitate thoughtful ethical considerations, such as preserving the anonymity of the participants who might appear in photos or videos that were used or produced during the research process. Even though creative visual methods can be empowering and give voice to participants, for example in approaches called 'photo voice' (Lapenta 2012, p. 206), they can also potentially harm the participants (Chalfen 2012, p. 194f.).

Due to the methodological advantages of creative visual approaches, their field of application is not limited to visual communication research. Rather, visual methods can enrich the repertoire of media and communication studies. In particular, audience researchers familiar with the genuine affordances of the visual mode can use this knowledge in the design of their research instruments, which does however require acknowledgment of the theoretical and methodological knowledge developed in visual communication. The common effort to further develop methods in media and communication research might thus contribute to breaking down the dominance of the verbal mode in scientific knowledge production, which has for too long neglected the unique methodological and epistemological potentials of visuals.

NOTES

1. Further information on participatory approaches such as reflexive photography or photo voice can be found in Lapenta (2012).
2. Several students in the seminar 'Mediatized Partner Communication' at the University of Bremen have assisted me in my study, recruiting respondents, conducting interviews, and producing transcriptions. I am very grateful for their enthusiastic and valuable contributions.
3. Photographs reproduced with permission. Even though the respondents gave us permission to reproduce the photographs in scientific publications without alteration, we decided to pixelate their faces in order to ensure anonymity. This is only one of the many ethical challenges that arise when using visual methods, which cannot be discussed here in detail (see, for example, Pauwels 2008; Wiles et al. 2012a, b).
4. See, for example, http://qmethod.org/ (accessed 10 March 2016).
5. See http://eresearch.informatik.uni-bremen.de (accessed 10 March 2016).

REFERENCES

Arthur, S., Martin M., Lewis J., et al. (2014) Designing Fieldwork. In J. Ritchie, J. Lewis, C. McNaughton and R. Ormston (Eds.), *Qualitative Research Practice: A Guide for Social Science Students and Researchers* (London: Sage), pp. 147–76.

Awan, F. and Gauntlett, D. (2011) Creative and Visual Methods in Audience Research. In V. Nightingale (Ed.), *The Handbook of Media Audiences* (Oxford: Wiley-Blackwell), pp. 360–79.

Berger, P. and Kellner, H. (1964) Marriage and the Construction of Reality: An Exercise in the Microsociology of Knowledge. *Diogenes* 12(46): 1–24.

Buckingham, D. (2009) 'Creative' Visual Methods in Media Research: Possibilities, Problems and Proposals. *Media, Culture & Society* 31(4): 633–52.

Chalfen, R. (2012) Differentiating Practices of Participatory Visual Media Production. In: E. Margolis and L. Pauwels (Eds.), *The SAGE Handbook of Visual Research Methods* (London: Sage), pp. 186–200.

Collier, J. (1957) Photography in Anthropology: A Report on Two Experiments. *American Anthropologist* 59(5): 843–59.

Collier, J. and Collier, M. (1986) *Visual Anthropology: Photography as a Research Method* (Albuquerque: University of New Mexico Press).

Davis, C. and Michelle, C. (2011) Q methodology in Audience Research: Bridging the Qualitative/Quantitative 'Divide'? *Participations: Journal of Audience and Reception Studies* 8(2): 559–93.

Dennis, K. and Goldberg, A. (1996) Weight Control Self-efficacy Types and Transitions Affect Weight-loss Outcomes in Obese Women. *Addictive Behaviors* 21(1): 103–16.

Fincher, S. and Tenenberg, J. (2005) Making Sense of Card Sorting Data. *Expert Systems* 22(3): 89–93.

Gamper, M. and Schönhuth, M. (in print) Zeigen, was sich nicht sagen lässt – Ansätze und Verfahren der Visuellen Netzwerkforschung [Showing What Can't be Said]. In: K. Lobinger (Ed.), *Handbuch Visuelle Kommunikationsforschung* [Handbook of Visual Communication Research] (Wiesbaden: Springer VS).

Gamper, M., Schönhuth, M. and Kronenwett, M. (2011) Bringing Qualitative and Quantitative Data Together: Collecting Network Data with the Help of VennMaker. In M. Safar and K. Mahdi (Eds.), *Social Networking and Community Behavior Modeling: Qualitative and Quantitative Measures: Qualitative and Quantitative Measures* (Hershey: IGI Global), pp. 193–213.

Grittmann, E. and Ammann, I. (2011) Quantitative Bildtypenanalyse [Quantitative Image Type Analysis]. In T. Petersen and C. Schwender (Eds.), *Die Entschlüsselung der Bilder. Methoden zur Erforschung visueller Kommunikation* [Deciphering Images: Methods to Research Visual Communication] (Köln: Herbert von Halem), pp. 163–77.

Hand, M. (2012) *Ubiquitous Photography* (Cambridge: Polity).

Harper, D. (1986) Meaning and Work: A Study in Photo Elicitation. *Current Sociology* 34(3): 24–46.

Harper, D. (2002) Talking About Pictures: A Case for Photo Elicitation. *Visual Studies* 17(1): 13–26.

Hawhee, D. and Messaris, P. (2009) Review Essay: What's Visual about 'Visual Rhetoric'? *Quarterly Journal of Speech* 95(2): 210–23.

Hepp, A., Berg, M. and Roitsch, C. (2014) Mediatized Worlds of Communitization: Young People as Localists, Centrists, Multi-localists and Pluralists. In A. Hepp and F. Krotz (Eds.), *Mediatized Worlds: Culture and Society in a Media Age* (London: Palgrave Macmillan), pp. 174–203.

Hess, R. and Hink, D. (1959) A Comparison of Forced vs. Free Q-Sort Procedure. *The Journal of Educational Research* 53(3): 83–90.

Lapenta, F. (2012) Some Theoretical and Methodological Views on Photo-Elicitation. In E. Margolis and L. Pauwels L (Eds.), *The SAGE Handbook of Visual Research Methods* (London: Sage), pp. 201–13.

Lobinger, K. (forthcoming) Visual Research Methods. In: J. Matthes (Ed.), *The International Encyclopedia of Communication Research Methods* (Oxford: Wiley-Blackwell).

Lobinger, K. and Brantner, C. (2015a) In the Eye of the Beholder: Subjective Views on the Authenticity of Selfies. *International Journal of Communication* 9: 1848–60.

Lobinger, K. and Brantner, C. (2015b) Likable, Funny or Ridiculous? A Q-sort Study on Audience Perceptions of Visual Portrayals of Politicians. *Visual Communication* 14(1): 15–40.

Lobinger, K. and Brantner, C. (2015c) Q-Sort: Qualitativ-quantitative Analysen bildlicher Rezeptions- und Aneignungsprozesse. Leistungen und Limitationen für das Feld Visueller Kommunikationsforschung [Q-sort: Qualitative-quantitative Analyses of Visual Reception and Appropriation Processes]. In K. Lobinger and and S. Geise (Eds.), *Visualisierung – Mediatisierung. Kommunikation und bildliches Handeln in mediatisierten Gesellschaften* [Visualization—Mediatization] (Köln: Halem), pp. 181–206.

Lobinger, K. and Brantner, C. (2016) Different Ways of Seeing Depictions of Politicians: A Qualitative–Quantitative Analysis Using Q Methodology. *Communications* 41(1), pp. 47–69.

Müller, M. (2007) What is Visual Communication? Past and Future of an Emerging Field of Communication Research. *Studies in Communication Science* 7(2): 7–34.

O'Neill, S., Boykoff, M., Niemeyer, S., et al. (2013) On the Use of Imagery for Climate Change Engagement. *Global Environmental Change* 23(2): 413–21.

Pauwels, L. (2008) Taking and Using. Ethical Issues of Photographs for Research Purposes. *Visual Communication Quarterly* 15(4): 243–57.

Pauwels, L. (2012) An Integrated Conceptual Framework for Visual Social Research. In: E. Margolis and L. Pauwels (Eds.), *The SAGE Handbook of Visual Research Methods* (London: Sage), pp. 3–23.

Robinson, T., Gustafson, B. and Popovich, M. (2008) Perceptions of Negative Stereotypes of Older People in Magazine Advertisements: Comparing the Perceptions of Older Adults and College Students. *Ageing & Society* 28(2): 233–51.

Rugg, G. and McGeorge, P. (1997) The Sorting Techniques: A Tutorial Paper on Card Sorts, Picture Sorts and Item Sorts. *Expert Systems* 14(2): 80–93.

Schönhuth, M. and Gamper, M. (2013) Visuelle Netzwerkforschung. Eine thematische Annäherung [Visual Network Analysis]. In: M. Schönhuth, M. Gamper M and M. Kronenwett et al. (Eds.), *Visuelle Netzwerkforschung. Qualitative, quantitative und partizipative Zugänge* [Visual Network Analysis] (Bielefeld: transkript), pp. 9–32.

Schwartz, D. (1989) Visual Ethnography: Using Photography in Qualitative Research. *Qualitative Sociology* 12(2): 119–54.

Stephen, T. (1985) Q-Methodology in Communication Science: An Introduction. *Communication Quarterly* 33(3): 193–208.

Stephenson, W. (1935) Correlating Persons Instead of Tests. *Journal of Personality* 4(1): 17–24.

Stephenson, W. (1953) *The Study of Behavior: Q-Technique and its Methodology* (Chicago: University of Chicago Press).

Van House, N. (2009) Collocated Photo Sharing, Story-telling, and the Performance of Self. *International Journal of Human-Computer Studies* 67(12): 1073–86.

Watts, S. and Stenner, P. (2012) *Doing Q Methodological Research. Theory, Method and Interpretation* (London: Sage).

Wiles, R., Clark, A. and Prosser, J. (2012a) Visual Research Ethics at the Crossroads. In: E. Margolis and L. Pauwels (Eds.), *The SAGE Handbook of Visual Research Methods* (London: Sage), pp. 685–706.

Wiles, R., Coffey, A., Robison, J., et al. (2012b) Ethical Regulation and Visual Methods: Making Visual Research Impossible or Developing Good Practice? *Sociological Research Online* 17(1): http://www.socresonline.org.uk/17/1/8. html (accessed 10 January 2016).

Innovative Methods in Media and Communication Research: An Outlook

Sebastian Kubitschko and Anne Kaun

Bringing together and giving a convincing overview of innovative research methods in media and communication research is without doubt an ambitious and ongoing project that needs continuous updating and revising. At the same time, as we have tried to make clear, it is a highly relevant project that needs to be approached from different angles if we take seriously the fundamental role of research methods for the elaboration of knowledge that deepens understandings of contemporary social constellations. Eventually, the question of how a changing media environment is part of transforming social life needs to be tackled from various disciplinary perspectives. This is above all the case because widening our comprehension of the relation between media and society relies on methods that allow us to grasp a wide range of communicative practices and processes.

In this regard, echoing Nick Couldry's formulation in the Foreword, innovating research approaches is an essential element of discovering how much methods matter for the quality of social life. The collection of

S. Kubitschko(✉)
University of Bremen (ZeMKI), Bremen, Germany
e-mail: sebastian.kubitschko@uni-bremen.de

A. Kaun
Södertörn University, Huddinge, Sweden
e-mail: anne.kaun@sh.se

© The Author(s) 2016   311
S. Kubitschko, A. Kaun (eds.), *Innovative Methods in Media and Communication Research*, DOI 10.1007/978-3-319-40700-5

research approaches to study media and communication brought together in this volume shows that methodological innovation to a large degree is about (a) *testing and transcending (disciplinary) boundaries of established research approaches*; and (b) *expanding the prevailing (disciplinary) themes and objects of investigation*. Accordingly, this book is less a call for methodological rejuvenation than an invitation to examine, revisit, and advance.

The overall objective we pursue is twofold. On a rather generic level, we intend to advance interdisciplinary scholarship on research methods to further understandings of media and communications; and on a more concrete level, we seek to inspire new research projects as well as inform teaching. The methodological repertoire at hand ranges from digital (self-)archiving practices (Baines, Chap. 2) and (self-)experiments (Despard, Chap. 3; Bucher, Chap. 5; Frigo, Chap. 8) to interdisciplinary reflections (Sak, Chap. 4), from digital research (Velasco, Chap. 6) and psychophysiological interaction analyses (Huskey, Chap. 7) to ethnographic accounts (LaDue, Chap. 9; Sartoretto, Chap. 10; Kumar, Chap. 11), from critical readings of visualization (Gray, Bounegru, Milan, and Ciuccarelli, Chap. 12) and urban sensing (Simeone and Patelli, Chap. 13) to topic mapping (Baya-Laffite and Cointet, Chap. 14) and participatory, visual approaches (Lobinger, Chap. 15). To bring the book's overall aim to life we relied on three major components: first, introducing research methods that deeply rethink established methods and bring new ones into being; second, promoting early career scholars who are applying these methods in empirical research around the globe; and third, nurturing dialogue between existing and emerging methods as well as between emerging and experienced scholars.

The contributing authors have combined a discussion of the distinctive opportunities for innovative engagement with research methods in the humanities and social sciences with critical reflection on their development, pitfalls, and consequences. In doing so, the chapters share the commonality that they ask the researcher to remain conscious and reflective about the potential and shortcomings of both traditional and innovative methods. In particular, methodological innovation needs critical reflection, as contemporary media change is not only co-constitutive of social, cultural, political, and economic life, but also carries with it potentially new ways of analyzing (mediated) life *per se*. Bringing together the essence of the volume's four parts—Materiality, Technology, Experience, and Visualization—eight correlated themes emerge that might best be read as an 'advisory register'.

A METHODOLOGICAL 'ADVISORY REGISTER'

Be Realistic To start with, commitment is a necessity, but is not sufficient. As Jess Baine' research experiences with the radicalprintshops.org wiki explicate, researchers have to be mindful regarding the resources at hand. In particular, sufficient time and expertise (knowledge, experience, and skills) are essential components of fruitful empirical work. No matter how dedicated one is, there is always need for a (realistic) alignment with the available capacities. This, however, does not exclude the possibility and productivity of naïvety. In some cases, as Erin Despard has shown in her chapter, experimenting with media in a reflexively naïve manner creates events of surprise, learning, and failure. However modest, these events in turn create openings that may result in a critical perception of relations between media and society. So, while it can be suitable and in certain cases even necessary to apply a specific method for the research question that one is eager to answer, resources and methods need to match. This is where collaborative work comes into play. Considering the complex entanglements of media, communication, and life *per se*, it will possibly become the most realistic way to tackle empirical challenges by bringing together researchers with complementary resources. A number of chapters in this volume already explicate the productivity of doing so: Richard Huskey, who builds on work with collaborators at the Media Neuroscience Lab; Gray, Bounegru, Milan, and Ciuccarelli, who bring together their different knowledge, skills, and experiences; Simeone and Patelli, who rely on their common abilities and the background of a larger research project; and Baya-Laffite and Cointet, who combine their expertise; not to mention the overall approach of the volume itself.

Stay Concrete Despite, or exactly because of, the quasi-omnipresence of media technologies and infrastructures, there is a need to specify the entanglements of media and society through empirical methods that are sensitive to context. That is to say, showing why, where, and how exactly media matters 'is necessary to push against narrow presumptions about the universality of digital experience' (Coleman 2010, p. 489). This also implies that instead of referring to meta-processes like globalization or individualization, there is a need for scholarly attention toward and explanation of media's on-the-ground manifestations. All chapters in this book follow this line of reasoning more or less explicitly. In particular, the contributions on ethnographic-driven research (LaDue, Sartoretto, and Kumar) explicate how context matters and how media become part of the everyday assemblage of signifying practices.

Care for the Detail Methodological rigor is one of the pillars of academic research, and part of it is the care for detail, when it comes to both data collection and analysis. Translating theoretical problems into empirically observable categories as well as generating theory from observed social reality are among the major challenges for every researcher. Part of this challenge is to elevate everyday explanations of social phenomena beyond banalities. This requires a thoughtful and in-depth engagement with the richness and details of the objects of study. As Lewis Mumford puts it when he points to the analysis of an ox moving over a winding, uneven road compared to the movement of a planet: 'it is easier to trace an entire orbit than to plot the varying rate of speed and the changes of position that takes place in the nearer and more familiar object' (Mumford, 2010[1934], p. 47). Similarly, Lev Manovich asks in his introduction to visualization for methods that allow for in-depth analysis despite the abundance of information.

Resist Temptations It can be tempting to apply the latest method simply for the fact of being excited by the 'new'. Yet, as has been argued convincingly elsewhere, 'it is not possible to apply a method as if it were indifferent or external to the problem it seeks to address, but that method must rather be made specific and relevant to the problem' (Lury and Wakeford 2012, p. 2–3). Resisting the temptation to jump on the bandwagon, the contributing authors consciously refuse to fuel the current hyperbole about 'the digital' (see Berry 2014). Echoing other elaborate readings of the relation between methods and object of study, the empirical studies collected in this volume emphasize that methods need to fit and their implementation needs to be adjusted to the specific circumstance. The emergence of 'digital objects' generates an opportunity to produce new methodologies, and specific research paths can emerge from what the affordances of novel digital objects bring up. In this context it is relevant, as Pablo Velasco highlights, that awareness of current computational epistemologies and an acknowledged intention of the researcher to restructure the social are key to identifying the opportunistic shaping of society. Methodological innovation is not about (re-)producing current hypes, but about questioning, (re-) developing, testing, and applying appropriate methods. Taina Bucher, for example, makes a strong case for applying well-known methods to new domains like online platforms and algorithms, which not only generates knowledge about emerging issues and practices, but also contributes to (re-)inventing methods.

Do Not Forget Where It Is Coming From Despite all the hype, we are not necessarily at a turning point or entering a new era. Despite the drastic transformations we are experiencing, yesterday the world looked just a little different than it does today. Innovating methods is not a sudden breakup, it is a perpetual effort. Of course, who would have foreseen only a few years ago the rapid rise of 'big data' mining or digital methods for accepted research approaches in the humanities and social sciences? Yet, as shown particularly by Alberto Frigo, methods do not emerge out of nowhere and are constantly in the making. Embedding his approach in a historical context, Frigo goes as far as envisioning lifelogging as a mean for generating knowledge—technical, empirical, maieutic, ethnographic, historical, and critical—beyond any fixed framework or dogma, but crafted by any humanist to conduct his or her tracking. In this respect, lifelogging as a method can be thought of as a way to deal with constantly increasing complexity and to transform surroundings by proactively involving the researcher producing data through everyday activities. To advance rewarding empirical research, both quantitative and qualitative methods need to be continuously rethought, permanently adjusted, and to aim to get rid of obsolete assumptions and noise. Having said that, it is essential to be aware of the 'evolution' and 'history' of a given methodological approach. Methods need to evolve and one needs to be aware of their roots; which also means that innovation is not an end in itself. After all, the pace and appropriation of innovating methods are what count.

Step Back and Reflect Taking the previous themes one step further, methodological innovation needs to be linked with critical reflection that questions the very categories of knowledge production. As has been argued convincingly, social media data, for example, tend to have 'methodological biases' that favor a highly particular type of social analysis, and may even 'call into question the relations between agencies of research' (Marres and Gerlitz 2015, p. 22). As Gray, Bounegru, Milan, and Ciuccarelli forcefully demonstrate, as visualization tools and practices become more and more ubiquitous, there is a need not only for the development of a critical *hermeneutics*, but also for new kinds of self-reflexive *praxis* for the creation and reconfiguration of visualizations that are attentive to different forms of mediation. Reflexivity also entails at least two more dimensions. First, one needs to consider how media centric a given research project is. Is a specific technology the starting point of inquiry or do we start, for example, from specific social relations or domains? With good reason, Paola Sartoretto emphasizes that research methodologies that are a result of reflexive efforts can help elucidate epistemological problems in a way that addresses their complexity. Sartoretto continues by arguing that when it comes to our relation to media, both as individuals and as groups, we must acknowledge the underlying structures in which this relation unfolds and the variety of media with which we interact. Second, one also has to take into account the researcher's subjectivity. Neha Kumar raises the question of how the quality and texture of research might be affected, for example, by the gender of the researcher. Similarly, as Kumar notes, religion, race, and class can act as boundaries as well as door openers. In both ways, they have an impact on the nature of the data collected.

Keep an Open Mind Although methods need to correlate with the object of investigation, this does not necessarily mean that various methods taken together do not enhance understandings of the problem that the researcher seeks to understand. On the contrary, there is not one method that contains the solution to all questions related to the contemporary media environments. Accordingly, one needs to stay open-minded and inclusive, and ideally to think in an interdisciplinary way. Segah Sak, for instance, brings to the table an architectural/urban viewpoint that enables her to explicate how studies of digital media do and can further benefit from socio-spatial research approaches. Richard Huskey's contribution is a formidable illustration of how thinking outside the box can enrich empirical research. Huskey's approach shows how in the context of video game addiction, for example, connectivity analyses can be used to identify a biomarker for psychological processes that are difficult to assess using more traditional media and communication approaches. Authors in this volume do not defend or advocate the exclusivity of one specific kind of (empirical) access to the world. Nicolas Baya-Laffite and Jean-Philippe Cointet combine traditional research methods and computer-assisted techniques, as well as manual and automated operations, to map climate change negotiations. Katharina Lobinger explicitly refers to the value of mixed-methods approaches in the context of Q-sort, and explores how creative visual methods can enrich media and communication research by working with non-verbal clues for self-expression. As already mentioned, one single researcher is not required to have all the required expertise or resources to apply multiple methods. Understanding a specific medium and/or communication phenomenon can (and probably has to) rely on the work of researchers with different disciplinary perspectives and methodological approaches.

Mind the Ethics and Politics On first sight, this volume does not explicitly cover the ethical dimensions of emerging research methods. While research ethics is a topic of such importance that there is a need to discuss its different facets more extensively, this volume does hint at some critical facets.[1] Emily LaDue—in her methodologically oriented wakeup call to visual and urban ethnographers—shows that innovative methods always also carry political meaning. Consequently, LaDue asks the sharp question of who we 'produce' our research for and for what purpose we 'mine' data. Luca Simeone and Paolo Patelli raise a similar point when they underline that the citizens as well as the related urban areas portrayed within the platform were not directly affected by the research project itself, in the sense that the artifacts generated through Urban Sensing (for example, data visualizations) never reached the actual spaces and the citizens it studied. Examining whether the work we do is being produced in common and for a community in resistance, or whether we use our work for placing ourselves on the market as academics, is key. How much *does* and *should* empirical research feed back into society and influence or co-determine social settings? This is an affirmation of the earlier call for critical reflection when we advance methodological approaches, and it emphatically points toward the ethical dimensions of empirical research in general. Simeone and Patelli also reflect on an additional ethical dilemma. The production of media content and mobile access to social networking services, both necessary to share geo-located contributions, is still limited to a segment of city inhabitants and visitors, let alone the world population. This raises the (ethical) question: Who do we reach/research and who do we not? Whose 'reality' do we perceive and interpret? Finally, Simeone and Patelli also accentuate that serious issues in terms of privacy need to be tackled when researching contemporary media and/or communication phenomena, since media are ever more embedded in people's daily lives, habits, rituals, behavior, and so on.

A Provocative Outlook

Boldly summarizing some of the current trends in media and communication research, we want to point to two fundamental flaws—inspired by Lewis Mumford's classical inspection of *Technics and Civilization*—that relate more deeply to the relationship of technology and society. The first flaw is the reduction of the complex to the simple by focusing on those events that can be counted or measured and by displacing large chunks of the living. The second flaw is a twofold neutralization of observers in respect to the data with which they work and agents in respect to the technical systems that they create to collect and analyze data. Mumford skillfully related these developments to the formation of physical science and the 'elimination of the organic' (2010[1934], p. 46 and p. 47). One could indeed phrase this in the following three provocations: What remains human and social about the humanities and social sciences if they are eager to apply the same principles and construct the same *Weltbild* that the natural sciences advance and corporate research institutions glorify? Is it advisable for disciplines that are generally confronted with space–time sequences that most of the time cannot be controlled, repeated, or investigated in isolation to eliminate any form of speculation and interpretation? Should the humanities and social sciences strive for predictive objectivity?

For several years now—and increasingly so—social inquiry and analysis in the context of media are no longer the exclusive province of researchers employed by academic institutions. Marketing research has been around for decades. Today, however, the commitment of corporately driven and financed research has reached unprecedented heights. The research divisions of large tech corporations gather excellent scholars in their 'laboratories' and maintain close collaborations with academic institutions (for example, Microsoft Research, Laboratoire des Usages Orange Labs, Research at Facebook, to name but a few large endeavors). One might even go as far as to state that 'Academic research in a digital age has been out-manoeuvred by freelance fact-makers in policy think tanks and corporate research' (Back 2012, p. 19). And something else has changed over time: tech corporations are at the same time the objects of study, the suppliers of large data sets, *and* increasingly research agents themselves. In other words, corporations have turned into the trinity of methods: producer, harvester, and analyst of data. Scholars are faced with the blurring of boundaries between the tools, the objects, and the analyses; and they will be so increasingly in the near future.

The fact that popular online platforms are now research agents in their own right and determine who has the right to access what kind of data brings with it restrictions and limitations. Corporations do not necessarily have the duty to make their data publicly available. Accordingly, in the context of changing application programming interfaces (API) and privacy settings, emerging research methods can be difficult and resource intensive (for example, technical know-how, skills, and experiences). Yet, as shown throughout this volume, there are valuable approaches to tackling these challenges (see also Hogan et al. 2016).

Etymologically, 'data' is the (nominative) plural of *datum*, which is Latin for 'something given' or '(thing) given'. To stretch this instruction in Latin even further, *datum* is the neuter past participle of *dare*, 'to give'. As has been illustrated throughout this volume, data are not facts somewhere out there for the taking. The process of giving is anything but banal and/or neutral. So, when we approach the process of 'giving' from a critical point of view, we need to ask ourselves as researchers: Who is giving, what is given, in what context is the giving taking place, how do we receive and approach the given, and who do we give to? Taking these provocations seriously, ultimately one is confronted not only with the question 'What is (relevant) data?', but more fundamentally with the questions 'How is knowledge generated?', 'How is knowledge diffused?', 'How is knowledge interpreted?', and 'By whom and to what ends?'.

NOTE

1. On ethics and qualitative research, see Nind et al. (2012); on ethics and digital methods, see Hewson (2016); on ethics and big data research, see Herman and Markham (forthcoming).

REFERENCES

Back, L. (2012) Live Sociology: Social Research and Its Futures. *The Sociological Review* 60(S1): 18–39.

Berry, D. (2014) *Critical Theory and the Digital* (New York: Bloomsbury).

Coleman, G. (2010) Ethnographic Approaches to Digital Media. *Annual Review of Anthropology* 39: 487–505.

Herman, A. and Markham, A. (forthcoming) Ethic as Method in an Era of Big Data. Special Issue of *Social Media + Society*.

Hewson, C. (2016) Ethics Issues in Digital Methods Research. In: H. Snee, C. Hine, Y. Morey, et al. (Eds.), *Digital Methods for Social Science: An Interdisciplinary Guide to Research Innovation* (London: Palgrave Macmillan), pp. 206–21.

Hogan, B., Melville, J., Philips II, G., et al. (2016) Evaluating the Paper-to-Screen Translation of Participant-Aided Sociograms with High-Risk Participants. *Proceedings of the 2016 CHI*, San Diego.

Lury, C. and Wakeford, N. (2012) Introduction: A Perpetual Inventory. In C. Lury and N. Wakeford (Eds.), *Inventive Methods: The Happening of the Social* (London: Routledge), pp. 1–25.

Marres, N. and Gerlitz, C. (2015) Interface Methods: Renegotiating Relations Between Digital Social Research, STS and Sociology. *The Sociological Review* 64(1): 21–46.

Mumford, L. (2010[1934]) *Technics and Civilization* (Chicago: University of Chicago Press).

Nind, M., Wiles, R., Bengry-Howell, A., et al. (2012) Methodological Innovation and Research Ethics: Forces in Tension or Forces in Harmony? *Qualitative Research* 13(6): 650–67.

AUTHOR INDEX

Note: Page number followed by 'n' refers to endnotes.

© The Author(s) 2016
S. Kubitschko, A. Kaun (eds.), *Innovative Methods in Media and Communication Research*, DOI 10.1007/978-3-319-40700-5

Subject Index

Note: Page number followed by 'n' refers to endnotes.

© The Author(s) 2016

S. Kubitschko, A. Kaun (eds.), *Innovative Methods in Media and Communication Research*, DOI 10.1007/978-3-319-40700-5

Printed in Great Britain
by Amazon